THEORIES OF SOCIAL WORK WITH GROUPS

THEORIES

OF

SOCIAL WORK

WITH

GROUPS

ROBERT W. ROBERTS AND HELEN NORTHEN
EDITORS

New York COLUMBIA UNIVERSITY PRESS *1976*

Library of Congress Cataloging in Publication Data

Roberts, Robert W
Theories of social work with groups.

Includes bibliographies and index.
1. Social group work—Collected works.   I. Northen,
Helen, joint author.   II. Title.
HV45.R6   361.4   76-4967
ISBN 0-231-03885-2

Columbia University Press
New York   Guildford, Surrey

Copyright © 1976 Columbia University Press
Printed in the United States of America

Dedicated to
Lois and Samuel Silberman
for their psychological and financial support
of social work scholarship during these very troubled times.

CONTRIBUTORS

Laura Epstein, Associate Professor, School of Social Service Administration, University of Chicago.

Charles D. Garvin, Professor, School of Social Work, University of Michigan.

Paul H. Glasser, Professor, School of Social Work, University of Michigan.

Margaret E. Hartford, Professor, School of Applied Social Sciences, Case Western Reserve University.

Elizabeth McBroom, Professor, School of Social Work, University of Southern California.

Helen Northen, Professor, School of Social Work, University of Southern California.

Howard J. Parad, Professor, School of Social Work, University of Southern California.

James Quinlan, Fellow, New England Medical Center, Tufts University.

William Reid, George Herbert Jones Professor, School of Social Service Administration, University of Chicago.

Robert W. Roberts, Associate Professor, School of Social Work, University of Southern California.

Eleanor Ryder, Associate Professor, School of Social Work, University of Pennsylvania.

William Schwartz, Professor, Columbia University School of Social Work.

Lola Selby, Professor, School of Social Work, University of Southern California.

Mary Louise Somers, Professor, School of Social Service Administration, University of Chicago.

Emanuel Tropp, Professor, School of Social Work, Virginia Commonwealth University.

Gertrude Wilson, Professor Emeritus, School of Social Welfare, University of California (Berkeley).

CONTENTS

PREFACE

Three major trends confront those interested in expanding social work practice theory. One is toward the development of theory for generic practice—that is, integrated theory that directs intervention with individuals, families, and formed groups. A second is the explication and codification of existing and developing models of practice, most of which address only one of the traditional intervention methods—casework, group work, or community work. The final trend is toward the empirical assessment of the effectiveness of social work practice.

Some see these trends as contradictory and mutually exclusive. We do not. We do, however, think they can and should be ordered in terms of priority and sequence. Specifically, we believe that existing theoretical models must be systematically defined, elaborated, and evaluated for logical consistency before valid integrated practice theories can be developed. In other words, it is our opinion that single-systems theoretical models will serve as the major building blocks of multisystem or integrated practice theories. If our belief is correct, this means that the profession will have multiple integrated practice theories, just as it now has multiple single-method theories. This seems appropriate for several reasons. First, practice models vary in their underlying value assumptions and philosophical premises. As it has been impossible to reconcile these differences and create an integrated and universally accepted theory of social casework or group work, so will it be impossible to merge them into one generic or integrated theory of practice. Second, existing single-method practice theories are, to a large extent, built on different and sometimes contradictory behavioral science foundations. Unless behavioral scientists resolve their contradictory explanations of human behavior and develop an integrated theory, a single theory for social work practice seems improbable. Finally, because existing models often address different social problems and needs, aim their intervention efforts at different target populations, and have different outcome objectives, their merger into one generic model seems unlikely. Instead, it appears that social work will develop integrated theories and not a unitary theory, and that any multisystem theory is no more likely to be effective for all types of situations appropriate to social work intervention than is any one single-system theoretical model.

Effectiveness research, we believe, will have more success and make larger contributions to theory development when the myth is laid to rest that all social work practice, clients, and target problems are essentially identical and that one set of outcome criteria is appropriate for all studies of practice. Instead, a more appropriate research question is what theoretical approach(es) to practice work most effectively with which types of clients with what kinds of problems under what sort of conditions? Before such comparative evaluations can be made, however, we must be able to specify our theoretical models.

An important step toward such codification of practice theory was taken in 1970 when *Theories of Social Casework* was published. The volume contained position papers by seven authors, each of whom followed the same topical outline in spelling out the details of the theoretical approach he represented.

Despite several efforts to delineate different theoretical approaches to social work practice with families and other groups, there is nothing comparable to the *Casework* volume. This is so despite the fact that there is less clarity about the similarities and differences among social work approaches to dealing with groups than there is for casework. To help remedy this situation, we decided to invite a select group of scholars to write position papers defining major theoretical approaches to social work with groups. These were to be supplemented by a paper tracing the historical development of theory for social work with groups and another giving an overview of the state of theory development. The hope was that the result would be a companion volume to *Theories of Social Casework,* and that most, if not all, of the position papers would articulate with those previously written on social casework. For several reasons, this goal was only partially achieved.

Social group work and social casework have different historical roots, and much of their development has occurred on parallel tracks. Foundation knowledge for the two methods has often been different. When they have drawn on similar bodies of behavioral science theory, theory development in the two methods was rarely integrated and, until recent years, it was a rare exception for scholars to develop theory for work with both individuals and groups. For this reason, there were not always existing practice models for work with groups that linked up with existing theories of social casework. Consequently, some of the authors had to take on the task of theory development rather than the codification of existing theory.

For unknown reasons, group workers have tended to avoid ideological splits and head-on confrontations of opposing theoretical schools. This may have been a result of observing the personal and professional tragedies that such theoretical conflict produced among caseworkers. Another possible explanation lies in the fact that group work developed as an interdisciplinary practice, held together by common values and knowledge concerning small groups. Untangling the use of groups in social work from their use in education and recreation preoccupied the efforts of early theorists and left little time or energy for developing distinctive theoretical approaches to social group work. Or, perhaps a strong belief in and commitment to the integrative and cohesive forces of group process led to an emphasis on similarities in the knowledge, values, and skills shared by the various approaches to work with groups. In any case, theoretical differences and incompatibilities were downplayed, and many of the contributors took on the job of highlighting theoretical differences *and* similarities with great reluctance and difficulty.

These factors led to considerable difficulty in making decisions about the selection of authors. While some group work theorists were clearly identified with a distinct theoretical approach, other prominent scholars had made more general contributions to theory development. And again, we were confronted with the reality that there were not existing theoretical models of group work that matched all of the casework approaches. The dilemma faced was whether to invite only those who had worked toward the development of specific models or to include those who had made significant, but more general, contributions to theory development.

The solution was to include both groups of scholars so that the papers in the volume would cover a range of stages in practice theory development: some are reasonably consistent theories *of* social work practice with groups, some are theoretical approaches that are in a relatively early stage of development, and others lack the characteristics of prescriptive practice models but are useful *for* social workers of almost any theoretical persuasion who work with groups.

Having established our framework, we then had to confront the challenging task of making decisions about possible contributors. The list grew rapidly, and it was soon apparent that not every one we wanted could be included. To narrow the list, several somewhat arbitrary criteria were set up. Priority would be given to those who had worked at developing distinctive theoretical approaches or those who, in our judgment, had the special knowledge base necessary for the development of an approach similar to those contained in *Theories of Social Casework*. Next a decision was made to include only those approaches that were well established and clearly identifiable as social work theories. This decision, of course, eliminated some of the newer approaches yet to be tested and those approaches which have been borrowed wholesale from other professions; most approaches omitted met neither of these criteria. An exception is behavior modification. This approach, while originating outside of social work, has been utilized by social work practitioners in a wide variety of settings. Early plans called for the inclusion of a separate chapter on behavior modification. Consultation with others closely associated with the approach, however, led to the conclusion that it is more often practiced as a component of broader theories—such as that developed at the University of Michigan—than as an exclusive approach.

A final limitation was physical rather than mental—the need to keep the volume down to a reasonable size and to avoid redundancies in theoretical orientations.

Following the format used in the casework volume, a suggested outline of topics to be covered was given to each author. While there was no intent to force authors into a Procrustean bed, it was thought that each paper would have to cover relatively similar topics to make possible rigorous and critical comparisons of approaches.

Construction of the outline was more complicated than we anticipated. Beginning with the outline used by the casework authors, we expanded it to include the additional components and complexities of social work practice with groups. The result was an outline longer than we had anticipated, and one that posed an extremely difficult task for the authors. Although many of them recoiled at the enormity of the request, all used the following outline as a basic blueprint for their chapters:

1. *Introduction.* Briefly describe the general characteristics of the theoretical approach under discussion. What were the origins of the approach and the major landmarks in its historical development?

2. *Philosophical considerations.* What value, philosophical, and ethical considerations are *central* to this theoretical approach?
3. *Behavioral science foundations.* What behavioral and social science knowledge is used by this approach as empirical and theoretical foundations? Identify the major constructs borrowed from each body of theory and describe how they are used by this approach. This may contain both descriptive and prescriptive components, but the two should be clearly differentiated.
4. *Target populations and organizational auspices.* Please describe, in terms of major social problems, types of clients, fields of practice, and organizational auspices, those considered most appropriate for workers using this theoretical approach.
5. *Classification of small groups addressed by the approach.* Describe the major kinds of groups for which this approach is considered appropriate. For theoretical approaches that are considered appropriate for several kinds of groups, a classification system is required. The following are some suggested dimensions around which such a classification system might be built.
   A. Types of groups:
      (1) Formed and/or natural or preexisting.
      (2) If preexisting groups are addressed by this approach, are both related (family) and nonrelated groups included?
      (3) Voluntary and/or nonvoluntary participation.
   B. Structural properties:
      (1) Open and/or closed memberships.
      (2) Time-limited and/or extended-time groups.
      (3) Variations in sizes of groups.
      (4) Residential and/or nonresidential settings.
   C. Composition of the group(s).
   Note: For all of the following topics, specific references will have to be made as to which of the above category(ies) of groups a given discussion applies. Depending upon the proclivities of the individual author, each section of the paper can articulate a given topic with the classification of groups described in suggestion 5, or each type of group can be discussed in terms of each of the following topics.
6. *Purposes.* What are the objectives? How are they determined? Are they shared with group members? Do they vary with the type of group being worked with? To be considered here are purposes as related to individual members, the group-as-a-whole, and extragroup systems.

7. *Assessment and selection of individuals and groups.* Discuss criteria (if any exist) for including or excluding applicants from the group, and how potential members are assessed. Some questions to be considered are the following: Are the purposes of the group defined before the selection process or does the composition of the group determine objectives? Are diagnostic assessments of individuals a part of this process? If so, what kinds of assessments of individuals are made and by whom? If individual assessments are not made, why not?

   In situations involving preexisting groups, are diagnostic assessments of the group made? If so, describe them. If not, why not?

   Describe any diagnostic classification schemes, and discuss their possible effects on the exclusion or inclusion of major types of social work clients.

8. *Group dynamics.* Is there a typical sequence of stages or phases of group process? If so, what are the manifestations and approximate length of each stage? Describe any ways in which this approach attends to the problems of engaging individuals and/or groups? What are the major group dynamics that work for or against achievement of objectives?

9. *Principles, methods, and techniques of professional social work intervention.* Discuss professional intervention in terms of content, methods, and techniques. If relevant, present a classification of intervention approaches, with reference to the diagnostic classification scheme included earlier. Appropriate questions to be addressed in this section are the following:

   A. What are the major roles, functions, or tasks of the social worker vis-à-vis the individual and/or the group?

   B. What concepts are used to describe what presumably leads to change in persons or environment? How are the dynamics of change explained?

   C. What is the worker's part in influencing change? What attitudes and skills should he have? What procedures or techniques of intervention should a worker follow?

   D. What is the client's role?

   E. Is there a method or systematic mode of procedure that should be used by the worker? If so, please describe. On what knowledge is it based?

   F. What criteria are available for judging the outcome of the service?

G. What are the relationships of intervention procedures to the approach's behavioral-social science base?

10. *Linkages.* What are the linkages between work with groups and work with individuals? Are there criteria for defining when a client is best served by the group method, by casework, or by a combination of the two? If so, what is the empirical justification or theoretical rationales for such criteria?

What if any behavioral science and practice theory concepts are shared with a major theoretical approach(es) to social casework? If such linkages exist, what additional concepts are involved in working with small groups and how compatible are they with the casework theory?

11. *Unsolved problems.* Discuss the major theoretical, research, and value issues and problems confronting your particular approach to work with small groups.

12. *References.* Give a list of major references.

ACKNOWLEDGMENTS

As part of the initial plan for a stock-taking of the state of group practice theory, the editors hoped that it would be possible to bring contributors to this volume together for several days where they could respond to each other's points of view and discuss issues and problems of current practice theory. Through the generosity of the Lois and Samuel Silberman Fund, such a conference was made possible. The meeting was held at the University of Southern California in September 1974, and its success can be measured by the substantial revisions in the manuscripts and the thinking of the editors that it inspired.

In addition to the authors, attendance at the conference included Gladys Ryland and John Milner, both of whom served as participant-observers and commentators. We thank them for their considerable contributions. We also thank Lilian Macon, Carole Noreen, Erving Ruhl, and Ronaele Whittington for recording the meetings.

Special thanks are also due to Gloria Byrd, Anita Morris, Ruby Smith, and Jacquie Mendelsohn for their careful and professional help in typing the final drafts of the papers.

The greatest recognition and acknowledgment of gratitude goes to those who agreed to write papers for this volume. In addition to their roles as authors, they contributed to this enterprise by a generous sharing of thoughts and feelings and a willingness to accept and use constructive criticism. It is our hope that their generous donation of time and their disciplined scholarship will be recognized as a substantial contribution to theory development in social work.

Robert W. Roberts
Helen Northen
University of Southern California
Los Angeles, California

THEORIES OF SOCIAL WORK WITH GROUPS

1

FROM PRACTICE TO THEORY:
A PERSONALIZED HISTORY

GERTRUDE WILSON

Service to people in need of help has always been a part of communal life throughout recorded history. In the nineteenth century the emphasis was upon need and the materials to meet it rather than the people who exhibited the need. Little attention was given to the methods used, whether problems were poverty, sickness, or some form of personal stress or depravity. Philanthropic organizations, religious and secular, saw people's problems as the result of either societal or individual misdirection.[1] The latter cases were seen as the responsibility of church or governmental agencies; the former were attacked through group organizations composed of concerned citizens and the victims of social situations.

WAR, IMMIGRATION, MUCKRAKERS, SOCIAL EXPERIMENTS, WAR

The latter part of the nineteenth century and the early decades of the twentieth century were years of social reform stimulated by the problems created by hordes of European immigrants seeking better living conditions in the "promised land" and by creeping industrialization.

The charity organization societies, organized in the 1860s, gradually became known as alms-givers to the worthy, resulting in the disapprobation of the word charity for many groups whose interest was in attacking the cause of the misery they and their neighbors confronted. The philosophical

[1] Many organizations with various social philosophies established the National Association of Charities and Corrections in 1873.

difference between these groups became apparent as the settlement idea adopted from the Toynbee Hall experience became known. This difference between "alms to the worthy" and "helping people to help themselves" may be seen today as a difference in theoretical approach as well as in philosophy of human relations.

THEORIES FOLLOW PRACTICE

A "theory," according to Webster's International Unabridged Dictionary, means "the completed result of philosophical induction from experience." Therefore, if a seemingly successful experience is to be repeated it must be translated into words, understandable to others, and tested at least by repetition before it becomes an acceptable professional practice. Applied to social work, service to people comes first, and *analysis* of the *means* through which that service is rendered is carried on through a philosophical screen of the analyzers. A theoretical approach, therefore, implies procedure in accordance with a preconceived idea based upon personal experience or the abstracted experiences of other persons, observed and/or recorded in social research.

Now no one does anything without an idea, which may be called an hypothesis for theory, because no one would do something unless he thought it would work. St Francis of Assisi, Clara Barton, Dorothy Dix, George Williams, Jacob Schiff, Canon Barnett, Jane Addams, Beatrice Webb, Mary Richmond, Charles Loring Brace, Grace Dodge, Lord Baden-Powell, Juliette Low, Lillian Wald, Joseph Lee, Luther Gulick—all these people and many others—had ideas and a philosophy about the welfare of people. Their experiences, based on ideas they dared to try out, were their "theories." Many of these proved to be guidelines for others, who in turn moved from small group associations into larger ones which today, under various names, are local, national, and international social welfare agencies.[2]

PIONEER HELPERS—DO WHAT COMES NATURALLY

During the second half of the nineteenth century and the first decade of the twentieth century, the people with ideas about the lives, living condi-

---

[2] National Catholic Welfare Council, National Jewish Welfare Board, American Red Cross, Settlements, Family Service Association, Child Welfare League, YMCA and YWCA, YMHA and YWHA, National Recreation Association, Boy Scouts, Camp Fire Girls, Salvation Army, and many others.

tions, and social atmosphere of many of their fellow Americans centered their activities upon health and welfare. They were out to help people—individually and/or in groups. The helpers soon found that some problems and some people could best be helped individually, while others benefited from a group approach.[3] Rendering the services frequently entailed enlisting the clients in enterprises to find solutions. The early helpers did not analyze the experience consciously nor did they seek to repeat on Wednesday a technique used on Monday. This can be seen by reading accounts of their experience (see first section of Suggested Readings).

Prior to 1900, settlements were established in several of the major cities by individuals influenced by the founders of Toynbee Hall (1884) in London.[4] It was believed that no one could understand the misery and deprivation of the poor unless he lived in their community and was in face-to-face contact with the people and their conditions; it was important that the worker be accessible when needed. Such a philosophy of helping resulted in the establishment of a living-in residency program which was the earmark of the settlement program until very recent times. Neighborliness was the watchword. Henry Steele Commager commented:

> The opening of Hull-House was the beginning of what was to be one of the great social movements in modern America—the Settlement House movement; here in a way, was the beginning of social work. As yet there was no organized social work in the United States—the beneficent program of Mary Richmond was still in the future—and as yet there was not even any formal study of Sociology. It was no accident that the new University of Chicago, which was founded just a few years after Hull-House, came to be the center of sociological study in America, and that so many of its professors were intimately associated with Hull-House—Albion Small, and John Dewey and the wonderful Miss Breckenridge and the two famous Abbott sisters, Edith and Grace, and thereafter two generations of academic reformers.[5]

These pioneers developed a structure for the provision of services. Few clients came by themselves to settlement houses. Instead they came in twos

---

[3] Eduard C. Lindeman, *Social Discovery* (New York; Republic, 1924).

[4] The Hudson Guild (New York) was established in 1876; the Neighborhood Guild (New York) in 1877; Hull House (Chicago) and the College Settlement (New York) in 1889; the Educational Alliance (New York) in 1890; the East Side House (New York), Andover House (Boston) and the College Settlement (Philadelphia) in 1892; the Chicago Commons in 1894; Henry Street Settlement (New York) in 1895; and the Union Settlement (New York) in 1895.

[5] Henry Steele Commager, in Preface to Jane Addams, *Twenty Years at Hull-House* (New York: Signet, New American Library, 1961). See p. 89 for reasons for living in a Settlement.

and threes or larger groups. Their motivation was based on curiosity, rumors from school or neighborhood, consciousness of perplexing problems, or a desire for friendly visiting. In the beginning, the helpers just responded to what they faced. They did not say to themselves, "Ah ha, here is the structure of a natural group!" They were unaware of structure until the sociologists called this to their attention. Those scholars had located the settlements and centers as ready-made laboratories to study the forms of society through which the agency was providing its services.

WORKERS WITHOUT TITLES

In the beginning, pioneer helpers were unclassified; they were just people helping people. When the houses established were named settlements, they became "settlement workers." When the Y's and Scouts became known as organizations, the helpers were designated as "Y" or "Scout" leaders. The helpers who worked on playgrounds were known as "recreation leaders." In other words, the helpers' functions became institutionalized as part of the agency system of which they were a part. Occasionally, some designated themselves or were designated as social workers. Jane Addams showed her acceptance of the National Conference of Charities and Corrections by accepting the presidency in 1910. Later, in 1917, she showed her identification with social work through her support of the change of its name to the National Conference of Social Work. It is interesting to note that Joseph Lee, father of the playground movement, was also on the board of the conference at that time. Speaking in favor of the change of name, Jane Addams said that in the first fifty years of the American settlement, "We had been afraid to be identified with the word charity, partly because the word itself was obnoxious to many of our neighbors and partly because we wished to be of service to self-respecting working people as well as to the very poor. As time went on, however, we found ourselves identified with the activities of the National Conference of Charities and Corrections." [6] Mary Richmond, who was a member of the special committee on change of name, made an eloquent plea for the change of name to the National Conference of Social Work: "Ours should be a common meeting ground for they [social workers] have no other. Every year we should make the name of the social worker mean more." [7]

---

[6] Jane Addams, *Second Twenty Years at Hull-House* (New York: Macmillan, 1930), pp. 24–5.

[7] Mary E. Richmond, *The Long View* (New York: Russell Sage, 1930), p. 422.

A few years later Mary Richmond wrote:

Everywhere the specialist is in danger of developing an insular habit of mind, and the phenomenon does occur occasionally even within the boundaries of social work. We have seen that a specialized form of skill has been taken into our homes, courts, schools, medical institutions and industries. But quite as important as this skill and quite as much needed in these institutions is the case worker's sense of the whole of social work and of the relation of each part to that whole. . . . The other forms of social work . . . are three—group work, social reform and social research.[8]

Throughout Miss Richmond's writing there is evidence of her intense interest in how to help people. But it was not until very near her death that she even envisioned the possibility of caseworkers serving the group. Their role was to make appropriate referrals. As early as 1922 she acknowledged that there was more to social work than just casework.

No better advice could be given to family case workers, I believe, than to study and develop their work to its point of intersection with social research, with group activities, and with social reform or mass betterment. This does not mean that they should drop their work or slight it in order to make special studies or engage in legislative campaigns, but it does mean that they should be more scientifically productive than they are now. . . .[9]

In the settlements the residents were the first volunteers, but soon others joined to provide the many services and to lead the multiple activities which were dictated by the interests and needs of the people from the neighborhoods. These helpers shared what they knew and could do. They did not receive training, nor participate in staff development. The quality of their contacts with the people who were the victims of the social and economic conditions of the time was largely related to the philosophy and convictions of the head resident and the other semipermanent residents.[10]

SOCIAL REFORM—KEYNOTE TO WORK WITH GROUPS

While the program and structure of the settlement "just grew" as residents became aware of the problems, interests, and needs of their neighbors, the program of most of the other organizations serving groups and individ-

---

[8] Mary E. Richmond, *What is Social Case Work?* (New York: Russell Sage Foundation, 1922), pp. 222–23.

[9] *Ibid.*, p. 225.

[10] *Educational Experiments in Social Settlements* (New York: American Association for Adult Education, 1937), p. 36.

uals was much more formalized. The Young Men's Christian Association, founded in London in 1844, was introduced into the United States in 1851. The original purpose—to improve the spiritual condition of young men in the "drapery and trades"—was gradually expanded to include the improvement of the mental, social, and physical condition of all young men of good moral character.[11] The Young Women's Christian Association was likewise born in London and introduced into the United States in 1866: "On March 3, thirty ladies met at the home of Mrs. Henry F. Durant in Mt. Vernon Street and adopted a constitution under the name of the Boston Young Women's Christian Association. Its object was the temporal, moral and religious welfare of young women who are dependent upon their own exertions for support." [12]

Throughout the rest of the nineteenth century many organizations were formed to promote the mental, moral, physical, social, and spiritual welfare of youth.[13] The purpose and programs of these agencies, when reduced to their constitutional language, provide very little opportunity for differentiating among them. Yet, the author's experience with most of them convinces her that they were and are each unique. They are unique because of the interpretation and program developed by large numbers of volunteers and a few employed people. The responsibilities were administration, program development, and direct leadership, which were shared by volunteers and employed persons, often with little distinction. The constitutions and various parts of the program were partially responsible for their designation as "character-building agencies." Many of these organizations were originated and sponsored by churches—Catholic, Protestant, and Jewish. Many, however, offered their services on an interdenominational basis.

Educating people about social, cultural, and economic conditions accounted for much of the content of the board and committee programs of these agencies. Most of them, in the early part of their history, developed

[11] *Social Work Year Book, 1935,* Fred S. Hall (ed.), (New York: Russell Sage Foundation, 1935), pp. 556–58.

[12] Elizabeth Wilson, *Fifty Years of Association Work Among Young Women* (New York: National Board, YWCA, 1916), p. 321.

[13] For instance, Girls' Friendly Society of the U.S.A., 1877; Boys' Clubs of America, 1906; Boy Scouts of America, 1910; Camp Fire Girls, 1910; Girl Scouts, 1912; Catholic Boys' Brigade of U.S., 1916; Big Brothers and Big Sisters Federation, 1917; Jewish Welfare Board, 1917 (YMHAs and YWHAs and community centers); Junior Achievement, 1919; Pioneer Youth, 1924; Catholic Youth Bureau (clearing House for Catholic youth organizations), 1933.

their own systems of staff and volunteer training, the content of which was, to a great extent, concentrated on *what* to do rather than *how* to do it. Leaders were trained to teach arts and crafts and other activities in a *class* structure even when the members thought of their group as a *club*. Knowledge of the laws of learning and the project method brought recognition of the value of learning while doing, yet there was little evidence that participation in the group was seen as a remedial process. In other words, group therapy was yet to be born.

These pioneer helpers apparently did not think in terms of theories, principles, techniques, or methods. Their thoughts were upon (1) the dreadful conditions under which many, many people were living, (2) the causes of the conditions, and (3) what to do to change the conditions. Faced with people struggling with unbearable conditions, helping behavior might be described as "doing what comes naturally." This principle is open to question if the helper consciously or unconsciously wants for others "the good things of life" he wants for himself—that is, if the worker does not appreciate his client's right to want a different way of life.

Workers engaged in these activities in the early part of the century ferreted out large social problems such as poverty, low wages, long working hours, poor housing and exploitation by landlords, inadequate sanitation, political corruption, and caste-class treatment of people. They provided direct service to feed the hungry and care for the sick, and created opportunities for cultural and recreational activities. They carried on programs of social action to alleviate or eliminate identified social problems through engaging the privileged and the oppressed in informational activities and by making bridges to local, state, and federal officials to secure social legislation and enforcement.[14]

AGENCIES TO MEET SPECIAL NEEDS AND MOVEMENTS
FOR FEDERAL AID

Throughout the first three decades of the twentieth century many specialized agencies were organized around problems of people, rather than people with problems. In other words, the people-centered agencies attempted to help particular people with whatever problems they happened to have, while the problem-centered agencies offered help to people with particular problems.

[14] The major references are contained in Suggested Readings at the end of this paper.

The Salvation Army (1865), the Settlements (1887), and the Family Welfare Association (1911) were oriented to provide service to people, particularly families, with different kinds of problems. The same was true of the youth-serving agencies, although they specialized in the problems of youth and the community, and gave only secondary attention to families. As sensitivity to the environmental and psychological as well as economic causes of many common problems increased, special-problem agencies were developed by and/or with the support of the "people-with-problems" agencies.

The development of the Immigrants' Protective League (1907) illustrates the circumstances that stimulated the development of many other agencies. Attempts to meet the needs of immigrants absorbed personnel and budgets of social agencies. In Chicago, as in every community, all residents of Settlements were aware of the variety and severity of the problems of their newly arrived neighbors. Grace Abbott, one of the residents of Hull-House, began organizing to protect immigrants, especially women and children, from exploitation in every area of living. At first, Hull House was the center, and efforts were carried on through the recently organized Women's Trade Union League of Chicago (1904). In 1907, with Grace Abbott as director, the Immigrants' Protective League (IPL) was incorporated with the objective of helping immigrants, regardless of sex.[15]

In addition to direct service to immigrants, the League engaged in efforts to secure more adequate service to immigrants from local, state, and federal governmental agencies. Travel and arrival information, job-finding, legal protection, income provision, and defense of immigrants' rights to participate in their new government were some of the services provided by the IPL. Immigrants faced large-scale exploitation. The failure of the federal government to assume some responsibility for the immigrant after he paid his head tax at Ellis Island was an especial grievance. Grace Abbott gave leadership to the effort to correct this situation.[16]

Jane Addams described the movement for public tax support of programs to meet the needs of the hungry and the sick:

> One of the first lessons we learned at Hull-House was that private beneficence is totally inadequate to deal with the vast numbers of the city's disinherited. We also quickly came to realize that there are certain types of wretchedness from which

[15] Sophinisba Breckinridge, *New Homes for Old* (New York: Harper, 1921).
[16] Grace Abbott, *The Immigrant and the Community* (New York: Century, 1917).

every private philanthropy shrinks and which are cared for only in those wards of the county hospital for the wrecks of vicious living or in the city's isolation hospital. . . .[17]

Attention to securing governmental aid on local, state, and federal levels occupied a prominent place in the programs of all Settlements and in most of the youth-service agencies. The YWCA was in the forefront of these agencies in the early part of the century, under the leadership of such women as Florence Simms, Lucy Carner, and Grace Coyle. Both the Settlements and the youth agencies were influenced by their professional associates, among whom were Mary Follett, Alfred Sheffield, A. J. Muste, Jacob Riis, John Dewey, W. E. B. Dubois, Paul Kellogg, Reinhold Neibuhr, Roger Baldwin, Paul Douglas, A. Phillip Randolph, Sidney Hillman, Agnes Nester, Eugene Kinkle Jones, Norman Thomas, Hilda Worthington Smith, and Horace M. Kallen.

EMERGENCE OF LEARNED SOCIETIES AND SPECIALIZED WORKERS' ASSOCIATIONS

The social and economic conditions of the nineteenth and twentieth centuries not only called for organized efforts to help with all kinds of problems but also brought strong "consciousness of kind" among the workers who had first-hand contact with people and their problems. Accompanying the organization of local, state, and national helping agencies was the organization of the workers who provided these services. The psychologists led the procession in 1844 with the American Psychological Association. The physicans were not far behind: the American Medical Association was organized in 1847 and the American Dental Association was formed in 1860. Education was early recognized as a national need, and the National Education Association (1857) succeeded in influencing the government to establish the Office of Education in the Department of the Interior in 1867. The American Bar Association claimed national recognition in 1878; in 1880 the Academy of Political Science was established, and one year later the controversial American Federation of Labor was organized. It was not until 1905 that the American Sociological Society achieved national status.

By the turn of the century, workers in the "service professions" had developed organizations for study and research in their specialized areas.

[17] Addams, *Twenty Years,* p. 219.

The operation of "consciousness of kind" was contagious.[18] Professional and semiprofessional organizations began emerging to answer different human needs.[19]

Medical social workers, who were in first-hand contact with the already organized medical personnel, were the first social workers to organize a professional social work organization in 1918. In 1919 the American Association of Visiting Teachers was founded. In the same year the eleven schools of social work became an association. Social workers from many fields and several specializations organized themselves into the American Association of Social Workers in 1921. Five years later the social workers specializing in service to mentally and emotionally ill persons organized the American Association of Psychiatric Social Workers, and twenty years later in 1946 the American Association of Group Workers claimed professional status.

THE GREAT DEPRESSION, THE SOCIAL SECURITY PROGRAM, AND WORLD WAR II

On the morning of the stock market crash of 1929, the author, who was the administrator of a youth-serving agency on the West Side of Chicago, came into her office as the phone was ringing long and seriously. She picked up the phone to hear Jane Addams ask: "What does your lobby look like?" "It's full of girls—every inch!" "Mine is full of men, women, and children—we must do something. . . . I have asked Paul Douglas to come down for lunch; will you join us?" That afternoon these three socially concerned persons mapped a program which included a little W.P.A. for Chicago (one of the patterns for the later federal program), campaigns for Unemployment Insurance for Illinois, and other emergency devices.[20]

Civic leaders and social workers, volunteer and paid, cooperated in hard work, night and day, to search for answers to the great questions of unemployment, poverty, and racial and national prejudices. The scene of the struggle shifted as efforts of more and more concerned people turned toward demands to lessen the burden of privately financed agencies through assis-

---

[18] Franklin H. Giddings, *The Principles of Sociology* (New York: Macmillan, 1896), p. 17.

[19] For instance, the American Association of Workers for the Blind was established in 1905; the American Association for Adult Education in 1926; the American Association of School Physicians in 1927; the Association of Church Social Workers in 1934.

[20] At this time *Standards of Unemployment Insurance* (Chicago: University of Chicago Press, 1932) was in preparation. Paul H. Douglas brought selected materials to this meeting.

tance from federal, state, and county governments. Finally, in 1935, the Social Security Program was enacted, ushering in a new way of problem-solving and new relationships in the federal, state, and local systems, public and private. Many social workers were active in this arena; the leaders, with a few exceptions, were the stalwart ones of the previous two decades.[21]

It is important to keep in mind that while personnel of the social agencies were painfully aware of the deprivation of the people whom they served, they never lost sight of the fact that institutional change was a prerequisite to the actual relief of the suffering. Washington, D.C., was familiar territory for most of the workers. Many leaders, members of organized groups, and clients went to Washington and state capitols to underscore the need for state and federal laws to protect the lives of the people. In the twenties the author accompanied groups of women employed in the silk mills of Allentown, Pennsylvania, to Washington to testify in favor of Unemployment Insurance. Other workers from many states were involved in similar programs. Social workers, teachers, and other professional and lay groups lobbied their senators and representatives in Washington to secure federal help. They were successful in establishing the Employment Service in 1907, the Children's Bureau in 1912, and the Women's Bureau in 1918. It was not, however, until pressure for the passage of the Social Security Act occurred that other objectives were achieved. For instance, the Federal Emergency Relief Administration, the Immigration and Naturalization Service, and the National Recovery Administration were all formed in 1933. Unemployment Insurance had to wait until an amendment to the Social Security Act was passed in 1936.

SOCIOLOGICAL AND PSYCHOLOGICAL CONCEPTS PENETRATE SERVICES TO GROUPS

Historically, the goals of most organizations which recognized *the group* (family, natural, and formed ones) as the unit of service were (1) to change social conditions of the poor, (2) to create the conditions and influences under which the people served could develop democratic social and moral characteristics, and (3) to enable participants to make emotional adjustments to situations in which they found themselves. As Jane Addams wrote,

[21] Eveline Burns, "Social Security Act," in Russell H. Kurtz (ed.), *Social Work Year Book, 1937* (New York: Russell Sage Foundation, 1937), pp. 472–80.

Settlements are trying through all these years to build up a technique, although with only a few generalizations to go upon *in order to use the group itself for educational ends.* Perhaps the best efforts in this direction have been carried out through the National Federation of Settlements. . . . Certain enthusiasts for creative discussion, such as the national Y.W.C.A. in their wide spread organization of committees, boards and clubs have accepted the growing change of basis in modern life from individual to organized activities, and seek ways by which people in group relations shall find the mutual stimulation and enhancement of shared purposes and pooled resources.[22]

In a discussion of whether neighborhood work could have a scientific basis, Burgess pointed out that the first stage toward a scientific basis is the search for knowledge and intimate contact with reality—that is, the concrete facts of life. He said that Settlement work represented the most devoted, idealistic, and intelligent phase of social work of the past generation. The residents, however, soon found that sympathetic understanding and intimate contacts failed to solve many problems.

The recalcitrancy of the boys' gang, the opposition and manipulation of the ward boss, the competition of commercialized recreation, the unsolvable cultural conflict between immigrant parents and Americanized children are only a few of the many perplexing conditions . . . which resisted the goodwill of the Settlement workers. They therefore began to study their communities in the attempt to state the factors at work by an analysis of the elements in the situation. . . . This interest in the discovery of factors in the social situation may therefore be called the second stage in the trend . . . toward a scientific basis.[23]

The Industrial Revolution eventually brought widespread mechanization and changed the meaning of work. But having no work is physical and emotional deprivation, an experience large numbers of people endured during the Great Depression and too many still experience. Yet today much work brings boredom and self-depreciation instead of self-esteem. Beginning in the mid-twenties, social work began to help people, individually and in groups, with resulting emotional problems. At that time the author worked with groups of women with personal and family problems, as well as in educational programs geared toward social action for unionization, employment insurance, and other protective legislation. In 1928, when writing a job analysis of an industrial secretary in the YWCA, she made the following comments:

[22] Addams, *Second Twenty Years,* pp. 410–11.
[23] Robert E. Park, Ernest W. Burgess, Roderick D. McKenzie, *The City* (Chicago: University of Chicago Press, 1925), pp. 142–43.

Economic, social and religious adjustment of women and girls to the life of today
is the general field of the Young Women's Christian Association. . . . Education
of women and girls in industry leads to personal development and participation in
activities within their own group and in the community. . . . The solution of individual and sometimes personal problems of girls in the club has come in for
special emphasis . . . such as (a) difficulties in spending wages wisely and (b)
personal problems when one is in love.[24]

The early beginning of a theoretical framework for work with groups
could be found wherever sociologists and other social scientists came in contact with youth-serving personnel. In New York City the faculty of Union
Theological Seminary and the national staff of the YMCA gave leadership to
the organization of the New York Conference on Group Work. In Chicago
the author was a member of a small group which had Sunday breakfasts
together around the fireplace of its teacher and leader, Robert E. Park. Here
the members discussed the practical and theoretical aspects of projects with
street-corner gangs. Members of this select group included F. M. Thrasher
and Horace Cayton, students at the University of Chicago. Everything happening through social processes was a demonstrated proposition. Chicago
social workers were aware of the various projects with groups sponsored by
social scientists at the University of Chicago and other academic institutions.
Some demonstration projects were sponsored by social agencies, notable
among them the camps run by Association House, where individualization
was the guiding principle. The camps were directed by Mrs. Eleanor Eells;
Dr. Irene Josselyn was a consultant.

Such experiments were carried on in many parts of the country, and the
findings resulted in a melding of the concepts of sociology and psychology.
Service to campers and members of clubs demanded an increased understanding of the meaning of interaction in groups. Two important questions
confronted the worker: what did the different behavior of members reveal
about their personal problems, and what did it do to the group-as-a-whole?
Such experiences demonstrated graphically that a *group is more than the
sum of its parts*. Such conclusions caused some, including one early sociologist, to call this phenomenon "the group mind." [25] Immediate controversy arose which resulted in discrediting the term, but it greatly increased current knowledge of the complex concept of group. Cattell, writing

---

[24] Gertrude Wilson, *Job Analysis of Industrial Secretaries, Young Women's Christian Association of the United States* (New York: National Board, YWCA, 1928), pp. 1, 16–17.

[25] William McDougall, *The Group Mind* (New York: Putnam, 1920).

of McDougall, said that ". . . many of his conclusions about group behavior are likely to prove correct, and his basic contention that it is rewarding to deal with groups as single entities remains the spingboard whence we take off into new research fields." [26]

Sociological concepts coupled with those drawn from psychology became the substance of group meetings, conferences, and seminars. The Chicago chapter of the American Association of Social Workers established a subcommittee to study group work: Claudia Wannamaker and Margaret Svendsen from the Institute for Juvenile Research were in leadership roles. The New York Conference on Group Work, also interested in basic concepts in the development of methodology, attracted, among others, John Dewey and Robert MacIver to their meetings. Agencies, especially the YMCA and the YWCA, turned regional conferences into seminars for the study of groups and the individuals who compose them. It was soon evident that more skill was needed both in conducting and participating in group discussions. As a consequence, the discussion method itself became a subject for study. The Inquiry, a small study organization, undertook the task of formalizing discussion as a method and of teaching this to interested groups. Alfred Sheffield's publications became popular.[27] Grace Coyle, who was studying for her doctorate degree at Columbia, participated in The Inquiry.[28]

During one summer in the 1930s, Grace Coyle, Lucy Carner, and the author spent part of their vacations on a walking and camping-out trip in the Green Mountains. Each took her turn carrying a book, just published in English, entitled *Systematic Sociology* by Leopold von Wiese.[29] Whenever there was a stop to rest, eat, or sleep, turns were taken at reading aloud. Since all had first-hand experience with small natural groups, formed organizational groups, and large social action groups, the concepts were tested by applying them to real experiences. Concepts defined, explained, and/or discussed in von Wiese are dynamic in nature—for example: ". . . in strictly sociologi-

---

[26] Raymond B. Cattell, "Concepts and Methods in the Measurement of Group Syntality," in A. Paul Hare, Edgar F. Borgatta, Robert F. Bales (eds.), *Small Groups* (New York: Knopf, 1955), p. 112.

[27] Alfred Sheffield, *Creative Discussion* (New York: Association Press, 1926, and *Training for Group Experience* (New York: Association Press, 1929).

[28] Grace L. Coyle, *Social Process in Organized Groups* (New York: Smith, 1930). This was Coyle's dissertation.

[29] Leopold von Wiese, *Systematic Sociology*. Adapted and amplified by Howard J. Becker (New York: Wiley, 1932).

cal analysis it is necessary to concentrate on inter-human relations as such, rather than on the purpose, aims or ends of these relations." [30]

The use of groups for therapeutic purposes received a great deal of support from Susanne Schulze and Fritz Redl, two social workers who emigrated from Germany and Austria, respectively, in the late thirties. Schulze stimulated interest in and increased the knowledge and skill of United States social workers in the constructive use of groups in children's institutions, while Redl humanized work with "kids" and helped group workers to relate "doing what comes naturally" to psychosocial theories and techniques.

Thus, step by step, a theoretical framework for the practice of group work was created out of the minds and experiences of many people.

EMERGENCE OF GROUP WORK AS A PROFESSIONAL DESIGNATION

By the mid-twenties the group was well established as a medium of service. Settlement houses, youth-service agencies, churches, and schools had their club programs, with leaders assigned by the agency. Many agencies offered training programs for their leaders, and some looked to the Adult Education Association and the National Recreation Association for materials and guides.[31] While many of the standard texts in the behavioral sciences had not yet been published, some workers and leaders in these agencies were associated with the yet-to-become-famous scientists through common membership in social action groups. Writings were exchanged, and informal conferences and intellectual "gab-fests" brought socially significant concepts into the consciousness of many who were in first-hand contact with small groups. In both the small program groups and the larger social-action groups there was an increasing awareness of the nature of group processes and of the techniques by which the processes could be affected to secure the purposes of the group.

The group process implied the participation of the members in (1) recognizing the problem to be solved, (2) picking the problem to pieces, (3) finding the relationship of the pieces, (4) setting up possible solutions, (5) identifying the one to be considered first, (6) trying it out, and (7) planning and carrying out a program to solve the problem. Emphasis was placed on

[30] *Ibid,* p. 46.

[31] For example, LeRoy Bowman, "Application of Progressive Education to Group Work," in Joshua Lieberman (ed.), *New Trends in Group Work* (New York: Association Press, 1938), and Joseph Lee, *Play in Education* (New York: Macmillan, 1915).

the worker's understanding as much as possible about the community and its resources, and knowing as much as possible about the background and interests of each member in order to understand his behavior in the group and his part in finding a solution to the problem undertaken by the group.[32]

In tracing the activities of social agencies, emphasis has been placed upon activities geared to social reform. This does not mean that the same personnel were ignoring personal problems of individuals or that they were referring them to caseworkers for service. Some agencies employed caseworkers as well as group workers to serve groups, but for the most part both group and individual service were given by the same worker.

A personal experience of the author illustrates this point. She was executive of a small agency on the West Side of Chicago; in addition she provided a job referral service for older teenage girls seeking employment in the neighborhood. Many of the girls attended educational-recreational activities. Boy friends were always welcome. Because the author had a personal contact with most of the participants, she became a personal counselor as well as job referrer. As might be expected, problems were manifold and she sought advice and consultation from staff at the Institute for Juvenile Research (IJR). This was the time when Karen Horney, having immigrated to the United States, was connected with the Chicago Psychoanalytic Society. Horney sought help from the IJR to understand Americanese as spoken by young girls. The IJR. sought the author's help, and this led to Dr. Horney becoming a consultant to the staff of the agency. Through meetings and individual conferences, the staff was helped to meet usual and unusual problems.

To summarize, it can be said that when a worker undertook the responsibility of serving a group, the prime requisite was that he have knowledge about and as much understanding as possible of the dynamics of three constructs: (1) groups, (2) human beings, and (3) social situations. He had to be familiar with the range of behavior implied in all three cases. He had to be aware that all groups are different because all human beings are different, as are all social situations. He had to know that the purposes of every group differ, even if the activities are similar.

Prior to the establishment of group work as one of the specializations at the School of Applied Social Science at Western Reserve University in the

---

[32] This outline is based on in-service training courses given by the author in the twenties.

mid-twenties, the term group records was practically unknown. In the twenties, when the author was on the staff of the Buffalo YWCA, she was the director of Camp Forty Acres. During part of this time, Gladys Ryland was the program director. Through her leadership, the program content was rich in the arts. Small groups expressed their interests and problems through the dance and in various forms of crafts. Observations of changes in behavior of campers as they participated in such activities were recorded in weekly reports. Ruth Perkins used some of this material for her book *Magic Casements*. [33] In 1930 Clara Kaiser edited the first book of group records; [34] they were written by students in the course in group work at Western Reserve University.

The reports, articles, and books written prior to the thirties reveal some common terminology, primarily related to social reform, physical problems, and behavior of neighbors or members. Sociologists who used neighborhood centers as laboratories began to build a conceptual language descriptive of a group and its activity. By the beginning of the thirties, such terms as *purpose, structure, social process, status and role,* and *stages of group development* became part of the worker's vocabulary. With increased awareness of emotional problems, many psychologists turned their attention from rats and mice to people and their social adjustment. Social psychologists increased in numbers and prestige, and various terms describing aspects of *interpersonal relations*—such as *acceptance, rejection, conflict,* and *control*—became part of the common vocabulary. By the late twenties and early thirties, psychoanalytical terms began creeping into social work terminology. Freud had visited the United States, Rank was active in the East, and Adler held seminars in Chicago as well as the eastern cities. Franz Alexander was at the University of Chicago.

Throughout the period covered, there was only marginal use of the term group work; in fact, only occasionally was the word group used except in abstract references. For agency purposes, the words clubs, classes, and committees were used to describe the structure through which the service of the agency was delivered.

Newstetter, one of the founders of group work as a specialized service in social work, accounts for the marriage of the words group and work to his

[33] Ruth Perkins, *Magic Casements* (New York: National Board, YWCA, 1927).

[34] Clara Kaiser (ed.), *The Group Records of Four Clubs at the University Settlement Center* (Cleveland: Western Reserve University, 1930).

associates: On a long train ride to the 1927 National Conference of Social Work, Newstetter and Walter Pettit were sharing the latest developments in their respective schools, Western Reserve University and the New York School of Social Work. Newstetter remarked that he had an interesting project going for which he had adequate financial support, but he had two problems: (1) he did not know what to call it and (2) he needed a director of research to evaluate it. After Newstetter's graphic description, Pettit said that it sounded to him as if the project would demonstrate the delivery of social service through groups, and that at his school they called the delivery of social service to individuals *casework;* why not call this Case Western Reserve University project *group work?* Newstetter was enthusiastic. Then he asked about a possible research director. Pettit hesitated and then said that a graduate of the New York School with a lot of experience had recently moved to the Chicago YWCA, but if she could be enticed away, she would be just the person Newstetter was describing.[35] The term group work became part of academia and, within less than a decade, an official part of the social work profession and practice.

It should be noted that the term group work was frequently used prior to this time in religious education and adult education circles. In these instances, the term usually either referred to a movement or to a program of activities. The method or methods used were regarded as adult education methods.

The concept of group work as a method was most popular with schools of social work. In 1937, according to Grace Coyle, thirteen educational institutions were offering courses in group work; of these, ten were schools of social work.[36] Western Reserve University, as it was then known, offered both courses and field work on a two-year graduate basis.

In the summer of 1934 Grace Coyle organized a two-week institute on group work methods at Fletcher Farm in Vermont. It was attended by forty workers from the YWCA and the Settlements. Similar institutes and seminars were offered under the auspices of the YMCA at George Williams

---

[35] In 1929 the author took the position in the Chicago YWCA vacated by Clara Kaiser who, in 1927, went to Western Reserve University. In 1934 Grace Coyle took the position vacated by Miss Kaiser when she left for advanced study. In 1936 the author joined the faculty of Western Reserve University to work with Newstetter and Coyle. In 1938 the author accompanied Newstetter to the University of Pittsburgh to help organize the new School of Social Work.

[36] Grace Coyle, "Social Group Work," in Kurtz (ed.), *Social Work, 1937,* p. 464.

College in Chicago by Hedley Dimock and at Springfield College by Paul Limbert, and at city and regional conferences. The other youth-serving agencies began to add "how to" instruction to "what to do," but it was not until people who called themselves group workers began to move toward organization that the term had professional significance.

In the fall of 1934, representatives from the New York Conference on Education in Group Work met in Ligonier, Pennsylvania, with group workers from Western Reserve, Ohio State, and Chicago's Committee on Group Work to discuss the need for consolidation of thoughts and people.[37] It may have been this group which was largely responsible for recommending to Katherine Lenroot, the president of the 1935 National Conference of Social Work (NCSW), that a section on group work be added.

Early in the spring of 1935, the author accompanied five other group workers [38] in a car driven by Roy Sorenson in an all-night trip from Chicago to Cleveland in order to join seven others [39] from New York City, Pittsburgh, and Cleveland for two days of planning the meetings for the first sessions of the Group Work Section of the NCSW. Thirty-six papers were presented. Four papers were presented by faculty of two schools of social work. The Settlements, the YMCA, workers' education, parent and community councils, and the YWCA were each represented by three papers. Workers from research and parent education, the National Recreation Association, and professors from sociology departments presented two papers each. One paper was presented by a worker from each of the following organizations: the Institute for Juvenile Research, a university physical education department, a department of a hospital, the Union Theological Seminary, the Girl Scouts, the Boy Scouts, the Boys' Clubs of America, the Children's Bureau, and the Agricultural Administration of the U.S. government. Since the 1935 Group Work Section of the NCSW is a landmark in the history of group work, the identification of the participants has been presented to demonstrate the variety of areas, backgrounds, experiences, philosophies, education, and training of people who contributed to the Group Work Section in 1935. This

[37] See Charles E. Hendry, "All Past is Prologue" in *Toward Professional Standards, A.A.G.W. 1945–46* (New York: Association Press, 1947); Marion Robinson, "Reminiscing with Louis Kraft," *The Group,* X, 1 (October 1947).

[38] Neva Boyd, Eleanor Eells, Dorothy Spiker, Margaret Svendsen, and Claudia Wannmaker.

[39] Henry Busch, Grace Coyle, Dora Einert, Charles E. Hendry, Leah Milkman, Clara Kaiser, and W. I. Newstetter.

galaxy of people, programs, and identifications enriched and broadened the field as well as created many questions for group work practitioners.

TRANSLATION OF CONCEPTS IN PROFESSIONAL LITERATURE

From 1935 to 1955, group work was a vibrant, growing movement with real promise as a force for social change. Psychosocial concepts were identified; the purposes, structures, and processes of different groups were seen as guidelines for new techniques; and psychological explanations of the behavior of individuals and the group as a whole gave guidance to the worker as he sought his appropriate role. As indicated earlier, there was much fermentation of these ideas in seminars and workshops, but the real impetus came from two papers presented at the 1935 NCSW by Grace L. Coyle and W. I. Newstetter. Coyle's paper is still a classic, one which bears re-reading many times.[40] The opening sentence provides the clue: "In a period like the present every human activity must test itself by its contribution to the vital changes that are making our society."

Newstetter's paper, the first public presentation of the theoretical operation of a group, was based primarily on sociological concepts available at that time. Since then all of the sociopsychological sciences have found much to study in all types of groups and the current social group work method is based on concepts derived from research in all sciences dealing with human relations. Newstetter first pointed out that "it is necessary to distinguish between group work as a *field,* group work as a *process,* and group work *techniques.*"[41] The confusion caused by the indiscriminate use of the term group work is a burden which has been borne throughout the last three and a half decades. Almost every agency which sought to serve two or more individuals at one time and in one place called themselves group work agencies. Many of the established leaders, however, were not interested in concepts and methods as such. Newstetter's speech was met with much ridicule, and terminology gleaned from the speech was quoted in derision throughout the conference.

However, by the time of the next NCSW in 1936, there was a large

[40] Grace L. Coyle, "Group Work and Social Change" (Pugsley Award), *Proceedings of the National Conference of Social Work, 1935,* (Chicago: University of Chicago Press, 1935), pp. 393–405.

[41] "What is Social Group Work?" *Proceedings, NCSW, 1935,* (Chicago: University of Chicago Press, 1935), pp. 291–99.

response to the invitation of the New York Committee on Group Work to meet for the purpose of discussing the formation of a National Association for the Study of Group Work (NASGW).[42] Membership in the Association was open to any person interested in its purpose, which was the advancement of group work through the utilization of knowledge gained from local study groups. Four study commissions were established: (1) Group Records—Grace L. Coyle, Chairman; (2) Standards—Hedley S. Dimock, Chairman; (3) Objectives—Clara A. Kaiser, Chairman; and (4) Leadership—Arthur L. Swift, Chairman.

Examination of the reports of these commissions reveals the confusion between group work as a method and a so-called group work agency. This was particularly noticeable in the reports of local committees studying the objectives of group work in 1936. The heritage of forty to fifty years of being a "Settlement worker" or a "Y worker" was not easily cast aside. The influence of the agency and its need to explain its work to the community hampered the development of professional identity—a first step in the development of methodology—until workers had the support of a professional association.

At the time of the organization of the NASGW, literature about group work was very scarce.[43] Recognizing this fact, one commission was created to collect and make available to the members reprints of all that could be found in various periodicals. Charles Hendry, commenting on this gap, said in 1937:

> . . . the literature on group work has grown largely out of an agency rather than an academic setting. Our literature is sectarian, not secular, and is oriented to the needs of a particular organization rather than to professional function.[44]

The NASGW attempted to meet this need by the establishment of a bulletin entitled *The Group—in Education, Recreation, Social Work.* Introducing the first issue, Hendry called this publication an instrument of inquiry.[45] *The Group* provided a media for workers in many fields of human

---

[42] See *Proceedings,* First Annual Report, NASGW, 1936–37, Indianapolis, May 26–28, 1937, pp. 2–3.

[43] Major writers are listed in second section of Suggested Readings at the end of this paper.

[44] Charles Hendry, "Cooperation Among Group Workers on a National Scale," *Proceedings of the National Conference of Social Work, 1937* (Chicago: University of Chicago Press, 1937), p. 279.

[45] *The Group,* 1(1):1 (February 1939).

relations. It was the only outlet for group service workers who were interested in methodology.[46]

It was in *The Group,* the annual conference reports of the NASGW, re-
named the American Association for the Study of Group Work (AASGW) in
1938, and the NCSW that group workers had the opportunity to report experiments in method as well as the many aspects of group work as a movement. Some books about group work methods, agencies, and movements
began to be published.[47] Many articles in educational, social science, and
specialized social work journals appeared in rapid succession over the next
twenty years.

The editor of Association Press, S. M. Keeny, wrote a strident criticism of the literature of group work for the 1940 Conference of Social
Work. He reported that Everett Du Vall, then of Temple University, had
identified 3000 volumes that were more or less related to group work; of
these, 1000 volumes were considered more closely related to group work
and seventy-six were classified as "group work methods and techniques."
One of Keeny's choice bits is quoted:

> Part of the difficulty arises from the intellectual indigestion of some of our authors,
> caused by their attempt to assimilate too many strange dishes too closely together.
> Three or four courses of new psychology have been served in the last fifteen years;
> as many of sociology; one or two of anthropology—all spiced in recent years with
> economic seasoning. Freud, Watson, Koffka, Lynd, Mead, Pareto, Marx—these
> are but a few that have been dished up to disturb us as we were quietly munching
> our vegetarian diet of Follett, Dewey, Kilpatrick and Lindeman.[48]

[46] *The Survey, Survey Graphic,* the *Compass* (a predecessor to *Social Work*), and *Staff,* the
magazine of the social service employees, published some articles on group work as a movement as it contributed to social action. Publications of other organizations such as the Visiting
Teachers' Association, the Family Welfare Association of America, and the American Association of Psychiatric Social Workers combined organizational matters with some contributions on
methods. Bulletins and magazines of national group service agencies produced some articles on
methodology. As early as 1937, the *American Sociological Review* published an article by the
author entitled, "Record Keeping in Group Work—A Contribution to Sociology," *American
Sociological Review* 11(2):237–46 (April 1937).

[47] See second section of Selected Readings. For additional references to pertinent publications prior to 1945, see "Bibliography on Group Work," compiled by Gertrude Wilson and
Gladys Ryland (New York: Association Press, 1945).

[48] S. M. Keeny, "A Criticism of the Literature of Group Work," *Proceedings of the National Conference of Social Work, 1940* (New York: Columbia University Press, 1940), p. 566.
It is important to note that Dr. Du Vall used the term "group work" in its most generic sense,
using all reference to the use of groups by social scientists, psychologists, educators, clergy-
men, politicians, and others in his identification of 3000 volumes, or even the 1000 volumes he
considered closely related to group work.

The literature in the field, albeit agency-oriented, reflects familiarity with many of the same scholars who were innovators in educational and social processes. As has been mentioned, Jane Addams' openness led to the dissemination of the concepts of such theoreticians as John Dewey, Albion Small, Mary Follett, Paul Douglas, and Robert E. Park. These contributions, along with those of other sociologists, economists, anthropologists, and psychologists, became integrated into a basic theory for the practice of group work. Wherever located, workers began to feel connected with each other because of a common knowledge of theories drawn from such scholars as MacIver, Parsons, Cooley, Jennings, Franz Alexander, Eubank, Anna Freud, Sigmund Freud, Fromm, Issacs, Mead, Moreno, Rank, Warner, and Lunt. Basic ideas were drawn from the research of such scientists. People working with groups tested their practical use and transmitted their experiences to their colleagues through papers delivered at workshops, seminars, and conferences of local, regional, and national organizations. Many of these papers were produced from theses written by the rapidly increasing number of students and faculty specializing in group work in schools of social work. This type of research might be called one of "trial and error": the results were accented on the basis of the deep conviction of the writers that the process described was helpful to individuals and society, and not because they were demonstrated by chi-squares or any other mathematical evaluations of the process through which human need is alleviated.

POSTWAR CONSOLIDATION AND INTEGRATION

In the preceding sections, the activities and ideas of people serving people individually and in groups throughout this century have been traced. Slowly these ideas began to crystallize, and were formulated into concepts upon which principles of practice could be based. The training of workers moved into colleges, universities, and graduate schools of social work. Leaders began to develop professional associations. Many questions were left unanswered. The central one that prevailed throughout was—and to some extent still is—the meaning of the term group work.

SOCIAL GROUP WORK: TREATMENT, PREVENTION, OR SOCIAL ACTION?

Relationship of group work to casework. There was, as indicated earlier, a great difference of opinion among both employed and volunteer workers about a social work identification.[49] Many thought of themselves as educators, with some identification with the adult education movement. The roster and the early writings of the early AASGW members demonstrates that many of its leaders regarded group work as an adult education method. The stereotype of caseworkers as alms-givers who were resistive to social change and were busy "adjusting" people to bad conditions was still a deterrent to social work unity.

The American Association of Social Workers (A.A.S.W.), organized in 1921, was almost entirely composed of caseworkers, many of them graduates of schools of social work. One of the items at the first annual meeting of the NASGW in May 1937 was a progress report by Louis Kraft on negotiations with the AASW to secure a change in membership requirements that would permit older, experienced, professionally able group workers who were not graduates of schools of social work to join the generic association of social workers. When some group workers were admitted to AASW, another link with social work was forged and a divisive element was introduced in the membership of AASGW.

For years, group service workers had little professional contact with caseworkers. In 1937 this author summarized the causes of their mutual exclusiveness as indifference, latent antagonism, and only intermittent cooperation.

> Vocabulary difficulties, differences in conceptual knowledge, even differences in fundamental philosophies have blocked progress toward complete and easy cooperation. . . . Back of this difference in vocabulary and the meaning of words lies a difference in actual concepts. For example, "the group as an entity" has a particular meaning to group workers which is not shared by most case workers. The group worker does work with the individual and is concerned with his growth and development, but also with the group, which, while composed of individuals, is in itself an entity and as such is an essential to the development of the individual. The individual not only uses the group to meet his personal need but also to obtain objectives which he could not have reached alone. The realism of the concept of the group as an entity is difficult to maintain except through the medium of experience and then words are unnecessary, for the feeling of "belonging to a group" carries its own reality. To the inexperienced this may sound mystical or at best on a deeper level than objective definition; it is doubtful, however, whether any phenomenon which involves human experience can be adequately described without the help of the empirical.[50]

[49] Addams, *Second Twenty Years*, pp. 24–25.
[50] Gertrude Wilson, "Interplay of Insights of Case Work and Group Work," *Proceedings, NCSW, 1937*, pp. 151–52.

The problem of acceptance by other social work practitioners was felt by many group workers. The scorn exhibited toward "those workers who play with children," "run dances," "go camping," or "teach arts and crafts" is well remembered. In 1936 it was reported that the California Conference of Social Work seriously questioned whether group workers were social workers.[51] Faculty members of the School of Social Service Administration of the University of Chicago minced no words in their exclusion of any study of an activity remotely connected with recreation. The general population of the country was still dominated by the "Protestant ethic."

Recognition of the importance of hand-foot-brain activities in the growing-up process of all human beings, and of their remedial values for the physically and emotionally handicapped, led the author and others to secure a grant from the Buhl Foundation to include an activities studio in its allotment for the development of the new School of Social Work at the University of Pittsburgh. Gladys Ryland, who at the time was teaching group work students at Western Reserve University how to use a great variety of activities in working with small groups of all ages, joined the Pittsburgh faculty and was assigned to equip the studio with the necessary tools and materials needed to teach graduate students how to use such activities as games, folk songs and dances, dramatics, music and art, design and crafts, clay modeling, woodwork, and photography in the service of members of groups and the enhancement of the group-as-a-whole.

The rationale for developing a strong group-activities component in the curriculum was clarified. The studio provided the optimum situation for helping students to make effective use of the "tools of the trade." The social worker began to serve as a resource of knowledge and skill in helping the group select and adapt content for the group experience. Members related to each other through a wide variety of activities; it was demonstrated that verbalization was not always necessary for the individual or the group to gain insight into the processes of adjustment and development.

Human experience involves activity on motor, verbal, mental, and affective levels, with close interplay among them; activity on one level stimulates the others. The worker must have the program skills, knowledge, and values "in his muscles," not just in his "notebook." Thus prepared, he can foresee what a given experience may mean to particular individuals with special needs and to the group's interpersonal relationships and develop-

[51] "Objectives of Group Work"—A Commission Report, NASGW (New York, Association Press, 1936).

ment; he may plan ahead, yet be flexible and able to change according to reactions; he may, with reasonable accuracy, forecast the outcome.[52]

The activity program of group service agencies was, and still is, difficult for many caseworkers to accept. It was not until psychiatrists and psychoanalysts began to write and give consultation and seminars on games, dancing, crafts, and other therapeutic activities that some caseworkers began to interest themselves in their use. Some workers and their agencies designated such services as "group casework;" others used the term group therapy, and sought consultation from psychiatrists rather than group workers.

An increasing number of agencies offering services primarily to groups began labeling themselves as group work agencies, casting off other titles such as "character-building" or "recreation and informal education." [53] This confusion was more pronounced than in agencies providing service to individuals. It was not until medical and psychiatric clinics and hospitals added group services that workers gained recognition for their professional knowledge and skill.

The use of groups in treatment situations became more and more popular; nevertheless, the words treatment and therapy carried an undemocratic meaning to some group practitioners—they became a "red flag" to some and a symbol of prestige to others.

It was the author's privilege to be one of the pioneers in the extension of professional education in group method to clinics and hospitals for physically and emotionally ill persons. Dr. Harry Little, who was a lecturer at the University of Pittsburgh School of Social Work and director of the Child Guidance Clinic, became interested in the content of the courses offered in social group work. At his invitation, one of the second-year students. Gisela Konopka, was placed in an experimental project in the use of groups to treat parents and children chosen from the clients of the Clinic. The following year, Konopka was employed by the Clinic, and then other students were assigned. The work spread rapidly to other schools and other cities.

Social service to groups whose members were suffering from physical,

---

[52] See Gladys Ryland, "The Place, Use, and Direction of Program Activities," in *Toward Professional Standards, AAGW, 1945–46* (New York: Association Press, 1947), pp. 51–63; Fritz Redl and David Wineman, *Controls from Within* (New York: Free Press, 1952), ch. 2; and *The Psychiatrist's Interest in Leisure Time Activities* (New York: Group for the Advancement of Psychiatry, 1958).

[53] Grace L. Coyle, "Not All Activities Are Group Work," and S. R. Slavson, "When is a Group Not a Group?" *The Group,* 7(1):10–11 and 12–13 (November 1944).

mental, and/or emotional problems was not new. Such service was given as a matter of course when the worker, be he a caseworker or a group adviser, encountered a family or friendship group. This has been true throughout the history of organizational help to people. As the social scientists and psychologists became increasingly interested in the role of groups in family and neighborhood life, caseworkers began to see service to groups as something different from service to individuals. The Settlement and youth-service workers began to distinguish between the problems of individual members of groups and to seek help from psychological and casework personnel to understand those members with "unusual" behavior.[54] Psychiatrists in private practice began referring patients with problems in relationships to group-service agencies. Most agencies could present examples of such service if they were fortunate enough to have workers with special skill:

(1) the ability to understand and to respond to the desires and needs of a group; (2) the facility to help the group express their desires in a constructive and progressive manner; and (3) the ability to focus attention of a group upon oneself. Every group needs an integrating and a unifying principle such as common interest, a cause, or an ideal. Before these are developed, however, this cementing factor is the personality of the leader.[55]

In *Group Work and Case Work—Their Relationship and Practice,* published in 1941, the bibliography lists twenty-seven references descriptive of a combination of group work and casework service for individuals and groups.[56] Eighteen additional references deal with administrative aspects. While group service workers had always served individuals as well as groups, some caseworkers now began to experiment with their role as group leader. In other words, group service per se began to penetrate agencies which formerly had provided primarily individual-by-individual service.

Developments in education. The question of where professional group workers should be educated continued to be debated. As the number of

[54] Gertrude Wilson, "Group Work–Case Work Cooperation—in Jewish Centers," A Symposium, AAGW (New York: Association Press, 1946), pp. 1–6; Florence Poole, "The Role of the Caseworker in a Group Work Agency," *Committee Report, NASW.* Chicago, 1958 (mimeographed).

[55] S. R. Slavson, "Group Therapy," *Proceedings, National Conference of Jewish Social Welfare, 1937.* See also *Creative Group Education* (New York: Association Press, 1937).

[56] Gertrude Wilson, *Group Work and Case Work—Their Relationship and Practice* (New York: Family Welfare Association, 1941). See also "Group Work and Case Work Relationships"—a symposium by Gertrude Wilson, Bertha Reynolds, Arthur L. Swift, and Alice Hatt Campbell, in *The Group,* 4(1):3–4, 6–8 (November 1941).

specializations in group work in schools of social work increased, group service agencies which had established training programs of their own were threatened. From the beginning of social work education for professional group workers, the Jewish Welfare Board and the Settlements were among its strongest supporters. The Jewish agencies were the first to abolish their sectarian school when the Graduate School for Jewish Social Work was closed in the late 1930s and prospective workers were advised to enroll in one of the existing schools of social work. One by one, the youth-service agencies closed their "schools" and concentrated their attention on short-term training through workshops, seminars, and conferences. The Settlements have never sponsored a separate educational institution to prepare their workers; they have chosen to draw from whatever college, university, or specialized school seemed appropriate.

Group work and group dynamics. Another controversy which blazed during the forties was that between the group work method and group dynamics. The first direct contact the author had with group dynamics was in the early forties when Kurt Lewin and Gordon Hearn came to the University of Pittsburgh to conduct an experiment to demonstrate this method of working with groups. Lewin requested the use of some groups led by students at the School of Social Work. The author objected on the basis of professional ethics and interference with the students' learning process in mastering group work methodology. It was Grace Coyle, however, who carried on the most vocal opposition against the philosophy and tactics of group dynamics, although she agreed that group work and group dynamics might be mutually beneficial.[57]

Literature on methodology. In spite of the criticisms from outside and the conflicts within agencies serving groups, there was a steady, slow growth of a common methodology. Even though there was interagency rivalry, these agencies had many common purposes and methods of service.

During the decade following the organization of the N.A.S.G.W. in 1936, the personnel in many types of agencies "took to the pen."[58] The increasing number of people teaching group work in schools of social work,

---

[57] Grace L. Coyle, "The Relation of Group Dynamics to Group Work," in *Journal of the National Associaton of Deans of Women,* 12(3):160 (March 1949), and "Group Dynamics and the Practice of Social Group Work," *Social Work in the Current Scene, 1950* (New York: Columbia University Press, 1950).

[58] Charles E. Hendry (ed.), *A Decade of Group Work* (New York: Association Press, 1948).

agency schools, departments of physical education, theological seminaries, and departments of education left their print in the journals of professional and trade organizations. The writings show continuing confusion or concern over the question, what is group work? Some continued to use the term in a threefold manner: as a movement, as a classification of agencies, and as a methodology. The cause-oriented person saw group work as a movement guided by a democratic philosophy; the community organizer used group work as a convenient way of classifying agencies for interpretation and money-raising purposes; and the practice theorists saw group work as a method to be used in any group situation—as a social process which could be used in accordance with the philosophy and purpose of any sponsor. In other words, group work, defined as a method, does not rule out agency purpose or the democratic movement. It simply isolates social structure as one particular vehicle of service. It is this distinction between method and agency which created the term social group work. Ironically, some of the most ardent defenders of the method definition encouraged organizations in recreation, religious education, and adult education to make use of group work as a method but discouraged their use of it as a classification.[59]

A professional organization emerges. The annual meeting of the AAGW in Buffalo in June 1946 was a turning point in the history of group work. Prior to this time, the chief purpose of the association was to study and develop group work as a method. In 1944 the Association had appointed a committee, representative of its various professional interests, to develop a plan for an *inclusive profession* based on the fields of recreation, physical education, group work, and leisure time. The report of this committee, plus revised bylaws and a suggested change of name, was submitted to the membership and approved by April 1946, prior to the meeting in June.

At this time the author, as chairman of the Group Work Section of the NCSW, and Miriam Ephraim, as chairman of the program for the annual conference of the AAGW, recommended emphasizing fields in which the group work method is germane to the NCSW program and insisting upon professional standards for the AAGW program.

[59] Grace Coyle, the author, and a few other group workers, participated in two National Conferences on Professional Training of Recreation Workers—one at the University of North Carolina in 1939 and the other in New York City in 1941. Lindeman was the leader of both conferences. Later the group work faculties of the schools of social work were instrumental in organizing a joint association of agencies and schools—the Conference of Schools of Group Work and Recreation, formed in Detroit, February 1943.

The 1946 meeting of the AAGW outlined the development of a scientific foundation of group work theory adaptable to any setting.[60] The following unsigned quotation was printed in *The Group:*

> Some wise observer of human life has said that the truly civilized man has one foot rooted in the past and the other in the future. If this is so, the reader of "Toward Professional Standards," the 1945–46 Proceedings of the A.A.G.W., could fairly conclude that the composite group worker of 1946 had reached an enviably civilized point in his regard of his chosen profession. For through these fifteen papers runs a common thread of careful sifting of past experiences and an eager freedom to consider the future.
>
> There can be no doubt that this volume will be a significant page—or rather, 183 pages—in the annals of group work. As the title suggests, this is a record of what a number of outstanding people in the field had to say at a time of professional consciousness.[61]

Because this was a tenth-anniversary year for group work, one is tempted to cite recollections of people and events during the decade of AASGW. Louis Kraft summed up his feelings about the early days when the idea of the AASGW was beginning to evolve: "It was one of the most satisfying associations of my entire career. . . . We were a group of zealots," he said smiling, recalling the days when fifteen or twenty group workers in the New York area began to meet together for informal discussions.

> It began about three years before the (1936) Atlantic City Conference. . . . We wanted to clarify an adherence to a group work philosophy. We all worked for different agencies, but we felt common elements in philosophy and method. Even then we saw the basis for a new movement that would add great meaning to our work. We started with one great advantage—we were congenial. It was a fellowship which cut across agency lines.[62]

In 1946 a majority of the 2043 members of AASGW, volunteer and employed, trained and untrained, voted to become the AAGW, a professional organization.[63] The steady focus of the organization was continued, but the major emphasis was upon *becoming* professional and there was less emphasis upon program and social action in other areas of common concern.[64] In the June 1947, issue of *The Group,* the Committee on Profes-

[60] *Toward Professional Standards* (New York: AAGW, 1947).

[61] *The Group,* 10(1):11 (October 1947).

[62] From an interview with Charles Hendry conducted by Marion Robinson and printed in *The Group,* 10:1 (October 1947).

[63] For information concerning the membership, see *Toward Professional Standards,* p. 172.

[64] Ann Elizabeth Neely, "Looking Ahead with AAGW (The Professional Tasks Ahead)," *The Group,* 9(1):3–5 (April 1947).

sional Education for Group Work Practice made its report, outlining (1) knowledge basic to practice, (2) application of basic knowledge to group work practice, (3) field work practice, and (4) research projects.

The proposition to change the AASGW into a professional association with educational requirements for new members was given considerable publicity. In the two-year period from 1944 to 1946, 1100 new members were enrolled in the AASGW, who thereupon became charter members of the A.A.G.W. The Association of 1946 was a far cry from the fellowship described by Louis Kraft. Some of the leaders who had virtually given staff service to the Association as a social movement were less interested in it as a fledgling professional association. S. R. Slavson left the Association and *The Group*, of which he had been editor from 1941 to 1946. Charles G. Mc-Cormick wrote of him in the June 1946 issue: "The American Association for the Study of Group Work has been richly privileged to have Mr. Slavson's service for so long. He is leaving us to devote full time to the science which has been signally dependent upon his skill and genius for development, namely, Group Therapy."

Meanwhile, during the 1946 NCSW in Buffalo, social workers interested in developing professional practice in community organization organized the American Association for the Study of Community Organization. Some members of the AAGW primarily interested in planning and social action on the community level left the group work association to devote their time and energies to study the process of community organization for social welfare.[65]

The people who attended the Group Work Section of the NCSW and the sessions of the AAGW in 1946 were united as representatives of many agencies concerned with youth and the constructive use of leisure time by people of all ages—adult education, education, group dynamics, labor education, physical education, agricultural extension, public housing, the children's bureau.[66]

However, the introduction of the concepts centering around a new profession gave many individuals second thoughts about the new organization.

[65] "Community Organization for Social Welfare," *Social Work Year Book,* 1949; Kenneth L. M. Pray, "When Is Community Organization Social Work Practice?"; Newstetter, "The Social Intergroup Work Process"; Lester B. Granger, Educational and Promotional Process in Community Organization," *Proceedings of the National Conference of Social Work, 1947* (New York: Columbia University Press, 1948), pp. 194–226.

[66] *Report*—Committee on Group Treatment in Family Service Agencies (mimeographed) (New York: Family Service Association, 1964).

For whatever cause, the majority of the leadership roles over the next decade were carried by group workers with degrees in social work or by supporters of professional social work education. The Association Press supported publications. Helen Rowe of the National Camp Fire Girls became the chairman in 1944, and was followed for two years by Ann Elizabeth Neely of the National YWCA. Charles Hendry, who might be regarded as having been the "father" during the previous decade, moved to the University of Toronto to become dean of the School of Social Work. Although Saul Bernstein, of the Boston University School of Social Work, and John McDowell, then executive of the National Federation of Settlements, preceded Harleigh Trecker as president, it was Trecker who carried the AAGW through its final transformation as it joined the other social work organizations to become the NASW in 1955.

The Growth of Group Services. Throughout the forties and the fifties the structure of the group was used by social workers in a great variety of settings—hospitals, family and children's agencies, correctional institutions,[67] public welfare,[68] psychiatric clinics and hospitals,[69] public schools,[70] and public recreation [71]—and continued in private leisure time agencies. Experimental group work by the Red Cross in military hospitals during World War II encouraged similar programs by civilian medical and psychiatric social workers.[72]

In 1948 the Social Group Work Program of the University of Pittsburgh moved into the Veterans' Hospital in Aspinwall, Pennsylvania, where, with the help of a grant from the United States Public Health Unit and the enthusiastic support of Claire Lustman, Director of Social Service, a unit of four

[67] The National Conference on Prevention and Control of Juvenile Delinquency, *Summaries of Recommendations* (Washington, D.C.: U.S. Government Printing Office, 1946), pp. 90–97.

[68] *Group Methods—Guide for Use of Group Methods in County Welfare Departments* (Sacramento, Calif.: State Department of Social Welfare, 1962).

[69] Committee on Practice, "The Psychiatric Social Worker as Leader of a Group," American Association of Psychiatric Social Workers Report (Washington, D.C.: 1955).

[70] *Social Work Year Book 1957* (New York: NASW, 1957), pp. 285, 509.

[71] Grace Coyle, "Social Group Work in Recreation," *Proceedings of the National Conference of Social Work, 1946,* p. 202; Gertrude Wilson, "The Social Group Worker in Public Recreation," *Recreation* 48, 9 (November 1955), 414 (New York: National Recreation Association).

[72] Cynthia R. Nathan, "Need for Social Casework as Revealed in Groups," *Proceedings of the National Conference of Social Work, 1944* (New York: Columbia University Press, 1944), pp. 208–18.

students and a social group work supervisor was established.[73] During the same period, the Pittsburgh School was using the Menninger Foundation Clinic and the Veterans Hospital in Topeka, Kansas, for block placements. During one summer the author, accompanied by Gladys Ryland, gave consultation and actively participated within the structure of the Topeka training program for psychiatrists under the supervision of Dr. Karl Menninger. This experience added not just to the *knowledge* but also to the *feeling* characterizing the use of social group work in a medical-psychiatric setting.

In the mid-fifties the AAGW received a grant from the National Institute of Mental Health to explore group work in psychiatric settings.[74] Three years later, the N.A.S.W. sponsored another such program.[75] The emphasis was upon group work as a method of treatment. As the use of group work methods became popular in both institutional and community agencies that customarily served individuals, the term group therapy, coined by Slavson, became attractive. Within the membership of the A.A.G.W., this added another source of conflict. The movement advocates saw the use of the term as a denial of social-action responsibility and as a threat to the democratic relationships between workers and members.

Workers, some volunteers, and some board and committee members of youth-service agencies held that the major use of the social group work method was for prevention, and that treatment was only for atypical groups. Some even held that the agency they represented was not organized to administer such groups. Criticisms of the movement toward a theoretical approach to group work service was not limited entirely to the untrained workers and volunteers. Irving Miller,[76] a lecturer in social group work at the New York School of Social Work, charged in 1955 that some agency leadership found that professionally educated social group workers (1) were overconcerned with methods and processes rather than with content and goals, (2) put greater emphasis on supervisory structure than on services to be

[73] Marion Robinson, "A Report of the Section and Associate Group Meetings," *The Social Welfare Forum, 1950*. Proceedings of the National Conference of Social Work, pp. 252–54.

[74] Harleigh B. Trecker (ed.), *Group Work in the Psychiatric Setting* (New York: Whiteside, 1956).

[75] National Association of Social Workers, *Use of Groups in the Psychiatric Setting* (New York: NASW, 1960).

[76] Irving Miller, "A Critical Appraisal of Some Aspects of Social Group Work Theory and Practice," *Group Work and Community Organization, 1955*. Papers from the National Conference of Social Work (New York: Columbia University Press, 1955), pp. 68–69.

given, (3) found greater interest in the "how" than in the "why," (4) saw a gap between what people were trained for and how the agencies used them, and (5) showed a lack of conviction about the role of social group workers in social action.

Some group service agencies, however, were enthusiastic about establishing scientific bases for the practice of social group work. The development in the fourth and fifth decades was one of integrating interested agencies, the AAGW, and the social group work specializations in the schools of social work and other graduate schools and departments where education for work with groups had been initiated.[77]

DEEPENING OF METHOD AND DISPERSION OF MOVEMENT

In the postwar period, social agencies and social workers pushed ahead, adapting old patterns and methods and at the same time experimenting with new ones. Jane M. Hoey wrote during the war:

> Social work concepts and methods are those that are recognized as underlying social work even though their use is not restricted to that profession. . . . Social work is not static; it must keep pace with changing social and economic conditions, scientific developments and evolving social concepts.
>
> Underlying social work are basic philosophical concepts that human personality represents the highest type of created being and each person is a unique individual who has an innate dignity because of his capacity to reason, his free will, his origin, and his eternal dignity.[78]

"The foremost problem of society today," said Supreme Court Justice Douglas, "is to cultivate and preserve incentive and independence for the individual and security for the masses of the people." [79] With this quotation the author opened her speech at the NCSW in 1949, a philosophical presentation on the challenge of "Today's Social Situation for Action," with special application to group work.[80]

The Industrial Revolution, two world wars, economic depressions, and

[77] Clara A. Kaiser, "Group Work Education in the Last Decade," *The Group,* 15(5):3–10 (June 1953).

[78] Jane Hoey, "Social Work Concepts and Methods in the Postwar World," *Proceedings, NCSW, 1944,* p. 36.

[79] Justice William O. Douglas, "The Human Welfare State," *Survey,* 75(4):209 74, 4 (April 1944).

[80] Gertrude Wilson, "Today's Social Situation—A Challenge for Action," *Social Work in the Current Scene.* Papers from the National Conference of Social Work, 1949 (New York: Columbia University Press, 1950), p. 210.

continual strife in many countries have kept in motion social forces which have denied many of the world's people both the physical and emotional nourishment for the development of mature relationships with their fellow men. Guided group experience based on the concept of self-determination can help cultivate this growth. The value of human experience in groups, substantiated by research in psychology and the social sciences, demonstrates:

1. That the capacity of human beings to develop cooperative living is directly related to the quality of their personal experience in groups.
2. That their personal and social patterns of behavior are molded by their experiences in family life.
3. That these patterns are further developed in small intimate groups.
4. That throughout life people need emotional support and intellectual stimulation from small, intimate groups as well as from larger groups, through which social goals of personal and social significance are achieved.

When individuals fail to have group experiences of this nature they are less able to contribute their share in building the road to a cooperative society. Society, in turn, has the responsibility to provide such individuals with supportive groups. It is essential that practitioners have the following philosophical strengths if they are to help group members achieve socially significant goals:

1. Acceptance that the quality and effectiveness of large representative groups are dependent upon the quality and effectiveness of small groups.
2. Recognition that conflict is the basis of integration.
3. Conviction that solutions to conflict are possible through the decision-making processes within groups.
4. Realization that democratic participation in groups is a skill to be learned through democratic group living.
5. Acceptance of the importance of evaluating the results against established professional criteria.

Throughout the decades of method consciousness, efforts were made to assess the success of the group-as-a-whole thoroughly, in terms of concepts, principles, and techniques, rather than one aspect and then another. To the experienced group worker, no one aspect remains real when separated from

its context in the interaction of the group as a whole. Practice concepts have
been adapted from research conclusions of psychosocial scientists and tested
by analyzing group records written by professionals and students.

The professional literature of the decade 1946 to 1956 was exceedingly
helpful in the formulation of the substance of social group work practice. A
landmark publication was the *Decade of Group Work,* published by Association Press in 1948. Only four of the twenty-five authors of the
chapters had graduate degrees in social work, and their affiliations included
posts with such federal departments as the Veterans' Administration, the
Social Security Administration and Extension Service of the Department of
Agriculture, the Adult Education Association, the American Labor Education Service, and some youth-serving agencies. Six of the AAGW chapters
were chaired by members from schools of social work providing specialized
education for group workers. The diverse backgrounds and the high degree
of agreement in basic philosophies, concepts, and principles is a tribute to
the communication among those providing a variety of services via the
group work method. The individuals affiliated with these services were contributors to a *Decade of Group Work* because of their knowledge, personal
background, and membership in the AAGW, not because they were employed by a particular organization.

In the same decade, articles in *The Group* indicated a predominate interest in methods of group work practice. Forty-four of the articles published
during this period were either methodological or descriptive of practice;
twenty-five dealt with group work service to clients with special problems or
in specialized settings; eighteen articles dealt with research problems and
reports; nine with social action; and six with casework–group work projects.
The membership at large had every opportunity to be up-to-date on the significant events in the development of group work throughout this decade.

The AAGW continued the tradition of the AASGW, which had published selected papers from its annual meetings and pamphlets on significant
subjects between 1936 and 1946. For instance, in 1946 a pamphlet reported
on the symposium, "Group Work-Case Work Cooperation." In 1949 a very
important document, the "Report of the Committee on the Function of the
Professional Group Worker," was published under the chairmanship of
Grace Coyle. This short sampling of the contributions of the AAGW to the
practice of group work is a small tribute to the skill of the leadership to unite
a large number of diverse people in a common concern.

Throughout the decade, all of the professional periodicals in social work and some in the social and behavioral sciences carried reviews of books about work with groups. The authors were identified with many professional organizations and many group service agencies. The books dealing with the actual practice of group work were to a large extent written by theoretician-practitioners who combined analyses of the processes internal to groups with the relationships of the worker to the members. Common objectives during this period of time were to help members accomplish their tasks, to grow and develop, to improve their adjustment to others and the society in which they lived, and, when necessary, to change their social situations.[81]

An analysis of the literature issued by the AAGW, its members, and other group theorists reveals that most of the authors tried to maintain a generic point of view or to be "jugglers," balancing the interests of education, recreation, social work, business and industry, and society as a whole. The point of view of many authors was that group work is a term which describes a process helpful to any cause which uses it effectively. Group work is a term which describes a process (1) which helps "normal" people to live more effective lives; (2) of service to people which prevents them from having "troubles;" and (3) through which society is forced to change social situations which are harmful to people. Many of the authors of commission reports, pamphlets, and books combine these various conclusions, and there are persistent examples of mutual quotations. To date, no one has succeeded in formulating a mutually agreed-upon statement of the purpose and function of group work. This is the situation in 1975, as it was in 1955 when the majority of the membership of the AAGW voted to unite with the other six organizations to form the NASW. Social group work then became definitely a social work service to groups.

The author of this paper was a participating member of the AAGW throughout its life, serving on national committees and the Executive Board, and was a member of local chapters. When the merger took place, she was elected as a member of the Executive Committee of the new Group Work Section of the NASW. At its first meeting in 1955 it was decided to accept

---

[81] Examination of the articles in professional periodicals supplies significant additional leads toward further professional definition. Many of these articles are written by authors who have published books in the decade 1965–1975. See also the final section of Suggested Readings at the end of this paper.

the recommendation of the last board of the AAGW that the first project should be a study to find out, as stated in the minutes of the board, "what current group work practice actually is, not what people think it should be. . . . Further examination may thus lead to formulation of what practice should be. . . . The entire membership of the section should be involved from the very beginning and throughout the various phases of the project."

The recommendation was referred to the Committee on Practice, chaired by the author, which consisted of fifteen core members, thirty-four corresponding members, and four subcommittees located in Berkeley, Los Angeles, Minneapolis, and Philadelphia. This was the most extensive and the only statistical study undertaken by the Group Work Section during its seven years of existence. It gathered data on the personal characteristics, practice experience, and professional educational background of 25 percent of the membership. In addition, it compiled information about the working conditions, work-time allocation, salary, and policies and procedures of employing agencies. The study, however, provided more questions than answers. One finding of the study was that there was no agreement on the purpose of group work. Qualified social work members did not want to face the deep implication of their social work identification. The dissent was voiced not only in the questionnaire itself but also in consequent commission meetings and articles in periodicals. What many members did not want to face was that work with groups is generic to all types of actions and issues, but social group work is unique because it is governed by the philosophy of the social work profession and the tenets of the Social Work Practice Commission of the NASW. The Group Work Committee regarded this study as a fact-finding and opinion-gathering one—upon which future studies could be based. The study did not include program content. Hence social action, as important as that function was and is, was not specifically included.[82]

Two other chairmen of the Practice Committee, Bernard Shiffman and Violet Tennant, carried on further studies of the practice of social group work for the Group Work Section. The Committee on Practice of the Group Work Section (1959–63) decided that, rather than attempt to formulate a precise definition of social group work, it would establish a frame of reference for social group work. A number of individuals were asked to prepare statements defining group work; ten such papers were printed in the find-

[82] "The Practice of Social Group Work"—Commission on Practice, 1955–58 (New York: Group Work Section, NASW, 1957; Summary, 1958).

ings. Again, the effort to define group work resulted in an endless stream of words, effort, enthusiasm, and frustration.[83]

It is regrettable that the Practice Committee approached its problem from a didactic point of view. In the author's opinion, progress is not made by the formulation of ideal definitions into which bits of practice are to be fitted. Perhaps greater progress could be made by studying and analyzing the actual behavior of social workers in group situations; from this it might be possible to identify the elements of social work methods in serving groups.

The Group Work Section was abolished in 1963. The Commission on Group Work Practice, under its first chairman, Ruby Pernell, who was followed by Helen Northen and then Miriam Cohn, was responsible for advancing knowledge and theory. It was hampered by inadequate staff service and financing from the NASW, which withdrew support of all of the commissions on social work practice in the mid-1960s.

CONCLUSIONS AND IMPLICATIONS

In 1964 the NASW celebrated its tenth anniversary with a symposium. Helen Perlman, in her article "Social Work Method: A Review of the Past Decade," wrote:

> When one looks at this range of practice embraced by group work, it is easy to understand the run of high feeling in its ranks about its definition and identity and the push by its leaders and formulators to develop further its practice models and principles. In the examination of its writings one sees some internecine struggles over whether its major commitments should be on the continuum of education-to-therapy or on the continuum of education-to-socialization. And sometimes these issues and questions are made murky by confusing personalities with positions.[84]

Writings by social caseworkers would seem to indicate many similarities in their struggle to define social casework.

It is often said that the social work profession was developed in accordance with the medical model; however, professional social work education failed to follow the medical education pattern. Pre-med courses are basic to the entire medical professional educational career. Basic medicine on a graduate level follows; then comes training in a specialization.

---

[83] Margaret E. Hartford (ed.), "Working Papers Toward a Frame of Reference for Social Group Work—1959–63" (New York: NASW, 1964).

[84] Helen Perlman, "Social Work Method: A Review of the Past Decade," *Social Work,* 10(4):166–78 (October 1965).

Historically, social workers were trained to provide the service of a particular agency concerned with the physical needs of people. Agency personnel—volunteer and paid—provided the training after they formulated the course content. It was natural that the training was focused on carrying out the function of each particular agency as determined by its board of directors.[85] In contrast to this pattern, the doctors-in-training were educated by M.D.s in medical schools, not under the jurisdiction of any hospital or community agency.

Doctors-in-training learn to be physicians; they provide medical service to clients of many different social systems, including patients of their own private practice. They may be employed by a medical, educational, industrial, or social agency, but they are not employed to carry out all of the functions of the agency. They are employed to provide the service of their profession. The advancement of the physician is dependent upon his skill in practice. He does not undertake to run the administrative aspects of the organization in which he practices. As a physician his first attentions are to the patient and to research about the various illnesses which threaten mankind. His professional and financial advancement is not related to stepping from direct service to supervisory responsibility to an executive role.

Social workers have never laid claim to providing a professional service without agency affiliation. Social workers with basic social work education qualify for practice in many areas in a great variety of institutions servicing human needs. They are needed in every community, as are the general medical practitioners. Later specialized training should qualify them for a designation comparable to that of the medical diplomat.[86]

It seems that the current flood of internal criticism in the profession is "baying at the moon." The social work system does not encompass the research and the consequent refinement of practice that is necessary. More research aimed at an unrealistic system only provides entertainment and use for more statistics and machines to count out infinitesimal data. The author agrees with George E. Erlich who deplored the recent emphasis upon research that has made the laboratory—and not the patient—the focus of medical education.[87] Without basic reorganization of the content of social work

[85] Ruth Fizdale, "The Voluntary Agency—Structure versus Accountability," *Social Casework,* 55(8):478 (October 1974).

[86] George E. Erlich, "The Future Society: Aspects of America in the Year 2000," *Annals of the American Academy of Political and Social Science* (July 1973).

[87] *Ibid.*

education to provide opportunity for generic, direct-service practice, the profession will continue to be dominated by the historic agency model.

Sociopsychological concepts, like all other concepts, are man's abstractions of his observations, tested by the scientific method as to their universal significance without reference to the value system of the people or of the social situation they describe. Their significance lies in the leads they provide to the applied scientists or practitioners for the formulation of principles of *how to do something* with people and groups.

The nature of the framework for the practice of group work depends upon the purpose of the group served. Generally speaking, group purposes may be classified as "task"- or "growth"-centered. In the former, the group worker's primary responsibility is to support the group to accomplish the task; in the latter, the worker's primary responsibility is to help members to use the group experience to resolve problems which are interfering with their personal growth and development. It must be understood that this designation of purpose is not as easy to determine as it is to state. Many task-oriented groups turn out to be growth-oriented, and some growth-oriented groups achieve their original purpose and continue with tasks chosen from common interests.

This discussion of causes, people, social situations, and theories related to services to groups over more than six decades provides a background for the author's theoretical model for serving it. The *theories* are meaningless without the *social situations* that move people to take up the causes that demonstrate the power of a group to find some solutions. By the sixties, social group workers began to accept themselves as social workers with less need to prove the social work aspects of their specialization.

During the last three decades we have witnessed a rapid shift in size and power of political, economic, and social organizations. This change has taken place through interlocking directorates, mergers, and direct legislation. Today, major policies, procedures, and programs of utilities, industrial goods, and services are made on a national-federal level. Social welfare agencies and the professions were not unaffected by the ideal of "bigness" which dominated these decades. The movement of the AAGW into the NASW is but one example of the shifts in the organizational life of the United States during this period.

It is noteworthy that even at the time of the transition from a study organization to a professional one, the majority of the officers of the AAGW were members of the A.A.S.W., the parent organization of the NASW.

This, however, was not true of the majority of the more than 2500 members of the AAGW scattered over the country. From its beginning in 1936, the AAGW demonstrated its ability to use, to organize, and to program local groups, and to maintain live lines of communication. Almost all of this was carried out by unpaid officers inspired by the value of developing a frame of reference for the practice of group work. The personal and written communication covering the United States in those twenty years produced a remarkable base for professional practice, as witnessed by the quality of articles in *The Group,* the Proceedings of the National Conference of Social Work, and the books published.

As time moved on, and almost every helping profession had some of its personnel using the group structure to deliver its services, such services became more prestigious. Confusion as to the nature of group service has spread into all aspects of service. It is time that social work move forward with clarity as to the nature and type of services to be expected from group service by social workers. The succeeding papers are a step in this direction.

SUGGESTED READING

ANTECEDENTS OF GROUP WORK THEORY

Addams, Jane. *Twenty Years at Hull House.* New York: Macmillan, 1910.

—— *The Second Twenty Years at Hull House.* New York: Macmillan, 1930.

Calkins, Clinch. *Some Folks Won't Work.* New York: Harcourt Brace, 1930.

Carner, Lucy P. "The Settlement Way in Philadelphia." Philadelphia: Delaware Valley Settlement Alliance, 1964.

Hall, Helen. *Unfinished Business.* New York: Macmillan, 1937.

Holden, Arthur C. *The Settlement Idea—A Vision of Social Justice.* New York: Macmillan, 1915.

Lee, Joseph. *Play in Education.* New York: Macmillan, 1915.

Lindeman, Eduard C. *Social Discovery.* New York: Republic, 1924.

—— *Pioneering on Social Frontiers 1896–1936.* Cleveland: Hiram House, 1937.

Rabinowitz, Benjamin. *The Young Men's Hebrew Association 1854–1913.* New York: National Jewish Welfare Board, 1948.

Simkovitch, Mary Kingsbury. "The Settlement Primer." New York: National Federation of Settlements, 1936.

Taylor, Graham. *Pioneering on Social Frontiers.* Chicago: University of Chicago Press, 1930.

Wald, Lillian. *The House on Henry Street.* New York: Holt, 1915.

Weinberg, Arthur and Lila Weinberg. *The Muckrakers—1902–1912.* New York: Simon and Schuster, 1961.

Wickman, E. K. *Children's Behavior and Teachers' Attitudes*. New York: Commonwealth Fund, 1928.

Williamson, Margaretta. *The Social Worker in Group Work*. New York: Harper, 1929.

Yeomans, Edward. *Shackled Youth*. New York: Harpers, 1921.

EARLY GROUP WORK THEORY (THROUGH 1945)

Baxter, Bernice and Rosalind Cassidy. *Group Experience: The Democratic Way*. New York: Harpers, 1943.

Blumenthal, Louis H. *Group Work in Camping*. New York: Association Press, 1937.

Busch, Henry M. *Leadership in Group Work*. New York: Association Press, 1934.

Coyle, Grace (ed.). *Studies in Group Behavior*. New York: Harpers, 1937.

DuBois, Rachel Davis. *Get Together Americans*. New York: Harpers, 1943.

DuVall, Everett. *Personality and Social Group Work*. New York: Association Press, 1943.

Kaiser, Clara A. *The Group Records of Four Clubs*. Cleveland: Western Reserve University, 1930.

Leigh, Robert D. *Group Leadership*. New York: Norton, 1936.

Lieberman, Joshua. *New Trends in Group Work, NASGW*. New York: Association Press, 1938.

Lowenfeld, Victor. *The Nature of Creative Activity*. New York: Harcourt, Brace, 1939.

Slavson, S. R. *Creative Group Education*. New York: Association Press, 1937.

—— *Introduction to Group Therapy*. New York: Commonwealth Fund, 1943.

Sullivan, Dorothy (ed.). *The Practice of Group Work*. New York: Association Press, 1941.

Tead, Ordway. *The Art of Leadership*. New York: McGraw-Hill, 1935.

THEORY AFTER WORLD WAR II (1946–1965)

Bernstein, Saul (ed.). *Explorations in Group Work*. Boston: School of Social Work of Boston University, 1965.

Blackey, Eileen A. *Group Leadership in Staff Training*. Washington, D.C.: Department of Health Education and Welfare, Children's Bureau Pub. 161, 1957.

Coyle, Grace L. *Group Experience and Democratic Values*. New York: Women's Press, 1947.

—— *Group Work with American Youth*. New York: Harper, 1948.

Hearn, Gordon. *Theory Building in Social Work*. Toronto: University of Toronto Press, 1958.

Klein, Alan. *Society, Democracy, and the Group*. New York: Morrow, 1953.

—— *Role Playing in Leadership Training and Group Problem Solving*. New York: Association Press, 1956.

Konopka, Gisela. *Therapeutic Group Work with Children*. Minneapolis: University of Minnesota Press, 1949.

—— *Group Work in the Institution.* New York: Whiteside, Morrow, 1954.

Konopka, Gisela (ed.). *Social Group Work: A Helping Process.* Englewood Cliffs, N.J.: Prentice-Hall, 1963.

Lowry, Louis. *Adult Education and Group Work.* New York: Whiteside, Morrow, 1955.

Maier, Henry W. (ed.). *Group Work as Part of Residential Treatment.* New York: NASW, 1965.

Maier, Henry W. *Three Theories of Child Development.* New York: Harper & Row, 1965.

Murphy, Marjorie. *The Social Group Work Method in Social Work Education*—Curriculum Study, XI. New York: Council on Social Work Education, 1959.

Phillips, Helen U. *Essentials of Social Group Work Skill.* New York: Association Press, 1957.

Redl, Fritz and David Wineman. *Children Who Hate.* New York: Free Press, 1951.

—— *Controls from Within.* New York: Free Press, 1952.

Schulze, Suzanne. *Creative Group Living in a Children's Institution.* New York: Association Press, 1951.

Slavson, S. R. *Recreation and the Total Personality.* New York: Association Press, 1946.

Sullivan, Dorothea. *Readings in Group Work.* New York: Association Press, 1952.

Trecker, Harleigh B. *Social Group Work—Principles and Practice.* New York: Women's Press, 1948; (rev. ed.; New York: Whiteside, 1955).

—— *Group Work: Foundations and Frontiers.* New York: Whiteside, Morrow, 1955.

Wilson, Gertrude. *Recreational and Informal Educational Service,* prepared for Mid-century White House Conference on Children and Youth. New York: AAGW, 1950.

Wilson, Gertrude and Gladys Ryland. *Social Group Work Practice.* Boston: Houghton Mifflin, 1949.

Wittenberg, Rudolph M. *So You Want to Help People.* New York: Association Press, 1947.

—— *The Art of Group Discipline.* New York: Association Press, 1951.

—— *On Call for Youth.* New York: Association Press, 1955.

2

GROUP METHODS AND GENERIC PRACTICE [1]

MARGARET E. HARTFORD

This paper examines a framework for understanding the use of group methods for service within the broader view of a generic or multimethods approach to social work practice.

Since the social worker's practice is in response to his assessment of a social problem or client need, he uses the methodological approaches most appropriate for the given situation. His efforts to provide service according to need may aim at any of the following objectives: enhancement, enrichment, learning, and growth of the participants; prevention of personal and social breakdown; support through crisis or recovery; correction of dysfunction; personal and social rehabilitation; or personal and social change. [2]

The emphasis of this paper, therefore, is upon the worker's understanding and use of the complexities, uniqueness, and intricacies of the group processes and his maximization of these group elements in order for

---

[1] While the views and theoretical formulations of this paper are my own, and have emerged from my experiences as teacher and practitioner, I must express my indebtedness to my personal friends and to my associates at the School of Applied Social Sciences, Case Western Reserve University, and students in the masters and doctoral programs who have helped to test out and clarify this position on the nature of social work practice with people in groups. Most particularly, I wish to acknowledge Mary M. Seguin, Marjorie W. Main, Edmond Jenkins, Paul Abels, Erlynne Davis, William Shalinsky, Norma Lang, Ruby Pernell, Sue Henry, Marcelline Tudor, and Josephine Daugherty. To these names must be added my professional heritage from W. I. Newstetter, Gertrude Wilson, Grace Coyle, Raymond Fisher, and Esther Test.

[2] A preliminary formulation of this continuum of practice objectives was first developed by the author when preparing Hartford, *Working Papers*.

the group-with-the-worker to become the instrument of service delivery or practice.

The social worker who takes a generic or multimethod approach to practice has available to him a repertoire of professional practice methods from which to select, including working with single individuals, total families or subsections of families, groups of unrelated people, and communities. While all of these approaches may fall within the boundaries of social work, each requires a somewhat different set of skills. For instance, a worker has different points of emphasis, as well as different parameters, when he is working in interaction with one person alone and when he is working with a collective of several people who are reacting to and interacting with each other as well as to and with him. While the content of the problem may be similar in a situation where the practitioner is working with one person alone, the process and the reaction to it differs once the collectivity extends beyond two people. For example, his counseling with one marital partner alone may differ from his work with husband and wife together or with the whole family together, though the subject of their discussion, whether alone or together, is the same conflict. His work with one child having school problems will differ from his work with a group of six children who have school problems, though the subject of school problems will remain the same.

The interaction of group members and the facilitation to work with each other, and to support and help each other, will be different when a worker is present. The worker can be supportive, encouraging, or reflective with a single older adult who is lonely, isolated, disengaged, and feeling severely his losses in occupational, family, and associational roles. The older individual may feel more worthy because the worker is attending him. However, when several older people are brought together, the worker's role is less concentrated in attention to each and more helpful in connecting them to each other. The group experience offers opportunities for its members to listen, to talk, to be heard, to be attached, and to be of value to each other; consequently, the worker is apt to play a less singular and central role.

Within the configuration of generic social work practice, then, this paper selects that framework which the worker employs when he is using group methods with the emphasis on group as the instrument for providing service. This discussion, of necessity, hits only the high spots of the basic elements which comprise a view of the theoretical and philosophical approach to the use of the group as the entity for the provision of service.

PHILOSOPHICAL AND BEHAVIORAL SCIENCE BASES

This view of the use of group methods in social work has its roots in the heritage of social group work. Social work practice through group methods emerged in the era from the 1890s to the late 1930s in the social settlement movement, boys and girls clubs and youth groups, the YMCA, the YWCA, adult education, mental hospitals, psychiatric and medical clinics, institutions for children and old people, public schools, and guidance centers.[3] While the practice within these settings developed in response to social need, the leaders in both practice and education for practice made use of the theoretical writings of the social scientists of that period who were developing views of the group. These included, among others, Cooley, McDougall, Durkheim, Simmel, Allport, and Mead.[4] Cooley introduced the concept of primary and secondary groups, and suggested that primary groups, such as families, peers, and work associates, provide the means and context of the socialization process or internalization of values and beliefs. MacDougall, who developed the concept of "group mind," suggested that people who come together in a group influence each other in such a way that they begin to think and act alike and together as a single entity. His formulation was a precursor of the concept of group contagion later tested by Polansky and Redl. Durkheim showed that the phenomenon he called personal anomie results from individual alienation and disassociation—that is, from a lack of belonging to groups of significant others. Anomic individuals often become

[3] Several reviews trace the history of the early theoretical development of the use of groups in social work, including Margaretta Williamson's *Social Worker in Group Work* (New York: Harper, 1928); Sara E. Maloney, "The Development of Education for Group Work in Schools of Social Work in the U.S. from 1919–1948" (D.S.W. dissertation, Western Reserve University, 1963); and Margaret E. Hartford, "Social Group Work, 1930–1960: The Search for a Definition," in Hartford (ed.), *Working Papers*.

[4] Mention is made of the writings of these authors in the early writings about group work by Henry M. Busch, *Leadership in Group Work* (New York: Association Press, 1928); Walter L. Stone, *Problems in Social Group Work* (Nashville: Informal Education Service, 1938); and Grace L. Coyle, *Social Process in Organized Groups* (New York: Smith, 1930). The references which they cite include: Charles H. Cooley, *Social Organization;* George Simmel, *Soziologie;* William McDougall, *The Group Mind;* Floyd Allport, *Social Psychology;* Emil Durkheim, *Suicide;* George Herbert Mead, *Mind, Self and Society;* Robert MacIver, *Community;* and E. E. Eubank, *Concepts of Sociology.*

so self-destructive that they commit suicide. From this concept was derived the idea of the importance to the person of belonging and attachment. Simmel's conceptualization of dyads and triads and supports and rivalries led to an exploration of interpersonal subgroups within groups. Mead's concept of the "looking glass self," or an individual's perception of himself as a result of the ways others respond to him, and his theories of roles in sets with each other, were utilized as ways of understanding personality and character development. His insight into how personal self-concept developed in groups had a strong theoretical influence on the development of programs in youth organizations. The social psychology of Allport had a strong behaviorist flavor and emphasized the influence of groups and leadership on changing individual behavior. While an analysis of the content of the major group work writings of the 1920s and 1930s shows the use of theory from other social scientists, these were the most frequently used.

The social philosophers such as Lindeman, Follett, Dewey, Sheffield, and Elliott had strong influence on the group work theory development of that period.[5] For instance, all of these people were active in the adult education and democratization movements and wrote social philosophies that grew out of their activity. Lindeman emphasized citizen participation in small groups not only for the intellectual and social enhancement of the individual person, but for strengthening the organization of the state as well. Follett also organized small groups for enlightened political action and wrote her beliefs in her book, *The New State*. Dewey taught and demonstrated learning by doing, working in small project groups, and logical problem-solving in groups. His theories are reflected in his books *How We Think, Human Nature and Conduct,* and *Democracy and Education*. These people and their writings were drawn upon widely for group work staff seminars of youth workers, Settlement workers, and the staff of the YWCAs and YMCAs. Sheffield and Harrison Elliott, along with Dewey and Coyle, were the prime movers of the adult education movement that produced the *Inquiry* and also resulted in their writing on discussion, thinking, and problem-solving in groups.

---

[5] A mimeographed outline for a theory of group work by Lucy Carner and Grace Coyle, dated 1928, contained the following references: John Dewey, *How We Think, Human Nature and Conduct, Democracy and Education;* Harrison Elliott, *The Process of Group Thinking;* Mary Follett, *The New State;* Edward Lindeman, *Social Discovery;* Alfred Sheffield, *Creative Discussion*. Other reports from this period also note these references.

From the assessed social and personal needs of their participants and the available social theory and philosophy, early social group workers constructed a formulation that groups in social work could be effectively used for inculcation of values, socialization, and education of individuals; personal growth and adjustment; and therapeutic and corrective purposes. They also believed that groups could be used for building a stronger democratic society and for changing social conditions through social action. These objectives appeared repeatedly in reports of conferences and training sessions offered during the 1930s, and were also reported by Clara Kaiser in her summary of the discussions of four work groups which had met in Los Angeles, Chicago, New York, and Cleveland for about a year to develop group work objectives.[6]

As new theories of personality began to emerge, the trend in the therapeutic uses of groups shifted from the group as a means for helping the individual adjust to society and to develop adaptive behavior, and for diversionary activity of the mentally and emotionally ill, to the use of the group as the means for participants to understand the nature of personality development and functioning, for working on an exploration of the causes of deviance and maladjustment, and for bringing about some change in the person. Therefore, the group was seen as the helping context in which the individual, aided by the social supports of other group members, could gain greater self-understanding, and begin to change. The emphasis of group therapy moved from adaptation and adjustment to change and rehabilitation of the person. The group thus came to be seen within social work as a therapeutic instrument as well as a means for the enhancement of normal growth and social action. Although the strand of therapeutic group work had been present mostly in mental hospitals, clinics, and institutions, this shift in emphasis also affected group work in some Settlements and community centers.[7] Freudian concepts, especially those of the group as a reactivation of

---

[6] These objectives were delineated in a report of four local study groups and a national conference roundtable on group work objectives. See Clara Kaiser (ed.), *Objectives of Group Work* (New York: Association Press, 1936).

[7] Neva Boyd reported a program of group methods for treating mental patients in Illinois in 1918 in "Group Work Experiments in a State Institution in Illinois," in *Proceedings of the National Conference on Social Work, 1935* (Chicago: University of Chicago Press, 1935). Grace Coyle has also traced this early history ("Group Work in Psychiatric Settings: Roots and Branches," in Harleigh B. Trecker (ed.), *Group Work in the Psychiatric Setting* (New York: Whiteside and Morrow, 1956).

the family and the attachment of group members to each other through identification with the leader, strongly influenced the therapeutic group work
which developed through the forties and fifties.[8] More recently, group
theory and group practice have been influenced by theories of ego psychology, especially the sociocultural-psychological approach of Erikson and the
writings of Robert White and Brewster Smith.[9]

While workers with groups involved in task-achievement and social
change have made some use of personality theory, their sources of knowledge were drawn more from sociology, political science, and social psychology.[10]

In recent years the philosophy and theory of the use of group methods
in social work has been influenced by the social scientific thought of Parsons, Bales, Merton, Goffman, Jennings, Moreno, Mills, Lewin, Homans,
Lippitt, Asch, and Sherif.[11] Parsons, Bales, and Shils' attempt to integrate
the concepts of society, culture, and personality, and especially their work
on the use and place of the small group in carrying on some of this integration, has had influence since the 1950s on the development of group work

[8] Grace Coyle, in 1930, made reference to Freud's contribution in *Social Process in Organized Groups* (New York: Smith, 1930). There was considerable infusion of psychoanalytic
content into group work in the 1940s and 1950s; Wilson and Ryland, for example drew heavily
on Freudian concepts of personality in their classic text, *Social Group Work Practice*. Saul
Scheidlinger also made direct application of Freud's writings in his text, *Psychoanalysis and
Group Behavior* (New York: Norton, 1952).

[9] Henry Maier developed an association between the developmental theory of Erikson and
group participation theory ("Application of Psychological and Sociological Theory to Teaching
Social Work with the Group," paper presented at CSWE annual program meeting, Salt Lake
City, 1967, mimeographed).

[10] Grace Coyle's *Social Science Knowledge in the Education of Social Workers* (New
York: Council on Social Work Education, 1958), summarizes the use of social science knowledge during this period.

[11] Talcott Parsons, Robert F. Bales, and E. Shils, *Working Papers Toward a Theory of Action* (Cambridge: Harvard University Press, 1948); Robert F. Bales, *Interaction Process Analysis* (Reading, Mass.: Addison-Wesley, 1950); Robert K. Merton, *Social Theory and Social
Structure* (New York: Free Press, 1957); Erving Goffman, *Encounters* (Indianapolis: Bobbs-
Merrill, 1961); Helen Hall Jennings, *Leadership and Isolation* (New York: Longmans Green,
1950); J. L. Moreno, *Who Shall Survive?* (Washington, D.C.: Nervous and Mental Disease,
1934); Theodore M. Mills, *The Sociology of Small Groups* (Englewood Cliffs, N.J.: Prentice-
Hall, 1967); Kurt Lewin, *Field Theory in Social Science* (New York: Harper & Row, 1951);
George C. Homans, *The Human Group* (New York: Harcourt, Brace, Jovanovich, 1961);
Ronald Lippitt, Jeanne Watson, and Bruce Westley, *The Dynamics of Planned Change* (New
York: Harcourt, Brace, Jovanovich, 1958); Solomon Asch, "Opinions and Social Pressure."
Scientific American, 193:31–35 (1955); Muzafer Sherif, *The Psychology of Ego Involvements*
(New York, Wiley, 1947).

practice theory. Bales' analysis of groups included the flow of emotional as well as cognitive currents in groups, the influence of affective and instrumental leadership, and the phases of group development through changes of various types of activities in groups. Merton's analysis of group elements and processes, and his conceptualization of the latent and manifest purposes of groups, have permeated the teaching and thinking about groups. Goffman's work on the interactions which affect the meaning and attachment of people to each other has also influenced current thinking about groups. Jennings and Moreno's work on sociometrics—the choices and attachments, rating and ranking of group members—and psychodrama—the playing out of life experiences through group activity—has been widely used by social work group theorists. Theodore Mills' work on the administrative function of group leadership; Homans' theory and analysis of small group processes; Lewin, Lippitt, and White's studies of leadership; Lewin's various researches on the group's effect on attitude development; and Lippitt's analysis of small-group processes all influenced the theory and practice of group work of the 1950s and 1960s. Sherif's work, as well as that of Solomon Asch, on the influence of groups on individuals has also been drawn upon by practitioners and educators engaged in specifying social work practice with people in groups.

While the social scientists and philosophers have undertaken research and built theory about human groups, social group workers have also developed a rich heritage of their own. The major social work theorists have been Newstetter, Coyle, Wilson, Boyd, Slavson, Kaiser, Klein, Phillips, and, more recently, Konopka, Fisher, Northen, Vinter, Bernstein, Glasser, Schwartz, and Hartford.[12] All of these practitioners and theorists have made major contributions to the development of a scheme for understanding the use of the group as an instrument for social work services to individuals, families, and other small groups, and social organizations.

RELATIONSHIP OF GROUP TO INDIVIDUAL AND COMMUNITY METHODS

The use of group methods within a generic or multimethods approach augments individual and community methods and is supported by them. Work with individuals may be combined with group methods from intake to post-

[12] Research on group work developed at Western Reserve University and was spearheaded by W. I. Newstetter. Other important researchers were Clara Kaiser, Helen Phillips, Grace Coyle, and Emory Bogardus.

termination, and is used by some workers to facilitate individual functioning in the group. Both individual and group methods are used with families. Group methods are used also as one of the major means for community organization, planning, and coordination, and for community development. Group methods augment, and may be supported by, intergroup methods, organization, and administration.

Groups are not a substitute for individual work, or vice versa. The group is used as the method of choice by a generic or multimethod social worker in a given situation, and other methods are seen as complementary. For instance, in a therapeutic situation an individual's problems often become clearer when expressed within a context of interaction with, or in reaction to, several others. Sometimes behavior in the group stimulates or surfaces problems which an individual has not dealt with in his interviews with a therapist. To take it one step further, a person meeting with a therapist may be able to work only on certain aspects of his problems, but in the context of the group he may be motivated to carry his work on his problems in additional directions. Also, when, in group deliberations, the focus is on some other person or problem, a participant may take the opportunity to see his problems in the perspective of their problems and ways of coping. Further, his reaction and behavior to others in the group may bring to the fore ways of functioning that do not appear in a relationship alone with a worker. Problems or insights that occur in this fashion can be understood and worked on in the group and, thereafter or simultaneously, be worked on individually if required.

People who need new or different social relationships, or who need help in becoming more skilled in relating to others, may find motivation through individual work. But only through group experiences, however, can they find opportunities to practice and enhance their social relationships and skills, and to connect with new peers. This is particularly true for socially immature adults, adolescents on the brink of social growth, older adults who have lost peers, mates, and companions, or new arrivals in an institution.

Persons who through individual help have made major personal changes, have begun to recover from an illness, have been motivated to control an addiction, or have begun learning to live with a chronic disorder may be referred to a group as the means of support for continued sustenance and progress while they continue their individual work outside of the group. Attachment to a collection of people with similar concerns and problems may provide "significant others" who make possible living through crisis or change and who give sustaining power as individuals attempt to make changes in their feelings, habits, life styles, or values.

Individual members of a family may find it helpful to work singly with a worker, to think out, talk about, or surface their feelings about conflicts and tensions within the family. It may be useful, away from the pressures of the presence of the other members, for each to be able to examine his own contribution as well as his reaction to family problems. On the other hand, talking out, working on, and experiencing the conflict together, as a total family group with a helpful worker facilitating the process and helping to focus the content, may give different insights and provide an opportunity to try a new way of working together on a condition that affects each one and all of them collectively. Thus, the social worker, by emphasizing the group in helping the family members to work together on their problems, may enable each of them to work for himself, on his individual problems, and also on the interpersonal problems and their total sets of relationships as an ongoing family group.

In the area of task-achievement, some jobs can be done better by people working alone and others can be better done by thinking and acting collectively. Groups may reach a low level of productive thinking in reference to certain problems. On the other hand, with other types of problems, when groups have a different composition or a higher level of group development, task-achievement may be facilitated by the interpersonal stimulation of many minds and emotions. In task-achievement and social problem solution, one social work method does not negate the other. In fact, several individual proposals or solutions resulting from people working alone may be brought together for new combinations of solution. Task-centered approaches in social work groups are as appropriate for neighbors, family members, peers, and for residents of institutions as they are for planning and organization.

In the intergroup approach at the community level, groups may be essential in the development of coalesced collectives which can be represented in the larger group with a community, coordination, or planning focus. Both group and community methods are interdependent in this instance.

An individual concerned with changing a system may be clear about dysfunctional structure, policy, or procedures, but may be less effective than a group of people in being noticed and bringing pressure to bear upon the situation. Yet the dysfunctional system may be causing individual and interpersonal conflict and disorder. Individuals working collectively can work for social change when they recognize their individual stake in the situation, are willing to risk taking aggressive action for change, and are prepared from their individual experiences to contribute to the group and work together with others to make some impact on the system. The thrust of collective action, based on the conviction of individual members, usually has greater effectiveness in winning a response from a large system than do individuals working alone. In the wider social scheme, the thrust of many groups working together, in convention or through their representatives, may have greater potential and social influence than a single group or a single individual. Therefore, intergroup action may augment a group's activities.

Group methods, then, can stand on their own as an essential aspect of social work. Within the generic or multimethod approach, group methods complement and supplement individual family and community methods; they are related to and are sometimes an integral part of the other methods in one unified approach. Thus, this approach to group methods in generic social work holds a central position in the theoretical scheme and in the practice framework.

For groups to provide the medium in which or through which social work objectives can be achieved, however, each group must develop into a social entity in which the worker and the participants can recognize their existence and work together for their agreed-upon objectives. Therefore, the social worker must acquire specific knowledge about the nature of groups and master skills in facilitating group development and functioning. This is necessary if he is to help a collection of individuals to become a group, or help an already organized group to begin to work on service-directed objectives.

CLASSIFICATION OF GROUP FOCUS

This view of the use of group methods in social work practice holds that groups may focus on a variety of primary and secondary expectations. An elementary scheme for categorizing group foci is as follows:

1. *Primarily focused on some effect on individual participants.* Such groups provide therapeutic, educational, socialization, and supportive experiences to help the participant himself, primarily, and provide opportunity for each participant to make gains for himself by participating with others while contributing to a collective experience which helps others in and through the group. The individual

participant may experience support, growth, change, or rehabilitation. Secondarily, there may be interpersonal and task-achievement gains, and resultant personal change may carry influence in the wider society.

2. *Primarily focused on some effect on the relationships between and among participants or on their relationships with others outside of the group.* Such groups provide therapeutic, interpersonal, or family relationship experiences aimed at correcting difficult or dysfunctional relationships of those who participate together in the group, or to enhance participants' capacity to function more adequately in interpersonal relationships with others outside of the group, such as with family members, colleagues, persons in authority, or friends. Secondarily, the group may focus on individual functioning and task-achievement, or may foster greater harmony within the community.

3. *Primarily focused on problem-solving or task-achievement.* These groups provide for collective activity focused on a specific task to be achieved or problem to be analyzed and acted upon. Through sharing ideas and cognitive notions, groups such as committees and task forces plan development to produce social results. Secondarily, the group influences individuals and interpersonal relationships, and may result also in community change.

4. *Primarily focused on affecting the context of the group.* Such groups seek to modify or influence the immediate surroundings of the group through collective action. Included here are ward management groups, tenant organizations, house organizations, and welfare rights, as well as some family therapy groups and some school social work groups. Secondarily, groups help modify individual participants and interpersonal relationships, and by modifying the context, lead to the completion of tasks and solution of common problems.

5. *Primarily focused on affecting an institution outside of the group or the wider society.* These groups provide collective action to influence a political or social system, the ecology, or community attitudes regarding groupings of society. Secondarily, group efforts may affect individual participants and interpersonal relationships, aid in task-achievement, and modification of the context within which the group exists.

The disciplined use of group methods within social work practice necessitates (1) an understanding by the worker of the nature of human groups and (2) the assumption of a defined professional worker stance, based on the knowledge of leadership functions in group process, as well as a philosophy and commitment to the meaning of groups to the participants and to the wider society. The remainder of the paper gives attention to these two aspects of social work practice through the use of group methods. It assumes that a social worker in generic or multimethod practice has, as part of his professional equipment, a dynamic understanding of individual behavior within a sociocultural context; an understanding of community, society, and social systems; a scheme for social problem analysis or an orderly system of problem assessment; and some knowledge about the social welfare system of which his service is a part. These aspects are therefore not discussed here.

THEORIES OF "GROUP" AND DYNAMICS OF GROUP PROCESS

The concept of "group" as used in this formulation is more than a sociological or psychological construct of interactions among the participants [13]—it implies a social reality; a human phenomenon with substance, process, and definable boundaries; the product of the interactions and emergent relationships among the members, and reflective of the context in which it is located. Groups are seen as developmental; from the initial gathering of potential participants to the termination of activity, a group experiences a constantly changing set of patterns of relationships and a cumulative history of experiences. The duration may consist of a single session in which the individuals coalesce into a feeling of entity and achieve collective activity and purposive outcomes, or the duration may be a series of sessions of a predefined or infinite number. The group may be distinguished from an aggregate of people by the development of a consciousness of self as a unique collective with shared purposes, direction, and goals; the emergence of norms and culture; patterns of collective behavior; and a mutuality of influence that results from the interactions of the participants. The level of cohesion achieved by participants may differ from group to group depending upon the capacity of the individuals; the time factors of duration and repetition; the nature of group purpose and the purpose of the service; the attractiveness of the content, composition, context, and purpose; and the level of group morale. But to the extent that an aggregate becomes a group, some

---

[13] This description and definition of group is drawn from Hartford, *Groups in Social Work*.

cohesion, some sense of entity, belonging, or bond will emerge. Group influence takes on a greater or lesser meaning for each participant, depending on the degree to which he has invested himself in the collective.

The group, then, is the social phenomenon by which, in which, and through which the social worker provides the opportunity for defined purposes. To do so, his activity includes working on the development of his relationships with the individuals and with the group as a whole. The worker also provides a bridge from the group to the social context in which the group is located and to the wider society. To accomplish all of this, the worker must have a dynamic understanding of the nature of human behavior—both individual and group. He must understand the dynamics of healthy or well-functioning behavior as well as individual pathology and dysfunctional behavior. Likewise, he must understand the principles of a well-functioning group as well as the pathologies of group behavior. He must understand the phenomena of scapegoating, destructive contagion, and transference reactions of members to each other as well as to himself. He must understand the destructive as well as constructive aspects of group process for the members and for society. Basically, he must develop his capacity to use his knowledge and his relationships to facilitate the emergence of the group in order that the group may become the medium by which the members work together to achieve their defined or contracted purpose—be that therapy, growth, task-achievement, systems change, or social change. The group can be used by the members to achieve these ends only when a group exists. Therefore, the social worker's responsibility is to use his expert knowledge of individual and group behavior to provide the skill needed to help participants develop their emergent group toward these ends.

Mention should be made of composition of the group. Obviously there are criteria for the composition of any social work group, based on the type of group and its purposes. Criteria are established by virtue of the nature or purpose of the service, the availability of potential members, and the problem being worked on by the group. For instance, people are selected for therapeutic groups because they have requested or been referred for service and are qualified for the group on the basis of some latent or manifest problem. Task groups, on the other hand, are composed of persons who have some special quality or interest in the subject to be worked on by the group. Criteria may at times be vague and unavowed. Composition of a specific group may be established by the agency, by an intake worker, or by the worker who will staff the group. Sometimes, groups are self-composed. This is especially true in autonomous groups who recruit their own members, and in families where members are acquired either through marriage or through birth. In these instances the worker has no influence on composition prior to his attachment to the group, but may have some influence thereafter.

Some groups have closed memberships with a definite composition that remains relatively unchanged from beginning to end. Other groups are established with the expectation of adding and losing members, and are referred to as open-ended groups. In closed groups there is likely to be a higher level of cohesion, greater continuity, long-range planning and goals, and deeper investment of members in each other and in the group. In open-ended groups there is lower cohesion, more reliance on the worker for continuity, more short-term goal-development and immediate activity, and less investment of persons in relationship with others and the group. Open-ended groups are more likely to leave the aggregational state and to develop cohesion and a sense of entity when the turnover is not rapid or dramatic. In order to maintain continuity there must be some stability of membership and more than just the continuity of worker. Greater frequency of sessions and time spent on review can make for better continuity in an open-ended group, whether its purpose is therapeutic, task-achievement, or social change.[14]

Early in the history of social group work, emphasis was placed on providing service through the assignment of a worker to autonomous or self-formed groups, cliques, gangs, and collections of people who had gathered together around some common attracting force, interest, or activity. Stimulated by studies of Mayo and Jennings, there arose the philosophy that work with autonomous or natural groups provided a better means for service.[15] This philosophy was appropriate for children and youth groups formed on a neighborhood or special-interest basis, and for adult education. For people needing help with personality problems or interpersonal relationships, groups convened by a worker or an agency were seen as more appropriate.

[14] Robert Ziller has done research on the nature and effects of open and closed groups. See "Toward a Theory of Open and Closed Groups," *Psychological Bulletin,* 63:164–82 (1965).

[15] Mayo's research showed that people who chose their work partners were more productive than those who didn't. Jennings' work on sociometrics revealed that people who chose their associates enjoyed them better and responded better to each other than those whose associates were chosen for them. Elton Mayo, *Social Organization of the Industrial Civilization* (Cambridge: Harvard University Press, 1945); Helen H. Jennings, *Leadership and Isolation* (New York: Longmans Green, 1950).

Actually, of course, people who had difficulty with relationships did not always belong to groups. People with common or similar problems did not always know how to connect with each other. In many contexts, therefore, social workers brought together people thought to have something to gain from working together. These have been referred to as agency-formed groups or, more accurately, agency-convened groups. The criteria for membership in these groups are usually established by the auspices or the worker, and defined by problem-task or target of change.

Regardless of method of composition, it is a basic principle that only the participants can form a group. The worker can select the participants, facilitate their participation, convene them, and direct the activity toward a focus, but only the members can interact with one another, attach themselves to each other, evolve purpose and contracts for the service, define their goals and boundaries, and develop their own cultural norms and cohesion. Only they, in other words, can develop the group to make it the instrument for service. The worker can direct or facilitate, but the group is a product of its members in interaction with the worker.

Work with families as a whole is of course a style of providing social work service to a group which is autonomous, self-formed, and self-directing. The worker's interventions—which often consists of a weekly one-hour session in a family group that continues to exist twenty-four hours a day, seven days a week—need careful consideration and focus. The worker enters a situation in which a structure exists, the culture is of long standing, norms are well established, and patterns of group control are in operation. The worker who enters a family makes use of all the knowledge available about working with autonomous groups as he attempts to help them to not only work on their problems but also to rearrange their interpersonal structure and change their group processes. He must establish his relationships with the group as a whole, and with each individual apart from and within the family context. He must tune in quickly to existing interpersonal structures, codes of behavior, and roles and statuses in order to pinpoint pathology and problems of functioning as well as health and strengths. His interventions must make use of existing group structure and processes and at the same time effect changes that will restore health and resolve the problems which brought the family to seek help.

In this scheme for social work practice, the worker may attach himself to already-functioning autonomous groups. On the other hand, he may convene a collection of individuals into a new configuration. Thus, this scheme encompasses providing services to both natural or formed groups, depending upon the circumstances and purposes of service.[16]

THE WORKER AND THE GROUP

Strategic to understanding this position regarding the use of group methods for social work service is an examination of the worker's role, stance, and activity. Reference has been made to the need for knowledge of individuals, society, and groups. It is also assumed that every social work professional carries values and ethics that commit him to work for the welfare of the person served and not for personal gain or profit, to use his knowledge constructively and not permit the group to be used destructively, and to maximize the sharing of his knowledge, especially when withholding knowledge would result in personal injury or loss. In terms of working with people in groups, this means that the worker shares with participants knowledge of the effect of group contagion and the powerful influence which a group may have over its members. He also shares with the group the reality that action directed at an outside system may bring retaliatory action against the group or its individual members. The worker should anticipate such reaction and discuss its possibility with members in advance. Since the worker understands group phenomena such as scapegoating and pairing, and the phenomenon of individual defenses, he is committed to use his expertise to help the group understand and work with these phenomena.

Ethical commitments based on knowledge—and skill in use of that knowledge toward the welfare of humankind—are particularly crucial in an area of work where the group can be used so powerfully to modify beliefs and behavior, for "brainwashing," or even for the destruction of an individual's self-image, personality, and feelings of competency. While the influence of the power in the role of the individual therapist, teacher, organizer, or problem-solver is great in the one-to-one relationship, research shows that the thrust of the group on an individual is even more tremendous, especially if the group members have taken on cathected meaning. The professional ethics of the social worker who provides service to people through groups mandate that he have mastery of small-group theory. He must be above corruption and personal fallibility lest he yield to destructive group process. He

---

[16] This phenomenon is discussed in greater detail in Hartford, *Groups in Social Work*.

must also be sensitively aware of and in control of his own needs for power. In addition, he must be able to recognize and deal with similar needs when they are expressed by participants in the group process.

The parameters of the social worker who uses group methods are broad in scope. His mind, his feelings, and his responses merge to form a wide-angle lens which allows him to simultaneously understand and integrate (1) the purpose of the service and its effect on the group; (2) the context of the service, including the auspices, whether they be agency, institution, or autonomous practice; (3) the nature of the individual participants and their needs, capacities, and interests relevant to group purposes; (4) the stage, phase, or level of group development, the accompanying or attendant individual and group behaviors and process, the deliberation and decision-making process, and the interpersonal substructure; and (5) the worker himself, including his effect on the group, his affective response to the group and its members, and his use of his capacity, talent, and professional skill, knowledge, and stance. Obviously the worker can have neither eyes in the back of his head, nor many lenses in his mind all of equal value and consistent attention. At times he will give more attention to one individual or to all individuals, to idea or task, to concerns about purposes, or he may focus totally on the group and its developing processes. But while his focus is on one part of the screen or another, the remainder of it remains present and in view.

The activity of the worker in this view is modified by a number of factors, encompassed in his wide-angle view. The role he takes with the members and with the group-as-a whole toward goal achievement within a social context depends upon each of these elements in interaction with the other. They come together and result in a multiplicity of stances a worker may take. While a given worker may rely heavily upon a single stance, this theoretical position is that the worker deliberately makes flexible use of the three specific ones. For purposes of clarification, and to distinguish each of the stances from the other, they will be described as discretely different. In actual fact, the approaches blend on the edges, and the worker may shift from one to another in the course of a session or a number of sessions in the process of working with a group.

THE DIRECTING STANCE

In the directing stance the worker assumes major responsibility for organizing, convening, and guiding the members, the group process, the discussion, and the flow of ideas and emotions. He remains central to the operations of the members and the group, constantly analyzing and assessing the behaviors and the expressions of the members, the level of group development, and the degree to which the members and group are moving toward the service goal. While his concern may be aimed at some effect on the participants, their interpersonal relationships, a task to be achieved, a context to be influenced, or a social-change objective, he plays a directive role in interventions or activities to enhance the group development so that he and the members together may maximize their collective success. While this directing stance may increase or even encourage individual and group dependency on the worker, his objective is to put or keep as much independence as is possible in the group.

Generally the worker takes this stance when the emotional state, the social stage, or the intellectual capacity of the members is such that they need a strong guiding force. He may also assume this role at the convening stage of the group and continue it until a level of group formation develops where the group can begin to coalesce and set norms, cultural patterns, and influence. In work with task-focused or problem-solving groups, he may maintain this stance to keep the group focused on the primary elements of their deliberation. On occasion, he may even assume the role of chairman. In long-term therapeutically oriented groups, even when members become well skilled in interpretations of personality and behavior, and the group achieves a high level of therapeutic milieu, he may retain this position out of a commitment to his own therapeutic expertise. In this case he may, at the same time, be maximizing the development of the group.

When the worker assesses that the participants, the group, the social situation, or the task demands it, the directing stance may be appropriately used for any of the group purposes mentioned in the classification of group focus.

THE FACILITATING STANCE

In the facilitating stance the worker views himself as a collateral member of the group, but with special expertness, and with a different role and function from other participants. He uses his professional skills to encourage individual members to assume responsibility in the group, and with the group and each other. He poses opportunities for exchange of ideas, affect, and interpretations among the participants. As these begin to take place he participates with the group members so that *his* contributions may be considered along with others, which he knows carry a different weight because he is in a professional role. As leadership and patterns of relationship begin to emerge within the group, he reenforces these and supports them. He clarifies focus and problems, assesses group processes and content, and encourages members to do likewise; he frequently gives the work back to the group-as-a-whole when a member or the group turns to him. He helps the group to keep focused on its purposes. Thus, the facilitating stance places the major responsibility on the group and its members, and maximizes its activity together. The worker, however, acknowledges that the auspices under which the group meets requires professional responsibility of him.

Generally, the worker takes this stance where the potential membership has experience or sophistication in group participation, and where members have social capability and some independent strength. Age and health of members may also be a factor in use of this stance, as well as the level of group development. For instance, an aggregate of potential members may respond initially better to the directing stance, but move quickly to a coalescense that makes the facilitating stance imperative with the first session.

The facilitating stance may be assumed in person-centered, therapeutic, or change groups, especially where members have clarity about the problems they are working on and have come to trust and respect each others' capabilities for help. In these instances, of course, the worker is part of the deliberations and shares his knowledge of problem-assessment and direction for working on problems, and his expertness in helping the members to examine and analyze various aspects of the problems. In groups focused on improved interpersonal relationships, the members themselves are working on the conflicts and tensions they feel, but the worker is very much part of helping them pose the situations to be worked on. In task groups, the facilitating worker will initiate ideas not seen by the group, and periodically he will help the group to summarize and take stock of its progress. In groups concerned with change of context or social situation, the worker taking a facilitating stance will share his knowledge of social systems and provide encouragement for members to collaborate on their collective action for change. He may also encourage participants who are less active, and inform the group of its minimal use of some of the members or some ideas.

THE PERMISSIVE STANCE

In the permissive stance the worker is nondirective, and assumes that if the correct composition has been made and the purpose and focus is clear, the group will emerge by virtue of the fact that the people have come together. Highly socially competent, strongly motivated people who know why they have convened and are experienced in group participation may make very good use of the nondirective worker. Groups that have coalesced and in which members are working well together, whether for therapy or task-achievement, may be able to move toward functioning with a minimum of leadership, guidance, help, or interpretation from the social worker. There may be periods in the life of many groups when they can achieve their purposes best if the worker just passively observes their activity. But even at the extreme of the nondirecting or permissive role, the worker never totally abdicates his responsibility for the social work function, nor the authority of his expertness in human relations and group behavior, nor his linkage with the auspices of the service. He is not only present in person, but his observation and nonintervention lend sanction to the behavior of individuals and the group. His nonverbal interventions also carry influence.

The permissive worker is constantly on the alert to note any evidence of internal group struggles for direction or of competition for internal leadership that is not resolved by the group. He may have to shift his stance if the group is spending more energy than is profitable on group process. If the group loses focus or becomes involved in deliberations or activities of which he has special knowledge, he is less than ethical if he does not share the knowledge and skill which he possesses. In these instances, he may be moving toward a facilitating role.

THE FLEXIBLE STANCE

In the flexible stance the worker, in the course of a session or series of sessions, deliberately changes his position and behavior in response to his assessment of the progress of the group toward its objective; the needs, capacities, and behaviors of members; the level of group functioning; and the problems of content or affect being considered in the group. He may move from a directing to a facilitating or perhaps even to a permissive stance if it appears that the group is doing its work and the members are showing the capacity to carry the therapeutic or task function. On the other hand, he may move quickly to a directing role if he assesses that the flow of group process is not functional for the members or the task, or if an individual seems not to be participating or producing for his own benefit or for the good of the group.

Within this framework, each of the stances may be appropriate in specific situations depending upon the purpose, the capacity of members, the level of group development, the content, and the worker's talents. Although some workers may use a single specific stance almost exclusively, the position of this writer is that a worker should remain flexible to modify his stance in response to the given situation, including his own comfort and capacity in response to it.

THE WORKER'S ACTIVITY IN GROUP DEVELOPMENT

This scheme for viewing group methods within a generic social work framework embraces a developmental theory of groups through phases and a consequent set of worker activities in facilitating the group development.[17] The group development phases are not time-bound, but are related to process and the achievement of a sense of group identity.

They begin with a pregroup period where decisions are made regarding the purpose of group service, potential composition, time of meetings, location, and size, and when potential participants become aware of the possibility of the existence of a group. The second phase is the movement of convening and the face-to-face beginning—where there is a "dance" around getting started and defining goals, roles, focus, and the direction for the future. The third phase is a formation process where there is some evidence of coalescense and sense of "we"—the new social creation, the group. The fourth phase is a period of distintegration or what Tuckman has called "storming." This is a postbeginning reaction where members begin to respond to the fact that the group may be "for real" and their ambivalence about getting to work with each other erupts in new resistance.[18] The fifth phase is one of reintegration, where the group pulls back together and gets to work on the purpose for which it was convened. In the sixth stage, there

[17] The full-phase scheme used by this author is developed fully in *Groups in Social Work*.

[18] Bruce Tuckman has done extensive research on phases of educational and therapeutic groups. A report of this study appears in the *Psychological Bulletin*, vol. 63 (1965), in "Developmental Sequence in Small Groups." His formulation includes "forming," "storming," "norming," and "performing."

is continuing work on both the purpose for which the group was convened and group maintenance—that is, improving the group interactions, culture, norms, cohesion, and control. The seventh phase is pretermination, working toward and through the impending ending. The eighth is the actual termination wherein the ending is ritualized in ways that highlight the group's significance to its members. The ninth is posttermination, or activity, if any, after the group has ended.

This is a simplistic overview of a phase theory of group development which the author has developed more fully elsewhere.[19] It should be emphasized that while time may be an element in group phasing, it is less important than the processes taking place between and among members, including the worker. Some or all of the phases may occur within one extended session, or over a period of several sessions. Phases are also influenced by composition, factors internal to the group, and external factors pressing upon the group. They may not always appear in exact sequence. For instance, a period of disintegration may recur in the life of an ongoing group, necessitating reintegration and reformation.

The existence of phasing within the life span of a collection of people moving from an aggregate to a highly coalesced group suggests behaviors for a social worker. If a social worker is committed to make use of the group as the means of service-delivery, then there are available to him some prescribed behaviors relevant to the group development process. He has proactive behavior related to actions around the decision to use a group; how to compose it; time, size, and space factors; long-range service goals; recruitment or selection devices; style and method of group process; and content.[20] He can facilitate the convening process to ease interaction, and connect participants to each other in ways related to group purpose. He can undertake activities in the formation process to facilitate interaction and coalescence, decision-making, and beginning attraction and attachment. He can intervene in the "storming" process and help the group to examine their disintegrating behaviors and their causes, and hopefully help the group to reintegrate. He can facilitate the group process toward doing its work. Finally, he can help group members to face termination, handle it, and work it through. Limitations of space permit neither the delineation nor the detailing

[19] Hartford, *Groups in Social Work.*

[20] The word proactive is derived from the literature on education, referring to behaviors on the part of a teacher before the beginning of a learning experience. In this instance it refers to work activity before he begins his work with a group.

of prescribed behaviors for the worker in each aspect of the group development process. Suffice to say that this view of making the group the essential instrument for service-delivery assumes worker activity in the phases as they appear, or as he is able to precipitate them.

All groups appear to pass through various phases and to repeat some of them as they progress through a sequence of experiences. When a worker helps a new group to convene and coalesce for the first time, a classic sequence of phases may occur. If, on the other hand, the worker intervenes in an already-existing group—such as an autonomous group, an ongoing group for which he was not the worker, or a family—he may enter at any place in the phase continuum. He will have to tune into group history and current functioning to know where the members are and what they have experienced previously. In a sense, however, his entry into the group in the role of a professional worker will of necessity cause some regrouping, with himself in the configuration. In essence, it may become a new group and go through the total sequence of phases. Or, it may begin with some "storming" and then reintegrate. The worker who is knowledgeable about group phases will be sensitive to these phenomena as he enters already-functioning groups.

Only the four aspects of worker activity which are most crucial in helping the group to emerge, work through, and terminate its activity as the means of social work service will be discussed in detail. These prescriptive behaviors are present regardless of the stance of the worker. In fact, his stance will affect only his style of working, not whether he has a role in the phases. To be considered are the worker's proactive behavior prior to group development, the convening activity, facilitation of group functioning, and termination.

PROACTIVE BEHAVIORS

To maximize the group as the instrument of service, the worker has important prescribed behaviors from the beginning to the end of his contact with a group. These range from proactive worker behaviors prior to the existence of the group, or prior to his relationship with an already-formed group, through termination or posttermination. His proactive behavior includes clarifying with the sponsoring body and himself the group's role as the instrument for service; spelling out service objectives; justifying the use of a group as method of choice for the particular purpose; determining actual composition from the range of possible members; assessing the duration, frequency, and number of sessions; setting feasible time limitations; considering location as related to purpose, problem, composition, and auspices; determining the open or closed nature of membership; and examining his own responses in relation to all of these aspects.

Once these aspects have been considered, the proactive work moves into the public stage. At this point, the worker who emphasizes the group will take particular care that potential members are oriented positively toward the meaning of group service. In therapeutic groups, they need to become aware from the outset that they will be giving as well as receiving help. They need to be assured that they will be working with and sharing the worker, and that the major instrument for their help will be each other, although the worker will always be responsibly present. In the task group the potential participants will know from the outset that they are to participate with a responsible contribution and that they will also be responding to, stimulated by, and expected to participate with others in the group. The worker's proactive behaviors are designed to infuse a collection of people with the anticipation of a group experience wherein the group will become the instrument within and through which the work will be done.

In an autonomous group which the worker will be joining, his own proactive behavior is the same. That is, he must determine how his service to this already-existing group—be it a family or a collection of unrelated people—is consistent with agency purposes. His initial contact with individual group members will set the expectations of work in the group as spelled out in the pregroup public stage.

From the beginning, individuals work on the process of making their collective into a group within which they will achieve their purposes. They acknowledge consciously that the group must be worked on through their relationships, their exchanges of feeling and thinking, their decisions, and their normative expectations. If they already exist as an autonomous body, then their acceptance of the worker means their rearrangement of preexisting relationships and culture to include the worker. In either case, there is an acknowledgement by members and the worker together of the group-with-worker as the milieu of their work together.

CONVENING THE GROUP

When the emphasis of the practice is upon maximizing the group's effectiveness as the instrument of service, activity from the first convening is upon the interactive nature of the collective. In groups where the focus is primarily on effecting change in individuals, each participant begins by seeing himself in relation to others in the group. Obviously, his primary motivation for coming to the group is to acquire something for himself. Thus, despite what he may have been told at intake or in the recruitment process, his anticipation may be that the group leader will be the main source of the service. In order for the group to become the instrument for service for all of the members, from the very beginning the process must focus on the group, the nature of giving and taking, sharing and receiving, and participating together. It is incumbent upon the worker, regardless of his stance with the group, to see that these processes begin to take place by the manner in which the group begins. The same principle holds for task groups and contextual change groups. Regardless of the purpose of the service or the nature of individual needs or capacities, if the group is to be the means of reaching the objective, there must be constant and deliberate focus on the development of the group. The responsibility for maintaining this focus rests primarily with the worker, but he shares the responsibility with the group members, since they, working together, compose the group.

If the potential participants are incapable of using a group or forming a group, then the question should be raised about the appropriateness of the use of group methods for these particular people. In some practice, known as "aggregational therapy," treatment goes on with a therapist in the presence of others and participants learn and gain some insight from observing the therapist with the others but they are not engaged in working with each other. Some people can only use this type of treatment, but it should be recognized in these instances that the group is in no way being used as the medium of help. In these cases the collectivity may be the context in which help is given, but it is not the means or instrument of help.

People have sometimes been convened for collective problem-solving only to contribute or react to ideas in parallel or disparate fashion, without a genuine sharing of ideas or cross-stimulation to develop new ideas. While such a procedure may produce a good list of potential problem solutions, it cannot be said that the result is a group product.

In essence, a collection of people must give some attention to working on their group development and group functioning as well as upon the purposes for which they were convened, if the collective is to come out with a group product. The role of the social worker is to help this process to hap-

pen as well as to help achieve the purposes which brought the people
together.

FACILITATING GROUP FUNCTIONING

As the group comes into being and forms into an entity, its processes may
flow along naturally. The participants may interact with one another, forming cathected relationships. Group norms and culture may emerge, and patterns of influence may begin to appear. When this is happening, the major
focus may be upon the purposes, the task, and the service. When the group
shows problems in functioning—such as loss of morale, rejection or
scapegoating of a member, disruptive behavior on the part of a member, or
deadlocks in the decision-making—the worker may need to have the group
stop and examine the group process to become aware of its dysfunctional behavior. Thus, throughout the course of the work together, the social worker
is conscious of the group processes as well as the content, and he works
with the individual participants and the group as a whole to help them develop awareness of what is going on within the group.

TERMINATING THE GROUP

Terminating the group is not as simple as completing the work, reaching
the terminal date, getting well, fulfilling the task, or bringing about some
change in the social situation. Usually, in addition to these matters, there is
the separation of the participants from the sets of relationships and the
dissolution of an entity that has become meaningful. While more of the person is usually invested in a group that exists with a personal focus, there
may be an equal sense of loss with the ending of a task group that has
worked well together or a social-change group that has achieved results. The
worker may need to assume responsibility for alerting the group to the impending ending far enough in advance that the members can work on their
sense of loss or jubilation. Discussing the termination of the group, sum-
marizing the achievements or reviewing unresolved conflicts, and rejecting
work or thrust toward work need time and some deliberation. The emotional
aspects of separating must be worked on. In a one-session group, this is
done during a brief period at the end of the meeting. In a short-term group,
at least one session should be set aside for this purpose. In longer term
groups, longer periods may need to be set aside. In assuming responsibility
for social work practice through group methods, the worker, regardless of

stance, should initiate the termination process and help the group to work on it. His activity comes from his knowledge of group theory and the effects of the group on the participants, and his knowledge of personality theory.

The social worker who emphasizes the group in his choice of social work methods helps the participants not only to work on the problems, pressures, tasks, needs, or crisis which brought them to the service, but to do so through their activity in the development of a group. Both the problem and the group must be worked on simultaneously and constantly. Both are interrelated if the group is the appropriate instrument for the particular problem or task.

MEASUREMENT OF OUTCOMES

Within this scheme, the objectives of the service are set, at least at an abstract level, by the auspices under which the group functions. More specific objectives are usually established by the worker, but the specific and concrete long- and short-range goals are determined by the group—that is, the members and the worker in interaction. These objectives may be stated as goals for the group in general and for the members individually. They may be arrived at through a contractual agreement, or they may be left as a general and flexible set of expectations. However, if there is some verbal consideration of expectations, and if they are periodically reviewed, then the group members, the worker, and others who have concern about the group have some way of measuring the degree to which the group is meeting expected outcomes. Change in a person's attitudes, values, behaviors, beliefs, personality, or interpersonal relations may be difficult to measure. Sometimes there is no apparent change in his behavior in the group, but the person reports greater comfort or production in other aspects of his life. Responses from others in the lives of group participants may indicate evidence of change. These results are or should be part of group consideration relative to evaluating effectiveness. In task groups, the achievement of a goal or completion of a project is a measure of outcome. The social-change group may have more or less concrete evidence that its work has been effective, depending on results. However, clearly formulated goals or objectives make it more possible to judge outcome.

The group method suggested here can be practiced within the same settings as social casework or community organization. It can be practiced in social work settings, or in other services such as schools, hospitals, clinics, industry, and churches. It can be practiced also in autonomous settings such as private practice or under independent citizens' auspices.

Suffice it to say that if one's theoretical position is that a group is a social phenomenon, that it comes into being out of the interactions, attachments, decisions, and coalescences of individuals into a new social entity, and that this social phenomenon can become the means by which individuals can be affected, the context of the collectivity modified, or the wider social scene influenced, and if one holds philosophically to the belief that such a social invention is a legitimate means of social work service delivery, then it is possible to practice social work through the use of group methods, with an emphasis on the group as the instrument for service.

AN UNSOLVED PROBLEM

A major unsolved problem is how to produce social workers who can practice within this scheme, with enough knowledge and practical experience to refine their skills in the use of groups within the present demands of professional education. The generic approach, which provides social workers with a broad view of their profession, and a comprehensive set of skills, at the same time limits the amount of intensive, in-depth preparation which a student receives in any single area. To this end, it would appear that fewer social workers have in-depth knowledge about groups, and fewer have mastery of group leadership skills, at the point in time when there is a more extensive use of group methods throughout the profession. As a consequence, many professionals who find themselves thrust into a position of working with collectivities do not have theoretical preparation and supervised practice in working with groups. While they may seek continuing education or consultation within their own profession, frequently they reach over to other professions for techniques and activities which are not necessarily compatible with either social work philosophy or theory. They may falsely assume that since they did not acquire enough knowledge in their professional education, such knowledge does not exist. Nothing could be further from the truth. The social workers who contributed to the development of this scheme for the use of groups have developed a carefully thought-out formulation of the nature of group behavior, a carefully analyzed set of formulations for the translation of this knowledge into practice, and an intensive educational program of prescriptive theory and practice. But this approach cannot be mastered by a single course, weekend workshop, or by reading a text or handbook.

If it is believed that there is one or several approaches which emphasize the group as the instrument for help, how, within a generic approach to social work practice which is crucial for current service demands, can practitioners also be equipped with the specific knowledge and skills needed to practice with people in groups, making maximum use of the group as the instrument for service? How can more small-group theory and prescriptive theory for practice with groups be built into social work curricula? The social worker who can swing from group method to individual method to community method and back, as indicated by assessing client need and social problem, and who has the ability to select from his repertoire of methodological skills in a definitive and deliberative way, is the ideal product of the generic social work educational system. The crucial issue for this paper is: how can he master enough knowledge and skill about groups? When the group is the method of choice, the capacity to use the group as the instrument in which and through which service is delivered is the only proof; and curricula need to be reexamined to determine whether enough is being taught about small-group theory and social work practice with people in groups, and whether enough actual field practice is offered, so that graduates are competent in their use of group methods. It is not enough to have solid theory in textbooks, or a beautiful framework for practice with groups. Social workers must be able to translate these into their own knowledge, skills, and beliefs. They must be able to emphasize group process in their use of group methods in their practice.

BIBLIOGRAPHY

Bernstein, Saul et al. *Explorations of Social Group Work*. Boston: Boston University Press, 1965.

Coyle, Grace L. *Group Work with American Youth*. New York: Harper, 1948.

Hartford, Margaret E. "Changing Approaches in Practice Theory and Techniques in Social Work in Group Services," in the National Association of Social Workers, Tenth Anniversary Symposium, *Trends in Social Work Practice and Knowledge*. New York: NASW, 1966.

—— *Groups in Social Work*. New York: Columbia University Press, 1972.

—— "The Preparation of Social Workers to Practice with People in Groups," *Journal of Education for Social Work*, III (1967), 49–61.

—— (ed.) *Working Papers Toward a Frame of Reference for Social Group Work.* New York: NASW, 1962.

Northen, Helen. *Social Work with Groups.* New York: Columbia University Press, 1969.

Schwartz, William. "The Social Worker in the Group," *Social Welfare Forum, 1961.* New York: Columbia University Press, 1961.

Simon, Paul (ed.). *Play and Game Theory in Group Work: A Collection of Papers of Neva L. Boyd.* Chicago: University of Illinois, Jane Addams School of Social Work, 1971.

Vinter, Robert (ed.). *Readings in Group Work.* Ann Arbor, Mich.: Campus Press, 1967.

Wilson, Gertrude and Gladys Ryland. *Social Group Work Practice.* Boston: Houghton Mifflin, 1949.

3
AN ORGANIZATIONAL MODEL [1]

PAUL H. GLASSER AND CHARLES D. GARVIN

This paper represents the continued development of an approach to group work practice known as the preventive and rehabilitative model.[2] It saw its inception at the University of Michigan in the mid-1950s in the writing of Robert Vinter and his colleagues.[3] The purpose of the current paper is to review the components of this approach as well as to present new developments which prescribe the role of the worker with reference to the organizational and environmental contexts of service.

The intent of this approach, since it was first conceived, has been as follows:

1. To provide a model of group work practice that brings it into the mainstream of the social work profession, and that places it on an equal footing with other social work methods. The intent never was to divorce it from other methods, nor to imitate them; rather it was to make social group work a distinctive but equal partner with other means of helping in the profession. The purpose was and continues

[1] The authors are indebted to Robert Vinter for the initial development of many of the ideas in this paper, and for his previous published efforts which layed the foundation for them. We would also like to express our appreciation to Harvey Bertcher and Norma Radin for their many constructive comments.

[2] Charles D. Garvin and Paul H. Glasser, "Social Group Work: The Preventive and Rehabilitative Approach," in *Encyclopedia of Social Work* (2 vols.; New York: NASW, 1971).

[3] Robert D. Vinter (ed.), *Readings in Group Work Practice*. (Ann Arbor, Mich.: Campus Publishers, 1967).

to be to provide a technology which is applicable to a great variety of people seeking services in many different settings.

2. To provide a model of group work practice that makes it possible to give attention to those among the population most in need of help and those most at risk concerning present or future social functioning.[4] When the model was conceived, the majority of group workers were concentrated in a few types of agencies, and one goal was to spread group work professionals into a much larger variety of settings. With this in mind, broad service priorities among potential client groups were suggested. Although the word treatment appears many times in the early formulations, its meaning was broadly conceived, and the model was always meant to include prevention as well as rehabilitation.

3. To provide a model of group work practice that furnishes the practitioner with a codified, systematic set of action-oriented concepts and principles that enable the worker to consciously develop intervention strategies as well as analyze past practice efforts. These must be at a level sufficiently concrete to be useful to the worker each time he or she acts in relationship to clients; nevertheless, a great many complex factors have to be recognized in the formulation.

4. To provide a model of social group work practice which codified already existing practice principles in a way that permitted their integration with new theories and findings in the social and behavioral sciences. Much effort has gone into this undertaking and a broad variety of disciplines has been used. The model always has been and continues to be open to material from many different sources. The intent has always been to bring new practice and social science knowledge to bear on professional activity. This includes systematic evaluation of worker activities by the professional as part of group work practice and by the researcher as part of more elaborate studies.

In this paper, by giving more attention to the organizational contexts for group work service, it is hoped that practice principles will be established that help the worker to focus more, and more easily, on the client's environment. Client reactions to organizational auspices will be specified and ways for the worker to deal with them suggested. The ways in which the professional achieves not only individual change but environmental change

[4] Robert D. Vinter, "The Essential Components of Social Group Work Practice," in Glasser, Sarri, and Vinter (eds.), *Individual Change,* pp. 9–33.

for clients with and through the group will be developed. The practitioner thus becomes a mediator, not only among members of the group but between the group and its social environment as well.[5] By providing broad definitions of organizational functions, and the group worker's activities within these limits, greater emphasis is also given to preventive work than in previous papers.

MAJOR CHARACTERISTICS OF THE MODEL

THE INDIVIDUAL AS THE FOCUS OF CHANGE

This principle stresses that the worker focuses on helping each member change either or both his individual behavior or his environment through the group experience. Specified group conditions are created only as they are seen to be helpful in the achievement of individual goals. These goals are referred to as intervention, terminal, or treatment goals, and refer not only to changes in some state of social functioning of the client but to the client's environment as well.

For some clients a highly organized group with an extensive division of labor is sought; for others, a loosely organized short-term group is chosen. For some clients, multiple activities are provided; for others, group discussion may be preferable. In every instance, however, the worker's primary attention is on how the group experience can facilitate each client's adaptation to a social situation, either by helping the member to change the reactions to and perceptions of that environment or by helping to change the member's life space so that anticipated or existing problems in social functioning are reduced.

While the worker's attention is directed at individual goals when interacting with the group, this is only one of many activities carried on in behalf of clients. The practitioner may find it necessary or useful to intervene in the environment of particular clients or of the group in order to make the agency or other community institutions and their representatives more responsive to the needs and wishes of each member. The worker may decide through negotiations with members to change group, agency, or community

---

[5] The specfic term "mediation" has been used extensively by William Schwartz. See "Social Group Work: The Interactionist Approach," in *Encyclopedia of Social Work,* pp. 125–63. Another discussion of this process can be found by Saul Bernstein in "Conflict in Group Work," Saul Bernstein (ed.), *Explorations in Group Work: Essays in Theory and Practice* (Boston: Boston University School of Social Work, 1965), pp. 54–80.

conditions with them or on their behalf. The decision to seek such changes, however, is always made with reference to the well-being of individuals in the group.

SPECIFICITY OF GOALS

This approach to group work stresses that goals must be expressed in precise, operational terms, whether they refer to some aspect of client social functioning or client environment, or the prevention or treatment of some problematic situation within the client or his social environment. It refers to a state or condition of the client or his situation which the worker would like to see changed at the end of a successful intervention sequence. The goals must be sufficiently concrete to measure their achievement when the group work process is over; a primary responsibility of the worker is to contribute to the improvement of his own practice as well as that of his colleagues.

Goals may be expressed in terms of any type of behavioral phenomena or any area of the environment. Thus, goals may relate to the individual's cognitive, affective, attitudinal, or instrumental behaviors. Goals are determined through client-worker deliberations; this is a process that can require much time in early contacts with the client and operates on a one-to-one basis as well as in the group. Under some circumstances, the worker may be required to develop explicit goals for clients which they cannot fully comprehend—as with psychotics or young children—or with which clients are not in full agreement—as with delinquents or criminals. In such circumstances, however, the worker should communicate these goals to the client and accept the client's decision to engage or withdraw from the group work process.

There may be one or more goals, related to one or several social positions and roles in the client's life. It is often necessary to establish priorities among these for attention in the group. Finally, there may be proximate as well as long-term goals because individual accomplishment and worker planning may best proceed through successive approximations to the final goal. For example, an imprisoned client's ability to select a career, plan and carry out appropriate training, and contact prospective employment agencies may be proximate goals to the long-term goal of becoming economically self-sufficient through regular employment on release from prison.

CONTRACT

An individual goal orientation and the specificity of goals make possible the concept of a member-worker contract, which is a set of agreements between the worker and group members regarding the problems to be dealt with as well as the means to be utilized in this process. In contrast to the legal contract, the group work contract is not a fixed document; instead, it represents a process with many subtle components. Modification in the understanding between members and worker concerning individual goals to be achieved and how group processes are to be used will occur as new information is secured or as problem-solving processes alter member-worker conceptions of the situation.

THE GROUP AS A MEANS FOR CHANGE

The group is conceived as a means as well as a context for the achievement of goals. The worker can promote group pressures, imitation among members, group rules and norms, group influences on the environment, and the like, to help members achieve their goals. The worker constantly seeks to enhance the way the members help each other attain goals.

The worker usually must set instrumental goals concerning such matters as group cohesion, decision-making procedures, or group structures and processes that facilitate the accomplishment of terminal goals. These instrumental goals are not ends in themselves. It is through their emergence as required by specific circumstances that the group becomes a viable means for change for the individual and/or the social situation.

INTERVENTION IN THE SOCIAL ENVIRONMENT

Before a decision is made to embark on an intervention method, it must be determined for each client whether worker or client intervention in the environment alone or one-to-one or group involvement with the worker over time will be required. On many occasions, actions to change the client's life situation must precede group work. For example, a child may have to be removed from an abusive home before it can be determined whether casework or group work efforts are needed to deal with other problems. Often, environmental changes and behavioral changes are sought at the same time in order to make it possible for the client to function in a manner acceptable to himself and to others.

AN ORGANIZATIONAL MODEL OF GROUP
WORK PRACTICE

Basic to this approach to group work practice is a formulation which places the individual not only in the context of the group but also in the context of the social environment. It is this environment which may have led to the person's seeking help or coming under the preventive function of an agency. The worker's efforts in the group, therefore, should be governed by an understanding of the forces that impinge on the client outside the group; he thus becomes not only the mediator among the members of the group but also the middleman between the group and its social environment.

The specific mediational issues differ from one setting to another; however, common elements are present among clusters of agencies, and these clusters form discrete conceptual categories. Because of this, it is possible to identify these categories of organizations and to demonstrate how each orientation affects group work services.

Organizations serve as society's attempts, on the one hand, to maintain consistent patterns of behavior among the majority of people for purposes of continuity, and, on the other hand, to allow for change as required by the society and its people and as demanded by conditions within and around a cultural group.

Related to this dichotomy are the social functions of organizations which employ social workers. These can be characterized as those that provide service to people in the midst of *transition* from one status or position to another, and those that provide service to people in the midst of a *social conflict*. The former primarily emphasizes socialization into new developmental positions, or choice among alternative and sometimes ambiguous norms in an anomic environment. The latter primarily emphasizes social control of those who have violated the legal and normative systems of the society or resocialization of those whose adaptation to their present environment is no longer functional. While the distinction between these two major types of organizations is not always clear in the minds of the public, the employees, or the clients, each tends to create a relatively different environment for group work practice. Despite the fact that many agencies try to fulfill both functions, and that many organizational problems stem from the ambiguities in organizational goals relevant to the functions associated with each category, as ideal types they are useful.

Each of the two ideal functional types can be further subdivided into two subfunctions: social transition includes *anomie reduction* and *socialization;* social conflict includes *social control* and *resocialization.*

ANOMIE REDUCTION

Practice settings which function to reduce anomie are among the newest emerging in social work practice. Workers in these settings seek to respond to persons in situations which have been characterized as "a state of societal demoralization, of normlessness, created by the disjunction of goals and norms for reaching these goals." [6] These persons often are headed toward deviant careers; thus, such organizations serve a preventive purpose.

This is a time when the mores and values of the society are in rapid change, and many individuals are unable either to understand what choices are open to them or to make decisions among the choices available. These are some of the difficult questions young people are asking: Is premarital sexual activity right for me? How important is it for me to complete my high school, or college, or graduate school education? Is my parents' emphasis on hard work for material goods the path I wish to take? Is it all right for me to experiment with marijuana or some of the other drugs? What are the real differences between the sexes, and how can I fulfill myself as a woman, a man?

Examples of organizations which have arisen to respond to these situations include teen "rap centers" associated with community mental health agencies and planned-parenthood clinics, women and minority group consciousness organizations, and many counseling programs associated with universities. In addition, a number of private organizations and institutes (some for profit) have formed to make this type of service available to the large number of people who feel in need of it. Services are usually short-term, and rarely is follow-up care provided. Increasingly, the approaches utilized by such organizations include "rap sessions," encounter groups, marathons, and gestalt therapy. Clients are generally self-referred and highly motivated to participate, although they may not always be clear about the experience they are seeking or likely to participate in. While clients feel they require such service, they generally are not having major difficulty in social functioning. Thus, the worker's focus is on clarifying alternative choices and widening the group members' perspectives. This usually includes help-

[6] Ann Hartman, "Anomie and Social Casework," *Social Casework,* 50:132 (1969).

ing clients understand themselves better, particularly their reciprocal reactions to others.[7]

SOCIALIZATION

The line between organizations which emphasize socialization functions and those which emphasize resocialization functions is sometimes blurred. However, the differences between the two are important. Socialization organizations serve clients who are not or are not likely to be in any form of conflict; instead, they are persons who are moving from one developmental level to another in a generally smooth pattern. The emphasis is not on giving up old attitudes, values, and behavior, but on anticipatory socialization and building on already-present knowledge and skills. Organizations which emphasize socialization functions include schools, settlement houses and community centers, family life and sex education agencies, nursery and preschool programs for children, and those serving the aged.

Adult clients who make use of these agencies tend to come voluntarily. Although some children are required to participate in some programs, there is an overall assumption that client motivation is high and resistance to learning is low. Focus of service is on career development in the broad sense, providing as many opportunities for learning as possible, and gearing the educational process to the needs and wishes of each individual. Ideally, agency rules are open and flexible, and there is opportunity for democratic decision-making.

SOCIAL CONTROL

This function is employed by an organization because society, usually through legislative and judicial processes, has given legitimacy to the agency to limit behavior classified as deviant. Organizations which emphasize social control functions include mental hospitals, residential treatment institutions, training schools for the delinquent and the retarded, drug centers, child-guidance clinics, and community mental health facilities. Central to their goals for clients is behavioral change—that is, the diminution or elimination of that behavior which got the client into trouble with the society. Service to clients is often involuntary as the agency's control over the population it is mandated to deal with is relatively high. The development of

---

[7] Carl Goldberg, *Encounter: Group Sensitivity and Training Experience* (New York: Science House, 1970).

new and more functional modes of performance to replace the dysfunctional behavior should be, but is not always, attended to in their goal orientation. The rules of these organizations tend to be authoritarian and coercive, especially in closed settings, and clients are allowed relatively little option on a number of issues.

Clients recruited to social-control organizations are often resistive to change, and often rebellious against the agency itself. This is sometimes fostered by the rigidity of agency rules and sanctions as well as by peer-group pressure for consensus about antiestablishment behavior. Thus, the initial motivation for change among such clients may be low or even nonexistent, and a beginning step in the intervention effort is to increase personal dissonance in their environment as a means to increase their wish to change. Further, it is often necessary to deal with peer-group resistance to change by dealing with the norms and values of the group.[8]

RESOCIALIZATION

Resocialization organizations emphasize the development of new values, knowledge, and skills to replace outdated or dysfunctional attitudes and behavior. While the client is or is likely to be in trouble in his environment because the world has changed around him or her, there has not been a major violation of social norms or legal sanctions. While there may be considerable environmental pressure on clients to do something about their situation, they usually seek help voluntarily because of personal discomfort. Organizations serving these populations generally allow clients many more opportunities for choice than social-control agencies, and their settings are apt to be open rather than closed.

Under these circumstances, clients are rarely resistive to change, and their motivation for resocialization is often high. However, they may find change difficult because of previous lifelong patterns. The worker's efforts are frequently directed at building on the motivation already present, and increasing the clients' comfort by relating the unfamiliar to the familiar. The peer group can be used to increase client motivation by reinforcing individual change efforts. There is much emphasis on education, which includes

---

[8] Mayer N. Zald, "The Correctional Institution for Juvenile Offenders: An Analysis of Organizational 'Character'," in Howard W. Polsky, Daniel S. Claster, and Carl Goldberg (eds.), *Social System Perspectives in Residential Institutions* (East Lansing: Michigan State University Press, 1970), pp. 58–72.

widening clients' perspectives and providing them with multiple choices in decision-making.

Organizations which emphasize resocialization functions include sheltered workshops and similar skill-development programs for the physically handicapped and the retarded, retraining programs for the unemployed, family-service agencies, medical social work departments, and family-life education programs for parents of low-income children. Many of the agencies specified under the social-control category claim interest in resocialization as well, although the environments of these two types are relatively different.

It is important to remember that organizations may fall between two of the categories. Specific programs within any particular organizations may have different functions, which may be a source of strain for the agency, its employees, and its clients. For example, when the school social worker is assigned to work exclusively with children who are classroom-behavior problems, that worker is functioning as a social-control agent in a setting emphasizing socialization. As a result the practitioner's activities may be seen as peripheral to the mandated goal of the organization.[9] This will affect the worker's relationship to education colleagues, clients, and the administration. Thus, the effects on group work practice will be considerable.

VALUE AND THEORY CONSIDERATIONS

SOCIAL FUNCTIONING

This model derives many of its principles from a conviction that the task of social work is to enhance the social functioning of individuals. Social functioning is conceived of as the ways in which individuals behave with reference to their social roles, through either seeking to change their own role performance or the social structures and processes relevant to their roles, or both.

Roles of interest to group workers frequently include those associated with the positions of student, spouse, employee, parent, and patient. Positions such as mental patient or prison inmate pose special issues because the goal of the group member, or of significant others in the life of the member, is to help this person to move out of these positions to others deemed more acceptable in terms of social norms. Role-related behaviors may include in-

---

[9] Rosemary C. Sarri and Robert D. Vinter, "Beyond Group Work: Organizational Determinants of Malperformance in Secondary Schools," in Glasser, Sarri, and Vinter (eds.), *Individual Change*, pp. 431–57.

terpersonal skills required by the role as well as the knowledge and values required for effective performance. Emotional responses such as dysfunctional anxiety or anger are also often the focus of change goals.

Social structures and processes which are problematic to role performances include role conflict or conflicting expectations for the behavior of the member, insufficiency of reinforcements from the environment for fulfilling role requirements, and lack of resources and opportunity structures to carry out roles successfully. Under some circumstances the desired role performances receive punishing responses from the environment.

As can be seen from the above discussion, the enhancement of social functioning is conceived in highly specific terms. The change orientation is clearly defined—whether it be with regard to the individual or the situation, or to the prevention of or changes in problematic behavior. When the actions of individuals—either group members or others—are concerned, these can be characterized in terms of observable behaviors.

RESPECT FOR THE INDIVIDUAL

A fundamental assertion is that respect for persons is the basic value in intervention and that other values, particularly that of self-determination, are derived from this value. Respect for this concern is embedded in the concept of contract which implies that a specific method to achieve a concrete goal is mutually agreed upon between group members and group worker. Many issues of technique, however, arise concerning how and when this agreement is reached. This is especially so when the member, by virtue of age or mental condition, is hindered in understanding its terms. All practitioners utilizing the contractual concept must seek to clarify and justify their approaches in these situations.

A major problem with operationalizing any value is that adherence to one value can be in conflict with adherence to another equally cherished value. Some illustrations of this dilemma follow:

1. The worker places a high value on the preservation of human life, and this may be in conflict with either the short-term or long-term consequences of the client's behavior.
2. Two clients in a group situation may desire goals which are mutually incompatible; or a client may strive toward a goal which infringes on a right of another individual.
3. The client's goals may be illegal, or illegal means may be required

to attain the goal. The worker holds values which prescribe obeying laws or striving to change them through legal processes.

As one analyst of these types of issues has stated:

> This is because principles do not form a single pattern in the way in which rules of a game do, and because in real life, situations are not artificially limited, so that these conflicts do not arise. If they are to be solved in terms of a morality or pure principles and not by considering, e.g., consequences, both proximate and remote, there would need to be a hierarchy of principles on a clearly indicated scale. *I do not know that any morality of principles has been able to set this up so as to give guidance in all possible conflicts;* at most some principles are held to be more stringent than others, and it is held that some ought not to be broken in any circumstances. . . . So in the end an element of moral judgement not fully specified by principles is inevitable.[10]

This approach, therefore, operates under the assumption that the worker has developed a personal hierarchy of values, and that these are shared with the agency, the group, and individual members to the extent that they are likely to be relevant to the intervention situation. The worker's communication of this hierarchy of values is a first step in enabling the organization and group members to take whatever actions they require to protect their values. An important further activity for the worker, however, is to help group members to understand the logical consequences of adhering to one value as opposed to another.

SOCIAL SCIENCE AND PRACTICE RESEARCH

Consistent with an emphasis on behavioral specificity in enhancing social functioning is the belief that group work practice should be derived from and tested through research. It is recognized that variations in group work methods will be introduced by the worker based on practice experience, and that these should be encouraged. Such variations, however, should be subjected to rigorous examination. All models should be open to continuous testing and change.

Until recently, research was conceived as requiring large samples and scientifically selected control groups. New methods are now available, specifically the single-case designs.[11] These may lead to the training of social

---

[10] Dorothy Emmet, *Rules, Roles, and Relations* (London: Macmillan, 1966), p. 50.

[11] Michael W. Howe, "Casework Self-Evaluation: A Single-Subject Approach," *Social Service Review*, 48:1–23 (March 1974).

workers who operate as practitioner-researchers able to test the effectiveness of practice innovations as well as examine hypotheses which range broadly across practice issues.

Specificity in group work also enhances its ability to draw upon related research in the social sciences: (1) for the purpose of assessing causal factors in group work situations in order to select appropriate change targets, and (2) to plan interventions to modify problematic behavior and dysfunctional situations. An example of the former is the analysis a worker makes to assess the influence of several powerful individuals in the group in terms of their relative access to communication networks. Much research in communication structures bears upon this issue.[12] An example of the latter is the worker who begins a new group by helping members to identify experiences they have had in common, using knowledge about the bases of interpersonal attraction and the influences of attraction among members on individual behavior.[13]

This emphasis on the development of a practitioner-researcher, and on the utilization of research, also leads to support for employment of carefully constructed instruments, used instead of or with traditional recording, to enable the worker to monitor the achievement of individual goals, changes in group conditions, and specified interventions. At times propositions tested in this way will articulate with larger scale research on practice and in the behavioral sciences.

SERVICE PRIORITIES

Another value issue has to do with service priorities. Although practice principles must be relevant to organizational variables, the profession of social work must not be co-opted by organizational needs and interests. The profession has historical commitments to those who as a result of being the most exploited, the most needy, or the most vulnerable, are impaired in their social functioning or are likely to become so. This legitimates the right as well as the responsibility of professionals to set priorities for social work services and to pursue organizational change. This also has implications for

[12] Barry E. Collins and Bertram H. Raven, "Group Structure: Attraction, Coalitions, Communication and Power," in Gardner Lindzey and Elliot Aronson (eds.), *The Handbook of Social Psychology* (2d ed.; Reading, Mass.: Addison-Wesley, 1968), 4: 102–204.

[13] A. J. Lott and Bernice E. Lott, "Group Cohesiveness As Interpersonal Attraction: A Review of Relationships with Antecedent and Consequent Variables," *Psychological Bulletin* 64:259–309 (1965).

the way social work training orients practitioners to service. Settings which have and continue to receive special emphasis by proponents of this model are those related to the social problems of poverty, mental illness, malperformance in educational situations, and crime and delinquency.[14]

BEHAVIORAL SCIENCE BASE

Modern social work practice has become increasingly dependent upon the social and behavioral sciences to (1) suggest new intervention strategies and techniques, (2) provide more useful and more comprehensive understanding for methods of change developed through practice experience, and (3) contribute empirical research methods that make possible the testing and refinement of various change-oriented processes. This approach shares with many others the view that problematic behavior is generated, maintained, and changed through interaction between the client and those individuals and institutions in his environment. The group worker, then, has been interested in drawing from all social science knowledge which can add to the usefulness of this interactional perspective.

In recent years, however, this knowledge has expanded rapidly into overlapping but specialized areas. Each practice model draws upon these and integrates them somewhat differently from others, and it is not always possible to make such distinctions explicit. But at this stage in practice development this is as it should be, for just as social and behavioral science theory is not ready for total integration, neither is social work practice theory. Each new approach makes its contribution by suggesting novel strategies or insights useful for evaluating in and through practice.

To make explicit the distinctive utilization and integration of social and behavioral science theory in this model is beyond the realm of this paper. Instead, some of the major elements from which it draws will be presented, beginning at the broadest level of society and community, and narrowing to the individual.

SOCIAL AND COMMUNITY STRUCTURE AND FUNCTION

The functions of organizations affect both the places where people seek help for their particular problems and the amount and nature of the help that is likely to be available. The most obvious effect of the former is on group

---

[14] Robert D. Vinter, "New Evidence for Restructuring Group Services," in *New Perspectives on Services to Groups* (New York: National Association of Social Workers, 1961), pp. 48–69.

composition. The latter affects the opportunity for and quality of service. For these reasons the worker and/or clients will seek to influence these interorganizational relationships. To do so effectively, an understanding of their power connections, communication patterns, and decision-making processes is essential.[15]

ORGANIZATIONAL THEORY

A preliminary examination of the effects of organizational functions on the composition and processes of the group has already been made. As a subsystem within the larger organizational system, the client group is both influenced by and has opportunities to influence the agency which sponsors it. Central to this analysis are the characteristics of transactions between the organization and individual clients and between the organization and groups throughout the intervention sequences.[16] For example, Hasenfeld has pointed to the effects on service of organizations which transact with clients singly, such as child-guidance clinics, as opposed to those which more frequently deal with clients in groups, such as street-gang agencies and correctional institutions. In the former, "group work practice . . . tends to be marginal and confronts the problem of formulating a common base for clients to interact as a group. . . . In an agency where clients often function collectively, group work encounters competition from other organizational units that transact with clients collectively in the pursuit of unit goals." [17] The social worker must understand—and help members to comprehend and analyze—power within the organization and the effects of the location of the group within this structure. Hasenfeld also refers to organizational location—that is, the space and time allocated to the group and the resources at its disposal, as "the ecological base" of the group, and notes there is insufficient research on this topic.

SMALL-GROUP THEORY

From its beginnings, group work has drawn heavily upon small-group and group-dynamics theory to understand and make use of the distinctive types

[15] John E. Tropman, "Conceptual Approaches in Interorganizational Analysis," in Fred M. Cox et al. (eds.), *Strategies of Community Organization* (2d ed.; Itasca, Ill.: Peacock, 1974), pp. 144–58.

[16] Yeheskel Hasenfeld and Richard English (eds.), *Human Service Organizations* (Ann Arbor: University of Michigan Press, 1974).

[17] Yeheskel Hasenfeld, "Organizational Factors in Service to Groups," in Glasser, Sarri, and Vinter (eds.), *Individual Change*, p. 309.

of interaction that take place within small groups.[18] For instance, those associated with this approach who have written about indirect means of influence—which include group purposes, selection of group members, size of group, group operating and governing procedures, and group development—have drawn heavily on this literature. In addition, topics such as group process, group structure, problem-solving, leadership, and cohesiveness have been discussed extensively from the group dynamics point of view.[19]

A social-role framework, which uses concepts such as position, role, expectation, norm, and status, has often been adopted by social psychologists in reporting research and theory development.[20] This framework has also been used by group workers in the application of such theory to practice. The concept of social functioning, for instance, is derived from the social-role framework, and used extensively in expounding group dynamic variables for practice.

A relatively recent development in small-group theory has been the application of learning-theory principles to the dynamics of small groups. Known as social-exchange theory, it characterizes persons as exchanging gratification within the context of the values and norms of the group which, in turn, were developed from historical and structural conditions.[21]

Some work theorists, including some authors associated with this approach, have drawn upon aspects of social-exchange theory to evaluate the potency of the worker and group members in terms of the rewards members receive.[22] The effectiveness of these exchanges are determined by individual, group, and extragroup conditions, and are amenable to change through worker and member actions. Thus, they are useful as a basis for intervention techniques. While this paper does not deal extensively with this topic, it is expected that workers operating within this framework will increasingly find this a fertile area for advancing practice theory.

---

[18] See, for example, Margaret E. Hartford, *Groups in Social Work.*

[19] See Glasser, Sarri, and Vinter (eds.), *Individual Change.*

[20] Bruce J. Biddle and Edwin J. Thomas (eds.), *Role Theory,* particularly the first four chapters.

[21] John W. Thibaut and Harold M. Kelley, *The Social Psychology of Groups* (New York: Wiley, 1959).

[22] Rosemary C. Sarri, "Behavioral Theory and Group Work," in Glasser, Sarri, and Vinter (eds.), *Individual Change,* pp. 50–70.

LEARNING AND SOCIOBEHAVIORAL THEORY

The original meaning and intent of sociobehavioral theory was the integration of modern concepts of learning with many of the concepts drawn from other areas of social and behavioral science. An example is social-exchange theory discussed in the preceding section. Learning theory is helpful to our understanding of the reasons for varied reactions to interventions in which the purpose is to increase, maintain, or decrease specific client behaviors. While some of these reactions may be understood in terms of internal or covert events, others may be better or more fully understood in terms of the context in which the exchange occurs.

The changes which take place in members' behavior can be viewed as a function of learning, with learning broadly defined in the classic way as a modification of behavior through experience. Group workers draw upon a variety of such theories, from the concepts of motivation developed by Bruner [23] to the operant principles of Skinner [24] and others. The latter theories seek to explain behavior in terms of the conditions that elicit responses (stimuli) and the consequences that these responses evoke (reinforcements). Group workers have applied this knowledge to help members behave differently in highly specific problematic situations. This practice has led to the identification and development of a number of new techniques such as individual and group contingencies, behavioral rehearsal, behavioral assignments, and token economies.[25]

EGO PSYCHOLOGY

This approach focuses on the stable response patterns of the individual, providing conceptualizations of the ways each person copes with the environment.[26] While some aspects of learning theory focus more on the immediate and present social environmental determinants of behavior, ego psychology is not necessarily inconsistent with this view, as Bandura and others

---

[23] Jerome S. Bruner, "Social Psychology and Perception," in Eleanor E. Maccoby, Theodore M. Newcomb, and Eugene L. Hartley (eds.), *Readings in Social Psychology* (3d ed.; New York: Holt, Rinehart and Winston, 1958), pp. 85–93.

[24] B. F. Skinner, *Science and Human Behavior* (New York: Macmillan, 1953).

[25] Arthur J. Frankel and Paul H. Glasser, "Behavioral Approaches to Group Work," *Social Work,* 19:163–76 (March 1974).

[26] Sidney L. Wasserman, "Ego Psychology," in Francis J. Turner (ed.), *Social Work Treatment: Interlocking Theoretical Approaches* (New York: Free Press, 1974), pp. 42–83.

have demonstrated.[27] As a cognitive theory, ego psychology helps the professional to understand how individuals perceive the environment, test reality, and deal with and protect themselves from stress. Intervention can be directed at defining and changing defenses, enhancing the expression of emotion, or reducing constraints in the problem-solving process.

SOCIALIZATION THEORY

As individuals and families move from one stage in life to another, and from one social group to another, they must learn to give up old patterns and take on new ones. Socialization occurs not only when the individual grows from an infant to a preschooler to an adolescent to an adult, but also when a client enters a group, an institution, or an agency seeking help.[28] Thus, a knowledge of socialization theory is important not only for professionals working in agencies which fulfill socialization functions or those involved with children and youth, but for all practitioners. An understanding of concepts such as reference groups and anticipatory socialization can prepare workers to assess and intervene more effectively in a great variety of situations.[29]

INTERVENTION

Clients for group work services are seen as those who have actually entered or are potentially interested in entering an organization whose functions are primarily one of the following: anomie reduction, socialization, deviance control, or resocialization. Group work intervention will vary within these organizational settings, but will follow, if this model is employed, a series of planful tasks. The purpose of this section is to present these tasks, and then to illustrate how they may be applied in each type of setting.

TASKS IN THE INTERVENTION PROCESS

Initial assessment. While organizational function determines to a considerable extent the type of client who seeks or is required to use an agency's

[27] Albert Bandura, *Principles of Behavior Modification* (New York: Holt, Rinehart, and Winston, 1969).

[28] Edward Zigler and Irvin L. Child, "Socialization," in Lindzey and Aronson (eds.), *Handbook of Social Psychology*, 3:450–589.

[29] Orville G. Brim, Jr. and Stranton Wheeler, *Socialization after Childhood: Two Essays* (New York: Wiley, 1966).

services, within these broad categories much individual variation exists. This means that assessment remains an important initial step in the intervention process. Further, while agency function sets limits on the types of group and other services that are available to clients in any particular setting, in many organizations a good deal of diversity is still possible. Therefore, the type of group formed, or the already-formed group chosen for professional intervention, continues to require worker judgement based on assessment of individual clients and the goals set with them in a one-to-one or a group context.

This assessment includes an identification of actual or potential problems in specific terms, and a study of their possible causes. These causes exist within the history, behavioral repertoires, and personality patterns of the individual, and within the dysfunctional social situations in which the client is located. Thus *both* the individual and the social situation must be assessed.[30]

Decision on contexts for change. Following assessment, a decision must be made as to whether social work intervention will be helpful to the client and, if so, which context is the most appropriate for the change effort. These contexts include individual, group, family, and environmental systems. In this paper, only the conditions for the choice of the group context and related environmental contexts will be described. Some elements for the choice of group work within each of the organizational settings identified will be discussed later.

In general, the following are among the criteria for the choice of the group context for individual and environmental change:

1. Some changes are required in the way the client feels about himself or the way in which he deals with present or potential problem situations.
2. The client wishes to pursue change through a group experience, and has made an informed decision to do this or at least wishes to try out group work.
3. A group or a pool of potential group members exists which will be helpful to this client.
4. The nature of the client's situation is such that a high emphasis on confidentiality is not an overriding consideration.

[30] Martin Sundel, Norma Radin, and Sallie R. Churchill, "Diagnosis in Group Work," in Glasser, Sarri, and Vinter (eds.), *Individual Change,* pp. 105–25.

5. The client is not likely to be destructive to other group members.
6. The client is capable, at some point in the life of the group, of receiving help from other group members.
7. The client has the potential for sharing the attention of the worker with other group members.

Additional criteria emerge from specific problems and organizational goals with reference to these problems. Important variables which the worker should consider in deciding on group treatment as opposed to other contexts when specific problems have been assessed were described in an earlier paper.[31]

Group composition. All persons who seek or require changes in themselves, their social situations, or both, may potentially use the group context for intervention. In some instances, already-formed groups, such as street gangs, patients on a psychiatric ward, or residents of a cottage in a training school, are the most appropriate focus of worker intervention. At other times it becomes necessary to purposely form groups. Decisions on the size and composition of these must then be made, including the balance between homogeneity and heterogeneity on descriptive and behavioral attributes.[32]

These decisions concerning size and composition derive from agency goals for the groups, members' goals for themselves, worker's goals for individuals, and the group goals which are likely to emerge as a result of group processes.

Worker interventions for change. With appropriate involvement of group members, the worker is continually required to make decisions regarding intervention. For purposes of analytic clarity, this complex process is divided into (1) selection of intervention targets, (2) selection of intervention strategies, and (3) selection of intervention techniques.

In previous formulations an analytic framework for practice was presented which separated out interventions in which the worker's intent is to change individuals in the context of the group (direct means) from interven-

[31] Charles D. Garvin and Paul H. Glasser, "The Bases of Social Treatment," in Glasser, Sarri, and Vinter (eds.), *Individual Change,* p. 497.

[32] Descriptive attributes "classify an individual as to age, sex, marital status, occupation, or other 'positions' he can be said to occupy," while behavioral attributes describe the way an individual acts or can be expected to act, based on his past performance. Harvey J. Bertcher and Frank Maple, "Elements and Issues in Group Composition," in Glasser, Sarri, and Vinter (eds.), *Individual Change,* p. 187.

tions in which the worker's intent is to change group conditions in ways conducive to individual change (indirect means).[33] The present framework is not meant to replace the other, but rather to supplement it as an aid in helping the professional to identify the most appropriate change efforts for individuals in the context of the group and the organizational auspices under which the group is meeting. The purpose is to provide a means to more systematically widen the perspectives and intervention methods of practitioners.

Selection of targets. The worker, with the participation of group members, decides whether the group will focus on client behavior and/or environmental systems in the client's life, and whether clients or the worker on behalf of clients will strive to effect the changes in the external systems. At this point only *client* efforts to change themselves or their situations will be dealt with.

Efforts by clients to change themselves or their situations can be classified into three types. The first are efforts to change personal behavior as an end in itself—for example, couples about to have their first child learn to handle the physical and emotional needs of infants, or employees learn to distinguish between work-related and personal criticism. The second refers to client acts intended to change an existing opportunity structure so as to better meet their requirements—for example, students ask a teacher to provide them with regular reinforcements, or public-assistance recipients request administrative changes to allow workers to respond more quickly and more flexibly to their needs. The third type involves clients' efforts to develop new opportunity structures, as when young people lobby for a youth employment program, or a group of aged persons develops a new neighborhood recreation center. In all three types of efforts, the worker must decide with group members whether to focus on changes in their affect, their cognitions, their activities, or some combination of these, in order to effect subsequent changes in themselves or their situations.

Selection of strategies. After targets are chosen, a general strategy of change must be adopted. A strategy is a plan encompassing a series of actions to attain the desired results. In group work practice such strategies have traditionally included the use of program tools as well as ways of facilitating problem-solving through discussion. Strategies which have

[33] Vinter, "Essential Components."

largely developed outside of group work but which have been drawn upon by group workers have included guided group interaction,[34] analytic group psychotherapy,[35] and group behavioral therapy. Social workers, however, must continue to create their own strategies as well as selectively incorporate effective elements of other approaches which are consistent with social work values, goals, and settings.

A typology of the components of strategies utilized within the group context is in its initial stage of development. This classification system is as yet not refined enough to represent mutually exclusive categories. Instead, it represents some of the current concepts regarding the elements from which any strategy must draw to derive particular techniques for specified circumstances. The categories consist of the following worker actions:

1. Change the content and pattern of communications in the group—for example, the worker asks a relatively nonverbal member to tell other members about her efforts to secure a change in agency rules.
2. Establish a *sequence* of stimuli—for example, the worker suggests that members play baseball.
3. Create the contingencies for reinforcement in the group—for example, the worker sets up a token economy.
4. Facilitate group problem-solving—for example, the worker suggests that members secure the facts regarding agency rules.
5. Elicit verbalizations and promote awareness—for example, the worker asks members if they can recall how they felt when he announced his resignation.
6. Modify affect—for example, the worker teaches the group a series of relaxation exercises.
7. Change norms—for example, the worker confronts the members with the consequences of their sexual promiscuity.

Selection of techniques. Once the strategy has been developed from session to session or within a session, the worker chooses particular techniques. These consist of specific worker behaviors derived from the strategy, appropriate to the ongoing group process, and often creatively enacted. Some of

---

[34] LaMar T. Empey and Maynard L. Erickson, *The Provo Experiment: Evaluating Community Control of Delinquency* (Lexington, Mass.: Heath, 1972).

[35] Dorothy S. Whitaker and Morton A. Lieberman, *Psychotherapy through the Group Process* (Chicago: Aldine, 1964).

these should be planned before each group session, but others will occur to the worker during the ongoing group process. The worker is aware that techniques affect individuals differentially and must, therefore, be consistent with and supportive of individual goals for all members. Techniques also affect group conditions and must help to create, or at least not break down, group structures and processes supportive of group goals.

Techniques are associated with particular strategies. Thus, one technique for changing the content of communication is to provide the members of a group with feedback about their behavior. A technique for introducing a sequence of stimuli (e.g., programming) is to provide a demonstration. A technique for enhancing problem-solving is to review with members the steps they have taken in the rational problem-solving process to deal with a difficulty in which they were all involved.

Illustrative consideration of how these worker tasks are used differentially in each of the organizational contexts described earlier is next.

ORGANIZATIONS WITH TRANSITIONAL FUNCTIONS:
ANOMIE REDUCTION

Assessment. Aspects of the client's functioning which should be assessed in order to decide whether group approaches should be used, and how they should be used, include the way the client has previously tried to make relevant life choices and the reasons for his failure. Failure may have stemmed from frustrated strivings, value conflicts, lack of role models, or deficits in the available opportunity structures. Many clients may be unaware of their own historical patterns and personal indecisiveness. Other aspects of client functioning to be assessed include capacity to use problem-solving methods to choose among alternative life styles, and the skills to involve self with others, particularly group members, in learning about experiences that foster decision-making.

Factors in the client's current life experience to be evaluated are the systems impinging upon the individual in which norms either are absent or put conflicting demands upon the person. These include disorganization in community, family, school, or work place, or inconsistent expectations among two or more of these settings. Another situation may be one in which punishment is meted out to the client for seeking to acquire norms different from the reference groups to which he or she belongs. Another consideration is the likelihood that the client will receive support from the social environment for making use of particular organizations and the accessibility of these organizations.

Context. Group work, within the general constraints noted earlier, is a highly desirable approach for anomic clients because the group offers each member an opportunity to meet others who have begun to consider various goal and value systems. Many anomic type persons voluntarily seek each other out for just this reason. The group can also provide substantial feedback and support for the client as each member vicariously or actually begins to select a career. Questions and reactions from other group members can also promote self-awareness.

Composition. A small group which is heterogeneous in descriptive and behavioral attributes may be both acceptable and valuable to the client, as he may feel less manipulated into a choice than might be the case in a homogeneous group. By virtue of its small size, the group will provide each client with an opportunity to voice concerns. Varied backgrounds of the clients may also provide knowledge about access to a variety of opportunity structures. Clients may also help each other to develop ways to make the social environment more amenable to their individual needs.

Targets. For the anomic individual, the attitudinal component with its related affects and cognitions is often central. The individual will seek to determine what goals are valued and what wishes are to be pursued in the environment. In working to reach this decision, some may discover that this task is hindered by a lack of community resources or by personal limitations. An institution that directly serves the client's needs may be absent, and its creation will then be a relevant target.

Strategies. One important strategy in dealing with problems of anomie is the structuring of stimuli in the form of new ideas and experiences which can be the basis for client options by means of the problem-solving process. Another strategy in this type of situation is for the worker to present alternative value systems as well as to present the likely short- and long-range consequences of client decisions and behavior.

Techniques. With reference to the strategy of structuring stimuli, the worker can help members to examine possible models existing within and outside of the group. The worker may also utilize such tools as simulation games so that members can play out the roles they contemplate assuming. For problem-solving, the worker can function as a resource in providing information relevant to life choices. The worker can also provide opportunities for reducing the tensions and fears incumbent on making decisions, as through social-emotional release in social events, the use of humor, and recreational experiences related to the choices clients are considering.

These clients often have difficulty establishing an awareness of their own identity as revealed in their history, aptitudes, and previous decisions. Some of the techniques developed in gestalt, sensitivity, and encounter groups, such as conversing with repressed aspects of themselves, may be helpful in resolving problems of anomie.[36]

ORGANIZATIONS WITH TRANSITIONAL FUNCTIONS:
SOCIALIZATION

When clients have decided, either through professional help or on their own, on a course they wish to follow, the relevant organizational function is one of socialization. The following are the tasks for planning interventions under that condition:

Assessment. Client attributes to be assessed include the individual's awareness of the tasks required in order to attain the desired position or role. Once these tasks have been identified, the skills needed to perform adequately must be examined. Utilizing the framework developed by Wheeler, the phenomena which must be assessed are the client's knowledge, skill, and motivation required to perform such tasks.[37]

Situational assessment appropriate to socialization requires that the opportunity structure be examined carefully. Does it exist in a form which will meet the client's requirements? Are the career steps adequately defined and appropriately paced for the client? Is necessary training available and will emotional supports be forthcoming? Have barriers been established because of the client's age, sex, race, or socioeconomic characteristics? What resources exist to overcome these barriers?

Context. When a number of clients are interested in pursuing similar socialization goals, group work is highly desirable. The clients can provide support to one another in acquiring difficult skills; they can also practice the performance of these skills with one another. Since they may encounter similar system barriers, they can bring the strength of numbers to social action

---

[36] Joan Fagan and Irma Lee Shepherd (eds.), *Gestalt Therapy Now: Theory, Techniques, Applications* (Palo Alto: Science and Behavior Books, 1970).

[37] Brim and Wheeler, *Socialization after Childhood,* pp. 51–106.

efforts to overcome these. Experiences in educational and training programs, as well as in a social work group, can be mutually reinforcing.

Composition. In contrast to the anomic situation, a group homogeneous in descriptive attributes is highly desirable in socialization settings. In some cases it may be helpful if group members have similar socialization problems, such as deficits in knowledge or skill. If problem-solving strategies are to be employed, however, it will be useful if each member possesses different information or skills so that this can be pooled in the problem-solving effort.

Targets. As implied from the above discussion, changes are often required in all target areas. The individual's own behavior is often the target in terms of motivation, knowledge, and skill. These involve all three behavioral components: affect, cognition, and activity. On the other hand, a behavioral repertoire may be useless if opportunity structures are deficient. Any program which fails to identify such deficiencies and fails to prepare group members to deal with them creates frustration, low motivation, and social dependency.

Strategies. The major strategies for socialization groups are problem-solving, prestructuring stimuli for anticipatory socialization, and mediating reinforcements. Anticipatory socialization includes a variety of discussion techniques and simulations which enable group members to predict demands, learn how to meet them, and practice the requisite skills. Motivation must remain high for meeting positional requirements, and this will require potent reinforcers. The workers must seek ways to help members provide this reinforcement to one another, but if this is insufficient, gratification also must be secured from others in the environment.

Techniques. One of the techniques which the worker in socialization settings will use frequently is that of coaching.[38] This intervention includes setting up intermediate goals, monitoring performances closely and quickly offering support as needed, giving advice, and participating *with* clients in tasks. Another technique which is useful for this purpose is role-playing or behavioral rehearsal, in which situations which closely resemble real life are created and practiced. At times, the worker will represent a client when a role model is needed. Many behavior-modification techniques will be useful as effective reinforcers, such as token economies and group contingencies.

---

[38] Anselm Strauss, "Coaching," in Biddle and Thomas (eds.), *Role Theory,* pp. 350–53.

ORGANIZATIONS WITH SOCIAL CONFLICT FUNCTIONS: SOCIAL CONTROL

Assessment. Individuals encountered in social-control organizations often assume norms which are labeled as deviant by major social institutions. These norms frequently have been developed by the participation of the individual in subcultures where such norms are acquired and maintained. Also, involvement in these subcultures may have been reinforced by society through labeling mechanisms.[39] Individual assessment, therefore, will include the degree of commitment which the individual has to these sets of norms, the presence or absence of conflicting norms within the individual, and the type of identification which the individual has with the subculture. The motivation of the individual to locate within another subculture with different norms, as well as his knowledge of such opportunities, are also important dimensions.

An analysis of the person's situation will include the family linkages which either maintain the individual within a subculture or which can serve as resources for new identifications. The kinds of opportunity structures which exist for the individual must also be studied. Barriers denying access to more legitimate organizations because of attributes such as race or sex, as well as prejudices regarding previous statuses such as delinquent or psychotic, must also be understood. A vital dimension is the degree to which the social-control institution supplies an alternative—as opposed to a custodial—orientation.[40]

Context. Group treatment can be very effective with individuals in social-control institutions because previous group forces often have molded the individual's norms, values, and behaviors. The opportunity afforded to the individual to change in a different and more benign group situation is a great asset. In some institutions, however, the pool of potential clients for a group might provide the basis for reinforcement of deviance. Under these circumstances individual treatment is more desirable. When family dynamics are maintaining the individual in a deviant role, family interventions also are effective.

[39] Edwin M. Lemert, *Human Deviance, Social Problems, and Social Control* (2d ed.; Englewood Cliffs, N.J.: Prentice-Hall, 1972).

[40] David Street, Robert Vinter, and Charles Perrow, *Organization for Treatment* (New York; Free Press, 1966).

Composition. A group which is too homogeneous in regard to a deviant behavior or values provides reinforcement to the members to maintain that behavior or those values. Heterogeneity in behavioral attributes is therefore desirable. When it is not possible, however, techniques of strong confrontation, as used by guided group interaction or by self-help groups such as Synanon, may be employed.[41] Even under such circumstances, though, these approaches seek to seed new groups with older clients who have already identified with the goals of the change milieu.

Targets. The targets in social-control-oriented groups are the cognitions and affects of the individual as these relate to attitudes toward social norms. Those attitudes manifested in behavior are focused upon also. As much of the literature regarding deviance suggests, deficient opportunity structures are seen as major forces for maintaining deviant subcultures, and these are the targets of modification.[42]

Value issues constantly confront the worker in social-control situations. Frequently the actual or potential group members fail to share agency goals and organizational purposes for the groups. Workers will experience many difficulties, therefore, in developing viable contracts with members. The intervention target involves, then, the transactions occurring between the individual, group, and agency. After each party to the transaction has made some changes, a contract for further client change can be established.

Strategies. Major group work strategies in social-control situations involve changing member norms as well as mediating reinforcements. More specific strategies for changing norms and supplying new reinforcements are sometimes borrowed by group workers from the experiences of those involved in guided group interaction, client-operated drug help programs, Alcoholics Anonymous, and organizations for former mental patients. These include elements of confrontation, creation of ambiguity, generation of strong peer-group pressures, and the introduction of positive models.

Techniques. The group worker confronts members with the consequences of their behavior as well as the way that behavior is seen by others. The worker also positively reinforces the group for problem-focused problem-solving efforts and concern shown for the actions and consequent suffering experienced by other members. Legitimate grievances about the agency as well as other social institutions are elicited and legitimate change efforts

[41] Lewis Yablonsky, *The Tunnel Back* (New York: Macmillan, 1964).
[42] Richard A. Cloward and Lloyd E. Ohlin, *Delinquency and Opportunity* (Glencoe, Ill.: Free Press, 1969).

supported; projection of problems on to social institutions, however, are strongly but supportively confronted.

ORGANIZATIONS WITH SOCIAL CONFLICT FUNCTIONS:
RESOCIALIZATION

It is difficult to separate the point at which social-control efforts recede and the resocialization functions of some organizations and groups predominate. There are, however, organizations and groups which focus almost exclusively on resocialization. The following are the tasks when resocialization functions predominate.

Assessment. In some respects, intervention for socialization and resocialization functions are similar. The differences are occasioned by the fact that the individual has been socialized into roles which are dysfunctional and which conflict, at times, with the resocialization emphasis. The assessment task for resocialization, then, is to identify conflicts between old and new roles and how the individual typically copes with these. Other individual evaluations parallel those for socialization, including awareness of socialization requirements, skills possessed, and knowledge and motivation for socialization tasks.

In addition to evaluating the opportunity structure for the new career choice, the worker will have to determine how much power former, non-useful environmental influences continue to exert upon the client (e.g., family or peer group). Ways to modify such influences, or to isolate the client from them, must be considered.

Context. Individuals can be helpful to one another when pursuing resocialization goals, and this again makes the group experience a good choice. Members can support each other in their efforts to separate themselves from previous dysfunctional roles. Beyond this, the same considerations as for socialization hold, which include working together to overcome system barriers and providing support for one another.

Composition. For resocialization functions, a group homogeneous in descriptive and behavioral attributes is preferred. Similarity in resocialization problems will enhance the cohesiveness of the group, promote relevant problem-solving, add to individual motivation, and promote changes in opportunity structures or the creation of new ones.

Targets. For socialization to occur, individual targets of change usually include affects, cognitions, and activities relevant to the desired roles. The affective component is particularly important for resocialization because of the conflicts the individual experiences in changing positions in society. In addition to problems with inadequate opportunity structures, a target often has to be to limit the effects of dysfunctional environments which continue to place inappropriate demands upon the client.

Strategies. Strategies continue to be problem-solving, prestructuring stimuli, and the mediation of reinforcements. Focus on anticipatory socialization is also relevant here. Problem-solving work will often emphasize the reduction of conflicts and stresses brought about by discrepancies between new and old careers. Also in the forefront will be anticipating and practicing ways of coping with institutions which continue to identify the client in terms of a former career rather than the one for which he or she is now preparing. Group sensitivity approaches which help increase client comfort with new life styles consistent with new roles are also valid.

Techniques. In addition to the techniques appropriate for socialization, the worker may use several others. One of these is values clarification, which has been found helpful to groups whose members are evaluating the personal meaning of conflicting norms.[43] Another is the development of supportive pairs of peers or subgroups which members use to cope with the conflicts and stresses of participation in new social situations. These approaches also help the individual, singly or with others, to work for modifications in the situation itself to facilitate the resocialization process.

STAGES IN THE TREATMENT SEQUENCE

As the client passes through each of the stages in the treatment sequence, the worker must (1) assess the client's situation with reference to problems, causal conditions of problems, and goals, (2) plan activities in relation to this assessment, (3) execute the plan, and (4) evaluate the outcome and, when necessary, revise the plan based on this evaluation. The way the worker utilizes these procedures depends on the stage of the client's career and the stage of group development. A general paradigm of the treatment process which involves these considerations follows.

FIRST PHASE: INTAKE, COMPOSITION, AND LOCATION

During this phase the worker locates potential group members for whom change efforts are consistent with the organizational functions of helping with transition or social conflict. Individual goals, as these relate to or are in

---

[43] Sidney B. Simon, Leland W. Howe, and Howard Kirschenbaum, *Values Clarification: A Handbook of Practical Strategies for Teachers and Students* (New York: Hart, 1972).

conflict with these organizational functions, are elicited, and the client's perceptions and expectations of the organization are identified. On this basis, as well as that noted under "Decision on Contexts for Change," members are selected for group service. Utilizing the compositional criteria discussed, groups are composed. Already-formed groups which meet these criteria may also be served.

When the group is composed, its location in the organizational structure must be clarified. Location refers to the specific linkages which are generated to the executive, technological, and resource-allocating subsystems of the agency. The worker's location in this structure is also important. This includes the status the group worker occupies in the organization, the worker's relationship to other people-changing and/or people-processing positions,[44] and the worker's channels of accountability for group processes and outcomes. These characteristics are important to identify because they may constitute constraints or resources in attaining group goals; the worker, and later the members, may be required to negotiate changes in these conditions or in group goals commensurate with such conditions.

SECOND PHASE: TARGET SELECTION AND
GROUP FORMATION

During this phase the group members and worker begin to meet together to develop specific group goals. These goals will be a result of goals for individual members already developed through member-worker contracts and agency goals for the group as related to organizational functions. Goals will be in terms of the prevention of or the reduction of problems in social functioning and they will specifically enunciate changes in targets in order to prevent or abate these problems in some way. They will also represent the result of the worker's mediational efforts between agency functions and individual and group needs.

Out of this process of selecting targets, group members and the worker will decide on immediate group efforts which constitute first steps toward change in targets. These steps will involve clarification of organizational resources and organizational changes required to accomplish group goals. Thus, early negotiations between the group and the organization, with the worker as mediator or advocate, will also occur during this phase.

[44] Robert D. Vinter, "Analysis of Treatment Organizations," in Edwin J. Thomas (ed.), *Behavioral Science for Social Workers*, pp. 207–21.

THIRD PHASE: PLANNING INDIVIDUAL AND SYSTEM CHANGE

During this stage the worker will negotiate with members the nature of the intervention strategy to be utilized. Some strategies call for the members to acquire detailed knowledge of them, often so as to function as co-helpers, while in others only the general outlines are communicated. Additional negotiations between the members and the organization often take place as resources are required, as the organization reacts favorably or unfavorably to the strategies selected, and as changes in organizational conditions are needed to make a strategy effective. For example, if the strategy involves a behavioral technique, the organization may have to provide resources for reinforcements; if some individuals who are influential in the organization are ideologically opposed to the strategy, they will have to be coped with; and the effectiveness of the strategy may require other individuals in the organization to monitor individual behavior change.

FOURTH PHASE: EXECUTING AND EVALUATING THE CHANGE PLAN

During this phase the worker, with member involvement, develops the techniques to be used within each group meeting. The worker also establishes a way to secure data regarding the consequences of his interventions. These data will be generated by events within group meetings—such as the number of fights engaged in by a child during meetings—as well as events occurring outside of group meetings related to intervention goals—such as the number of fights engaged in by a child in the classroom. It is important to remember that changes are with reference to targets and, therefore, include not only the behavior of the member but also changes in environments. When the worker, on behalf of members, seeks environmental changes, these are also measured. For example, if either a child or the worker on his behalf seeks regular reinforcements from a school teacher for desired behavior, the extent to which this reinforcement contingency appropriately occurs must be noted and evaluated.

FIFTH PHASE: CONTRACT RENEGOTIATION OR TERMINATION

When a particular goal has been chosen it will be pursued until it has been attained, appears unlikely to be attained, or is no longer appropriate. In situations where the goal is not attained, the client will either terminate or a new goal and/or new strategies to achieve this goal will be negotiated.

Ideally, termination occurs because intervention goals have been achieved. The worker's task, then, is to reduce the nonfunctional attachments that the client may have formed with the worker and other members, as well as with the organization, that may prevent realization of the new potential. The worker may also attempt to strengthen the changes that have occurred. There are two types of evidence that the termination decision was correct: (1) when the client places higher value on leaving the group than on staying and (2) when there are data indicating that there is transfer of changed behavior into contexts other than the intervention group.

The worker also takes responsibility for estimating whether the environmental systems have stabilized to the point where they are supportive of the client's functioning. Under some circumstances the worker may terminate with the client and/or group but still provide some help to these systems. An example is when a worker continues to provide consultation to a teacher whose students had been the focus of effort even when group work with these students has been terminated. The teacher in this hypothetical example may require the worker to express confidence in his or her ability to work with the children who had been referred for group work service; he or she may also need to feel secure in the approaches learned as part of this consultation.

Finally, the worker engages in a terminal assessment, which includes an evaluation of changes in both the individual and the situation, including organizational changes in the agency itself. The worker will then seek to draw conclusions about the degree of effectiveness of service, considering agency, client, and extraorganizational variables as they are related to the kinds of targets that were chosen, the strategies that were adopted, and the specific techniques that were employed. This is a complex task but one to which practice must continuously address itself.

ENVIRONMENTAL CHANGE

In the intervention section of this paper a variety of strategies and techniques were discussed for influencing client behavior and dynamics within the group to achieve improvement in social functioning for each member. Emphasis was not only on helping clients change their reactions to their social situation but also on helping them develop ways to change their environment more directly—that is, to open up or create new opportunity structures. This can be done through their own efforts or together with other group members and/or the worker. Therefore, the professional requires an accessible set of strategies for changing the environment to complement those useful in intervention in the group.

Such strategies have been suggested in earlier publications. These include choosing targets for environmental change efforts and involving clients in these endeavors. The strategies are organized according to whether persons or systems in the service organization or other community organizations are the focus of planned change. Attention is given to the focus of practitioner activity on and in the client's environment. Examples of these strategies are the following:

1. Manipulation of the social and/or physical situation—for example, the worker recommends that a hospitalized patient be moved to another ward more conducive to his recovery.
2. Education of others—for example, the worker informs prospective employers of the kinds of jobs that can be performed by handicapped clients and reviews the excellent work records of those employed.
3. Interpretation—for example, the worker illustrates to cottage parents how their reactions to a client set off the antisocial behavior which led to institutionalization.
4. Evaluation—for example, the worker gathers data to demonstrate to public assistance personnel how certain policies and procedures maintain clients in a state of economic dependency, thus costing the government extra money.
5. Co-optation—for example, the worker invites an antagonistic law enforcement official to a meeting of predelinquent adolescents to discuss community problems in the hope that the official will better appreciate the difficulties the group members have to deal with, and will wish to be more helpful.

Among the other sixteen techniques discussed are confrontation, bargaining, use of influentials, alliances, advocacy, consultation, use of mass media, and passive and active resistance.[45]

[45] Paul H. Glasser et al., "Group Work Intervention in the Social Environment," in Glasser, Sarri, and Vinter (eds.), *Individual Change;* Robert D. Vinter and Maeda J. Galinsky, "Extra-Group Relations and Approaches," *ibid.,* pp. 281–91.

ORGANIZATIONAL PREREQUISITES

A major orientation of this paper is that the organization in which group work is practiced has important effects on the intervention process. As such, the organization, and the professional as its representative, mediates between the client and client group, and the broader social environment. For this reason, this formulation began with a discussion of some of the effects of organizational function on the milieu in which group work is practiced.

Consistent with this approach, this section discusses some of the prerequisites in the organizational environment required for effective group work practice. Few organizations are able to maximize all of the criteria, but some are so limiting that successful practice is difficult to achieve. An understanding of these factors will not only help the worker to comprehend the constraints put on professional activities but also provide better understanding of needed organizational change.

The way in which the organization defines limits on service to clients with a variety of social and personal characteristics has a significant effect on group composition. Some agencies, like prisons and mental hospitals, are constrained by legal and other requirements to accept only specific types of individuals into their program. Others, such as community centers and settlement houses, have much more open membership policies. The development of heterogeneous groups among the former agencies is more difficult than in the latter. This can be a problem in some situations in which the emphasis should be on resocialization or dealing with problems of anomie.

The way in which the organization approaches the group worker's access to clients makes it possible for the worker to select from the full range of clients in some situations; in others his access is more limited. Such access may be enhanced or limited by either formal procedures or informal channels. For example, some school social workers may be allowed to have contact only with those students defined as having behavioral or learning problems in the classroom; in others, the worker may establish priorities for group service. Or the group worker in a juvenile correctional facility may not be permitted—for security or other reasons—to mix clients from different cottages, buildings, or wards. Under the more limiting set of circumstances, individual and group goals may have to be narrowly defined.

The type and amount of resources made available to the group by the organization influences practice. Resources include not only the place where the group meets and the equipment available there but many other things as well. Included may be funds for craft materials, refreshments, and trips, access to transportation, and the time the worker has available to devote to the group members. Without such resources the worker may be unable to successfully carry out certain strategies and techniques.

The approach which the organization takes to decision-making within the group varies. In some organizations the rules are permissive; in others they are so restrictive that opportunities for clients to change themselves or their environments are minimized. In some settings variations in routines are not permitted, clients are not allowed beyond certain geographic boundaries, and particular legitimate activities are denied to them. These conditions prevent the group and its members from making autonomous decisions about their own behavior or ways to make their environments more conducive to maximum social functioning.

The willingness of the organization to respond positively to organizational change affects the group. As environments change, and the nature of client problems change, agencies must be flexible. It is often the group that points up the need to restructure staff or change agency rules. Is long hair for men or short skirts for women necessarily a sign of behavioral deviance requiring sanctions? Is the agency willing to consider new policies that make more sense in the light of new developments, and at the same time provide clients with a sense that they do have the power to open up or create new opportunity structures?

The degree to which the organization encourages cooperation by other personnel with the group and its worker varies. In this matter, informal channels are often more important than the formal ones. Some clients are readily available for group meetings, but others are restricted because personnel have assigned them different tasks. Employees in some settings are more willing than others to discuss with worker or clients changes in their own behavior which may facilitate client change. These matters are often crucial for the achievement of individual and group goals.

The facilitation of communication by the organization may be characterized by the openness of information channels which is crucial if the group and its worker are to deal with this environment effectively. Without this, individual and group goals may be set which are inappropriate, and group decisions made which cannot be carried out. This can only serve to discourage and disturb group members in their efforts to change themselves and their social situations.

The degree to which the organization and the worker have control over and access to the client's social environment outside the organization is an important consideration. Efforts in closed institutions must be directed at the social functioning of clients in the environment to which they are to return. But even in open settings, workers are sometimes directed to limit their activities to efforts within the agency itself. When this occurs the worker's and members' efforts are diminished considerably. The ability of the group and its worker to plan and carry out endeavors making it possible for clients to adapt more successfully to their social environments is essential to this model.

Central to all of these criteria, as well as others that could be developed, is the worker's power within the organization. Both the worker's legitimate power through his or her position in the institutional structure and the worker's informal influence are crucial in terms of ability to facilitate the intervention process. This is an area of social work practice that needs much more attention in future literature.

EVALUATION

A major feature of this model is that an emphasis on precise, operational goals for individual members, groups, and the social environment makes testing its utility feasible. Further, the specification of targets, strategies, and techniques—which has only been partially achieved in this and other papers—makes it possible to evaluate particular aspects of the model without having to necessarily test it as whole. This, in turn, allows for its revision as new evidence concerning the usefulness of particular practice concepts is gathered. However, this major task has just begun.

A number of studies explicitly using aspects of this model have been reported in the literature. Navarre, Glasser, and Costabile, working with public-assistance clients, found that groups with precise goals on which workers focused throughout the intervention process were helpful in increasing mothers' responsibilities for their children, especially in school-related tasks.[46] Sarri and Vinter also have reported on the effectiveness of this approach for improving school performance of children.[47]

In other spheres, Garvin has demonstrated that agreement on purposes

---

[46] Elizabeth Navarre, Paul H. Glasser, and Jane Costabile, "An Evaluation of Group Work Practice with A.F.D.C. Mothers," in Glasser, Sarri, and Vinter (eds.), *Individual Change*, pp. 387–403.

[47] Sarri and Vinter, "Beyond Group Work."

between workers and members was associated with group movement in problem-solving.[48] Feldman has revealed how different forms of group cohesion and integration are useful for setting conditions in the group which facilitate individual change.[49] In addition, Rose, Rose and Sundel, Lawrence and Sundel, Lawrence and Walter, and Frankel have all used behavior-modification approaches within the context of this model to reveal its effectiveness with a variety of client types, including delinquent children and their parents, spouses with marital problems, and youngsters referred to a child guidance clinic.[50] Radin, and Radin and Wittes have made extensive use of the model to work in the preventive area with paraprofessionals and with mothers of culturally deprived preschool children.[51]

It is evident, however, that these studies are merely the beginning efforts in the kinds of evaluations required to improve and refine the model. Work needs to be done to replicate existing studies as well as to determine the precise interrelationships among client characteristics, environmental situations, factors in group composition, and alternate intervention strategies.

LINKAGES

The writers of this paper are committed to a concept of interpersonal change in which workers adapt their strategies, targets, and techniques to meet the needs of clients. They support the aim, therefore, that social welfare agen-

[48] Charles Garvin, "Complementarity of Role Expectations in Groups: The Member-Worker Contract," in *Social Work Practice, 1969* (New York: Columbia University Press, 1969), pp. 127–45.

[49] Ronald A. Feldman, "Modes of Integration and Conformity Behavior: Implications for Social Group Work Intervention," in Glasser, Sarri, and Vinter (eds.), *Individual Change,* pp. 149–68.

[50] Sheldon B. Rose, "A Behavioral Approach to the Group Treatment of Parents," *Social Work,* 14:21–29 (July 1969). Sheldon B. Rose and Martin Sundel, "The Hartwig Project: A Behavioral Approach to the Treatment of Juvenile Offenders," in Glasser, Sarri, and Vinter (eds.), *Individual Change,* pp. 404–19; Martin Sundel and Harry Lawrence, "Behavioral Group Treatment with Adults in a Family Service Agency," *ibid.,* pp. 325–47; Harry Lawrence and Claude Walter, "The Effectiveness of Behavior Modification with Adult Groups," paper presented at Association for Advancement of Behavior Therapy Conference, Chicago, November 2, 1974; Arthur J. Frankel, "A Client-Mediated Token Economy for Disturbed Children in an Open Setting" (Ph.D. dissertation, School of Social Work, University of Michigan, 1972).

[51] Norma Radin, *Early Education Program: Analysis of Changes During the Year* (Ypsilanti, Mich.: Ypsilanti Public Schools, 1969); Glorianne Wittes and Norma Radin, "Two Approaches to Parent Work in a Compensatory Preschool Program," paper read at National Conference on Family Relations, Washington, D.C., October 1969.

cies should be able to offer a choice of individual, group, family, and environmental change contexts to all clients. Although social group work has been emphasized, the implicit concept of practice is broader. For this reason, the effort has been made to create a model with generic elements underlying interpersonal helping in a variety of contexts. These generic elements are described below.

First, it is proposed that the various approaches to interpersonal helping have the same goal: to enhance the social functioning of individuals. This may be for preventive or treatment purposes. Casework, group work, and family treatment can all work to help individuals to change either themselves or dysfunctional aspects of their situations.

Second, all of these contexts for practice can follow the intervention sequences described. This includes assessment, choice of context, composition of the intervention system and its location in the organizational structure, selection of intervention targets, planning for individual and system change, executing change, and termination or renegotiation. There are different compositional issues in family and group contexts, and in executing change in all of the contexts. It is not the contention, certainly, that work in all contexts is identical, but rather that a general model is feasible.

Third, the social science knowledge base described here is useful for all approaches to interpersonal helping. Casework, group work, and marital and family therapy all constitute work with small, primary groups; and small-group theory in particular is one of the major theoretical resources in all of these contexts. The authors have drawn upon reports which have considered the similarities and differences between dyads and larger groups, and have usefully applied some small-group concepts to two-person as well as to larger groups.[52] There are differences in two-person situations and between groups with related and unrelated members, and these must, of course, be considered when one context is chosen instead of another. In addition, other theories such as community structure and function, organizational, ego psychological, sociobehavioral and socialization theories all describe dynamics that can be seen to operate in a variety of social aggregates.

A fourth type of linkage lies in the possible usefulness in various contexts of the typology of intervention strategies described above. Garvin has taught these as generic approaches to helping in an interpersonal change

---

[52] Garvin and Glasser, "Bases of Social Treatment."

methods course, and students have been able to deduce from these the specific details of strategies in a variety of intervention situations. Some of the differences among interpersonal methods lie, most likely, in the way techniques are utilized to implement the strategies. Techniques focus on the ways in which group members can help one another, and the ways in which the worker can enhance mutual support and problem-solving capabilities in group situations. Similarly, the worker must employ techniques to deal with the special emotional meanings which a worker often comes to represent in casework and marital and family therapy situations, although it is argued that many similar phenomena emerge in group work settings. Also, because techniques may have different effects in different contexts, the worker may have to utilize different criteria for the choice of a specific technique in casework, group work, and marital and family therapy. These criteria are as yet in the area of practice wisdom, and a good deal of research remains to be done on the relationship between contexts and intervention choices.

FURTHER WORK

The material in this paper represents an extension and modification of earlier formulations. As such, much work is required to integrate the approach of this paper with previous work and to systematically test its feasibility and effectiveness. In more precise terms, priorities for future efforts are as follows:

1. To integrate further the developments in social science theory and research into this approach to group work.
2. To continue to test the applicability of social science research findings to social work settings.
3. To devise and carry out research on the practical application of this modified model, as well as to determine the effectiveness of this model in changing individual behavior and relevant environmental conditions.
4. To generate a more sophisticated typology of worker interventions which integrates environmental change efforts with change efforts within the group. This typology should build upon previous work on direct, indirect, and extragroup means of influence.
5. To expand this paradigm which articulates the components of intervention (choice of target, strategy, and technique) with organizational functions of anomie reduction, socialization, social control, and resocialization.

Throughout this process the authors are mindful of the value to group work practice of identifying common elements among various group work models. Also, they see the importance of identifying goals and interventions compatible with casework and community work models, thus assisting in the evolution of more comprehensive social work services available to all clients.

BIBLIOGRAPHY

Bandura, Albert. *Principles of Behavior Modification*. New York: Holt, Rinehart, and Winston, 1969.

Biddle, Bruce N. and Edwin J. Thomas. *Role Theory: Concepts and Research*. New York: Wiley, 1966.

Cartwright, Dorwin and Alvin Zander (eds.). *Group Dynamics: Research and Theory*. New York: Harper & Row, 1968.

Cloward, Richard A. and Lloyd E. Ohlin. *Delinquency and Opportunity*. Glencoe, Ill.: Free Press, 1969.

Glasser, Paul, Rosemary Sarri, and Robert Vinter. *Individual Change Through Small Groups*. New York: Free Press, 1974.

Hartford, Margaret E. *Groups in Social Work: Application of Small Group Theory and Research to Social Work Practice*. New York: Columbia University Press, 1972.

Hasenfeld, Yeheskel and Richard English (eds.). *Human Service Organizations*. Ann Arbor: University of Michigan Press, 1974.

Shaffer, John B. P. and M. David Galinsky. *Models of Group Therapy and Sensitivity Training*. Englewood Cliffs, N.J.: Prentice-Hall, 1974.

Thomas, Edwin J. (ed.). *Behavioral Science for Social Workers*. New York: Free Press, 1967.

Zald, Mayer N. (ed.). *Social Welfare Institutions: A Sociological Reader*. New York: Wiley, 1965.

4

PSYCHOSOCIAL PRACTICE IN SMALL GROUPS

HELEN NORTHEN

Psychosocial practice in work with groups has evolved from developments within social work, as influenced by the values and expectations of society, the burgeoning knowledge available from the psychological and social sciences, and theory development and research related to practice itself. It is a theoretical approach to practice that views work with individuals and work with groups as closely interrelated and interdependent. Indeed, there seems to be emerging a psychosocial approach to practice that holds promise of integrating values, knowledge, and methods across the boundaries earlier designated as social casework and social group work.[1] For purposes of this paper, the theory domain is the social worker in the group. This boundary does not negate the importance of service to individuals apart from the group, of work with others in behalf of group members, or of social workers' efforts to change the environment.

The distinguishing characteristic of this approach is its psychosocial orientation. The purpose toward which practice is directed is the enhancement of psychosocial functioning. The emphasis is on the interrelationships between psychological and social forces and the interactions between the

---

[1] In a survey of the literature on collaboration between casework and group work, it was found that the psychosocial model of practice was predominant. See Jerry Flanzer, "Conintegration: The Concurrent Integration of Treatment Modalities in Social Work Practice" (D.S.W. dissertation, University of Southern California, 1973) and Anne-Marie Furness, "Three Formulations of Social Case Work."

person, the small group of which he is a member, and the environment. It is thus a systems approach. The major behavioral science foundations consist of psychoanalytically oriented ego psychology, knowledge of problem-solving as a process, and a framework of concepts that explains the relationships and dynamic interactions among individuals in small groups and in their networks of relationships in the community. The knowledge base is used for differential assessment, planning, intervention, and evaluation. The approach is in agreement with Hollis' statement that "treatment must be differentiated according to the need of the client," [2] but in work with groups it is necessary to realize that treatment is also differentiated according to the nature and functioning of the group. The small growth-oriented group is the appropriate unit of service when the client's needs can be met through interaction with others, as distinguished from treatment apart from others.

The group is a principal means for problem-solving and goal achievement, supplemented by the social worker's direct influence on members. A small group is simply defined as a number of persons gathered together on the basis of some common purpose and forming a recognizable unit. The family falls within this definition of small group: it is one example of a continuous autonomous group, utilized and served in social work practice. In this approach, the group is used as both the context and means through which its members sustain or modify their attitudes and behavior, develop and maintain social relationships, and cope effectively with those obstacles in the environment which work against the achievement of objectives. Thus the social worker recognizes the "potency of social forces that are generated within small groups and seeks to marshall them in the interest of client change." [3] The interdependence of people one on another, a form of mutual aid, contributes a major dynamic for growth and change. The small group is effective in bringing about positive changes if it combines psychological support for efforts to change with adequate stimulation from others to enhance motivation toward the achievement of goals. Prevention and enhancement as well as restoration or rehabilitation are functions to which the approach is directed.

[2] Florence Hollis, *Casework: A Psychosocial Therapy* (2d ed. rev.; New York, Random House, 1972), p. 36.

[3] Mary Louise Somers, "The Small Group in Learning and Teaching," in *Learning and Teaching in Public Welfare*, Report of the Cooperative Project on Public Welfare Staff Training (Washington, D.C.: Bureau of Family Services, Welfare Administration, U.S. Department of Health, Education, and Welfare, 1963), I, 160.

This psychosocial view of social work practice is evolving and changing as new knowledge and demonstrations of practice modify or enrich earlier formulations. The development of practice theory is interwoven with and dependent upon the state of knowledge about the systems with which the practice is concerned and knowledge about the methods and activities of the practitioner, as its usefulness is demonstrated through practice itself. Thus, it is an open system of thought, incorporating new knowledge as its applicability is tested and dropping off ideas no longer useful.

Influential in the development of this approach were a number of distinguished formulators of practice theory who consistently focused on understanding and helping the person in his situation, working with either or both the person and selected aspects of his environment, and providing differential service to meet the individual's particular needs. From the literature on practice with individuals, some of the major contributors have been Annette Garrett, Ruth Gartland, Gordon Hamilton, Florence Hollis, Helen Perlman, Bertha Reynolds, Mary Richmond, Ruth Smalley,[4] and Charlotte Towle.

More influential perhaps were contributions by numerous practitioners and educators who specialized in work with groups. Studies on the interrelationships between casework and group work led to an understanding of the generic base of values, knowledge, and methodology, as well as of some important differences in the interactional skills required for effective service to individuals or groups.[5] The experimental research on the group adjustment of disturbed children in a summer camp, begun by Wilber I. Newstetter in 1927, demonstrated the value of several basic constructs necessary to understanding the interrelatedness of individual and group behavior.[6] Later, in an article entitled, "What is Social Group Work?," Newstetter set forth the first formal definition of social group work as a method and process within social work, and pointed out some of its commonalities shared with casework.[7] Two books, one edited by Grace L. Coyle and one authored by

[4] Ruth Smalley is now associated with the functional approach to social work, but earlier in her career she made contributions to the diagnostic approach.

[5] For a survey of the historical development of the relationships between casework and group work, see Flanzer, "Conintegration."

[6] Wilber I. Newstetter, Marc J. Feldstein, and Theodore Newcomb, *Group Adjustment: A Study in Experimental Sociology* (Cleveland: School of Applied Social Sciences, Western Reserve University, 1938).

[7] Wilber I. Newstetter, "What Is Social Group Work?" *Proceedings of the National Conference of Social Work, 1935* (New York: Columbia University Press, 1935).

her, described the application of major concepts concerning group structure and processes to practice in youth-serving agencies.[8] Gertrude Wilson has had a direct influence on the development of this work through her first book on the relationship between casework and group work,[9] her many papers, and the seminal book, *Social Group Work Practice,* co-authored with Gladys Ryland.[10] Wilson and Ryland have consistently assembled knowledge selected from psychoanalytic and other theories about human development, small groups, program media, and culture—including social class and ethnicity. They have described the use of this knowledge as it has been integrated with practice wisdom and the value system of the profession. Gisela Konopka's extensive writings on the application of concepts and principles of group work to psychiatric clinics, hospitals, correctional settings, and residential treatment further illustrated and elaborated the approach developed by Wilson and Ryland.[11] Another contribution was made by the work of Saul Bernstein and his associates on stages in development in social work with groups and on conflict and decision-making processes.[12] Margaret E. Hartford's continuous work on explicating knowledge concerning groups for use in social work has been influential.[13] A host of other writers, although varying in important theoretical respects, have also made contributions which have been incorporated into psychosocial work with groups.

More recently, treatment of the family system or its subsystems has developed as an important facet of social work practice with groups.[14] While it is true that many of these contributions were made by persons who were educated as caseworkers, numerous others whose roots were primarily in group work or in combined casework-group work have also contributed to

[8] Grace L. Coyle, *Group Work with American Youth* (New York: Harper, 1948).

[9] Gertrude Wilson, *Group Work and Case Work: Their Relationship and Practice* (New York: Family Welfare Association of America, 1941).

[10] Wilson and Ryland, *Social Group Work Practice.*

[11] Gisela Konopka, *Therapeutic Group Work with Children* (Minneapolis: University of Minnesota Press, 1949), *Group Work in the Institution—a Modern Challenge* (New York: Whiteside, Morrow, 1954), and *Social Group Work.*

[12] Saul Bernstein (ed.), *Explorations in Group Work* (Boston: Boston University School of Social Work, 1965).

[13] Hartford, *Groups in Social Work.*

[14] See, for example, David Freeman, "Social Work with Families: A Systems Approach to a Unified Theoretical Model" (D.S.W. dissertation, University of Southern California, 1973) and Elsbeth Couch, *Joint and Family Interviews in the Treatment of Marital Problems* (New York: Family Service Association of America, 1969).

the development of practice with families. Important group work contribu-
tors on work with families include Robert Brown, Grace Coyle, David
Freeman, Paul Glasser, Alan Klein, Gisela Konopka, Florence Ray, Mary
Louise Somers, Gertrude Wilson, and Gladys Ryland.

PHILOSOPHICAL CONSIDERATIONS

The ultimate value that underlies this approach is that each individual should
have opportunities to realize his developmental potential in ways that are
both personally satisfying and socially constructive. Implied in this basic
value is simultaneous concern for the dignity and worth of the individual and
the integrity of collectives.

Values are translated directly into principles of practice. Prevention as
well as treatment is essential if people are to fulfill their potential. Service
should be differentiated according to the needs of an individual as these interrelate with the needs of others. Experimentation and flexibility—rather
than conformity—are valued, based on a belief that differences can enrich
relationships and experiences. A commitment to social justice and equity
guide the social worker's direct service and activities in behalf of his clientele. Client participation in all aspects of the social process is fostered, with
respect for the members' rights to make and implement their own decisions
within certain mutually understood limits. Relationships between the worker
and his clients are based on acceptance and respect for both likenesses and
differences among people. A safe and socially beneficial atmosphere in
which members have freedom to express themselves, but also have the right
to privacy of feeling and thought, should be provided. The means used by
the social worker must be consistent with the ends sought.

Seeing social work practice as unitary is valued; work with groups can
be separated from work with individuals and communities only for purposes
of analysis. Social work practitioners have a responsibility to give service
according to client need, not according to the unit of service they value
most. Furthermore, the worker has responsibility to use findings from scientific inquiry in order that clients will receive service based on the best available knowledge and tested methodology.

PURPOSES, CLIENTELE, AND AUSPICES

PURPOSES

Within social work practice, it is proposed that the group is an appropriate
unit of service when the needs of people can be fulfilled through group asso-

ciation. The purpose is the enhancement of social relationships as these interact with obstacles in the environment. As indicated earlier, one major purpose for which psychosocial practice is considered to be most suitable is the enhancement of capacity for satisfying and functional social relationships so that the gap between actuality and potentiality is reduced. The other major purpose is the prevention and treatment of problems in social relationships. The specific goals that are selected are based on the client's and worker's assessment of the current problems, motivations, and capacities of the individual. In the case of natural groups, assessment also includes the adequacy of patterns of relationships within the system being served.

There is no single suitable typology of purposes toward which work with groups is directed nor of the problems in psychosocial functioning with which members of groups seek assistance. From one perspective, the problems or capacities in social relationships may be conceived in terms of fundamental interpersonal orientations: intimacy or social distance appropriate to the situation, love and affection or hate and indifference, and the need to be controlled by others or to control others.[15] The problems here may be in lack of complementarity of one's own needs with those of others, in distortions of a person's perceptions of himself and his relationship with others, or in patterns of behavior that mitigate against giving to others and receiving from them.

Another set of problems often requiring social work service is comprised of situations in which there are lack of opportunities for developing and maintaining relationships. There may be loss of significant persons through change of residence, death, desertion, divorce, or hospitalization. A person may lack knowledge about, or have inadequate resources for use in, developing new relationships. There may be a need for some form of compensation or substitution for missing relationships, as in placing children in foster homes or providing Big Brothers or Big Sisters.

Frequently, problems may be categorized as difficulties in the interaction of a person with others in specific role relationships. There may be dysfunctional relationships within the family as a total system or in parent-child, marital, or sibling subsystems. The difficulty may be with a person's relationships with people in positions of authority or with dysfunctional peer relationships. Conflict with others may be related to inadequate patterns of

---

[15] William Schutz, *The Interpersonal Underworld* (Palo Alto, Claif.: Science and Behavior Books, 1960).

communication, distortions in perceptions of others' intents or behavior, or prejudice based on sex, ethnicity, or religion that is directed toward clients or by them toward others. There may be conflict in values between individuals or groups and other persons or groups; such conflicts often are related to changes in the value system of society and its various subsegments.

The purpose of prevention is often carried out through services for populations considered to be vulnerable to stressful situations. Goals may include preparation for new demands resulting from a move to a new community, transitions from one level of education to another, or changes in attitudes and behavior necessary for success in new roles or coping with changing roles—for example, of men and women who challenge traditional stereotypes. Here problems of role-functioning are interpreted as difficulties in relationships with others, occasioned by lack of congruence concerning expectations for behavior, or lack of knowledge or skills necessary to the achievement of competence. The need is for opportunities for socialization.[16]

The enhancement of capacity for the development and maintenance of functional and satisfying social relationships seems to be a crucial need that can be achieved best through the means of group experiences. There is evidence that many people describe their own personal and social difficulties in the realm of relationships. In a survey of over 2000 Americans, 83 percent reported that, when they had sought help for problems, they defined them as difficulties between themselves and other persons or circumstances.[17] Similarly, a study by Ripple, Alexander, and Polemis indicated a preponderance of problems in interpersonal relationships.[18] And Scherz has described family therapy as concerned with bringing about change in the relationship systems in the family unit or its subsystems: "Family therapy seeks to modify or change those aspects in the family relationship system that, although stabilized, are for some reason no longer functional or satisfying and hence are interfering with management of life tasks." [19]

---

[16] See Elizabeth McBroom, "Socialization and Social Casework," in Roberts and Nee (eds.), *Theories of Social Casework*.

[17] Gerald Gurin, Joseph Veriff, and Sheila Feld, *Americans View Their Mental Health: A Nationwide Interview Study* (New York: Basic Books, 1960).

[18] Lilian Ripple, Ernestine Alexander, and Bernice Polemis, *Motivation, Capacity, and Opportunity* (Chicago: School of Social Service Administration, University of Chicago, 1964).

[19] Frances Scherz, "Family Therapy," in Roberts and Nee (eds.), *Theories of Social Casework*.

CLIENTELE AND TYPES OF GROUPS

Psychosocial practice is generic in its application to persons and groups with actual or potential problems in psychosocial functioning. In this way of working with people in groups, there are no specific prerequisites for accepting an individual or a group for service. It is not necessary, for example, that the members be able to relate to others in an interdependent way or that they be able to participate actively in group problem-solving. It is necessary that the social worker begin with the members at their current level and then help them to move from there as they become able to do so. The approach has been applied to such diverse populations as regressed, withdrawn schizophrenic patients, acting-out disturbed adolescents, and adolescents with normal difficulties in making a transition from one level of education to another.[20] The approach has been used with persons in various stages of the life cycle, ranging from preschool children to the aged. It has been used in social agencies in all fields of practice and in both open community and institutional settings, so long as there is a service designed to meet an established need for enhancement, prevention, or treatment of problems in psychosocial functioning. It has been used by social workers in private practice with family units, formed peer groups, and multiple family systems.

The approach has been used with both formed and preexisting groups. The formed group is one developed through the initiative of practitioners in bringing together individuals thought to be suitable for a particular group. These groups have been composed of peers of the same or both sexes, intergenerational groups of families, and subsystems of families. The formed group may have varied structures such as a social club, play group, or discussion group, or combinations of these forms. Groups may have either open or closed memberships and they may be either time-limited or extended in duration, depending upon the particular purpose of the group as it is defined in relation to the needs and characteristics of the members. Groups that have had a life prior to the entry of the practitioner, often referred to as preexisting groups, have been served. In addition to families and

[20] See, for example, Dorthea Lane, "Psychiatric Patients Learn a New Way of Life," in *New Perspectives in Service to Groups* (New York: NASW, 1961); Helen Northen, "Social Group Work: A Tool for Changing the Behavior of Disturbed Acting-out Adolescents," in *Social Work with Groups, 1958* (New York: NASW, 1958); Lola E. Buckley, "The Use of the Small Group at a Time of Crisis: Transition of Girls from Elementary to Junior High School" (D.S.W. dissertation, University of Southern California, 1970).

subsystems of families, these include living groups, hospital wards, and gangs of young people.[21]

Although voluntary participation is desirable, initial experience in the group may be required, either as a condition prerequisite to probation, for example, or for receiving other kinds of service—for example, when a child-guidance clinic requires that the family accept treatment as a prerequisite to the child's use of service. In some instances, the group experience may be prescribed by physicians, as are other forms of treatment.

Excluded from this approach is work with task-oriented groups in which the purpose is to achieve a goal other than the enhancement of the members' own psychosocial functioning or the more effective functioning of the family or other preexisting group.[22] Most of the concepts described here are thought to be equally applicable to task-oriented groups, but the difference in purpose necessitates some change in focus and in the constellation of interventions by the worker.

BEHAVIORAL SCIENCE KNOWLEDGE

Concepts from the behavioral sciences have been selected for their pertinence to the effective use of small groups for the achievement of some purpose or goal within the realm of enhanced psychosocial functioning. Psychosocial functioning is concerned with the complex gestalt of emotion, cognition, and action, motivated by both conscious and unconscious forces in the personalities of the persons involved, and the resulting patterns of relationships between people in defined situations. It may be desirable to increase the adaptive skills of the ego, to improve the functioning of the system in which the difficulty lies, or, frequently, both. The hoped-for change may be in the individual's attitudes, emotions, and behavior, in the group structure and process, in the environmental situation, or, most commonly, in the interactions involving person-group-situation. Thus, the integrating idea is the dynamic interplay between person, group, and situation.

Three interrelated constructs are essential to understand the behavioral science base of practice; psychosocial functioning, complex adaptive systems, and social interaction.

---

[21] For descriptions of the variety of groups served, see Konopka, *Social Group Work,* ch. 9, and Northen, *Social Work with Groups,* ch. 4.

[22] For the distinction between task-oriented and growth-oriented groups, see Gertrude Wilson, "Social Group Work—Trends and Developments," *Social Work,* 1(4):66 (1956).

PSYCHOSOCIAL FUNCTIONING

The person is regarded as a constantly developing being in necessary and significant interaction with others. He is a biopsychosocial entity—a whole person—and he is also a component of a network of social systems. His behavior is purposive, and motivated by both conscious and unconscious forces. His attitudes and behavior are understood in terms of his unique attributes, his idiosyncratic perceptions of self, others, and situations, and the particular meanings that experiences have for him, as these are evidenced in specific situations. Those reference groups which have salience for him influence his attitudes and behavior; changes in personality and in relationships with others are inseparable because "personality is shaped by and expressed through the interaction of the person's basic equipment and his environment." [23]

The major content areas that have been selected to describe and explain an individual's psychosocial functioning are:

1. Biological influences on psychosocial functioning—for example, physical health, illness, effects of drugs, and physiological maturation.
2. Phases in development throughout the life cycle. Each stage has its own needs, tasks, and opportunities for achievement: the influences of family and other group associations on human development, the importance of earlier experiences on subsequent development, capacity to grow and change throughout life, generational differentiation, and environmental forces and conditions that hinder or support development.
3. Structure of personality: the interplay among the id, ego, and superego, and conscious, preconscious, and unconscious forces.
4. A range of interdependent ego functions: the ego as a creative force which serves to mediate between a person's diverse conflicts and drives and between the person and his environment; perceptual and cognitive functions; ego autonomy and mastery; capacities for withstanding and coping with stress and conflict from both internal and external sources; capacity to solve problems and adapt to changing needs and conditions; and interlocking modes of adaptation to group situations.

[23] Bernece Simon, *Relations between Theory and Practice in Social Casework* (New York: NASW, 1960), p. 24.

5. Stress and types of responses to stress that threaten the adaptive resources of the organism: effect of earlier modes of resolving stressful situations on current adaptation, and the range of adaptive and maladaptive reactions to stress.

6. The significance of culture: values, norms, and traditions associated with varied age, ethnic, religious, and social class populations influence human development and psychosocial functioning; prejudice and discrimination affect human development.

7. Characteristic patterns of social relationships are significant to psychosocial functioning and related to interpersonal needs and social roles.

8. Groups to which a person belongs and other reference groups are the context and means for effecting changes in attitudes, interests, and behavior; these changes often endure beyond the existence of the groups themselves.

SYSTEMS THEORY

Systems theory—or, more correctly, a framework of concepts for describing and analyzing systems—is useful for purposes of alerting the social worker to the interrelatedness between an individual and the systems of which he is a part, and for understanding the interrelatedness between systems. A system is defined as "a complex set of elements or components directly or indirectly related to a causal network, such that each component is related to some other in a more or less stable way within any particular period of time." [24] Such a construct permits us to view the interdependence of parts of a system and the interrelatedness between systems. An individual is a biopsychosocial system that both influences and is influenced by his environment and he is a component part of multiple social systems; likewise, a family or formed group is a system that is interconnected with a network of other systems. There is continuous interaction of a system with its environment. [25]

The major areas of content selected to describe and explain a complex adaptive system are:

[24] Walter Buckley, *Sociology and Modern Systems Theory* (Englewood Cliffs, N.J.: Prentice-Hall, 1967), p. 41.

[25] For a full discussion of systems theory as applied to social work with families, see Freeman, "Social Work with Families."

1. Identification of the mutually interacting elements held together by an open boundary within which there is greater interaction and interdependence of members than with people outside the boundary; the extent to which the boundary is permeable to inputs and outputs of matter-energy.
2. The channels and nature of communication or feedback loops through which information is exchanged; the exchange of information between system components and their environments; feedback as a regulatory process involving a combination of correct and incorrect maneuvers.
3. The tendency of a system to maintain a balance between its parts and between its own internal needs and environmental expectations and conditions; a steady state is defined as a shifting, dynamic balance rather than as a static equilibrium; stress and conflict disturb a steady state; disturbing forces are reacted to by resistance or accommodation.
4. Processes to reduce a system's natural tendency toward entropy or a mechanism to produce negative entropy processes; capacity for adaptation to stress within the system or from without.
5. Ongoing structural-functional tendencies lead to a general increase of organization, complexity, and differentiation of parts from the whole over time.
6. Goal directedness and adaptive mechanisms help systems to survive over time; the principle of equifinality indicates that the same end result can be achieved through different means; and goals are achieved by means of a process of development of a system through a series of stages or phases.

SOCIAL INTERACTION

Social interaction, the dynamic interplay of forces in which contact between persons results in a modification of the attitudes or behavior of participants, is another major integrative construct. The basis of social interaction is human communication, a complex social process through which information is transmitted, received, and interpreted. Communication consists of the verbal, explicit, and intentional transmission of messages between people; it consists also of the nonverbal processes by which persons influence one another. It is dynamic, directional, interactive, and contextual. Essentially, it is a process of making and exchanging common meanings. As persons communicate with others, they learn about each other's feelings, hopes, ideas, and values. As members of a group exchange feelings and thoughts or participate in activities, there is a reciprocal and cyclical influence of members upon each other.[26]

People come together in a group through some common need or interest that gets translated into purpose. A complicated network of social relations comes into play. Members communicate their acceptance or rejection of each other and they engage in selected activities. As they do so, roles become established; values and norms emerge or are modified; there is mutual influence through such means as group deliberation, identification, suggestion, or contagion; conflict occurs and is managed or resolved in some way; and a degree of cohesiveness develops sufficient at least for the survival of the group.[27]

Knowledge from personality and systems theories are brought together so that individual dynamics and environmental influences are understood within the small-group system. The major content areas necessary to understand social interaction are:

1. Functions of small groups in society and in different cultural populations: special functions of the family as a primary group and of its subsystems; and characteristics of different types of groups as these influence practice.
2. Group development: the family life cycle and its developmental tasks and phases as these interlock with developmental phases of individuals and with the development of the family as a group; the development of groups through stages from the initial impetus to termination and follow-up.
3. The potential in group experiences for restricting or enhancing individual growth and group functioning: causes of dysfunction in groups as distinguished from dysfunction in individuals.
4. Influence of group purpose or goals on its values and norms, patterns of communication, role expectations, and activities: the influence of goals on group development and outcome; purpose as a composite of the expressed goals for the group held by agency and members; ways in which desires and needs become blended and

[26] For a fuller discussion of communication and references to it, see Northen, *Social Work with Groups*.

[27] For a full discussion of the behavioral science base, see *ibid.*, ch. 2. See also Hartford, *Groups in Social Work*.

developed into specific goals; understanding of covert and unconscious goals as well as consciously avowed ones; and identification
of the extent to which there is clarity and consensus about purpose
and congruence of aims of individuals with general purpose.

5. Determination of membership and group composition: criteria for
group composition, both formal and informal; homogeneity and
heterogeneity of membership related to group purpose; factors of
sex, age, ethnicity, socioeconomic status, personality variables,
and problems of members related to composition; and the effect of
changing membership on group development.

6. Structure as an important influence on the quality of group experience: formal and informal arrangements influence the distribution
of authority and responsibility, the development of governing procedures, and the coordination of activity; elements of time, space,
size, and physical environment as they affect human behavior.

7. Development of patterns of relationships through a discernible process by which people are related to each other and around which
the group takes its shape and form: [28] affective ties that comprise
the emotional bond among members; nonverbal communication as
the principal means for expressing and exchanging emotions;
sources of problems in social relationships related to cognitive mis-
understandings, differences in culture, stereotyping, or transference reactions; identifications that are formed with the worker or
with other members; differences in members' basic interpersonal
needs for inclusion, affection, or control; and complementarity or
conflict between needs.

8. Patterns of relationships as influenced by processes of status-rank-
ing, differentiation of roles, and evolution of subgroups as these
interact with the emotional ties among members: expectations for
behavior that both affect and are affected by the individual in the
role, the social system, and expectations and demands of the wider
milieu; definition and redefinition of roles as agreements develop
about what is to be done, by whom, in what way; assigned roles
and interpersonal roles; subgroups of temporary or relatively stable
alliances that develop as expressions of common interest; and complementarity of interpersonal needs.

9. The common system of values that develops in a group and determines the norms of behavior for the members: norms as a product

[28] Coyle, *Group Work with American Youth*, p. 91.

of social interaction, based on consensus about values; group pressures toward conformity; ability to resist pressures toward conformity, related to sense of identity, rebellion against authority, convictions, contagion, or need for acceptance.

10. Problem-solving and decision-making: steps in the problem-solving process; rational and nonrational influences in deliberation and decision-making; reflective discussion; conscious and unconscious distortions of the group process; conflict as inevitable; means for coping with and managing conflict; and conflicts and their solutions as the central core of any activity.[29]

11. The influence of group cohesion on development and productivity: essential conditions for the development of a cohesive group; and internalization of values and norms through identification with a reference group.

USE OF CONSTRUCTS IN PRACTICE

A social worker uses knowledge to develop a model of a type of group that is viable for social work purposes. Purposes are shared, and the member's role is a collaborative one; relationships are characterized by a predominance of positive ties and interdependence; communication is characterized by freedom from usual taboos, openness in emotional expressiveness, attentive listening and responding, and respect for individual differences and privacy; and the values of the group are supportive of healthy growth toward adaptive behavior. Such a group is cohesive; it becomes a reference group for its members.

It is to be noted that understanding of each of the major constructs requires knowledge from ego psychology, small-group theory, and individual and group connections with other significant systems.

PSYCHOSOCIAL DIAGNOSIS

GENERAL CHARACTERISTICS

Psychosocial diagnosis is here defined as a careful investigation of the facts necessary to understand and to formulate an opinion concerning the nature of the client system in its environment. Skill in diagnosis of individuals interacting in a social situation is a chief resource of the social worker, requiring ability to use a conceptual framework for organizing observations.

[29] Wilson and Ryland, *Social Group Work Practice,* p. 52.

The major purpose is to gain understanding of the individual, the group, and the situation sufficient to plan and conduct treatment. Diagnosis is essential for individualizing treatment and for assuring that the goals, structure, and processes of the group are appropriate for meeting individual and group needs. The initial development, and later reformulation, of goals and the focus of treatment depends upon sound diagnostic thinking.

Usually, when an individual or an existing group seeks assistance, there is uncertainty, if not anxiety, about the functioning of the applicant's system or of its interaction with other systems. Major attention is given to the discomfort in the current situation, but selective attention is paid to past experiences as they impinge on the present. Evaluation of the individual in his social systems takes into account knowledge of a continuum of psychosocial functioning, as distinguished from a dichotomy of normal and abnormal or sick and well behavior. Although norms for evaluating functioning are necessary, rapid changes in life styles and expectations pose problems for both the client and the social worker in assessing functioning. Understanding of problems is insufficient; there must also be understanding of opportunities in the environment, and members' positive motivations, preferences, and capacities are given attention. Such strengths are used and built on as the applicant becomes a member of a group or as a preexisting group enters into a relationship with a social worker.

To a considerable extent, the content of diagnosis varies with the many facets of the service, particularly its purpose and structure. The understanding of the client-group-situation gestalt that is sought cannot be inclusive of all aspects of the client's or group's functioning, but is limited to what is essential for effective service toward the achievement of particular goals. The structure of the group provides boundaries for the exploration concerning the client in his situation—for example, in a short-term, formed group the goals are usually specific to a difficult situation shared by members and the content of diagnosis is thus limited to that which is most pertinent to the focus of the group. The need is to begin working on the particular difficulties, and exploring for the feelings, experiences, and information that is essential to the work at hand.

Exploration for facts is an integral part of the social work process. As facts are revealed to individuals and to the worker, their meanings are summarized in terms of the service sought or offered. In formulating a preliminary diagnostic statement, certain questions guide the worker's thought processes: (1) What are the core interpersonal, family, and family-community problems that have put stress on clients and interfered with adequate functioning? (2) What goals and aspirations, recognized by the client or members of a preexisting group, might serve as a beginning focus for treatment? (3) To what extent is the client motivated to accept and use the help of the worker and other agency personnel? What are indications of positive motivation and what are the nature of resistances to the use of service? (4) What are the strengths in individual and or group functioning that can be supported and further developed?

From this preliminary and tentative diagnosis, an initial plan for service is developed, with full participation of all persons involved. It covers the particular persons to be included, the mode or modes of treatment to be offered to individuals or groups, and a plan for coordinating services if more than one service is to be given. The rationale for these decisions develops from the diagnostic statement, the clients' reactions to it, and their own preferences.

DIAGNOSIS OF INDIVIDUALS

Diagnosis is an on-going process as distinguished from a separate step preceding treatment. Beginning with what facts are relevant to the decision to accept a person for service and his placement in a particular group, the worker continues the diagnostic process as he judges what additional information will be helpful to him in serving individuals and the group as a whole.

Problems and goals are closely interrelated: problems are indications of unmet needs.[30] A concern with the goals of an applicant should be paramount: a person's positive motivations and aspirations are at least as important as his problems. The worker starts with an applicant's interest in having something be better. The applicant may be clear about what he hopes for, or have only vague feelings of discontent with himself or something in his situation. He may be articulate or need help to express himself. Accompanying the positive motivations toward the opportunity for assistance available, resistance may be evident. Problem formulation takes into consideration the presenting request, the reason for application, and the source of referral; the

---

[30] For a fine presentation of the relationship between needs and problems, see *ibid.*, p. 19.

origin in time of the felt difficulty; whether there is a state of crisis; and prior efforts to deal with the problems.

As the worker seeks to understand the applicant, he tries to assess the constellation of factors that might be contributing to the person's stress, usually some combination of internal and external circumstances. Personal characteristics—age, sex, role in family, ethnic origin, religion, socioeconomic status—are significant in understanding the person in his phase of psychosocial development. Major events in the life history of the individual and family have relevance for the definition of the problem and goals. Particularly relevant are the person's attitudes toward himself as reflected in self-esteem and sense of identity, the adaptive operations being used as these relate to typical patterns of coping with stress, and capacity for accurate perception of reality. Physical or intellectual strengths or disabilities and psychiatric or medical diagnoses that bear on adequacy in psychosocial functioning are taken into account. The member's capacity for object relations is indicative of personality integration. Behavior is seen within a range of normal functioning in terms of complementarity of interpersonal needs. The nature and quality of a person's social relationships within the family, with peers, and in other social roles are particularly pertinent, as they interrelate with some of the above qualities. Ability to give and receive love and affection, reach out to others, and make one's desires known; the balance between the need for inclusion and privacy; and attitudes toward authority figures and toward being in authority or sharing positions of authority are usually relevant. A person's feelings about his roles, the way he interprets them, his responses to the expectations of others, and his interpretation of and responses to the roles of others will give clues as to the functioning of personality in interaction with environment.

DIAGNOSIS OF GROUPS

The facts about individuals are used not only to understand each one of them but to develop a profile of the group to indicate the way in which differences and similarities among members may influence group interaction and development. Thus, attention is given to understanding group structure and process. Here, concern is with individual goals as these intermesh to become group goals. The difficulties as seen by each member and his views of hoped-for outcomes are explored. As the relationships between the worker and the group develop, there is considerable emphasis on members' capacities for responding to feelings of others, the extent of mutuality of need-meeting, and modes of relating as used for constructive and destructive purposes related both to individual growth and to group maintenance and development. Patterns of role relationships, the appropriateness of role structure, the degree of congruence or conflict concerning expectations for role performance, the distribution of power and authority, and the flexibility or rigidity of roles are noted.

When entering into a family system or other preexisting group, the worker assesses the extent to which the steady state is disrupted and the nature of the stresses and tensions that produced imbalance. Often, the feedback system is not working adequately and the worker must take into account the processes of intragroup and intersystem communication, the weight of the information load, the adequacy of inputs into the system, or distortions in the interpretation of information. He notes whether patterns of communication are faulty and whether there are blocks to the expression of feelings, desires, and opinions; severe restrictions on the content of communication because of norms concerning what is taboo; double binds; inconsistency between verbal and nonverbal messages; or inability to listen to others. As a formed group develops, the worker is alert to the existence of these types of problems in group functioning, and uses knowledge of them as a basis for influencing the problem-solving efforts and the way in which the group develops.

In any group there is need to understand the sources of conflicts within the group and between the group and community, the ways in which conflict becomes recognized and handled, the nature of decision-making (by whom and by what means), and the growth-producing or dysfunctional effect of conflict on individuals and on group development. Patterns of communication and ways of handling conflict are closely related to the goals, values, and norms of behavior of the group. It is therefore important to sort out the values that are important to individuals and the group; the sources of these values in religious, ethnic, and other reference groups; and the nature of agreement about or conflict in values and norms or rules of behavior that govern the interaction and behavior of members. The goals of individuals and of the group are considered as they either motivate the group toward achievement or create undue stress and conflict. If the group has achieved cohesiveness and is attractive to its members, it is important to know the nature of the satisfactions that members receive from belonging. The cohesiveness may be associated with conformity or with individualization and differentiation.

Any group is interdependent with other systems in the community, and conditions and resources have an impact on individuals and groups. Knowledge about the deficits and obstacles in the individual's or family's material circumstances, the availability of resources and the group's use of them, prejudice and discrimination toward the group by others or by the group toward others, and the nature and extent of isolation from or participation in groups and associations in the community give important clues to the functioning of individuals and the group.

GROUP COMPOSITION

The composition of formed groups is related to the purpose of the group, and the needs, problems, and personal and social characteristics of the members. Concern is with who can benefit from a particular group experience, and a decision entails the assessment of the likely effects of members on each other. The particular constellation of persons who interact with each other is an important determinant of whether or not a group will be satisfying to its members and suitable to the pursuit of goals. If the composition of a group is faulty, it is less likely to become a viable and cohesive social system. Knowledge of the factors that influence the participation of members is used by the worker to determine which ones seem most crucial to the purpose and anticipated content of the group. The basic questions concern the extent to which an individual might benefit from the group, and his ability to participate in such a way that his presence and his behavior will not interfere seriously with the realization of the purpose of the group for others.

There are many opinions, but little research, about criteria for group composition. A generally accepted principle is that groups should be homogeneous enough to ensure stability, and heterogeneous enough to ensure vitality.[31] This statement is based on the premise that the two major dynamics operating in groups are support and stimulation. Some balance is necessary so that no single member represents an extreme difference from other members, for this usually makes integration into the group unlikely. When considering grouping, most practitioners take into account com-

---

[31] Fritz Redl, "The Art of Group Composition," in Suzanne Schulze (ed.), *Creative Group Living in a Children's Institution* (New York: Association Press, 1953).

monality of needs, problems, readiness, and prior group experiences that are related to developmental phase, sex, ethnicity, and social class.[32]

In work with natural groups, the social worker's control over the composition of the group is limited, but important. Although the group's membership is already established, there are still contributions to be made by the worker. In instances in which the family is the unit of service, for example, there is a need to define the boundary for purposes of the service, and to decide whether the total family, one of its subsystems, or members of the extended family should be served. Similarly, in serving an existing gang, the social worker must determine whether he will regard the entire gang as his client system or select some core group or segment of the gang for his major attention. To be accepted for service, there must be some agreement concerning an initial goal and some readiness on the part of at least some members to enter into a trial relationship with the worker.

PHASES OF GROUP DEVELOPMENT

INITIAL PHASE

Prospective members are usually interviewed at least once prior to attending a formed group. The particular focus and content of the interview varies with the initial request. The interview combines orientation of the person to the general service purpose and to the structure, composition, and anticipated content of the group. Enough information is secured about the person and his situation to assess whether the group is a viable modality for meeting his needs and whether his goals and needs have a chance to mesh with those of others. Sometimes referral to a group precedes a period of individual service, sometimes it follows it, and sometimes the services are concurrent. Assessment provides the worker with sufficient knowledge regarding the client to individualize the experience for him and to develop a relationship to ease his transition into the group. The basic question for consideration by the worker is: Do the person's characteristics make it possible for him to have an opportunity for finding something in common with others and to have a chance to be accepted by others? If placement into an ongoing group is considered, the person's readiness for entry, the readiness of group members to accept him, and his effect on the group's development must also be considered.

---

[32] For a fuller discussion of group composition, see Hartford, *Groups in Social Work;* Northen, *Social Work with Groups;* and Wilson and Ryland, *Social Group Work Practice.*

With families or other preexisting groups, the initial contact may be with the member or members who inquire about the service; usually interviews are conducted with as many members of the group to be served as can be brought together. Thus, there is usually a combination of interviews with some members individually, with subsystems of the group, and with the group as a whole. Again, there is need for sufficient information about the individuals, their reasons for seeking or being referred for service, and a preliminary assessment of the group's functioning to allow a preliminary decision by both members and worker about the suitability of the group for continued service. Initial interviews focus on a demonstration of common themes underlying what members consider to be the difficulty so as to establish the existence of a group problem, to develop a therapeutic alliance, and to demonstrate the intragroup or extragroup aspects of the problem rather than allow it to be projected onto one member.[33] When the social worker enters into the life of a preexisting group he must learn where this group is in its life cycle, for in this instance it is the worker who is the newcomer and stranger. Families have typical stages in their life cycles, associated with the number and types of ascribed roles of their members. Other natural groups have histories which need to be understood. But when the worker serves a preexisting group he needs to take into account its changing development through phases in the process of treatment.

The purpose of the original interview and the first meetings of the group is to enhance motivation for purposeful participation in the group's endeavor. Positive motivation is enhanced when a person feels that the worker is interested in him, accepts him, and desires to understand his capacities and difficulties from his own point of view; thus the initial development of relationship between worker and each member is crucial. Positive motivation is enhanced when a person understands how his own goals and desires can be met through the service medium and how these mesh with those of other members; thus, there is focus on member-to-member relationships and communications. Feelings of stigma associated with the use of the service must be dealt with. Attention is given to help the client understand that his needs can be met through the particular service, and assess what is expected of him and what he can expect from both the worker and other members. The worker supports the client's desire to change something

---

[33] Scherz, "Family Therapy," in Roberts and Nee (eds.), *Theories of Social Casework.*

about himself and his situation, and strengthens any feelings of optimism that things can be better.

The major tasks for the social worker in the initial phase of group development are to assist the members in becoming oriented to the worker, each other, and the group; to develop and clarify goals and expectations; to begin to develop relationships with the worker and each other; and thus to become engaged in the process.[34]

OTHER PHASES

Involvement of members in a group does not occur only through a period of orientation. There needs to be ample opportunity for members to work through the ambivalence that is characteristic of new experiences, but often particularly true of the decision and subsequent effort involved in becoming part of a group. Resistance is heightened if anxiety becomes too great; thus, support from the worker is essential. The acknowledgment that ambivalence is commonplace, coupled with the provision of a safe atmosphere in which positive and negative feelings toward the experience can be explored, tends to reduce resistance and enhance positive motivation. A mutual agreement between each member and the worker and between the worker and the group (sometimes referred to as a contract) concerning the major purpose and focus of the group's activity and the mutual expectations is a major dynamic in enhancing motivation toward participation in the group. As members express themselves, patterns of social interaction develop. The interaction is characterized by exploring and testing out the situation and by unrest, tension, and conflict. There is exploration of the interpersonal potential in the group, development of patterns of relationships or shifts in existing patterns, differentiation or redifferentiation of roles, clarification of norms, and perceptions of individual and common goals. As members explore each other in relation to the group, their awareness of similarities and differences among them becomes acute, resulting in ambiguity and conflict. Through dynamic decision-making processes, members modify their original ideas about the service. A group develops with which they can identify, or members of a preexisting group now perceive themselves as being, for a time, a special group while they are meeting with the worker.

Clarity of purpose is essential; the general purpose provides the basic

[34] For further elaboration of stages of group development, see Northen, *Social Work with Groups*.

guide for both worker and members. There seems to be an association between the worker's clearly formulated objectives which he communicates to the client and the latter's accurate perception of these objectives. When there is clarity about goals and commitment to them, the group is able to resist and to cope with disruptive forces. An absence of discussion concerning purpose may lead to considerable misperception by clients of the worker's objectives, and vice versa.[35] Often there is not a single objective but a cluster, suggesting desired changes in both social and psychological aspects of functioning. One task associated with this early phase of treatment is that of clarifying the desires and outcomes sought by the members. The underlying assumption is that a worker's ultimate aim grows from his perception of members' needs, capacities, and goals, and that the relationship revolves around purposes recognized by both worker and participants.

The major tasks of the worker during the period of exploration and testing are to develop understanding of the group as a social system, support the members in their exploration of the group, clarify the various facets of the situation as necessary, engage the members in decision-making processes concerning the group and their use of it, regulate conflict, and strengthen the positive ties among the members. Essentially, a major outcome of the process of exploration and testing out is the achievement of considerable congruence between each member's perceptions of the group and the worker's perceptions of it. Members of groups tend to perceive quite clearly the contributions of the worker to the group.[36]

In the next stage of development, sufficient cohesion has developed so that members are truly interdependent and use the group as a vehicle for work related to the group's purpose. The group has become a means for both supporting and stimulating its members toward the achievement of individual and group goals. Members are able to accept their differences and

[35] Some findings from research tend to support these statements: for example, Florence Clemenger, "Congruence between Members and Workers on Selected Behaviors of the Role of the Social Group Worker" (D.S.W. dissertation, University of Southern California, 1965); Margaret E. Hartford, "The Social Group Worker and Group Formation" (Ph.D. dissertation, University of Chicago, 1962); Marjorie Main, "An Examination of Selected Aspects of the Beginning Phase in Social Work with Groups" (Ph.D. dissertation, University of Chicago, 1965); Patricia McGuerty, "Individual Group Members' Expectations of Social Work Help as Compared through Time in a Delinquent Adolescent Group" (M.S.W. thesis, University of Southern California, 1963); Julianna Schmidt, "Purpose in Casework: A Study of Its Use, Communication, and Perception" (D.S.W. dissertation, University of Southern California, 1966).

[36] Clemenger, "Congruence between Members and Workers."

utilize them for collaborative work on problem-solving. The task of the worker is to maintain the viability of the group so that increasingly the members are able to help each other. His own activities are directed toward supplementing what the members themselves are able to accomplish.

In the final phase the major efforts of the social worker are directed toward helping the members to stabilize the gains they have made and to prepare them for termination. Termination is viewed as a process through which a social service to an individual or a group is discontinued. In the case of natural groups such as a family, the group itself continues, but without the assistance of the social worker. The worker evaluates each individual and the group in relation to goals and to agency policies concerning length of service and criteria for termination. He makes plans for maximizing the use of remaining sessions. The purpose is to stabilize gains that have been made, and to help the members separate from the social worker and, in the case of formed groups, from each other. An important task is to help the members to cope with the stressful situation of ending this particular experience, a situation which is fraught with complex and ambivalent feelings. He supports efforts to cope with the stress. He makes plans for supplementing the group service and for possible follow-up services.

SOCIAL WORK METHODOLOGY

THE WORKER AND THE GROUP

An influential group is one in which the member's role is defined as a collaborative one in relation to the social worker and to other members. A member not only receives help but gives it as well, belonging and participating in the group in interdependence with others. Thus, a mutual aid system is developed and used.

The worker is an interacting participant in the process of problem-solving. His roles are those of facilitator of relationships among members, direct influencer of individuals and of the development of the system based on interpersonal trust as well as on the authority of knowledge and competence, and supporter of individual and group efforts. His attention is directed to individuals, to the relationship between individuals, and to the gestalt of the group entity.

The social work method is an orderly and systematic approach. It consists of (1) the use of procedures and the development of conditions to make possible the formation of a group or the acceptance of a service by a natural group; (2) exploration and study to secure facts necessary to understand individuals, the group, and the network of social systems to which each individual and the group is connected; (3) assessment of the meaning of the facts for individuals, the group, and significant others in the environment; (4) participation with an intent to support or to challenge feelings, cognitive processes, or group interactions; and (5) evaluation of the effects of his interventions and the participation of others on individuals and the group. These are ongoing components of the method, and not discrete steps. The content varies according to its relevance to the group purpose and the goals of individual members. The method is based on knowledge concerning the processes of scientific inquiry, problem-solving, and group process.

Problem-solving takes place in the context of multiple points of view about the problem and the situation, and within a context in which the important reference groups of each member have an impact. Thus, the role networks and multiple reference groups of members increase the complexity of the interaction with which the worker is involved. In general, the worker's responsibility is to support the group process when it contributes to goal achievement and to intervene when, in his judgment, the group process is counterproductive. The nature and degree of direction varies with the capacities of the members to meet the demands of group life and to direct their own activities. When the members are not able to cope with a situation, the worker actively uses his authority; when they are able to participate responsibly, he is less active.[37]

DYNAMICS OF CHANGE

The group is both the context and means through which members, with the assistance of the worker, stimulate each other to support, strengthen, or change attitudes, feelings, relationships, thinking, and behavior. The context sought is one in which the group becomes an influential reference group for the individual. Participation of members according to their abilities leads to some degree of involvement of each in pursuing individual and group goals. The process of goal-setting and clarification of expectations provides an agreed-upon framework for meeting of mutual needs. This, in turn, contributes to the building of cohesive forces.

The attainment of vital relationships provides a degree of gratification

[37] Wilson and Ryland, *Social Group Work Practice,* pp. 67–68.

for the client which enables him to be involved in the group experience and sustains him through periods of change. As Perlman puts it, "The human drive and need for social connectedness and social recognition are life long movers and shapers of personality." [38] This is akin to what Slavson calls social hunger, the craving to belong to an accepting group.[39] In the group, the experience of being both accepted and respected by other members—whether in peer or intergenerational relations—and being able to accept and respect others contributes an additional dynamic.

The support provided by the worker and group members tends to enhance self-esteem, lessen the need for dysfunctional ego defenses, and free energies for problem-solving and for group building and maintenance. Support has as its function the preservation and enhancement of those elements in the group process that are adaptive. It is an important motivator not only because it tends to enhance self esteem but because it is a prerequisite to change through other means as well. The importance of support is suggested by research that showed that the revelation of important information about oneself in situations of trust and mutual support was beneficial to participants, but that self-disclosure before the group was able to respond constructively was not helpful.[40]

Interruption of dysfunctional patterns of behavior, through confrontation offered by the worker and particularly by other members in a spirit of mutual aid, disrupts the steady state, making possible the system's openness to new inputs. Feedback from other members may lead to recognition of distortions in perception of self, others, and situations. Cognitive understanding of the reality may break down false perceptions of self in relation to others, thereby making it possible for a person to make choices and to develop object relationships appropriate to his developmental phase. Through the process of feedback from others, blocked channels of communication can be opened up and defective patterns of communication can be corrected.[41] If a person perceives relationships and situations differently, he can use that changed perception to act differently, and a personality change occurs. According to Hollis, "A change in personality has occurred whenever a new

[38] Perlman, Social Casework, p. 150.

[39] S. R. Slavson, A Textbook in Analytic Group Psychotherapy (New York: International Universities Press, 1964), pp. 173–74.

[40] Morton A. Lieberman, Irvin D. Yalom, and Matthew B. Miles, Encounter Groups: First Facts (New York: Basic Books, 1973), p. 359.

[41] Robert A. Brown, "Feedback in Family Interviewing," Social Work, 18(5):52–59 (1973).

way of responding or behaving has been sufficiently incorporated into the personality to enable the individual to respond consistently in a changed way to repetitions of the same event or its equivalent." [42] Learning is dependent upon the person's capacity and readiness to take responsibility for his part in the problem or, for that matter, to take responsibility for his positive contributions.

Finally, change is facilitated when a person has the resources of knowledge and competence to behave in such ways that his own positive feelings and strengths are reinforced by accurate feedback from others as he participates in common interests and endeavors. Change is also facilitated when environmental obstacles to a person or group's achievement of goals are reduced or eliminated.

USE OF RELATIONSHIPS

The nature and quality of the worker's relationships with individuals, subgroups, and significant persons in the network of systems has an important effect on each member's use of the group and on the development of the group itself. The worker develops a unique relationship with each member, based on respect for and understanding of him. But if he is to help members to use group relations, "he will need to modify the many diverse, individual strands of his relationships with the members so that they will be in process with each other and so that he will have a connection with the group as a whole." [43] In Coyle's words, development of a helpful relationship with a group "involves the capacity to feel at ease, in fact, to enjoy the social interplay among members and to be able to perceive both individual behavior and its collective manifestations . . . as well as to become a part of the relationships and to affect them." [44] If the worker has a connection with the group, he also simultaneously views the individuals, the network of relationships, and the group's connections to its environment.

The social worker seeks to develop a relationship based upon sensitivity to feelings, respect for others, and trust. There is substantial evidence from

[42] Florence Hollis, "The Psychosocial Approach to the Practice of Casework," in Roberts and Nee (eds.), *Theories of Social Casework*, p. 60.

[43] Helen U. Phillips, *Essentials of Social Group Work Skill* (New York: Association Press, 1957), p. 145.

[44] Grace L. Coyle, "Some Basic Assumptions about Group Work," in Marjorie Murphy (ed.), *The Social Group Work Method in Social Work Education* (New York: Council on Social Work Education, 1959), p. 100.

research to indicate the importance of the qualities of acceptance or unconditional positive regard, genuineness, and empathy to the outcome of service.[45] These qualities are conveyed to the members by the worker's verbal and nonverbal behavior, and these qualities are facilitated among the members when they identify with a common purpose and have similar interests. Members usually have realistic views about the qualities of the worker. At times, however, erroneous perceptions and expectations concerning his role, or transference reactions from earlier meaningful relationships may distort perceptions. Self-awareness is essential if the worker is to avoid distortion of his own perceptions of the members through countertransference. If transference components are inimical to the progress of an individual or the development of the group, they need to be understood and clarified. Attention is given to understanding and working with both the transference and reality aspects of the worker-individual and member-to-member relationships.

The social worker's efforts are directed to noting and evaluating both positive and negative cues to the quality of relationships among the members, and, acting on the basis of his evaluation, he helps the members to recognize and clarify the nature of their relationships with each other. Particularly, in early sessions, he notes and builds on positive efforts to relate to him and to each other. The worker is the model for members in their efforts to develop functional relationships with each other. The worker's attributes can be conveyed to members in short-term as well as long-term involvement.

USE OF PROCEDURES OF TREATMENT

The social worker has responsibility for the differential application of procedures and techniques of treatment, according to the needs of each individual and the conditions of the group at a given time. He recognizes occasional conflicts between the needs of different individuals, but works with the group to find the common strands and to use these. He cannot meet all needs of all members at a given time, but he can assure that some needs of each person will be met. Based on diagnostic evaluation of individual needs

---

[45] For a review of research, see Alfred Kadushin, *The Social Work Interview* (New York: Columbia University Press, 1972).

related to the group, he may have interviews with individuals to supplement or complement what is achieved in the group. According to his knowledge of the group, he uses specific techniques to directly influence an individual or the group. The procedures are implemented through varied forms or techniques of verbal and nonverbal communcations between the worker and the members. The worker's acts are related to the threads of identifications or common interests: even when the worker addresses an individual, he is aware that other members are influenced by however he deals with one. The worker's acts may be classified into a set of basic procedures that are directly derived from knowledge concerning the dynamics of change. The major procedures are support, exploration, clarification, confrontation, direct influence, and providing structure.[46] As the members become able to help each other, the social worker becomes less active. He supports the ongoing process. When the interactions among the members become dysfunctional to progress, he actively intervenes in the process.

The purpose of support is to sustain or maintain the current level of functioning. The worker gives sufficient support to the members so that they learn from him, but in time the major support will come from the group itself. Supportive communications sustain the motivation and capacity of a person to seek certain experiences or outcomes and to develop confidence in the group as a means toward growth. Support is given to the strengths and constructive defenses of a person in order that he maintain a level of functioning and become motivated to attain a better one.[47] The worker expresses support through the relationship itself and through such means as encouragement, realistic reassurance, approval, recognition of effort and achievement, expression of realistic expectations, and universalization of feelings and conditions. The members become supportive of each other as they become aware of their common purposes, aspirations, interests, and needs, and as

[46] This classification of procedures was developed by Fatout from a content analysis of major texts in social work with individuals, families, and small groups. See Marian Fatout, "A Comparative Analysis of Practice Concepts Described in Selected Social Work Literature" (D.S.W. dissertation, University of Southern California, 1975). This listing of procedures is consistent with those enumerated by Hollis in Casework: A Psychosocial Therapy.

[47] For further information concerning support, see Louise Frey, "Support and the Group: Generic Treatment Form," Social Work, 7(4):35–42 (1962), Hollis, Casework: A Psychosocial Therapy; Northen, Social Work with Groups; and Lola Selby, "Supportive Treatment: the Development of a Concept and a Helping Method," Social Service Review, 30:400–14 (1956).

they work out their positive and negative feelings toward each other. They become supportive of each other as they feel security and trust in the worker; as they come to identify with him, they begin to integrate into themselves some of his ways of giving support.

Exploration is a common procedure in social work practice. Its major function is to discover the varied feelings, ideas, and facts that bear on a situation—in short, to get information necessary for the worker and the members to work together effectively. Exploratory forms of communication search out common interests, themes, and problems within the diversity among the members. Through exploration, there is an increase in the members' views of and responses to the group as a whole. This, in turn, provides a storehouse of shared experiences on which to build. The worker's part in the process of exploration is to encourage sharing of information, ask relevant questions, aid in the ventilation of feelings and opinions, summarize and test for common and diverse understandings, and guide the flow of material so that it remains relevant to the group purpose. Exploration is an important component of the decision-making process; it is essential in defining and understanding the felt difficulty and in seeking and considering alternative choices.

Clarification is the process of making understandable the meanings of communication and behavior. The content of clarification may be a situation, the emotions and actions of a person, interpersonal relationships, or the connections between one or more of these elements.

Clarification goes beyond exploration to promote understanding of persons, group and social situation. As Goldstein notes, "a movement toward change or the attempt to devise new principles for action stirs some measure of apprehension and anxiety that impedes or disables the problem solving process." [48] There is then dissonance in the form of discomfort or ambivalence. Clarification reduces dissonance. Clarification of ambiguous elements is requisite to adequate coping with the problem.[49] Clarification of communication itself is important. One of the aims of the worker is to provide opportunities for each member to participate more effectively with other people. The worker thus is concerned not only with communication within the group but with a member's abilities to communicate effectively

[48] Howard Goldstein, *Social Work Practice: A Unitary Approach* (Columbia: University of South Carolina Press, 1973), p. 102.
[49] *Ibid.*, p. 305.

in relationships with other people in his daily living. The concern is with communication both as a tool in working toward other goals and with ineffective communication as a problem in itself.

One of the values of group experience is the opportunity afforded for reality-testing. Feedback from other members as well as from a professional helper enables people to check their perceptions against those of multiple others. But there are great differences in the way members share with others and the responses they receive from others. If a member is able to share with others and then use the experiences of others for cognitive learning, feedback tends to be beneficial. But feedback which engenders negative feelings within the self seems to be associated with negative outcomes. Active participation in understanding oneself is far different from only being the recipient of opinions of others.[50]

The social worker intends to help members to recognize and identify the various aspects of a social situation, then extend or elaborate on their understanding, and move ahead to clarify the problems and the situations. There are three major aspects that need clarification by members of a group: the social situation, including the group, agency, and environment; patterns and content of communication; and the attitudes and behavior of the members in various social situations. Exploration and clarification of the influence of environmental conditions in precipitating, maintaining, or exacerbating individual and group difficulties may lead to individual or joint decisions to take action toward environmental change, or to accept what cannot be changed. Establishing the nature of the situation and patterns of behavior is most usefully done by the members themselves, but the worker adds ideas, facts, and value concepts which are not available to the members. At times, interpretation of the meaning of behavior is essential. As a general rule, such interpretations deal only with conscious or preconscious material, but recall of the past is facilitated when helpful to the solution of current problems. The group is assisted in finding its own meanings through such means as the worker's recognition of ambivalences and obstacles, explanations of connections between events and between feelings and reality, requests for consideration of consequences, restatements or reflections of feelings or throughts, interpretation of the meaning of behavior and situations, and evaluations of individual or group problems and progress.

Confrontation has been described as a procedure, closely linked to clar-

[50] Lieberman, Yalom, and Miles, *Encounter Groups: First Facts,* p. 366.

ification, which has as its major intent the interruption or reversal of a course of thought or action. Members or the worker may interrupt to point out the unproductive direction of a discussion or activity, or may call attention to a discrepancy between perception and reality. Confrontation challenges a person to acknowledge his behavior, makes him face the reality of a feeling, behavior, or situation, and makes continued denial or projection difficult. It challenges the person with some inconsistency between his own statements and those of others, or with the consequences of his behavior. Respect for the ego's defenses is essential, but in some instances they may need to be opened up to examination through confrontation within a supportive relationship.

Providing a structure that defines the rights and responsibilities of the group and its members for self-determination is another procedure. Within the policies of the agency, group members participate in determining such limits. In order to function adaptively, a person's behavior needs to meet the realistic demands of the environment. Members need to learn to meet these demands and to be protected from the destructive tendencies of themselves and each other. Within the prescribed limits, there is ample room for individual choices. Because people need to feel free to experiment with new ways of behaving, the worker needs to balance the use of limits with permissiveness.

Although the social worker's major emphasis is on facilitating the capacities of the members to make their own decisions and to act on the basis of these decisions, he at times must use direct influence in the form of advice, suggestion, or direction with the intent of promoting a definite step or action. He uses these techniques within the general principles of practice, and should be willing to share with the members his reasons for taking such direct action.

EVALUATION OF OUTCOME

In view of the purpose of the service, evaluation of outcome is in terms of changes in individuals' attitudes toward self and others and in their patterns of behavior in relationships with other people. The goals set with individuals and the group provide the specific criteria for judging movement. Individual changes are thus evaluated with respect to that individual's own goals.[51]

[51] For a fuller discussion, see Helen Northen, "Evaluating Movement of Individuals in Social Group Work," *Group Work Papers, 1957* (New York: NASW, 1958), pp. 28–39.

Evaluation of outcome is related to changes that can be observed within the group and with regard to the situations with which help was originally sought or service was offered. Such change may be in the form of enhancement of relationships or in the prevention or treatment of problems in relationships. Thus, evaluation of outcome considers the interrelatedness of changes in individuals, the group, and the broader situation.

In instances of work with families or other preexisting groups that will continue after termination of social work service, the purpose is not only to foster changes in individuals and their situations; in addition, changes are sought in the structure and dynamics of the group's functioning, so that the group itself continues to bring satisfaction to its members and enhance their personal and common goals.

The behavioral science base, combined with knowledge of professional theory, is directly related to the methodology of practice and to evaluation of outcome. The major constructs from behavioral science provide a conceptual framework for use in the assessment of individual development, ego capacities, and behavior in social relationships. They provide a systems perspective for perceiving the individual as he is a part of the group and other interlocking systems, and for perceiving the group as it is connected with other systems. Systems constructs provide the worker with guidelines for assessing the group's steady state and forces of disruption. They provide a schema for analyzing phases in group development, including assessment of structure and processes as they promote or integrate individual and group movement toward goals. Knowledge of the dynamics of change processes, as these are congruent with the purpose and goals of the service and the characteristics of the members, directly influence the delineation of treatment procedures and techniques and outcome. The art of practice is the way in which the worker flexibly applies the basic knowledge and acquires competence in translating this knowledge into communications with other people in a scientific and humane way.

LINKAGES TO CASEWORK

Social work practice with groups is linked to social work with individuals through common values, knowledge, purposes, methodology, and types of interventions used. Indeed, the use of groups is regarded as an approach to working with individuals and families, but through the group rather than the one-to-one interview. Social work practice in direct services is viewed as a single method of serving individuals, families, and other groups based on common values, behavioral science knowledge, and skills requisite to effective service. Even when a social worker is serving an individual singly, he needs to understand that person's status and role and his transactions within his family, membership groups, and other social relationships. In this sense, there is nothing unique in the knowledge about human behavior and complex adaptive systems required for serving individuals as compared with serving groups. The differences involve not the values, knowledge, and interventive procedures but the need, in working with more than one person at a time, to plan for and structure the group and to make use of the group as a major means toward goal achievement. The worker needs additional skills in simultaneous assessment of individuals and of group development and process, and additional interactional skills that focus communication so that the members interact with each other for mutual support and stimulation.

This approach to practice with groups seems most congruent with the psychosocial formulation of casework theory. It shares many similarities also with the problem-solving, socialization, and crisis-intervention approaches to work with individuals.[52] All these approaches seem to be rooted in a common base of values, psychoanalytic-ego psychology, and social science theory that connects the individual to his network of role relationships and to his situation. There is emphasis on goal-directed activity, the importance of relationships, individualization, client participation, phases in process, and the use of resources. All use a conception of method, with an emphasis on diagnosis, planning, and treatment which are seen to operate throughout the length of service and incorporate the principle that treatment is based on differential diagnosis. The major differences between the approach described here and the casework approaches are in the particular constellation of knowledge and procedures and in the ways in which certain social science concepts are used. In casework, social science concepts are used to understand the individual in his situation; in group work, they are used to understand the individual and group structure and process in order to be able to intervene directly into the process. Bifocal vision of individual and group is required: the focus is on the maintenance or change in the group's development as well as individual development; the social worker's communications are intended to develop members' abilities to support and stimulate each other, rather than to depend solely upon the direct influence of the practitioner.

[52] Roberts and Nee (eds.), *Theories of Social Casework.*

UNSOLVED PROBLEMS

There is recognition that the preceding description of a psychosocial approach to work with groups is incomplete and requires further elaboration and testing. As in any effort to develop theory, there are unsolved problems.

1. Unevenness in research substantiation for parts of practice theory is a problem. Recent research has contributed some understanding of the social work relationship; the influence of motivation, capacity and opportunity on the use of treatment; clarification of purpose and role expectations; classification and use of procedures of treatment; and evaluation of outcome. But, much more research is needed on these topics and also on the relationship between the length and structure of treatment and outcome, as related to different types of purposes and client characteristics; the dynamics of change processes; the connection between diagnosis, planning, and treatment; and differences in worker activities in direct treatment of individuals and in the use of group process.

2. There is need for further work on the selection and integration of concepts drawn from varied foundation disciplines. Particularly, knowledge concerning social relationships has not been assembled, assessed, and integrated for use in social work. There is need for a classification system of different levels of psychosocial functioning, with special reference to human relations.

3. There do not seem to be tested criteria for determining when a person is best served through this approach or other ones; when individual, family, or other group is the most effective modality for meeting needs of people; and when and under what conditions service through a group should be provided simultaneously with individual treatment.

4. Since emphasis is on competence in social relationships, there is the need to explore new approaches to such compelling problems as intergroup conflict and prejudice.

5. The breadth and depth of knowledge and skills required for competence in practice has direct relevance for social work education. Curricula need to be strengthened in both classes and field instruction. The length of professional education may be inadequate to assure that clients receive the quality of service to which they are entitled.

BIBLIOGRAPHY

Beck, Dorothy Fahs and Mary Ann Jones, *Progress in Family Problems*. New York: Family Service Association of America, 1974.

Furness, Anne-Marie. "Three Formulations of Social Case Work and Three Formulations of Social Group Work: A Comparison." D.S.W. dissertation, University of Southern California, 1971.

Hamilton, Gordon. *Theory and Practice of Social Case Work,* 2nd ed. New York: Columbia University Press, 1951.

Hartford, Margaret E. *Groups in Social Work.* New York: Columbia University Press, 1972.

Hollis, Florence. *Casework: A Psychosocial Therapy,* 2nd ed. New York: Random House, 1972.

Konopka, Gisela. *Social Group Work: A Helping Process,* rev. ed. Englewood Cliffs, N.J.: Prentice-Hall, 1972.

National Association of Social Workers. *The Family is the Patient: The Group Approach to the Treatment of Family Health Problems.* New York, NASW, 1965.

Northen, Helen. *Social Work with Groups.* New York: Columbia University Press, 1969.

Perlman, Helen Harris. *Social Casework, A Problem-Solving Process.* Chicago: University of Chicago Press, 1957.

Roberts, Robert W. and Robert H. Nee (eds.). *Theories of Social Casework.* Chicago: University of Chicago Press, 1970.

Wilson, Gertrude and Gladys Ryland. *Social Group Work Practice.* Boston: Houghton Mifflin, 1949.

5

A FUNCTIONAL APPROACH

ELEANOR L. RYDER

A functional approach to social work makes distinctive use of three particular concepts: the nature of man and his institutions, the significance of social purpose, and the use of social process as a helping dynamic.[1] In order to understand the importance of these ideas for social work with groups, each must be examined in relation to: (1) the social context for social work with groups, (2) the nature of groups, and the members' perceptions of needs, purposes and goals, and (3) the role of the social worker as a facilitator of change with and within the groups.

BASIC CHARACTERISTICS

SOCIAL CONTEXT

Traditionally the social context within which social work with groups has been practiced has been either a group service agency such as a Y or settlement, or a host setting such as a public school, prison, or hospital. Both types of agencies, in developing services to groups, have recognized the potential of a group experience for helping people to make use of the resources of the setting to accomplish the purpose for which the agency exists. In either kind of setting, the particular institutional arrangement, the social purpose of the institution, and the time frame within which the service is begun, developed, and terminated provide form and focus for the group and for the role of the social worker with the group. The dominant cultural norms of the community within which the agency operates and the values and expecta-

[1] Ruth E. Smalley, "Social Casework: The Functional Approach," *Encyclopedia of Social Work* 2 vols.; New York: NASW, 1971), 1195–96.

tions of the auspice which supports that agency and to which it is accountable, provide both limits and resources for use by agency groups. The sanctioning community, through the agency which it structures, provides a social
purpose that is the basis for development of agency function and service.
The time frame—for example the camp season or the school year or the
prison sentence—provides additional structure for the development of a
group process, with an opportunity for the social worker to help the group
exploit the potential of each phase of the process for movement toward
group and individual goals.

Social work with groups has never been limited to traditional settings,
however, and the question is frequently asked as to whether a social worker
in private practice or with a community-based group that is not affiliated
with a social agency can use a functional approach. There has been a tendency to associate the functional approach with—indeed to assume it is
based upon—the existence of a particular piece of agency structure spelled
out in the organization's formal documents of incorporation. If instead, as
Hofstein suggests, we recognize the central concept of functional social
work to be that of a process in which function is the embodiment of the values of society,[2] it becomes apparent that the social purpose of the group, the
context within which it operates, and the professional purpose of the worker,
provide the structural dynamic. Thus a social worker in private practice can
meet with a family or other client group and involve himself with it in group
interaction to help individual members and the group as a whole attempt to
identify their purpose, consonant with societal norms and the social worker's
professional purpose. In recent years, the development and proliferation of
community-based organizations, many of which are protest groups with little
or no community sanction outside their own membership, has led to a
deeper examination of the usefulness of clearly defined and agreed-upon
social purpose as a viable form of the structural concept that is also inherent
in agency function.

INDIVIDUAL AND GROUP PERCEPTIONS OF NEEDS,
PURPOSES, GOALS

Margaret Hartford has defined a group as two or more people

gathered with common purposes or like interests in a cognitive, affective, and
social interchange in single or repeated encounters sufficient for the participants to

[2] Saul Hofstein, "The Nature of Process," *Journal of Social Work Process,* 14:14–15
(1964).

form impressions of one another, creating a set of norms for their functioning together, developing goals for their collective activity, evolving a sense of cohesion so that they think of themselves and are thought of by others as an entity distinct from all other collectivities.[3]

Group characteristics important to the social worker are: membership, purpose, relationship, and process, from which emerge group norms, goals, bond, and boundaries.

Group members may participate voluntarily in an agency program—(as in a youth center) or under coercion (as in a prison). They may be members of a natural group that comes to the agency as a group for agency program (a teen club), or they may be assigned as individuals to become part of a formed group (a group of foster parents in a child-care agency). They may come for socialization purposes (a group of older people in the leisure-time program of a senior citizens center). They may come for help with a special kind of individual problem which all share (a preparole group in prison). They may have a common problem which they need to solve collectively (a neighborhood club seeks to develop a cooperative food purchase plan); or they may have an external task orientation (a group of ADC mothers in a welfare rights organization who are seeking a change in legislation).

Whatever their ages, interests, or concerns, whatever their previous association with each other, individual members come with their own perceptions of what they want from the group experience—their own definitions of need. As the group develops, there emerges a group perception of its need or interest, and this may or may not be entirely congruent with the perceptions of various members. If it is a natural group, this perception of need may be the factor that brings it to the agency. If it is a formed group, one of the early tasks will be to arrive at some agreement on purpose—a task which requires some shared understanding of need. In any case, both individual and group perceptions of needs and goals will be tested against agency or social purpose and function, with the worker helping the group as a whole and individual members to identify and work on the options available to them within that particular setting, using both the range of resources offered and the limits set by social purpose and function to cope with present reality. As group members engage with each other and with the social worker over a period of time, assessment and reassessment of needs and goals continue to be part of the process which they work on together, for perceptions of these change as the group process develops.

[3] Margaret E. Hartford, *Groups in Social Work,* p. 26.

THE SOCIAL WORKER AS CHANGE FACILITATOR

The primary task of the social worker with a group is to help members engage effectively in the group process as they identify and work toward the achievement of group goals. This means that the worker must understand group structure, characteristics, and process. He must have skill in developing relationships with members and helping them to relate to each other. He must carry within himself and present for their use an understanding and acceptance of the social and institutional purpose which provides the framework within which the members discuss and select, reject or modify group goals. It is his responsibility to increase the options open to members wherever possible and to help them test and push back or accept the limits of reality when their choices are unreal or unacceptable. Another task is to help them take responsibility for the choices they make, to assess the results, and use that assessment for growth and future action.

Social change may occur in a group or as a result of its activity, whether or not a social worker works with it. It is the responsibility of the worker, however, to help members make maximum use of the group experience, both in selecting the *direction* of change and in working for a particular level or quality of social change.

A KNOWLEDGE BASE FOR A FUNCTIONAL APPROACH

The chief architect of a functional approach to social work with groups is Helen U. Phillips, who for twenty-four years was professor of Social Group Work at the University of Pennsylvania School of Social Work. Her book, *Essentials of Social Group Work Skill,* published in 1957, still stands as the single most comprehensive description of this theoretical formulation. Since publication of this book, the social work profession, the social welfare system, and the institutions which provide the framework of operation of both, have changed substantially. With those changes and with the ever-increasing knowledge base upon which the profession of social work draws, there have developed some changed perceptions and additional insights about the application of functional theory to social work practice with groups. Some of these will be explored here, but within the general framework developed by Phillips.

Historically, the functional approach to social work practice developed out of the association of Jessie Taft and Virginia Robinson with Otto Rank, an association which was rooted in a professional interest in child therapy and child welfare and carried over into the development of a base for professional education for social workers. The focus was on work with individuals and families within the context of a clearly defined agency purpose. The literature of this early period shows concern for and interest in issues that foreshadow current developments. Most notable for this paper are two: a concern for the social worker's skill in and responsibility for development of individual and institutional change, and the conviction that principles of practice are generic for all practice modalities.[4]

The psychological base for functional social work practice is rooted in the works of Otto Rank. Nowhere is Rank's contribution to functional theory clearer than in his premise that the human will, as a creative and organizing force in the life of the individual, provides a difference and a strength which can be used by that individual for his own growth and development. In social work with individuals, this has led to the assumption that the center for change resides within the client, and the social worker's responsibility is to engage him in a relationship process that frees him for choice and growth. Phillips developed this concept for use with groups by identifying the responsibility of the social worker to engage the members of a group in a relationship process that frees both individual members and the group as a whole to choose the nature and direction of their change and growth.

The concept of the use of social process is also a derivative of Rankian psychology. The focal point of process in functional social work is the present moment, recognized as the only time dimension available for use by the client or group or social worker. The worker and the group, as they interact, use knowledge from the past and make plans for the future, but this occurs within the confines of current opportunities and limitations. As Phillips wrote:

> It is only the present, given moment of time that is available to a person for growth as he wills it. . . . The crux of the matter is how one *uses* his past in the present to move forward toward the future that holds his goals and aspirations. What has gone before and what is to come meet in the present. . . . It is that pivotal point, the present moment of time, that is available to the group worker for

[4] Virginia P. Robinson, "The Meaning of Skill," *Journal of Social Work Process,* 4:2 (1942).

his help to group members in their use of relationships with each other and with himself.[5]

The concept of social purpose derives from social work practice rather than from psychology or one of the social sciences. It has several components: professional social work purpose, societal purpose as defined by sanction and support, and agency or organizational purpose. It is out of the last of these that Jessie Taft identified the significance of agency function for the helping process, and suggested some of the questions and directions of social work practice in the seventies.

> We . . . leave to the individual the freedom as well as the responsibility of testing out his peculiar needs against the relatively stable function of a particular agency. There remains to us a large and comparatively unexplored area in which to learn how to maintain our functions intelligently and skillfully, and how to isolate whatever can be isolated from the particular situation in terms of the law, the nature, the general pattern of the helping process.[6]

It is to this "unexplored area," beyond the "relatively stable function of a particular agency," that social workers address their attention in the seventies, and it is out of this that the expanded concept of social purpose has developed.

The specifics of the three key concepts for a functional approach to social work thus come from, but are not limited to, Rankian psychology. Functional social work, like other social work theories, derives its knowledge about group structure and process from the findings of a variety of social scientists.

The early work of Phillips drew heavily upon the educational theories of John Dewey, A. H. Kilpatrick, and Alfred Whitehead, and the behavioral science formulations of George Herbert Mead, Charles Cooley, and George Simmel. Later influences that have added to an understanding of group behavior and group process include the work of Kurt Lewin and Ronald Lippitt and associates on field theory and group dynamics; the studies by George Homans of the properties of small groups; and the organizational and systems-theory contributions of Talcott Parsons. Additional knowledge has been drawn from the writings of numerous social workers, including Clara Kaiser, Gertrude Wilson, Gladys Ryland, Grace Coyle, Gisela Konopka,

---

[5] Helen U. Phillips, *Essentials of Social Group Work Skill*, p. 134.

[6] Jessie Taft, "The Relation of Function to Process in Social Case Work," *Journal of Social Work Process*, 1:5 (1937).

Helen Northen, Ruth Middleman, Robert Vinter, William Schwartz, and Margaret Hartford. For a thorough analysis of the behavioral science and social work research which provide the knowledge base for social work with groups, the reader is referred to Margaret Hartford's *Groups in Social Work.*[7]

In addition to the base of knowledge about groups, the social worker with groups also needs knowledge about individual behavior and development, and knowledge about the dynamics of social work practice. Early sources of these for functional social work with groups have been indicated, along with later sources of practice knowledge. To these should be added the use of other psychological formulations for understanding human behavior, with special reference to the works of Charles Moustakas, Helen Lynd, and Frederick Allen.

For the social worker to translate relevant concepts from this broad knowledge base into professional action, he must first identify the value base from which he operates. The role he assumes, the acts he performs, and the skill he develops grow out of the knowledge base but are given direction by his value system.

A VALUE BASE

As the social work profession moves away from the confines of specific methodological approaches toward the identification of a generic base for practice, there is increasing recognition of the significance of group action and interaction for the offering of help. Gertrude Wilson, in her paper written for this volume, has traced the history of the development of social group work as a method in social work, and the value base on which that practice has been built. The community organization literature is replete with examples of the use of groups to accomplish community tasks, drawing on ideas that go back to Mary Parker Follett, Clarence King, Eduard Lindeman, Wilber Newstetter, Kenneth Pray, and, more recently, Murray Ross, Robert Morris, Arnold Gurin, and many others. In social casework, which for a long time focused on work with individuals almost to the exclusion of consideration of the significance of group interaction, the use of groups is somewhat newer. Even here, there is now general acknowledgment of the value of working with families and peer groups in helping clients.

[7] Hartford, *Groups in Social Work.*

Man is a social animal; whatever his goals, he works toward them in association with like-minded people. In today's world, we are reminded anew that group experiences can be used in diverse areas of life for the destruction of the common good as well as for its enhancement. Social work, as a helping profession which deals with *social* problems and relationships, has both a special contribution and a special responsibility to work with people in groups for achievement of a *social* purpose.

Social work has developed its practice with groups on the premise of a universal need for group association and on the value assigned to such association by our culture and by our profession. It has its own unique forms and methods for meeting this common need, and for using groups to perpetuate or change cultural norms and social institutions. Community people demand group services of their social agencies. Social workers, responding to this demand, provide opportunities for participation in groups as a means both for individual development and for social and institutional change.

Phillips says that "the fundamental unshakable value that undergirds all of the helping professions" is the recognition that every person has the capacity to change and the right to decide whether, when, and how he will change.[8] Kenneth L. M. Pray developed the idea in this fashion:

> The client, whatever his strengths and weaknesses, carries responsibility for his own life. . . . At least he has not asked us, and we cannot consent, to take that responsibility from him. He has asked us, rather, to help him carry that responsibility . . . and in the very act of seeking this help he has disclosed at least some of the elements of strength for dealing with this responsibility. The worker's task is to enable him to build on this latent strength. . . . The problem remains his own. . . . Furthermore, this approach . . . starts with the assumption—indeed the profound conviction—that the helping dynamic, the source of healing power, is also in the client himself as he reaches out for help. It is not primarily in the worker.[9]

A functional approach then, recognizes not only the right but the inherent capacity of people to work individually and collectively on matters of common concern or on like interests. This supports the belief that growth and change can result from group interaction, and places on the social worker the responsibility for active engagement with the group to help the members use the group experience for that purpose.

[8] Phillips, *Essentials of Social Group Work Skill*, p. 44.
[9] Kenneth L. M. Pray, "A Restatement of the Generic Principles of Social Casework," in Kenneth Pray (ed.), *Social Work in a Revolutionary Age*, p. 249.

Within this value base are the roots of a potential dilemma for the social worker—the dilemma posed by the conflict in values between individual and group, group and agency, or group and the larger society. As values are operationalized in expression of purpose, in delineation of goals, in planning, and in carrying out of activity, the issue may be sharpened for both social worker and group as they struggle to find a common ground. For example, prisoners in a state penitentiary, feeling oppressed and helpless within the walls of the institution, may join a group for the purpose of trying to get a few extra privileges within the prison, or to work toward the possibility of early release, or even to plan for escape. The social worker will share their values at an abstract level—that is, in the belief in the right of human beings to be freed from the oppression and injustice that pervades much of the correctional system. But he also has other sets of values that have to do with (1) the right of society to be protected against violent criminal acts and (2) the belief in the capacity of many prisoners to learn to cope with society and its pressures without resorting to acts of violence, such as planning a prison riot and escape or returning to a criminal career after release. Prison administrators may or may not share the social worker's belief in the rights and capacities of the prisoners. Even if the basic value stance is shared, the social worker is constantly faced with the necessity to work with different perceptions of what will be the most effective expression of those values within the limits of the prison setting. The way in which he uses himself with the group as the members work on choosing and carrying out a course of action will affect that course of action. If the value base is not widely shared within the prison, if the basic premise under which the prison operates is one of an institutional responsibility to punish and dehumanize the inmates, his dilemma is even greater. Can he work within the system? Do his goals, in fact, lead to acts which will increase the vulnerability of prisoners, or can he help them learn to negotiate the system? If he cannot help, does he leave the prison because it violates his value system? What, then, happens to the prisoners?

In another setting, a district director of the Department of Public Assistance recently commented to a college class that a welfare rights organization group was the agency's best friend. She and the unit supervisors had spent hours in negotiation with that group and it was obvious that the group did not make the staff job easier or increase efficiency. What the group did that was useful was to provide a consumer expression of protest against oppressive policies, thus reinforcing the values and goals held by staff as they work for change within the system.

One sometimes hears the comment that a social worker walks a thin line as he strives to find a balance between his values and the values of the group as the members engage in joint activities. The elements of professional skill emerge as he combines his value system and his professional knowledge in involving himself with the group. The remainder of this paper will examine some of those elements which seem to have particular significance in a functional approach to social work with groups.

COMPONENTS OF SKILL

Helen Phillips has identified four components of social work skill with groups:

1. Skill in use of agency function.
2. Skill in communication of feeling.
3. Skill in use of time, with special emphasis on exploiting the present moment of reality for use by the group.
4. Skill in use of group relationships.[10]

Ruth Smalley, in writing about a generic base for social work practice, identified five principles which incorporate these components but provide a broader base for analysis.[11] The components identified in her paradigm, made specific for social work with groups, include:

1. Involvement of the worker and the group in a continuous process of diagnosis and reassessment.
2. Use of process—that is, the exploitation of time phases for group movement.
3. Use of agency function and social purpose to further productive engagement of the group and its members.
4. Use of structure which evolves from function and process to further the effectiveness of the group.
5. Use of relationship to help the group accomplish its purpose.

Underlying the elements described by each of these writers is the concept of process, the notion that the group and its members change as they move through time. A combination of the elements defined by the two au-

[10] Phillips, *Essentials of Social Group Work Skill,* pp. 51–166.
[11] Ruth E. Smalley, *Theory for Social Work Practice,* pp. 133–76.

thors, developed for purposes of examining the components of skill required of the social worker with a group, produces the following:

1. Skill in helping the group to diagnose or assess and reassess itself, including goals, purpose, expectations, structure, programs, achievements, and frustrations or failures.
2. Skill in helping the group to assess and use the reality of each part of each time phase for achievement of the group purpose.
3. Skill in helping the group to assess, use, and/or modify various levels of social purpose, including agency function.
4. Skill in helping the group to develop and use structure and the relationships within the structure to further its own effectiveness.
5. Skill in communication of feeling between worker and group, along with skill in facilitating communication of feeling between group members.

SKILL IN USE OF A DIAGNOSTIC PROCESS

From their first engagement with each other, one of the key tasks of worker and group is to engage with each other in the process of making a diagnosis. The diagnosis emerges as the worker assesses the hopes, aspirations, and needs of individual members. As the members gradually yield to a common purpose, the "how" and "whether" become the basis for diagnosing further movement.

In connection with a well-baby clinic, for example, a social worker had a number of teenage mothers referred to her. The young mothers were referred because, although they brought their babies to the clinic regularly, they did not follow instructions on infant care between visits.

Before getting the mothers together to explore what they might want or need additionally from the clinic, the social worker had only a brief medical resume on each child, and the name, address, and age of each mother. Five of eight mothers came at the invitation of the worker. In the course of the first session the worker learned that all eight knew each other; all were school dropouts, all received public assistance, and all lived in their parents' households. Their addresses had let the worker know they all lived in the impoverished, run-down neighborhood in which the clinic was located.

A diagnosis of "poor motivation" would have been an obvious, accurate, but sterile one. As the worker helped the young mothers evolve a purpose around their common concerns, six of the eight stayed with it and became a group, investing themselves with the worker on assessing and working through a heavy emotional problem which involved the parents of one member. In reaching this point they went through a time of testing each other and the worker; a time of rising levels of motivation and involvement as interests were taken seriously and acted upon; a time of expressing anger and frustration and, later, fear of never being able to change things. But as they worked as a group to deepen and broaden the group purpose, as the worker shared her assessment with them and they worked together on evaluation of the situation, they began to sense a new freedom to hear and to learn, and to use the services that were there for them. They developed the capacity to work together on problems of health care for themselves and their children, on finding new housing, on making use of the opportunity for job training. In other words, they were involved in a continuous process of diagnosis, in which worker and group engaged together to clarify the group situation, to identify work to be done, and to evaluate program, structure, process, and individual and group progress.

SKILL IN USE OF TIME PHASES

Every group process has its beginnings, middles, and endings. Perhaps the most difficult phase, and in many respects the most critical from the worker's perspective, is the beginning.[12] From the moment a social worker begins to think about the possibility, purpose and potential membership of a group until an aggregate of people who meet together give evidence of becoming a group by developing some sense of collective purpose, program, structure, and group bond, the social worker carries a special responsibility for using himself to further the active engagement of each potential member in the group-formation process.

This period is apt to be characterized by ambivalence deriving on the one hand from the awkwardness of new relationships and the doubts about self, on the other from enthusiasm, hopes, and aspirations not necessarily based on reality. For the social worker who is sure that a group experience

[12] Certainly more has been written about this phase than about other time phases. See for example Grace L. Coyle, *Group Work with American Youth,* pp. 45–90; James A. Garland, Hubert E. Jones, and Ralph L. Kolodny, "A Model for Stages in the Development of Social Work Groups," in Saul Bernstein (ed.), *Explorations in Group Work,* pp. 21–37; Margaret E. Hartford, "The Social Group Worker in the Process of Group Formation"; Marjorie W. Main, "An Examination of Selected Aspects of the Beginning Phase in Social Work with Groups"; William Rosenthal, "A Theory of Beginnings in Social Group Work Process."

will be useful to mental hospital patients, for example, the period in which members are joining and withdrawing, are accepting of agency function or trying to bend it to meet individual desires, can be a painfully difficult one. If, as Smalley suggests, the worker can "stay with the beginning and let it be a beginning in all its inevitable awkwardness and tentativeness," [13] he will be able to free individuals to choose for themselves whether they will invest in a group process within the limits of purpose and resources offered by the agency.

If terminating is less difficult for the worker than beginning, it is only because by this time the group as a group has learned to carry responsibility for its own process. It shares an awareness of the burden of ending that it did not share in the sense of responsibility for beginning. Most group endings contain elements of both sadness and joy: sadness at the termination of a meaningful relationship, the dissolution of group bonds, the loss of support of the group experience; joy at the completion of the task at hand or the achievement of the desired goal and at the prospect of moving toward a new beginning. Sometimes group members experience one of these sets of emotion almost to the exclusion of the other. A group of hospitalized veterans awaiting discharge may feel some regret at saying goodbye to the hospital group but are more likely to be so caught up in the fear and joy of release to the outside world that the significance of the group quickly fades. A group of campers returning from a canoe trip, on the other hand, may have developed such close ties in an experience of wilderness living that the departure from these friends for the more familiar ties of home and family may generate great feelings of sadness. Most terminations carry some of both types of feelings. A student graduating from school, for example, may be sad about leaving classmates and the structured school life but at the same time he can be enthusiastic about anticipating the new experiences that lie ahead. A worker, helping group members to terminate responsibly with each other and with him, needs to be able to help them understand and accept both kinds of feelings. His skill lies in helping group members to use the trauma of ending for the purpose of moving into a new beginning, neither hanging on to a form that has outlived its usefulness nor denying its validity as one part of the life process now past.

Beginnings and endings—which contain the seeds of new beginnings—

---

[13] Smalley, *Theory for Social Work Practice*, p. 144.

have much in common. In between lies that more or less undifferentiated time-space called middles. Much of the writing about this phase of group process focuses on tasks rather than on use of time. Yet everyone who has ever worked with a group is aware of the unique quality of this time phase; during it there is a leveling off of activity, frequently followed by a slump from which the group does not fully recover until the end is in sight, and a sense of time pressure stimulates a new burst of activity. In this period, the worker is called upon to hold the group to a steadiness of movement, to break up the time period and the tasks in a way which gives group members some sense of newness of purpose or activity and a feeling of successful accomplishment in small time units within the broader space. Here especially, the worker's understanding of the rhythm of group process and his skill in helping the group to exploit the present moment of reality will be called into play.

SKILL IN USE OF PURPOSE AND FUNCTION

The centrality of the concept of social purpose, derived from a combination of sources including the sanctioning community, the profession, the agency, and the group, has already been discussed. All of these purposes are there for the worker's use with a group, to give the group focus, direction, and content for its activity. In a stable agency, the most useful and powerful statement of purpose tends to be agency function, for it is this that provides the social worker with the sanction and the resources to work with a group. His major accountability is to the supporting community through the agency. Grace Marcus has said that the social agency "is the place where the interests of society and the interests of the individual are joined." [14] The agency provides opportunities for growth; it also sets limits, holding the aspirations of worker and group to the limits perceived as possible within agency purpose and resources. The worker consciously uses the agency function which he carries within himself to effect change in group goals, process, and relationships. His skill lies in his capacity to direct efforts toward carrying out agency purpose and helping the group to select and work for goals consonant with that purpose—or, if necessary, to identify and come to grips with a conflict between group purpose and agency function.

There is a danger in this emphasis on agency function, the danger that a

[14] Grace Marcus, "The Necessity for Understanding Agency Function." Philadelphia: unpublished, undated paper.

dependent or authoritarian social worker may view purpose and function as fixed and unchangeable. While purpose and function do provide a relatively stable base for operation and for accountability, they cannot be helpful for long if they are perceived as providing a static set of rules and regulations. In an agency with a commitment to a social purpose, there is an exchange between client and policy maker, frequently through a staff person but sometimes more directly. As this exchange flows freely, it serves to shape and reshape agency policy and purpose. In addition, the expertise—derived from professional knowledge and experience—which staff members bring to bear upon client problems, is an important source of information for policy determination and change. Agency purpose, like client purpose and professional purpose, is involved in a developmental process and is subject to change. The skillful worker carries his responsibility in this part of the process both as a concerned staff member and as a social worker with a group that may have a part to play in reshaping agency policy.

SKILL IN USE OF GROUP RELATIONSHIPS

As group members interact with each other during the process of group formation, group norms are established, roles are taken or assigned, social bonds are developed, and the structure for working relationships emerges. The worker is responsible for helping members to develop and use these relationships in a way that will help each to have a full and meaningful part in the group process. The worker must be aware of each individual member and his interaction with others as well as his connection with the group as a whole. He must be attuned not only to the feelings of success and failure in activity, the feelings of like and dislike of each to the other, but also to the sense of connection of each member to the purpose and process as a whole. He must know when and how to put in his point of view, his "differentness" as agency representative, in order to further the process, and he must know when to be silent and let the group members carry their own process and the conflict inherent in it. Phillips suggests that containment and trust are important aspects of this skill component if the worker is to free the group to use the group process creatively. She further distinguishes between controlling group *members* and controlling group *process,* noting that only as the worker avoids the former and engages in the latter can he free members to take part in the process.[15]

[15] Phillips, *Essentials of Social Group Work Skill,* pp. 148–66.

SKILL IN COMMUNICATION OF FEELING

Purpose, task, process, and role are essential parts of any social work with groups, but they do not comprise the whole. No discussion or interaction between worker and group or among group members would be complete without consideration of the significance of the affect that develops as part of that process.

A capacity to be concerned about others, to feel with them, is one of the most highly valued qualities in social work. For the worker to be useful in a professional, helping way, he must acknowledge and discipline this quality of caring so that he is free to use his feeling, and not be controlled by it.

Awareness of feeling and acceptance of it with all of its positive and negative aspects is a first step for a social worker with a group. Only then can he present his feelings for the group's use. His skill is in being able to use his feeling genuinely with the group, but focused on the members' need to know and experience it rather than his own need to express himself. Of this skill, Phillips wrote:

> He must contain the two sides within himself—the spontaneous, outgoing quality, and the disciplined, controlled consciousness of how he is using himself in relation to his group. If his primary concern is for the feelings of his group members and the freeing of them for responsible use that can lead to their relatedness to him and to fellow members, he discovers an inevitable control on a licensed expression of his own emotions. He is with the group to help it, and his consciousness of that fact gives direction to responsible communication of the feeling part of himself in a genuine though disciplined way. . . .[16]

A second aspect of the skill in communication of feeling is to be found in the worker's capacity to help group members understand, accept, and express their feelings in a responsible way. It is not enough for the worker to *know* how they feel. Group relationships grow, and group process is enhanced when members are helped to acknowledge and use their feelings with each other. Part of the skill is in eliciting and using positive feelings; part is in the worker's capacity to elicit negative feelings and help the member deal with them before they become aggressively overpowering to the member and disruptive to the group. It is difficult to confront a member with some reality that may be painful for him. To deny the reality, or to

[16] *Ibid.,* p. 99.

allow him to deny it, is to avoid coming to grips with an issue that can block growth. A group of hemiplegics in a rehabilitation center, for example, can plan movies, craft programs, and patient parties without ever facing the reality of their need for rehabilitation. As the members are helped to face the reality of their physical problems and to acknowledge their hopes, fears, and anger, they can begin to work on a constructive, mutually supportive approach to therapy. A social worker with such a group needs to be sensitive to each member's feelings about himself and other members, and help each individual use such feelings for his own growth. In addition, the worker must be alert to the members' feelings about his own wholeness, and their need to discuss this and the pain it may evoke.

With any group, then, the social worker confronts a complexity of feelings—his own, each member's, and frequently a group feeling that grows out of the interaction of all of these. Each has its positive and negative aspects, and the worker's capacity to help members acknowledge and use both aspects can have a great effect on the usefulness of the group experience.

SUMMARY AND CONCLUSION

A functional approach to social work with groups is based in the distinctive use of three concepts: the nature of man and his institutions, the significance of social purpose, and the use of social process. In the past, these three concepts have been applied to a social group work methodology for use primarily in group service agencies or in host settings in which there was a clearly defined agency function.

The social upheavals of the sixties and the proliferating service forms that have continued to develop into the seventies require of social work a more flexible approach to service delivery. This paper is an attempt to review traditional concepts and current thrusts to discover how a functional approach to work with groups can be and is being used by social workers in a variety of traditional and nontraditional settings to develop and implement programs of individual and social change.

BIBLIOGRAPHY

Bernstein, Saul (ed.). *Explorations in Group Work.* Boston: Boston University School of Social Work, 1965.
—— *Further Explorations in Group Work.* Boston: Boston University School of Social Work, 1970.

Coyle, Grace L. *Group Work with American Youth.* New York: Harper, 1948.

Hartford, Margaret E. *Groups in Social Work.* New York: Columbia University Press, 1971.

—— "The Social Group Worker and Group Formation," Ph.D. dissertation, University of Chicago School of Social Service Administration, 1962.

Konopka, Gisela. *Group Work in the Institution.* New York: Association Press, 1970.

Lewis, Harold. "The Functional Approach to Social Work Practice—A Restatement of Assumptions and Principles," *Journal of Social Work Process,* XV (1966).

Main, Marjorie W. "An Examination of Selected Aspects of the Beginning Phase in Social Work with Groups." Ph.D. dissertation, University of Chicago School of Social Service Administration, 1963.

Middleman, Ruth R. *The Non-Verbal Method in Working with Groups.* New York: Association Press, 1968.

Middleman, Ruth R. and Gail Goldberg. *Social Service Delivery: A Structural Approach.* New York: Columbia University Press, 1974.

Northen, Helen. *Social Work with Groups.* New York: Columbia University Press, 1969.

Phillips, Helen U. (ed.). *Achievement of Responsible Behavior Through Group Work Process.* Philadelphia: University of Pennsylvania School of Social Work, 1950.

—— *Essentials of Social Group Work Skill.* New York: Association Press, 1957. Reprinted, Philadelphia: University of Pennsylvania School of Social Work and Norwood, Pa.: Norwood Editors, 1973.

Pray, Kenneth L. M. (ed.). *Social Work in a Revolutionary Age.* Philadelphia: University of Pennsylvania Press, 1949.

Rosenthal, William. "A Theory of Beginnings in Social Group Work Process." D.S.W. dissertation, University of Pennsylvania School of Social Work, 1970.

Shoemaker, Louise P. "Adaptation of Traditional Methods in Services to Individuals in Families and Groups," in *Source Book of Teaching Materials on the Welfare of Children.* New York: Council on Social Work Education, 1969.

—— "The Significance of Group Services to Public Welfare Clients," in U.S. Bureau of Family Services, *Helping People in Groups,* 1965.

Smalley, Ruth E. *Theory for Social Work Practice.* New York: Columbia University Press, 1967.

Vinter, Robert D. (ed.). *Readings in Group Work Practice.* Ann Arbor, Mich.: Campus Publishers, 1967.

Wilson, Gertrude and Gladys Ryland. *Social Group Work Practice.* Cambridge, Mass.: Houghton Mifflin, 1949.

6

BETWEEN CLIENT AND SYSTEM:
THE MEDIATING FUNCTION

WILLIAM SCHWARTZ

THE SCIENTIFIC PARADIGM

The profession of social work was born and raised under the influence of a scientific model which showed an objective investigator at work, exploring his materials, learning their properties, and developing skill in manipulating them for the good of society. The scientists and the engineers studied their objects, found the laws that regulated their behavior, and used the knowledge to make nature operate to man's advantage. So, too, in the helping professions: the physician, faced with a person whose machinery had gone wrong, examined it, diagnosed the difficulty, and proceeded to put it back in working order. Following closely, the psychiatrist, the psychologist, the educator, and the social worker took over this view of the helping relationship. They posed the same problems, set themselves the same tasks, and laid their claims to science in the terms laid down by this positivist view of the world. In this conception, an independent worker-*subject* acts upon a client-*object* from a distance, to understand him, to change him, to fix him, using standards drawn from his own special area of expertise.

In its time, this image of science worked very well. It brought man into his age of enlightenment and helped him gain greater control over the world in which he lived. It taught people that they were products of their experience and could, like nature itself, be studied and understood, tested and improved. And it helped create new attitudes toward people in need: if men were made by events, we needed to understand both men and events and not simply judge people in abstract moral terms; further, we had to do something about the conditions of the poor, rather than rely entirely on exhortations to be "worthy" of society's help. To the budding human-relations professions of the Progressive Era, the spirit of science and experiment lent a view of the client-worker relationship that reflected the modern spirit. It was historical, rational, determinist, prescriptive, individualist, objective.

But something went wrong in the adaptation of this model to the art of human relations. In fact, the very qualities that helped bring these professions into being soon began to tear them apart. The historicism that brought them to the study of causes and effects created a determinism so rigid as to magnify the importance of the past until it blocked out the worker's vision of the present. The rationalism that valued knowledge and logic (Freud's term for his therapy was psycho-*analysis*) turned into what John Dewey later described as the "quest for certainty," where knowledge was considered more elegant than action, and the nonlogical and the intuitive became elements in a lower, "unscientific" order.[1] The prescriptiveness that we borrowed from the doctors helped us to think more specifically about human problems, but it soon came into conflict with our growing emphasis on the importance of self-determination. Further, the stress on individual differences served to focus our attention on the study of human behavior, but the increased preoccupation with early character formation made it too easy to underplay the social and interpersonal forces that continue to change people throughout their lives, as they move from situation to situation. And the objectivity that brought us closer to science and research also created a detachment so formidable that the client suffered from the distance put between him and his helper. In fact, professionalism itself came to be defined as the ability to maintain one's distance from the client; we thus found ourselves bound to what Rollo May called "the traditional doctrine, so limiting, self-contradictory, and indeed often so destructive in psychology, that *the less we are involved in a given situation, the more clearly we can observe the truth.*"[2]

A new vision was needed to illuminate the nature of the helping pro-

---

[1] John Dewey, *The Quest for Certainty: A Study of the Relation of Knowledge and Action* (New York: Putnam, 1929; Capricorn Books, 1960).

[2] Rollo May, "The Origins and Significance of the Existential Movement in Psychology," in Rollo May, Ernest Angel, and Henri F. Ellenberger (eds.), *Existence*, p. 27. Emphasis in original.

cess. Fixing broken things was not the same sort of work as helping people to mobilize their own energies in their own behalf. The worker-client relationship was one in which the client was not an object at all, but a dynamic force with a will and energy of his own. The client did not hold still to be examined, labeled, and treated, and the engagement was not between a detached expert and malleable entity—between fixer and fixed, teacher and taught, changer and changed. The person in need retained the ultimate power—using it both consciously and unconsciously—to accept help or reject it, and much of the impetus for change came from the client. Thus, even as the worker strove to "enable" his client, he was himself being enabled by the latter's own motives and energies.

A SHIFTING OF PARADIGMS

In response to these persistent realities, some professionals began to move to a new model of the helping process. This move represented a revolution in thinking similar to that described by Kuhn in his work on the history of science. In his *Structure of Scientific Revolutions,*[3] Kuhn showed that science advances not through a gradual accumulation of bits of knowledge but in a series of dramatic leaps from old ways of looking at the world to radically new ones. As the gestalt changes, the "ducks become rabbits;" the field of inquiry shakes itself loose from the "normal science" of its day and shifts to a new paradigm from which there emerge new kinds of questions and brand new problems for research.

The old paradigm, as Kuhn defined it, is a set of "received beliefs," written into the textbooks of its time and defining the legitimate areas of inquiry. Normal science, productive in its time, sets the tasks for the paradigm, creating a climate in which the professionals all "know what the world is like." They talk the same language, ask the same questions, and work on the same "games and puzzles"—that is, on problems in which the answers are already embedded.

It is the very solidity of this world, however, that makes it necessary ultimately to suppress novelty, motivated by fear that diverse viewpoints might be subversive of the paradigm's basic commitments. "A paradigm can, for that matter, even insulate the community from those socially important problems that are not reducible to the puzzle form, because they cannot

---

[3] Thomas S. Kuhn, *The Structure of Scientific Revolutions.*

be stated in terms of the conceptual and instrumental tools the paradigm supplies." [4] This effort is not conspiratorial; it is simply part of a historical process through which a field of inquiry moves as it passes from the preconsensual stage, to that of normal science, to the transcendant revolutionary leap. In any event, the jump from normal science is precipitated by the fact that science cannot suppress its novelties indefinitely, since it is not in its nature to tolerate the arbitrary for too long. In time, the paradigm begins to spring leaks; and it develops a number of anomalies—phenomena that are contradictory and do not square with expectations.

It is at this point, said Kuhn, that there "begin the extraordinary investigations that lead the profession at last to a new set of commitments, a new basis for the practice of science." [5] He showed how such revolutions took place in the fields of light, heat, electricity, astronomy, and others, describing how scientists emerged, after the crisis, into a world that was almost literally transformed:

> Led by a new paradigm, scientists adopt new instruments and look in new places. Even more important, during revolutions scientists see new and different things when looking with familiar instruments in places they have looked before. It is rather as if the professional community has been suddenly transported to another planet where familiar objects are seen in a different light and joined by unfamiliar ones as well. . . . In so far as their only recourse to the world is through what they see and do, we may want to say that after a revolution scientists are responding to a different world. [6]

In all this, the analogy to social work development can be overdrawn; the social sciences in general are still in what Kuhn called the preparadigm state. But the similarities are striking, nonetheless. We too have our received beliefs, embodied in the paradigm of study-diagnosis-treatment as it was taken over from medicine, research, and positivist science. We have our consensualized language, and the games and puzzles that frame only certain kinds of questions and can imagine no others. [7] We have our stubborn contradictions, the anomalies that face us at every turn: the need to hedge on the sequential character of study, diagnosis, and treatment, maintaining that each step occurs simultaneously, since the imagined process is so obviously at odds with what actually happens between worker and client; the vexing

---

[4] Ibid., p. 37.   [5] Ibid., p. 6.   [6] Ibid., p. 110.

[7] A colleague asked, incredulously: "If you don't teach diagnosis and treatment goals, what can you teach at all?"

inability to reconcile the demands for both prescriptiveness and self-determination; the call for both professional detachment and deep empathy in the same relationship; the problem of integrating concepts of changing people with those of helping them; and many others. And the crisis is unmistakable as professionals try to live with the traditional subject-object view of the helping relationship.

The problem that faces the social work profession, and the other helping disciplines as well, is to describe an art whose achievements depend only partly on the skill of the artist. Since his power is a function of the power of his materials—his clients—a model is needed that will show the acts of the professional as a force exerted not only on people but in interdependent relations with them. The worker-client engagement is one in which, in Parson's terms, "the *relations* determine the properties of its parts." [8] Or we may view it as Frank's "organized complexity," where "we need to think in terms of circular, reciprocal relations and feed backs . . . through which the component members of the field participate in and thereby create the field of the whole, which field in turn regulates and patterns their individual activities." [9] The language of description will have to be a language of action, showing how the worker *moves,* and not only what he knows, what he values, and what he hopes to achieve. In effect, such a model undertakes to describe *separately* a number of professional acts that are virtually *inseparable* from those of clients around him. It is indeed a different world for the professional who changes his image from that of a fixer of broken objects to that of a participant in a network of active, reciprocal relationships, where he finds his own special piece of the action and then fashions the skills necessary to carry it out.

THEORETICAL FOUNDATIONS

The new gestalt that springs from all this does not abandon what was useful in the old. Kuhn himself noted that "the new paradigm must promise to

[8] Talcott Parsons, *The Structure of Social Action* (Glencoe, Ill.: Free Press, 1949), p. 32. Emphasis added.

[9] Lawrence K. Frank, "Research for What?" *Journal of Social Issues,* Suppl. Ser. No. 10 (1957), p. 12. Frank also refers to Albert Einstein and Leopold Infeld, *The Evolution of Physics* (Cambridge, England: Cambridge University Press: New York: Simon and Schuster, 1938), p. 259, where these authors point out that "it needed great scientific imagination to realize that it is not the charges nor the particles, but the *field in the space between* charges and the particles, which is essential for the description of physical events. . . ." (emphasis in original).

preserve a relatively large part of the concrete problem-solving ability that has accrued to science through its predecessors." [10] In fact, many of the necessary themes are there in our history, running underground for part of the way but surfacing in certain features of the old paradigm itself. When they do, they are frequently honored more in the breach than the observance—as when we devise a "treatment plan" for a client without reference to his work on the problem, even as we stress his right to self-determination. For when two sets of desirable but opposing aspirations cannot be reconciled, we tend to act on one and pay homage to the other.

It was, in fact, a version of the reciprocal construct on which John Dewey based his interactionist view of the teaching-learning process, although he found few, even among those in progressive education, who understood what he meant and could translate his vision into a theory of pedagogy. [11] Martin Buber tried to find a reciprocal language, distinguishing between the interdependent relationship of "I-Thou" and the detached, subject-object encounter that he called "I-It." [12] As Buber explored the "dialogical" character of human relations, he showed us two men observing each other:

> The essential thing is not that the one makes the other his object, but the fact that he is not fully able to do so, and the reason for his failure. We have in common with all existing beings that we can be made objects of observation. But it is my privilege as man that by the hidden activity of my being I can establish an impassable barrier to objectification. Only in partnership can my being be perceived as an existing whole. [13]

Buber's "barrier to objectification" is the central theme of any reciprocal, transactional approach to the helping process. [14] The tradition from which it draws is part of the historic revolt against Descartes' early 17th century polarization of the self and the environment, his dichotomy of feeling and intellect, and his rigid definition of science as the study of that which is

---

[10] Kuhn, *Structure of Scientific Revolutions,* p. 168.

[11] The most systematic presentation of Dewey's ideas on education can be found in John Dewey, *Democracy and Education.*

[12] Martin Buber, *I and Thou* (2d ed.; New York: Scribner, 1958).

[13] Martin Buber, "The William Alanson White Memorial Lectures, Fourth Series," *Psychiatry,* 20:106 (May 1957).

[14] For further elaboration of Buber's ideas on "objectification" in human relations, see Maurice Friedman's introductory essay in Martin Buber, *The Knowledge of Man: Selected Essays,* edited by Friedman (New York: Harper & Row, Torchbooks, 1965), pp. 11–58.

external and visible.[15] The opposition to this individualist and objectivist thesis has surfaced in every generation since, taking one form or another as part of the history of philosophy, the physical sciences, and the social sciences. Wherever it appears, its ideas are expressed through a curiosity about processes, the nature of experience, the influence of feelings on human behavior, and the conduct of people in interaction.[16] Gordon Allport has traced the development of two antithetical traditions: the one, engendered by John Locke, an admirer of Descartes, stresses the "scientific," environmental, behavioristic factors in human psychology; the other, begun by G. W. Leibnitz soon after the death of Descartes, emphasized the purposive, internal forces of man, and led toward the work of Kant, Herbart, Wundt, and the gestalt psychologists.[17]

Soren Kierkegaard, a contemporary of Freud's who went unnoticed by the new human relations professions, pointed out that "truth exists only as the individual himself produces it in action." [18] Rousseau's intuitionism, Jame's phenomenology, and Dewey's analysis of the emotional aspects of human experience, all helped to translate the tradition into a new view of the educational enterprise. Mary Follett, a social philosopher of the Progressive Era, helped lay the foundations of social work thinking with her observation that "experience is the power-house where purpose and will, thought and ideals, are being generated." [19] And in the present day, social workers with an existential perspective have stressed the antiindividualist theme:

> To understand existentialism it is essential to have a feel for its conception of man's most fundamental need that distinguishes him as a human being. This may be described as the hunger for unity, belonging, eternalization of personality by somehow overcoming the separateness he feels between parts of himself, as well as between himself, others, and the universe as a whole.[20]

[15] Rene Descartes, *Discourse on Method and Other Writings,* translated with an introduction by F. E. Sutcliffe (Baltimore: Penguin, 1968).

[16] See Rollo May, "Origins and Significance of the Existential Movement in Psychology," in May, Angel, and Ellenberger (eds.), *Existence,* pp. 3–36. See also Fritz Heider, "On Lewin's Methods and Theory," *Journal of Social Issues,* Suppl. Ser. No. 13 (1959), pp. 3–13. See also William Schwartz, "Social Group Work: The Interactionist Approach," *Encyclopedia of Social Work* (2 vols., 16th ed.; New York: NASW, 1971), 2:1252–63.

[17] Gordon W. Allport, *Becoming: Basic Considerations for a Psychology of Personality* (New Haven: Yale University Press, 1955).

[18] Cited by May, "Origins and Significance of the Existential Movement," p. 12.

[19] Mary P. Follett, *Creative Experience* (New York: Longmans, Green, 1930), p. 133.

[20] Donald F. Krill, "Existentialism: A Philosophy for Our Current Revolutions," *Social Service Review,* 40:292 (September 1966).

In fact, the ideas that helped fashion our concepts of social interaction and social influence, as well as the empirical work that elaborated these ideas, have flowed from so many sources that it would take an essay as long as this one merely to trace its barest outlines. For those interested in the most recent philosophical implications of the existential view as it is joined to latterday phenomenology, Luijpen's book on the subject has interesting implications for a professional's view of human behavior.[21]

In psychiatry, Freud himself, representing as he did the prototype of positivist science, also provided entry for the dark forces of subjectivity and irrationalism in his therapeutic emphasis on feeling, instinct, and the unconscious. And his successors—Adler, Horney, Rank, and others—developed and enriched his concept of the ego and its efforts to gain control of its immediate environment. In psychology, the theoretical and experimental work of Carl Rogers directed attention to the details of the helping process, stressing the powers of the patient and the efforts of the therapist to enter into a genuine collaboration with him; Gordon and others carried the Rogerian implications into work with groups.[22]

In sociology, the stream of thought flows from Cooley and McDougall, who gave us our first real glimpses into the entity of group, over and above the properties of its individual members,[23] to the contemporary work of Parsons, Frank, and Grinker, whose emphasis on the organic whole brought the interactional insight to its most dramatic development and helped us begin to grasp the idea of group-as-client.[24] In social psychology, we learned about the uses of spontaneity from Jennings and Moreno,[25] the effects of group

[21] William A. Luijpen, *Existential Phenomenology* (rev. ed.; Pittsburgh: Duquesne University Press, 1969).

[22] Carl R. Rogers, *Client-Centered Therapy* (Boston: Houghton Mifflin, 1951.) See also Carl R. Rogers, "The Process Equation of Psychotherapy," *American Journal of Psychotherapy*, 15:124–46 (1961); Thomas Gordon, *Group-Centered Leadership* (New York: Houghton Mifflin; Cambridge, Mass.: Riverside Press, 1955).

[23] Charles Horton Cooley, *Social Organization* (New York: Scribner, 1909); and W. McDougall, *The Group Mind* (New York: Putnam, 1920).

[24] Talcott Parsons, *The Social System* (Glencoe, Ill.: Free Press, 1951); Frank, "Research for What?"; and Roy R. Grinker et al., *Psychiatric Social Work: A Transactional Case Book* (New York: Basic Books, 1961).

[25] Helen Jennings, Leadership and Isolation (New York: Longmans, Green, 1943); Jacob L. Moreno, *Who Shall Survive* (Washington, D.C.: Nervous and Mental Diseases Publishing, 1934) Jacob L. Moreno, "Foundations of Sociometry," *Sociometry*, 4:15–35 (February 1941).

pressure on individual judgments from the experiments of Asch [26] and Lewin,[27] the analysis of interaction from Bales,[28] the effects of different leadership styles from the work of Lewin and his colleagues,[29] and, most recently, the history of the nonverbal, "beyond science" tradition embodied in the sensitivity and encounter movements from Kurt Back.[30]

In an interesting way, we may also be said to have learned from the behaviorists and their concern with action; their interest in external behavior is akin to our preoccupation with the observable skills of the worker in interaction with his client. In fact, whether or not we agree with his methods, B. F. Skinner has shown a greater concern with the process of teaching than have the proponents of progressive education themselves.[31]

Again, a thorough review of all the appropriate theory and research that has led us to our present understanding of a way in which "the word of address and the word of response live in the same language," [32] would take a long effort of its own; this writer has essayed three such reviews, from the perspective of the history of small-group study.[33]

Thus, it can be seen that the basic elements for a radical shift in our view of the helping process have been developing for generations, contribut-

[26] Solomon E. Asch, "Effects of Group Pressure Upon the Modification and Distortion of Judgments," in Eleanor E. Maccoby, Theodore M. Newcomb, and Eugene L. Hartley (eds.), *Readings in Social Psychology* (3d ed.; New York: Holt, 1958), pp. 174–83.

[27] Kurt Lewin, "Conduct, Knowledge, and Acceptance of New Values," in Lewin, *Resolving Social Conflicts: Selected Papers on Group Dynamics* (New York: Harper, 1948), pp. 56–68.

[28] Robert F. Bales, *Interaction Process Analysis: A Method for the Study of Small Groups* (Cambridge, Mass.: Addison-Wesley, 1950).

[29] Ronald Lippitt and Ralph K. White, "An Experimental Study of Leadership and Group Life," in Maccoby, Newcomb, and Hartley (eds.), *Social Psychology*, pp. 496–511.

[30] Kurt W. Back, *Beyond Words: The Story of Sensitivity Training and the Encounter Movement* (New York: Russell Sage Foundation, 1972).

[31] See, for example, B. F. Skinner, "Why Teachers Fail," *Saturday Review*, October 16, 1965, pp. 80–81, 98–102. See also, for an excellent summary of the behaviorist contribution to the tasks of practice, Robert D. Carter and Richard B. Stuart, "Behavior Modification Theory and Practice: A Reply," *Social Work*, 15:37–50 (January 1970).

[32] Buber, *I and Thou*, p. 103.

[33] William Schwartz, "Small Group Science and Group Work Practice," *Social Work*, 8:39–46 (October 1963); "Neighborhood Centers," in Henry S. Mass (ed.), *Five Fields of Social Service: Reviews of Research* (New York: NASW, 1966), pp. 144–84; "Neighborhood Centers and Group Work," in Henry S. Mass (ed.), *Research in the Social Services: A Five-Year Review* (New York: NASW, 1971), pp. 130–91.

ing steadily to social work—and group work—theory, but always somehow in contradiction to the accepted positivist gestalt and never put together in a coherent and consistent pattern of ideas that would help us build a reciprocal model of the worker and his clients in action. What was actually called for was a kind of "relativity theory" of human relations, along the lines of the uncertainty physics of Bohr and Heisenberg, and in the sense that Polanyi meant it as he discussed the discovery of relativity. "When Einstein discovered rationality in nature," he wrote, "unaided by any observation that had not been available for at least fifty years before, our positivistic textbooks promptly covered up the scandal by an appropriately embellished account of his discovery." Polanyi then continued:

> There is an aspect of this story that is even more curious. For the programme which Einstein carried out was largely prefigured by the very positivist conception of science which his own achievement so flagrantly refuted. It was formulated explicitly by Ernst Mach, who . . . had extensively criticized Newton's definition of space and absolute rest on the grounds that it said nothing that could be tested by experience. He condemned this as dogmatic, since it went beyond experience, and as *meaningless,* since it pointed to nothing that could conceivably be tested by experience. Mach urged that Newtonian dynamics should be reformulated so as to avoid referring to any movement of bodies except as the relative motion of bodies with respect to each other, and Einstein acknowledged the 'profound influence' which Mach's book exercised on him as a boy and subsequently on his discovery of relativity.[34]

TOWARD A THEORY OF PRACTICE

Polanyi's admonition "to avoid referring to any movement of bodies except as the relative motion of bodies with respect to each other," is apt for social work as well. The model of the open, organismic system offers us the opportunity to put together all the dimensions we need into an image of the helping relationship in action. The systems idea is far-reaching, ranging across the whole scientific spectrum; Bertalanffy called it "a new world view of considerable impact." [35] But we do not need the whole technology for our purposes. What we do need are certain basic features to which the model calls attention: bodies in motion within a limited space, the inter-

---

[34] Michael Polanyi, *Personal Knowledge: Towards a Post-Critical Philosophy* (New York: Harper & Row, Torchbooks, 1964), p. 11. (Emphasis in original.)

[35] Ludwig von Bertalanffy, *General System Theory: Foundations, Development, Applications* (New York: Braziller, 1968), p. vii.

dependence of parts, the division of labor and the interplay of functions, the specificity of purpose, and the permeability of boundaries between the organism and its environment.[36]

The systems terminology is growing in popularity, precisely because it promises to meet the need for an active and reciprocal view so sorely missed in our traditional descriptions of the helping process. But too often it is only the words that are used, rather than the total gestalt; the latter would require a surrender of the old paradigm, rather than simply garnishing it with up-to-date terms. The models are in fact irreconcilable: either the ducks become rabbits or they remain ducks. The effort to have it both ways produces strange effects, as when the worker is said to intervene in the client-worker system. The idea of intervening in a system of which one is an integral part violates the whole model and obscures the tasks it sets before us.

In social work these tasks are as relevant to the worker-individual relationship as they are to the worker-in-the-group. The tasks begin with the search for a function for which the professional should be held accountable, whatever the relational system in which he operates. The statement of function must be phrased in active terms, describing what social workers *do,* showing how these acts affect, and are affected by, the acts of others within the system in which they meet. Further, the description must make it clear that the worker operates within an immediate sphere of influence, touching directly only those with whom he interacts, within the limits of his specific function within the system.

By the function of the profession is meant not its hopes and visions of the outcome, but its specific part in the division of labor, both in the larger social system from which it takes its assignment and in the smaller subsystems in which its practitioners work—the one-to-one, the family, the com-

---

[36] Definitions vary in complexity, but these are the most concise: "A system is a set of objects together with relationships between the objects and between their attributes." "The analytic model of system demands that we treat the phenomena and the concepts for organizing the phenomena as if there existed organization, interaction, interdependency, and integration of parts and elements." And "system is typically understood as a whole made up of interdependent and interacting parts." A. D. Hall and R. E. Fagen, "Definition of System," in Walter Buckley (ed.), *Modern Systems Research for the Behavioral Scientist: A Sourcebook* (Chicago: Aldine, 1968) p. 81; Robert Chin, "The Utility of System Models and Developmental Models for Practitioners," in Warren G. Bennis, Kenneth D. Beene, and Robert Chin (eds.), *The Planning of Change: Readings in the Applied Behavioral Sciences* (New York: Holt, Rinehart, and Winston, 1962), p. 203; Irma Stein, *Systems Theory, Science, and Social Work* (Metuchen, N. J.: Scarecrow Press, 1974), p. 3.

mittee, the peer group, and others. In each of these, the worker's acts are adaptations of his general function, showing his part in the division of labor: how he translates his knowledge and purpose into skill.

Practice theory—what Loeb called a "professional science" [37]—leans heavily on both knowledge and philosophy, but it cannot end there. For a theory of practice is a theory of action, and action is not deducible from either knowledge or intention working alone. If we knew everything there is to know, we would still have to decide what to do; and if our purposes were impeccable, the action based on them would still not be self-evident. Each of these areas influence and limit each other in every specific situation: given the appropriate evidence, and given a set of valued outcomes, the principles of action provide the implementing force. Throughout any practice theory we might build, every step must show how we bring together science, policy, and action within a total scheme. [38]

A CONCEPT OF FUNCTION

The effort to find a general function for social work in our society is complicated by the very wide range of jobs and settings in which it has worked over the past hundred years—from rent-collecting to psychotherapy, recreation leadership to social action, family counseling, neighborhood organization, athletic coaching, child placement, and other functions, performed in settlement houses, family agencies, sectarian community centers, camps, playgrounds, hospitals, children's institutions, industry, and many other auspices. The common themes have not been easy to uncover. But there is one that has asserted itself continuously over the years: the preoccupation with the "social" begins with the name of the occupation itself and repeats itself in its attention to the psychosocial, social relationships, social functioning, social action, and the like. Still, as they stand, such terms are inchoate, expressing more a concern and an aspiration than an active function for the profession. To do that, there must be some description of the forces into which social workers wish to move, and how they plan to affect such forces. To say that we are concerned with the social is almost tautological, since it

[37] Martin B. Loeb, "The Backdrop for Social Research: Theory-Making and Model-Building," in Leonard S. Kogan (ed.), *Social Science Theory and Social Work Research* (New York: NASW, 1960), p. 11.

[38] For further discussion, see William Schwartz, "Toward a Strategy of Group Work Practice," *Social Service Review,* vol. 36 (September 1962).

is hardly possible for any profession to exist without some sense of urgency about the conditions in which it works. As Pray noted:

> The word "social" has none of the precision of such words as "medical" or "legal". . . . It is obviously not enough to say that social work treats "social" problems. For virtually every life problem of every individual in this modern world is, in reality, a "social" problem in one sense or another.[39]

The tendency to see the social merely as the situation, and to demand simply that "it" be taken into account, fails to find the specific processes we want to address. Historically, it has set the scene for the ancient quarrel between those who would—as if they could—choose one or the other, the individual or society, therapy or social planning.[40] And those who have urged that we do both, or assign primary and secondary emphases to one or the other, have helped to maintain the dualism and failed equally to find what Jessie Taft called the "living relationship" between individual needs and their collective, institutionalized forms.

The author's reading of history suggests that social work's function in the society we know has been most powerfully expressed when it directs itself not to the individual *or* the social but to the relationship between the two. Social workers seem clearest about what they are doing when they are addressing themselves to the energies that flow in both directions between people and their institutions—to the reaching and pressuring and straining that goes on between them as both strive to carry out their sense of need and purpose. The relationship between people and their environment begins as a symbiotic one, with each needing the other for its own life and growth, and each reaching out to the other with all the strength it can command at a given moment.[41] In any complex system, however, and particularly one in which great power exists and is unequally distributed, a force is needed to guard the symbiotic strivings and keep the interaction alive when each party is tempted to dismiss the other as unreachable. But whether the relationship is harmonious or conflicted, the function of social work is to mediate the

[39] Kenneth L. M. Pray, "When is Community Organization Social Work Practice?" in Pray, *Social Work in a Revolutionary Age and Other Papers* (Philadelphia: University of Pennsylvania Press, 1949), p. 275).

[40] For further discussion of this issue, see William Schwartz, "Private Troubles and Public Issues: One Social Work Job or Two?" *Social Welfare Forum, 1969* (New York: Columbia University Press, 1969).

[41] For further discussion, see William Schwartz, "The Social Worker in the Group," *Social Welfare Forum, 1961* (New York: Columbia University Press, 1961).

transactions between people and the various systems through which they carry on their relationships with society—the family, the peer group, the social agency, the neighborhood, the school, the job, and others. The mediating skills are designed to create not harmony but interaction, based on a sense of strength, feeling, and purpose, drawing on the often all-but-forgotten stake of people in their own institutions, and of the institutions in the people they are meant to serve. The worker's job analysis, in any specific system in which he and client find themselves, can thus be expressed as follows:

> If each service system is . . . regarded as a special case, or small version, of the individual-social relationship, the social worker's skills are fashioned by two interrelated responsibilities: he must help each individual client negotiate the system immediately crucial to his problems; and he must help the system reach out to incorporate the client, deliver its service, and thus carry out its function in the community.[42]

The relationship of forces is presented diagrammatically below. This model may be used at two different levels of abstraction: on the one hand, it shows the general function of social work in society; on the other, it depicts the specific relationships at work in any given situation.

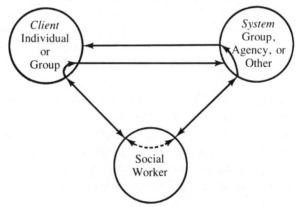

This arrangement shows the impetus of the client (individual or group) toward its system, and the system (group, or agency, or family, or school, or other) toward its member or client. It also shows the lines along which the social worker uses his skills to encourage the approaches of each toward

---

[42] Schwartz, "Social Group Work," p. 1258.

each. These approaches may involve conflict, cooperation, confrontation, negotiation, or any other form of exchange emerging from the realities of the situation. Again, the demand is not for conciliation, but for a realistic exchange, based on the actual business between them.

THE WORKER AND THE GROUP

When we consider this arrangement as a picture of the social worker in the client group, we have the characteristic two-client responsibility well known to group workers. In part of his work, he addresses himself to each member—in the member's part-whole relationship to the group which he needs to negotiate. In the other aspect, his client is the collective itself, the group-as-a-whole, as it moves to negotiate the larger systems of which it is a part—the agency, the neighborhood, the peer-group culture, and others. As the worker moves into this small-group system, he finds himself in *a collection of people who need each other to work on certain common tasks, in an agency that is hospitable to those tasks.* The group is a project in mutual aid, focussed on certain specific problems, and set within a larger system— the agency—whose function it is to provide help with just such problems. It is an alliance of moving, interdependent beings, each pursuing his own purposes together with others similarly engaged.

The worker is one of those moving parts, and his professional function is conceived in action terms, which are then elaborated in the specific acts and skills designed to carry it out. The worker's movements must reflect the movements of the others, as he acts to help others act. His moves are directed toward specific purposes, limited in scope and time, and touching only those within his immediate reach.

The definition of group as presented above is specific enough, and yet broad enough, to include any of the client groupings in which social workers are apt to function. It has four major features: the group is a *collective,* in which people face and interact with each other; the people *need each other* for certain specific purposes; they come together to *work on common tasks;* and the work is embedded in a relevant *agency function.* The designation is *specific* in that it demands an identifiable group purpose, and is stated not in vague, aspirational form but in active, understandable tasks. And it is *broad* in that it makes few requirements other than that the people need each other and can work together, with help, on tasks they accept and understand.

In this sense, the formulation is not limited by whether the group is natural or formed, therapeutic or task-oriented, open or closed, voluntary or captive, time-limited or extended, age-or-sex homogeneous or heterogeneous, or other quite legitimate small-group distinctions that will of course affect the nature of the group processes, but will leave intact the model diagrammed above and the professional function illustrated there. The requirements are simply that people can give and take from each other however slight their capabilities, that the agency and the worker have some stake, however slight, in allowing the freedom to work, and that there is some real reason for the people to be together.

The professional acts that are fashioned by this arrangement of separate and interdependent forces, each pursuing its own function and purpose, can be described most clearly with reference to the time in which they occur. The sequence of acts divides itself naturally into four phases, extending from the worker's preparation for entry, to his beginnings in the group, to the actual work on the tasks that brought them together, to the processes of ending and separation. These phases can be viewed both as they cover the entire life of the group and the events of a single meeting: from either perspective there is a preparation, a beginning, a period of work, and an ending that is either permanent or transitional to the next encounter.

THE PHASES OF WORK

There is space here only to develop a general strategy for each phase of work, with just enough specificity to demonstrate the mode of analysis. In response to the aforementioned need to bring together the elements of science, policy, and action, each phase must address three major questions. First, what *assumptions* can we make about the laws of nature appropriate to the tasks of the worker in this phase? Some of these assumptions may have been tested, some not, but in either event the judgments are operative and need to be brought into the open in a form that is clear and arguable. Second, what are the immediate *valued outcomes* that need to be brought about? The key here is immediacy: the worker's expectations are focussed on next steps rather than long-range goals that are only abstractly related to the work at hand. And third, given these assumptions and these immediate expectations, what are the *implementing acts* which the worker may bring to bear?

THE "TUNING-IN"

As the worker prepares himself to enter (or reenter) the group, he must understand that the life-processes with which he is about to join forces began long before he came, will continue after he leaves, and will, even during his tenure, be subject to many influences other than his own. The worker is about to move toward processes already in motion, establish his function quickly, do his job, and leave. These preparations, which he will go through each time he readies himself for a new beginning, are based on a number of assumptions about human behavior. He knows, for example, that there is a continuity in human experience, which means that people's expectations in new situations will be built on their memories of old ones. Thus he knows, too, that people will tend to respond, in these new situations, as they think others expect them to respond. Further, he suspects that beginnings tend to stir up feelings of self-doubt and hesitancy about one's competence to play the new game. With regard to the worker's own reception, he may assume that a new authority will engender both a fear of new demands and a heightened initial dependency, with expectations of reward and love. And he expects that these cues and others will be communicated in a kind of code; that his clients will convey directly, to him and to each other, only a small part of how they feel.

There are, of course, many other assumptions relevant to this phase of work, governing the members' ambivalence about work itself, the group climate in the opening stages, the members' demands on each other, and more. What is important is not that the worker build a ready-made inventory of all the possible hypotheses, but that he identify as many as will help him sensitize himself to the possibilities inherent in the forthcoming encounter.

The valued outcomes of this opening phase consist in the worker's ability to "tune" himself to the coded messages and disguised meanings through which the members will be communicating their messages as they begin the work together. His is a kind of preliminary empathy, as illustrated by the young worker who had tuned herself so keenly to the feelings of old people in a home that when they commented on how young and pretty she was, she smiled and replied: "I know, but I'll do the best I can." In such an exercise, the worker is less interested in drawing pictures of the outcomes (goals) and analyzing the structures of each client (diagnoses) than in visualizing the terms of the future encounter—the actions and reactions through which he and the members will deal with each other in the opening stages of the experience. He does not ignore prior knowledge of the class of clients or the specific personalities, but operationalizes this knowledge by anticipating the possibilities and rehearsing his expectations. He wants to bring himself to understand how they may perceive him, how his own sensations will connect with theirs, and how he may decode their meanings from the symbols they use.

The skills of the tuning-in phase are largely empathic, invoking demands similar to those made on the actor, who must generate from his own imagination the feeling and color of another's experience, particularly when the one is as yet unknown to him. It is something like the Stanislavskian effort to help actors create a new experience by using both their knowledge and their feelings, their observations and their instincts. The worker's exercise in preliminary empathy demands a similar ability to connect his thoughts and his emotions as he readies himself for his opening moves with the clients. In addition, he needs skill in both generalizing and partializing the data at his command—both organizing the bits of information into a pattern of expectations and breaking down his general knowledge into smaller propositions that are relevant both to the class of clients he is to meet (the aged, or foster children, or parents of the handicapped) and to the particular members (*these* aged, *these* children) whose folders he has before him. The process of generalizing must make the worker *more* receptive, rather than, by stereotyping ("poor people don't verbalize," "deaf children can't conceptualize"), less so. Thus, it is important that the worker's heightened attention to certain expected cues not serve to cut out his peripheral vision for those he does not anticipate. And finally, the tuning-in skills are strategic in nature, involving his plans for bringing clients and agency together in the work that lies before them. Using his knowledge of both the client stake and the agency interest, he prepares to ask both members and agency representatives to enter into open, unjargonized recognition of what the work will be about.

THE BEGINNINGS

The second phase is that in which the worker moves into the group and asks both members and agency to make their beginnings under clear conditions of work. In the group he asks for an explicit understanding of what they are there for; and in the agency he verifies the nature of the service and the contract that exists between the agency and the group. To the worker, this relationship between these clients and this agency is a special case of the processes through which people and their society reach out to each other, and the terms of this particular engagement will first show themselves in the opening stages of their relationship.

The heart of these beginnings is the contracting process, and several assumptions underlie the work. First, the new relationship will engender certain demands and expectations of each upon the other, and these demands will create certain behaviors and forces at work, whether or not they are verbalized, or even recognized, by clients and agency. Second, these demands and expectations are further complicated by the small group itself, where there is a complex interaction of individual stakes, where there is a shifting consensus of how these should be expressed, and where the new client—the group itself—is put into interaction with the agency. Third, and for reasons not well understood, any direct statement of what these demands and expectations are is experienced by both sides as embarrassing and taboo. In fact, the theoretical importance of the contracting process lies precisely in the fact that direct statements of mutual expectation are perceived as rude and impolite, that consequently the client-agency engagement is often replete with hidden agendas, and that a force is needed that is uninhibited by such taboos. Fourth, the taboo about explicit purposes creates an ambiguous framework within which it is difficult for the clients to choose their responses. Fifth, the vagueness also tends to create a prolonged period of testing during which the members make covert attempts to discover the nature of the enterprise, the rules of the game, and what the worker represents. Building from one consequence to the next, a sixth assumption would be that the ambiguity and the testing creates a greater fear of the power of the agency and the worker's power, under cover of clarity, to invade their lives without restriction. Contrariwise, a further assumption is that a clear consensus on group purpose limits the claims of each upon the other—client on service, service on client, and even client on client. There are a number of other propositions dealing with the more general problem of beginnings—on the effects of new situations, on the interactions they foster, on the fear of being tested in unfamiliar situations, on the hopes engendered, and more. In addition, further hypotheses are needed to explicate the ways in which each meeting of the group constitutes an entity with its own beginning, middle, and end.

Moving to the valued outcomes, what the worker wants to help bring about in this phase is an opening consensus: from the members, on what they need, and from the agency representatives, on what they offer. The worker also wants a partialization of tasks, beginning to break down the work before them into some of the specific jobs of which it is composed.

And he seeks to help establish some of the ground rules and procedures designed to move them as quickly as possible to a collaborative and independent style of problem-solving.

The skills of the beginning phase begin with the worker's ability to feel his way so deeply into both the client need and the agency service that he can make a simple statement of their connections. If there is a viable relationship—not necessarily harmonious—between the agency and its clients, and a real service and an urgent need, then an agent is needed who will understand both the service and the need and accept both stakes without reservation or embarrassment. If there is not such a relationship, the contracting process is defeated from the outset, and the defeat lies hidden behind jargon and obscure agendas that none is brave enough to pierce. The worker's skills also extend to his ability to reach for feedback and encourage specifics, refusing to allow comfortable but fuzzy formulations to rest undisturbed. He must also learn to make the "demand for work" with which he challenges the members to move through their timidity to the words and feelings they need to express in order to own their problems and aspirations without coloring them in euphemisms. In this stage, the worker prepares himself to monitor the terms of the contract; later, he may have occasion to ask both group and agency to renegotiate as they pass through the various stages of the work.

THE TASKS

The tasks of the middle phase have been elaborated elsewhere in some detail.[43] Briefly, there is the search for common ground between the needs of clients and those of the systems they have to negotiate. There is the process of detecting and challenging the obstacles that come between the members and their systems. There is the worker's responsibility for contributing ideas, facts, and values, as he feels these data may be useful to the members in the course of the work. Further, the worker needs to share his own vision of the work, his feelings about the process, and his faith in the clients' strengths. Finally, he must help to define the limits and requirements of the situation in which the work takes place. Each of these tasks requires its own framework of professional assumptions, valued outcomes, and strategies for action. For example, the worker's search for common ground proceeds

---

[43] Schwartz, "Social Worker in the Group," pp. 156–70.

partly from the assumption that an individual's major access to new ideas lies in his sense of their usefulness to him, and in his consequent ability to invest feeling in the job of making them his. Similarly, with respect to the common-ground task, the worker will have in mind the valued outcome of having the client examine his self-interest, situation by situation, in very specific terms. And, with regard to his strategy, he will be reaching repeatedly for feelings of self-interest that are buried under considerations of politeness, self-denial, and the desire to cooperate with one's oppressor.

In this fashion, each of the major tasks of the worker in this phase is powered by specific assumptions, valued outcomes, and actions:

> . . . all call for explicit variations on the symbiotic theme; each demands specific hypotheses on the nature of self-interest, the relationship between people and their systems, the group processes through which pooled self-interest yields a social product, how both individuals and systems strive simultaneously for equilibrium and change, the role of the mediating authority, and others. The immediate outcomes, throughout, are envisaged by the worker as the investment of affect, the engagement of energies, the expression of conflict, and the translation of feelings and ideas into work. And the professional skills involve the ability to decode messages, to reach for ambiguities, to probe for negatives, to show love and energy in the work, to partialize tasks, to point up the connections between fragments of experience, to find and mobilize resources, and, throughout, to make the "demand for work" inherent in the contract and in his helping function.[44]

TRANSITIONS AND ENDINGS

In the final phase of work, the essential task is to make a transition from one stage of experience to the next. In both the temporary endings that mark the passage from one meeting to the next and the final separation that brings the entire experience to a close, there are a number of problems concerning the uses of time, the way energy is distributed in beginnings, middles, and endings, and the relationship between the opening and closing phases of group experience. There has been little experimental work on the subject of time and the group experience; the most valuable studies have been philosophical and poetic. However, we might hazard a few assumptions based on experience with groups.[45] For example, group records indicate that, as part

[44] Schwartz, "Social Group Work," pp. 1260–61.

[45] For an excellent description of developmental stages in groups, based on analysis of agency records, see James A. Garland, Hubert E. Jones, and Ralph L. Kolodny, "A Model of Stages of Development in Social Work Groups," in Saul Bernstein (ed.), *Explorations in Group Work* (Boston: Boston University School of Social Work, 1968), pp. 12–53.

of an ebb and flow of productive work, there tends to be a rush of energy toward the closing moments of the group meeting. This phenomenon can be called "doorknob therapy," in which the members seem to save their most important disclosures for the time when they are on their way out of the door. Subsequent attempts by the worker to tack these subjects onto the following meeting fail almost invariably, revealing another interesting fact about group experience—namely, that the meeting does not end when it is over, but moves, via the informal system, into an interim phase of communication in which the difference is that the worker is not present. This is another way of saying that the life of a group does not proceed in quantum jumps, but in a continuous and unbroken process, with the meetings constituting a special—but not an isolated—event in that process. Thus, in a group that meets weekly for ten weeks, there is a considerable difference in whether the life of the group is regarded as ten meetings or ten weeks.

The permanent ending that brings the group life to a close seems to go through a number of stages, protracted or brief depending on the variables of *authority* (their use of the worker) and *intimacy* (their use of each other). There is an evasive period, in which the prospect of ending is ignored and denied. There is a sullen, angry stage, in which the worker finds himself back in the beginning aspects of the relationship, resisted and suspected. There is a period of mourning, in which the members are close to their complex feelings about the worker and the others in the group, and are capable of intensive work on the meaning to them of the experience. Finally, if there is time and skill in dealing with the mourning period, there is a kind of graduation effect—the future is regarded with optimism, there is a tendency to reject the worker, and there is considerable rehearsing for new stages of experience. The resistance to endings seems to be marked by a general reluctance to tear down a social structure built with such difficulty, and to give up intimacies so hard to achieve. Members may also experience a sense of guilt that is based on feelings that they could have played their roles more adequately. There are strong feelings, often, that members could be better members if they had the chance to do it again. There may, in fact, be a kind of inverse logic in the relationship between group members' satisfaction with the experience and the emotional intensity of the closing phase: successful groups seem to end more easily and go through their ending stages more quickly than those whose experience has been more frustrating, with the latter generating more dependency and pain in the separation process.

The valued outcomes in this final phase include the following: that the members make the ending a serious part of their work together, attentive to what is happening to them and learning from it as they have from the events of the work phase; and that the endings-work be regarded as part of the contract, rather than a kind of farewell party in which the worker is eulogized, the negatives obliterated, and the experience suffused in a rosy glow. Another way of putting this is that the ending should have substance as well as feeling: where the content is stressed and the feeling repressed, there is apt to be a kind of mechanical recital of what the members "learned in school"; and where the reverse is true, there is an orgy of expressiveness, equally evasive of the total reality. The valued outcome is that the ending be not a moratorium of the work but a significant episode in it. In considering the transitional endings, the worker wants the members to respect the interim events in the life of the group, valuing the informal system and accepting its workings as legitimate. He wants them to weave these between-meeting themes into the continuity of the group meetings themselves, bringing in as many of the negatives, the afterthoughts, and the rethinking as they can muster for his notice. While he does not try to eliminate the private, informal system of the members—for that would be neither possible nor desirable—he wants to include their productions in the official working system. The wider the gap between the meeting-work and the interim developments, the more mechanical and ritualistic grows the work for which they have gathered as a group.

Moving to the action implications—but staying with the temporary endings—the worker credits the informal system, accepting its existence and legitimizing it with his own interest and curiosity. He reaches for this material, leaving room for it at the beginning of meetings and urging its relevance. In effect, the worker's activity in this regard constitutes an extension of the *demand for work* to the entire time period of the group's existence rather than merely to the meetings themselves. The worker also monitors time, developing a sense of the rhythm of the meeting and the transitions from the opening stage, to the body of the work, to the closing moments which carry with them a sense of achievement or self-doubt, vagueness or clarity, hope, frustration, and other feelings affecting the outlook for the next meeting.

In the permanent endings, the monitoring of time safeguards the amount needed to allow the group to pass without haste through the various stages in which they come to grips with one aspect of the problem at a time. The worker calls attention to the imminence of the ending, and watches for and reaches for the cues that emerge in devious forms from stage to stage. Here again the demand for work is made in specific terms: the worker asks the members to recollect their time together, to review both positive and negative experiences, to deal with their present feelings about him and about each other, and to think about next steps. And again, the confrontation of feelings is not undertaken simply because the feelings are there, but because their work at this phase is as much a part of their contracted tasks as all the rest. Also, and for the same reason, the demand upon the worker is that he involve himself closely in the separation experience, sharing his own feelings even as he retains his function as the authority within the system.

GENERIC LINKAGES

Given what has gone before, it is hardly necessary to dwell on the helping process as a pattern of activity that retains most of its salient characteristics regardless of the number of people within the system. The worker's sensitivity to cues, his ability to read human behavior, the generalization and partialization of tasks, the reaching for feelings that lurk beneath those which are expressed, the integration of feeling and substance in the work, the uses of authority, the demand for work, the contracting and the separating—all of these acts are as relevant to the worker in the one-to-one interview as they are to the worker in the group.[46] Certainly differences do occur when the group element, the dimension of mutual aid, is introduced. As the intimacy theme appears alongside the theme of authority around which the casework process is built, the worker finds himself in a situation where there is not just one helping relationship but a multiplicity of them; and this calls for some new knowledge and some new skills. The worker is now put to the additional task of helping people not only to help themselves but to help each other as well. There are also certain strains attached to the distribution of authority, the de-monopolizing of professional control, and the new skills needed in fostering group interaction and decision-making. But the knowledge of human behavior, the aspirations for client autonomy, and the communications arts indicated above all remain the same and are familiar to the

---

[46] For further discussion of the use of groups by caseworkers, see William Schwartz, "Discussion of 'The Group Method with Clients, Foster, Families, and Adoptive Families' ", *Child Welfare,* 45:571–75 (December 1966).

caseworker in another context. The historic reasons for the original tripartite arrangement of casework, group work, and community organization are interesting to pursue,[47] but it has certainly lost whatever functional validity it may once have had.

As to any criteria which may exist for a differential assignment of clients to either group or individual help, there is little evidence that such criteria actually have been formulated. Further, it is questionable whether they are needed. It is this author's impression that all people—"sick" or "well," with severe problems or ordinary ones—need and use both the personal help of authority figures and the peer help of people in the same "boat," often at the same time. To suggest that social workers can decide which form is more appropriate is to defy the social processes through which people use others, and to try to mold their lives to the profession's ways of working, rather than the other way around. Group demands may be difficult for some clients, as those of the one-to-one relationship may be for others; but such difficulties are often productive, and not reason enough to substitute a professional prescription for an actual experience skillfully conducted.

SOME PROBLEMS

The symbiotic view of the client-agency relationship is a difficult one to grasp, in the face of considerable experience with the antagonisms between the two. That the tensions exist is beyond question; but the problem remains as to how to deal with them in the helping process. If the adversary relationship is accepted as normal, and seen only as a continuous running battle between the two, the social workers can only see themselves as collaborators in further separating the institutions from the people to whom they belong. The professional strategy that emerges from this view is a war strategy, and as in most wars, the intellectuals do the planning and the people do the suffering. If, on the other hand, the troubles between client and agency are seen as a relationship under stress, then a professional strategy can be developed to help both parties re-address the work they are meant to do together. In keeping both client and agency in the field, the client is helped to establish his claim, service by service, through the worker's knowledge and skill, the strength of the group, and, when necessary, confrontations with the agency.

[47] For some historical background on this development, see William Schwartz, "Group Work and the Social Scene," in Alfred J. Kahn (ed.), *Issues in American Social Work* (New York: Columbia University Press, 1959), pp. 110–37.

In all this, the theoretical problem is to develop a more dynamic view of agencies. This involves eschewing the devil theories, always a feature of war strategies, and finding the forces within agencies that need novelty and change as much as they do equilibrium and the status quo. Social workers have learned to do this with individuals, balancing the analysis of pathology with the search for ego strengths, and thus deepening their understanding of the forces that drive clients toward society as well as away from it. In the same manner, more work needs to be done on the symbiotic-mediating model so that it more clearly depicts the forces that drive agencies both toward and away from the people they are designed to serve. Here, systems theory and organizational theory can be most specifically useful in helping to identify the agency structures and processes to which the worker might best address himself as he carries out his mediating function.

The need for a more detailed exposition of the elements that keep client and agency together in a working relationship is but one of the problems of the triangular model showing the forces that keep client, agency, and worker operating in the same orbit. The others are located on the lines of energy running between worker and client and worker and agency. Here the model makes its case on its ability to call attention to the moves by which a professional is judged, translating the worker's states of knowing, being, believing, and aspiring into acts of skill. The difficulty lies in achieving more refined degrees of specificity without becoming trivial, prescriptive, or vague. By focusing on the worker's *function* within a system, a new realm of specificity is entered. When this function is partialized into its component *acts,* yet another step is taken. But a step remains: the move from *acts* to *skills* has yet to be made with confidence—from *what* the worker does to *how* he does it in its most economical and effective form. There is still a tendency to equate the what and the how, thus settling for an insufficient measure of operationalism.

Finally, more study is needed of the problems involved in analyzing the phases of work in the double perspective of both the single meeting and the life of the group. Using the time sequence is undoubtedly a productive way of identifying and ordering the worker's moves, for they are in fact located somewhere along a time continuum, and each measure of time reflects a different task. But the array of knowledge, outcomes, and skills in each phase has not yet been worked out in detail. In each phase, the skills must be seen in interaction with both client and agency people, and reflecting on both lines the same degree of sensitivity, awareness, and clarity of purpose.

The problems and questions that emerge from this model call for a research program, just beginning to emerge, that stresses analysis of processes rather than the study of outcomes and long-term effects. For until more is known about what goes on in the helping process, social workers will be unable to decide what "it" was that worked or did not. It is believed that the main progress for a time will be in studies of process and limited effects. In the course of learning to ask the right questions, the major devices will for a time remain descriptive, exploratory, and theory-developing, and the primary tools will be the group record, the life-history, the critical incident, and other techniques for codifying and conceptualizing the experience of practice.

BIBLIOGRAPHY

Bertanlanffy, Ludwig von. *General System Theory: Foundations, Development, Applications.* New York: Braziller, 1968.

Bronowski, J. *Science and Human Values.* New York: Harper & Row, Torchbooks, 1965.

Buber, Martin. *I and Thou,* 2d ed. New York: Scribner, 1958.

Buchler, Justus. *The Concept of Method.* New York: Columbia University Press, 1961.

Coyle, Grace L. *Group Experience and Democratic Values.* New York: Woman's Press, 1947.

Dewey, John. *Democracy and Education: An Introduction to the Philosophy of Education.* New York: Macmillan, 1916.

Kropotkin, P. *Mutual Aid, a Factor of Evolution.* New York: Knopf, 1925.

Kuhn, Thomas S. *The Structure of Scientific Revolutions.* Chicago: University of Chicago Press, 1962.

May, Rollo, Ernest Angel, and Henri F. Ellenberger (eds.). *Existence: A New Dimension in Psychiatry and Psychology.* New York: Basic Books, 1958.

McGrath, Joseph E. and Irwin Altman. *Small Group Research: A Synthesis and Critique of the Field.* New York: Holt, Rinehart, and Winston, 1966.

Reynolds, Bertha. *Learning and Teaching in the Practice of Social Work.* New York: Rinehart, 1942.

Robinson, Virginia. *Training for Skill in Social Work.* Philadelphia: University of Pennsylvania Press, 1942.

Schwartz, William and Serapio R. Zalba (eds.). *The Practice of Group Work.* New York: Columbia University Press, 1971.

7

A DEVELOPMENTAL THEORY

EMANUEL TROPP

The roots of this approach started with the contributions of Grace Coyle, from which this model derived its first principle, that group self-direction toward a common goal is the most effective group vehicle for the social growth of its members.[1] Wilson and Ryland extended and richly elaborated the productive uses of group autonomy and group decision-making.[2] Phillips added a considerable sharpening of focus on leader skill in relation to group purpose, a stress on the importance of the here-and-now, and a view of the main source of growth as residing within the member rather than the leader.[3] Schwartz probed more deeply into an analysis of group function and leader role, and developed the concepts of mutual aid and the contractual relation between leader and group.[4]

It always seems strange when people view this approach to group work as a "very special" one, because it is a direct descendant of a mainstream, for without the formulations described above, it would have been unthinkable to have developed these views *de novo*. This attribution of "special" qualities to this approach means either of two things: one, that the approach is increasingly *specific* in its methodology (which tends to make it special because it *is* specific or because it becomes easier to distinguish it from

[1] Grace Coyle, *Group Experience and Democratic Values* (New York: Women's Press, 1947).

[2] Gertrude Wilson and Gladys Ryland, *Social Group Work Practice* (Cambridge, Mass.: Houghton Mifflin, 1949).

[3] Helen U. Phillips, *Essentials of Social Group Work Skill.*

[4] William Schwartz, "The Social Worker in the Group," pp. 7–29.

others) or two, that it is most assuredly different from, and actually at odds with, the predominant forms of group psychotherapy which have attracted far more social workers (and they are—by sheer numbers—overwhelmingly caseworkers) than has group work, as so clearly noted by Barbara Solomon.[5] The various models of group psychotherapy are more likely to be associated with the concepts of invididual study, diagnosis, and treatment. Although some group work theorists are associated with these concepts, this writer has clearly separated his own thinking from those ideas, which seem to him to be special offshoots rather than within the mainstream of group work development.

This approach may also appear more specific because it is *not* eclectic. The purest form of eclecticism—the potpourri—appears to have the virtue of infinite tolerance and is hard to attack for having any posture at all. Few, if any, practice-oriented theorists in social work have not been affected by ideas from multiple sources. Even though the effects may have been felt well before the theories were publicly announced—or the social work theorists may not have paid their respects to each theory by its title—what school of thought has not been touched by role theory, communications theory, or systems theory?

What has been attempted, at every stage of formulation, is to develop a centrally organized, ordered, and internally coherent system of analysis and action. Such a system is obviously an easy target, but it is also subject to clear usage. Anything tangible can be both used and attacked. But pure eclecticism appears to be above criticism, until one realizes that it faces two options: to avoid any attempts at integrating all the diverse pieces, which then makes it dysfunctional as a coherent approach; or to integrate the pieces in some selective way within some unified system on a new level, at which moment it ceases to be eclectic and becomes a new formulation.

BASIC CHARACTERISTICS

The central features of this model are derived from many sources, but have been re-integrated into a coherent system, which is not closed but rather selectively open to any new ideas that can deepen its analysis and effectuate its operation. These characteristics can be described as follows:

[5] Barbara Bryant Solomon, "Social Group Work in the Adult Outpatient Clinic," *Social Work*, 13(4):55–61 (1968).

1. It starts from the proposition that people attain enhancement of their social functioning most effectively through *specific kinds* of group experiences.
2. The kinds of experiences that are most productive of this enhancement are seen as those in which the group has a *common goal*— that is, a goal which the members share for the group goal-achieving process and with each other in relation to it.[6]
3. The common goal may take the form of a common concern or common interest or common life situation, each of which results in a *peer relationship* among the members.
4. In order for the members to have maximum opportunity to achieve their individually needed gains, the effectiveness of the group goal-achieving process becomes the *primary target* for both the members and the leader.
5. Within the context of group goal-achieving, the members achieve *differential individual gains* in social growth and contribute to other members' gains to the extent and in the ways in which they engage themselves. The leader relates to all members as though he *expects* them to be able to engage. Thus, individual gains are *available* and can also be maximized by leader intervention.
6. The group becomes the medium for the members' actions, for their perception of each others' actions, and for the leader's perceptions of both—all of which create a base of *commonly perceived behavior,* to which members and leader can jointly relate their perceptions, evaluations, and actions. This behavior is dealt with on a conscious level.
7. All of this process is carried out on the basis of open agreements, openly arrived at and openly pursued, resulting in a *mutuality* of understanding and effort between members and leader.
8. The group is essentially *self-directing,* within varying limits, and each member is self-directing in relation to what he wants to give to and get from the group; there is no intention to change anyone, for it is seen as each member's right to decide how to lead his life and to then benefit or suffer from the consequences.
9. For the leader to conduct himself in this open manner, he must locate himself in a *humanistic* perspective, which is defined here simply as ''a view of one human being by another,'' though each

---

[6] See Emanuel Tropp, *A Humanistic Foundation for Group Work Practice,* pp. 7–28.

have different functions to perform and different resources to bring to bear.[7]

10. This approach is *phenomenological* in that its crucial focus is on what is happening currently, whether in the group or in the life situation outside the group, or both.

11. This approach is *developmental,* in that it sees people as being continually able to move forward in a lifelong process of self-realization, or fulfillment of potential in social functioning.[8] This is in sharp contrast with the treatment-of-illness orientation.

12. This approach regards the social system of a common goal group as a specialized (although very common) system of peer relations, which, in turn, requires a *specialized* body of knowledge, method, and skill to utilize as a mode of professional group work practice.[9]

All of the above characteristics lead to a two-part definition of this model, which aims (1) to help people in the enhancement of their social functioning through group experiences in which the members are involved in common engagement with common interests or concerns and (2) to help such groups to function effectively and responsibly in the fulfillment of those purposes.

KNOWLEDGE AND VALUES

Statements have already been made in such a way as to imply a view of human beings as being free, responsible, and capable of self-realization. These are conceptions commonly ascribed to those of the existential-humanistic persuasion, and they are often relegated by others to the category of glowing ideals without substance or proof or method. The issue boils down to the classical controversy generated by the philosophical school known as logical positivism, which claims that what cannot be quantitatively measured cannot be taken as a given. This school has been in the saddle in the behavioral sciences in this country for some time now, and it insists upon "empirical" proof, in quantitative terms. Therefore, it is necessary first to deal with the issue of empiricism directly in order to clarify why empirical evidence will *not* be offered as *thus* defined.

The concept of empiricism entered social work theory fairly recently, at least in the form of carefully designed research evidence as the basis for

[7] *Ibid.,* pp. 65–94   [8] *Ibid.,* pp. 31–45.   [9] *Ibid.,* pp. 47–56.

making valid statements. It is, of course, of much longer standing in the social sciences. Rather than delude the reader into expecting to find, further on, researched evidence for *anything* stated (let alone everything), let it be quickly said that there seems to be little, if any, such evidence on appropriately posed target problems, which would either support or contradict the position of this paper.

If, by empirical, we assume the basic meaning of "depending on experience and observation alone," then this is truly the way group work practice theory has evolved. If we include the criterion of being based upon rigorous research methods, then, as so many social work writers have noted, we are likely to have on our hands studies of inappropriate end-results of various social work methods. In a volume that evaluated thirteen studies of social work intervention, a sober view was taken of their unpromising results; but it was generally conceded that serious questions had to be raised about what was studied, with the only clear continuing thread of conviction among the various writers being generated by a comparative study by Reid and Shyne of two different approaches, which does not lead to any conclusion about effectiveness per se.[10]

If we mean by empirical, unquestionably sound and thorough research investigation of validly stated hypotheses, replicated sufficiently, and based upon a clearly framed theory and methodology, then we would be hard put to locate such findings. But social work is not the first discoverer of this difficulty. Others in the social sciences have been plowing that soil for a long time and many have reluctantly come to conclusions that lead this writer to be content (until contrary evidence develops) to rely on the simplest meaning of empirical—that is, depending on experience, or what social workers have usually called practice wisdom.

The need to organize this practice wisdom is enormous, but the possibilities of proving it may, at this time, be illusory. Therefore, the challenge to this paper is not perceived as scientific proof that something results from something else, but rather to organize a structure of concepts and principles that correlates values, knowledge, purposes, and methods in a systematic manner and that is derived from and leads to certain claimed results derived from experience, even though no adequate means has as yet been found to quantify what has resulted.

[10] Edward J. Mullen, James R. Dumpson et al., *Evaluation of Social Intervention* (San Francisco: Jossey-Bass, 1972).

In the absence of a more useful current equivalent, "empirical" will be used to refer to accumulated descriptions of the applications of the described methods and first-hand responses that are seen, heard, and felt by those who use this approach to social group work services, in such a way as to indicate what they attained with them. The claims that will be made in this model are in the nature of *available gains* for *any* member of a given group. Such gains are dependent on the methodology, the skill of the practitioner, and—as a concomitant of the stated value system—on the choices of each member as to how to use the group experience so that no results for a given individual can be either guaranteed or predicted. This is not an escape-hatch from responsibility, but a realistic recognition of the very ground rules of the social work profession, which respects the rights of individual self-direction and does not intend to remake people despite themselves.

Evidence of gains for members is constantly being received and replicated by professional observation, which indicates that a wide variety of people in a wide range of settings do use this kind of group experience to become more socially functional. The gains they receive vary not only with the skill of the professional but with what the members give to the group and what they use from it. These gains, however real or great they are, may still be limited in application as a result of external conditions that are beyond the control of the member in his private life. That is, while his gains may be quite clearly observable in the group and can be checked against a clear set of criteria for social growth, external limits may block their visibility outside the group. However, such a member may still be making substantial *internal* gains in knowing how, and having increased strength, to cope more effectively with these external limitations. These gains may not show up until much later on and in ways that we may not have begun to evaluate—or even consider worthy of evaluation.

An approach to a humanistic, developmental, phenomenological base for group work practice will be presented here, resting on the thesis of the validity of logical deductions from stated assumptions, values, purposes, and knowledge induced from practice. And this means the beginning of some ordered system of looking at human behavior in general and at group behavior in particular.

To return to the view of humans as being free, responsible, and capable of self-realization is to state three *assumptions,* which are not likely to be subject to proof or disproof. Behind these assumptions rests an important duo of values, which are recurrent themes in established positions taken by such leading social work spokesmen as Bartlett and Boehm [11]—namely, that people should be treated with respect for their dignity and for their capacity to fulfill their potentials, and that people should also be expected to be responsible in their relations with others in society. "Should" statements represent desirability or value and, as such, are beyond the domain of proof.

These two classical values of social work are in very close correlation with the assumptions of this model, for people cannot be expected to be responsible if they are not free to make choices, and they must be treated with respect for their dignity if they are to be granted the freedom to choose. In this perspective, to treat people as the objects of change-endeavors becomes tenable only when they have been classified as *not* responsible for their own behavior, which public law has established as the basic guideline for mental illness. [12]

For those who are either so distorted in their perceptions of reality or so withdrawn from reality that they cannot be asked to cope responsibly with that reality, becoming the objects of someone else's change-endeavors is a viable, and perhaps the only, alternative. But for all others—and they constitute the vast majority of those who use social services—*freedom must be respected* and *responsibility must be expected.* The vital end-product of this dual view is a mode of relation between practitioner and user of service identified as *mutuality,* which is defined here as open agreements, openly decided, and openly pursued in a joint effort, yet with differing roles. [13]

This view of human beings is sometimes challenged as being utopian, because of the internal and external forces impinging on each person. Viktor Frankl provides the clearest foundation for this composite value-assumption posture. [14] Writing from the experience likely to be the most extreme form of duress ever known to humans—the Nazi concentration camp—Frankl persuasively argues that choices still remained even there, if sometimes only in-

[11] Harriett M. Bartlett, "Toward Clarification and Improvement of Social Work Practice," *Social Work,* 3(2):6 (1958); and Werner W. Boehm, "The Nature of Social Work," *ibid.,* pp. 11–12.

[12] Emanuel Tropp, "Approaching the Concept of Change in Education for Social Work," *Journal of Education for Social Work,* 9(3):99–106 (1973).

[13] Emanuel Tropp, "Three Problematic Concepts: Client, Help, Worker," *Social Casework,* 55(1):19–29 (1974), and "Expectation, Performance, and Accountability," *Social Work,* 19(2):139–49 (1974).

[14] Viktor Frankl, *The Doctor and the Soul.*

ternal choices on what attitude to take in order to survive and transcend. He further notes how many determinisms have been offered to justify a person's lack of freedom to choose, such as economism, sociologism, or psychologism. And he convincingly makes out the case that, no matter what the limitation, there is always some room for choice—and so it is essentially a matter of degree.

The traditional argument against the belief in freedom of humans to decide for themselves has been that, when we know enough about causation of behavior, we will be able to explain all behaviors as being determined, thus converting the appearance of freedom into a mere illusion. It is time to place the shoe on the other foot: to state that the sense of choice that all people experience at just about every moment is a genuine experience and *to demand proof* that all choices *can* be explained as having been determined. Until such proof arrives, there is no reason not to go on believing in one's subjective experience.

Once it is recognized that such proof is really nonexistent, then Frankl's thesis that people need to be helped within the conscious aspects of their experiences and the volitional aspects within their control becomes a clear foundation for further development of principles in relation to the enhancement of social functioning. If something is not consciously perceived by a person or easily available to stimulated awareness, it is not a reality that this person can be asked to cope with; if it is beyond volitional control, he cannot be asked to be responsible for it.

But this does not mean that the areas subject to a person's control are narrowed down so severely as to become almost meaningless. We need only follow our own daily lives for any given day and check out the choices of action we could have made *at any moment,* in order to discover that what we actually did was one of several choices available at each moment. For example, one could decide not to go to work; the fact that this would create difficulties does not mean that it is not a viable choice, but simply that there are always consequences for various alternatives, and one must weigh them. The troublesome choice may create the need to make easier ones, but at other times we may prefer the trouble.

The choices with which social work is concerned have to do with social functioning. In the developmental perspective, people are not seen as being sick or healthy, but on a scale ranging from socially functional to dysfunctional to eufunctional. The major social situations that confront people in our society, and which also bring them to the social services, are: the family, school, work, play-and-friendship, and community. In each of these areas of social living, *socially functional behavior* can be defined as management of self in such a way as to cope with social relations or tasks. This management (or self-direction) and coping (or coming to grips with) may be assessed on the scale of functioning described above. People are seen as being continually able to move up this scale in a life-long developmental process of self-realization.

To strive for self-realization is to attempt to tap the vast unused potential that resides within all people and which is generally used only fractionally—in the spheres of physical, intellectual, aesthetic, and interpersonal development, of which the last is the direct concern of social work.

Allport has been a source of great illumination for this model by providing a basis for the concept of the self.[15] From Szasz[16] there has been derived the concept of the social transaction, with its rules and roles, by which to function and evaluate. Szasz is also that great defender of the rights of people *against* the misdirected intentions of those who would "help" them by insisting that they become something else and he is that everlasting challenger (to those whom he defends), encouraging them to take their lives in their own hands and to refuse to lean upon others' explanations of their behavior as a basis for avoiding their responsibilities.

Parsons[17] provided the major constructs for the analysis of groups. With the plethora of groupings that exist in society, some means must be found to develop a scanning device to determine the typologies and characteristics of each. Building on the structural-functional analysis of social systems by Parsons, this writer developed a three-way analysis for determining the basic nature of any group; the *purpose,* or why the group was formed; the *function,* or what it was established to do in order to carry out its purpose; and the *structure,* or how it will arrange power to get these things done.

TARGET POPULATIONS AND ORGANIZATIONAL AUSPICES

This approach has been organized, taught on the graduate level, and repeatedly evaluated in use with a cross-section of social service auspices, through

[15] Gordon W. Allport, *Becoming,* pp. 41–51.

[16] Thomas S. Szasz, *The Myth of Mental Illness.*

[17] Talcott Parsons, *The Structure of Social Action;* also Talcott Parsons and Edward A. Shils (eds.), *Toward a General Theory of Action* (Cambridge: Harvard University Press, 1954).

student field experience, and the work experience of graduates, and has been found applicable for an across-the-board usage, with minor adaptations under limited circumstances. The one issue of any substantial importance created by organizational auspices has been related to the matter of nonvoluntary membership in the organization and/or group.

There are two major settings which create an *involuntary* situation: corrections and public welfare. Although people may apply voluntarily for public assistance, they cannot be legally required to attend any kind of group "rehabilitation" sessions as a condition of their continued eligibility. However, when they are invited to belong to a counseling group and agree to join it, then there is usually a suspicion in their minds of a presumed hidden agenda on the part of the agency—that is, that the purpose of the group may be to "get them off welfare" by some unknown means. If the intent of such a group is indeed to effect the removal of members from the welfare rolls, then there is clearly an enforcement function here that represents a type of police function. It would not be consistent with this model to regard "involuntary rehabilitation" as a viable goal.

In corrections, whether in institutions or in probation and parole, there is an even clearer base of law enforcement and thus a more tangible police function. In both welfare and corrections, group work can be *offered* as a service. If the offer is accepted in good faith by the potential members, then a voluntary agreement can be reached as a basis for proceeding with the work of the group. Further, even in organizations that can legally require enrollment in such groups, it is still possible to get started at the first meeting by converting the requirement into an offer and then granting the right— after one or two trial sessions—to drop out of the group, in which case it once again becomes a voluntary agreement. Szasz has made out a compelling case when he says that, in the choice for confined offenders between therapy and justice (which he defines as fulfillment of a contract by such means as deprivation of liberty), "just actions afford more protection for the self-defined interests of others than do loving actions" and ". . . in the Therapeutic State, care, help and treatment are not what the involuntary 'patients' request but what the 'humanitarian' psychiatrists impose." [18] Whatever has been said, therefore, about corrections and public welfare, would apply to any other auspices that use involuntary means.

[18] Thomas S. Szasz, "Justice in the Therapeutic State," *Comprehensive Psychiatry,* 11(5):442–43 (1970).

Beyond these specific limitations are the limitations of age and capacity. Because self-direction is perceived as the major means for both group effectiveness and individual gain, it is necessary that the maximum feasible amount of self-direction be a feature of the group experience. There are limits to feasibility even in society at large, so that no group is ever without *any* constraints in its work. In social work, there are not only the usual legal or communal constraints applicable to all people but also the policies of the sponsoring agency.

Just as legal classifications of minor or incompetent status establish the conditions of limited or nonresponsibility for individual actions, group work has always recognized the need for a leader to take more responsibility in directing the group to the extent that the members are not capable. However, the intent of the leader would still be to enable the group to grow toward increasingly responsible decisions for its own life. It is a necessary condition of the criterion of self-direction that the group be *asked* to take some basic responsibility that is central to its purpose, such as deciding on *what to do* in activity or action groups or *what to discuss* in counseling groups, as well as *how* to go about it. While the practitioner may assume the role of direct leadership, this does not detract from the fact that the group is expected to make these key decisions and to take responsibility for fulfilling its commitment to those decisions. Thus, in this format of practitioner as direct leader, while the usual full democratic process of self-elected leaders is not operating, the already-defined condition of self-direction is clearly there. The role of the leader is one of literally empowering the group to take its own life in its hands in order to carry out its own formulated plans, even though he may need to make proposals to facilitate the process.

TYPES OF GROUPS SERVED

Peer groups. This is the single most important population criterion of this approach. However, since just about all kinds of groups *but one*—and that is the family group—can be considered peer groups, this is again not a very restrictive influence. If groups to be served are organized around a common concern, interest, or life situation, then any of these commonalities automatically becomes the criterion for establishing peer status. Patients on the same ward of a hospital are in a peer relationship which, at that moment, is of greatest consequence as the immediate life situation and tends to predominate over differences. A group that gathers to pursue a common interest—such as social activities—or a common concern—such as being parents of mentally retarded children—similarly creates a peer relationship among the members.

There are further refinements of peer status, such as age, sex, and ethnic background, which are sometimes given in terms of the available population to be served or sometimes structured in advance.

The only significant group in which the members do not have this distinctive peer quality is the family group. Although all the members may have an interest in or concern about common matters, they do not relate to these matters from *comparable* (that is, peer) vantage points. The roles, and consequent perspectives, of a father, a mother, an adolescent, and a young child are vastly different. Not only are there role differentiations in our society *between* the two parents, but they both have, as the societally and legally perceived function in the family unit, the responsibility for acculturating and providing care for their children. Thus, as Bach has observed, the family is "inherently hierarchically structured." [19] Erickson has noted that family group therapy is a modality that is neither the same as nor a derivative of casework. [20] This writer would add that the same statement can be made for its relation to group work. Family group counseling is built on the dynamics of a highly unique and specialized group system and requires a specialized knowledge base and methodology of its own.

Formed and natural groups. Groups that are natural (street gang), preexisting (patients on a ward), or formed (mental health center group) are *all* appropriate for this model.

Voluntary and nonvoluntary participation. The nature of an open agreement between members and leader at the very beginning, around the purpose, function, and structure of the group, implies the necessity for voluntary participation, because an individual who has not accepted a group placement need not feel any obligation to live up to the expectations built into membership status, nor can he be legitimately asked to do so. However, this cannot be simplistically defined only in terms of voluntary *affiliation*,

---

[19] George R. Bach, *Intensive Group Psychotherapy* (New York: Ronald Press, 1954), p. 326.

[20] Gerald Erickson, "Teaching Family Therapy," *Journal of Education for Social Work*, 9(3):11 (1973).

which, while desirable as an indicator of motivation, is not the only route to voluntary involvement. A *voluntarily joined* group represents a motivational thrust that becomes the most effective beginning base of operation, but there are other ways in which groups *become* voluntary after affiliation.

Even though the initiative for joining may have come from outside the member, it is the way in which any individual handles this offering that determines whether he can use the group experience. If the group is a required assignment, the experience will have little or no value unless the individual begins to voluntarily accept membership in it. Therefore, under such conditions, the leader's first task is to ask the members to accept the reality of the group, to see its potential values, and to give it a chance. A good deal can be accomplished at a first meeting to develop confidence in the group's value. This is done mainly by giving the group the right to select, from within the offered purpose and function, those areas it wishes to discuss or those activities or social actions it wishes to engage in, so that it feels it has control over the significant content of its experience. To be more specific, it must be made clear that any area of content will be pursued only with the group's consent.

Until voluntary acceptance becomes a reality for the group as a whole and for individual members, very little can be accomplished with the group or some members. Therefore, in working with a compulsory group, an option needs to be left open: to the effect that, after giving the experience a chance, any member who is still not committed to the group's purpose need no longer attend. If he is still required to attend regardless of his wishes, he is likely to seriously interfere with the sense of group vitality that is so necessary for its effectiveness. To insist upon continuing the requirement of physical presence beyond a reasonable trial period is to take on a police function and is contradictory to the value system of social work.

STRUCTURAL PROPERTIES

Power relations. The most important structural characteristic is the one that answers the question of where the power resides for making decisions. There are varying structural patterns of groups, but they tend to fall into a few simple categories. At one end is the pattern whereby all authority is vested in the leader, claimed as a fundamental premise by analytic group psychotherapy. At the other end of the spectrum is the self-governing group, including elected officers, or at the very least a chairman who conducts the meetings. In between, there is a widely used pattern in which there is no formal self-government and the practitioner serves as the group leader, but the group proceeds on the basis of *its* choices and agreements, made mutually with the leader. Such a group is self-directing within the limits of its function and is expected to take responsibility for its life as a group, with the leader serving as a facilitator of the processes needed to enable the group to achieve its purposes.

Those groups that have full authority vested in the practitioner do not have the group dynamic properties deemed to be most productive of social growth, although they may well be productive of other kinds of gains. On the other hand, groups that are given the opportunity to elect their own officers can be very socially productive, but they call for differential skills from the practitioner, who is not seen here as the leader but as the advisor, who will need to respect the role of elected chairman and work through that person. The pattern of electing officers has no realistic utility for a counseling group and is, in that instance, dysfunctional because the skills of the discussion leader require professional competence. For activity groups, the self-elected pattern of leadership is quite realistic and even desirable within the limits of ability to lead, based on age or capacity. In social action groups, this is clearly the pattern of choice, since experience has indicated that practitioner-led action groups too easily fall prey to manipulation by the professional toward *his* desired social changes and means to those ends. While groups can be led to follow in the belief that the choice is their own, this is not in the best interests of the members or of the community.

Open or closed sessions—and time limits. The admission of others into the group after the initial agreement is made makes it very difficult for later arrivals to feel party to the commitment. A working axiom might be that the shorter the group's lifespan, the less desirable it is to add new members after the first session.

In the extended-time group, where the probability of continuing indefinitely is very great, there are ways of partializing the process. In an activity group, a yearly rhythm of renewal, with a fresh start and a renegotiated agreement, is needed at the beginning of the program year. If the group is a social action group, it may be terminated by plan based on goal-attainment or nonattainment, or the group may decide to pursue another action with its own time limits. In the extended type of counseling group, the time pattern can be divided into manageable segments by reaching an agreement on what to accomplish, say, in eight sessions, with a new agreement for the next eight, in order to avoid a sense of endlessness which may create a feeling of futility.

PURPOSES

The concept of purpose is both the philosophical and methodological core of this model, from which everything else radiates. There is first the purpose of the profession, and it is stated most clearly in that simple phrase, "the enhancement of social functioning." Then there are the purposes of a given social service, and those of a larger organization that offers this service as one of many. It is here assumed that professional purposes are of the highest order of importance, and that a social worker would work for an organization only if there were concurrence between professional and organizational purposes. Further, a group work practitioner carries with him, as he approaches a group or prospective members, some workable composite of both of these purposes, now sharpened in its directions in accordance with the nature of the target population served by the agency and the type of service offered. In addition, each group leader needs to appraise this composite in relation to the particular group he is to face, and this becomes the most specific formulation of purpose, as viewed from the service-provider's perspective.

Then there is the composite of individual and group-as-a-whole understanding of purpose for that particular group. The first operational directive for the leader is to arrive at a reasonably clear understanding with the group about the purposes both are considering to undertake. A prior, indirect task is for the leader to prepare, in his own mind, some formulation of how he sees the composite purposes, how he believes the group may see them, and how he can best ask for and present these purposes for group consideration.

In order to have a firm basis for identifying organizational purposes, the practitioner must first have a screen of professional purposes that is broad enough to be adaptable to any auspices and any group within this purview, yet specific enough to provide clear guidelines for his own formulations. A three-dimensional set of criteria provide the end-purposes, the working purposes, and the evaluative guides for achievement of purposes.

END-PURPOSES

The three end-goals in the process of enhancing social functioning are: *effectiveness* in role performance, *responsibility* to others in that role, and *sat-*

isfaction of self in that role. The specific social roles under consideration determine the ways in which these ultimate purposes become more concretely explicated. In viewing any specific role performance, the implications of this screen are that people who are having some difficulty or seeking greater self-realization in that role are not viewed as abnormal or pathological. Rather, all are seen as people who face stressful developmental stages, life situations, challenges, and crises with which they must cope in some way.

WORKING PURPOSES

To realize these end-purposes, common-goal groups go through four basic purposive processes, which are the major dynamic elements in achieving the social growth of the members through the group experience.

1. *Release.* This is a release of those feelings—anger, fear, guilt, and affection—that tend to block effective social task performance if not openly expressed and unburdened, preferably in the presence of others who are in comparable situations and can thus appreciate and respond to these expressions.
2. *Support.* This is a receiving of acceptance and affection through belonging and a group recognition of self-expression that is thereby translated into achievement, which encourages the tapping of further strengths, with a resultant gain in self-esteem.
3. *Reality orientation.* Through seeing others in similar situations, seeing how they handle themselves, and seeing how others see oneself, each member can gain a clearer orientation to his own behavior among peers.
4. *Self-reappraisal.* This involves attaining from all of the above a clearer perspective on oneself and others, new options for handling situations, increased ability to make judgments, and a more responsible taking hold of one's own life in relation to the reasons for being in the group.

EVALUATIVE GUIDES FOR ACHIEVEMENT OF PURPOSES

To determine the degree of enhanced satisfaction of self, a combination of asking the member and perceiving his behavior will usually suffice. The determination of effectiveness and responsibility can be explored on two levels: behavior within the group (in the role of member) and outside the group (as the members discuss a common life situation). The criteria are the same but the means of evaluating them are quite different. The criteria for evaluation are seen as: (1) enhanced awareness of self and others; (2) enhanced ability to place value on self and others; and (3) enhanced ability to mobilize oneself, activate oneself, and interact with others.

These prospective gains, operational purpose, and criteria for evaluation, as specified for a given group, are seen as available to all members of the group. Although the practitioner can use his method in the most skillful manner, thereby insuring the greater likelihood that more members will utilize more of this availability, he cannot predict or guarantee how any given member will use it because of the unpredictable variables within a given person and the external limitations on that individual's personal life outside the group. However, *the greater the worker skill and the greater the group commitment and effectiveness in its work as a group, the more probable it is that more members will internalize significant gains—of varying kinds, in varying degrees, and with varying time delays in visibility.*

Since the group agreement in advance is that each member will decide for himself how to contribute and how to gain, only likelihoods or probabilities for the totality of the membership can be realistically considered linked to practitioner effectiveness. The gains are also seen as essentially similar in nature for all the members, with variants determined on the basis of individual performance in the group. Also, there is no presumption of the need for anyone to "change," since any member is respected in his right to choose to reaffirm his present means of coping, either as truly the most appropriate choice or the best he can do at this time. However, even reaffirmation can have its strengthening qualities after having been checked out against an intensive group experience, since it is now clearer and based on others' perceptions. If reaffirmation has any unhappy consequences, the member will need to deal with that result, either in anticipation or after the fact.

This three-stage perspective on purposes is, then, the totality of the purposes as they can be perceived and agreed upon in some specified form with a given group. This, in turn, converts it into the group's work and each member's work simultaneously, thus making it also the leader's work.

FUNCTION AND STRUCTURE

Having formulated purposes even at such length still leaves out two tremendously important parts of the agreement needed to be concluded with a group as a basis for beginning operation: namely, *function* and *structure*. Function and purpose are often used to mean the same thing, but they are clearly different in meaning. The purpose of a group is *why* the group has been organized—that is, the aims it intends to accomplish. The function of the group is *what* it will be doing in order to achieve its purpose. For example, any specific type of social service may have a clearly stated set of purposes but may have many different functions as vehicles to carry out those purposes.

The term purpose is used in this paper to refer to the ultimate or long-range purpose of a group, while the term goal is used to refer to a specific task agreed upon for a specific session, as one means of achieving that purpose. In this sense, "goal" bears more relation to function.

The three most common functional modes in group work practice are: the *activity* group, which is gathered to pursue a common interest; the *counseling* group, which is gathered to discuss common concerns or common life situations; and the *action* group, which is gathered to effect some improvement in its social environment. There are also possible composites of these types, though these are less frequent in practice. The action group might appear to resemble a grass-roots community organization group, but the essential distinction is that, to be considered a group work service, its central purpose would need to be the gains of the members as individuals, with the societal effects seen as instrumental means to those ends; the community organization group would have the priorities reversed—namely, that the societal gain would be central and the individual gains seen as the possible by-product.

It is, in fact, in the area of function that the group can be most substantially involved in determining its own course of action. While the leader, as a representative of an organization, offers a set of purposes for the consideration and approval or modification by the group, he operates in quite the opposite manner in relation to function—that is, he *needs to know* from the members what *they* would like to do or discuss. Even though he must come prepared for each session with his own proposals in this area—known as "program content"—to use as a stimulant or additive as needed, it is most appropriate and effective to elicit these proposals first from the members. In the process, he demonstrates that he not only wants to help them to work in areas of *their* greatest interest or concern but that he *expects* them to take increasing responsibility for determining program content within the realistic bounds of group and agency purposes and policies.

In regard to structure, the worker needs to make clear from the first what the organization's ground rules are for this kind of group. He must clarify what *power* the group has in order to determine the content of its sessions and what *role* he will play in facilitating that determination. It is very important that this structural component be clearly understood and agreed to from the start. In effect, purpose and structure are mainly agency "givens," while the specifics of a particular function (i.e., program content) is *always* the group's area of decision; and it is a vital one because it involves not only what to do but in what ways to go about it.

One closing commentary is needed here, and that relates to the options for group *and* leader under those conditions where the agency's policies *appear* to be in contradiction to the group's sense of purpose. If these policies are realistically tenable by professional standards but create dissatisfaction in the group then the role of the leader is to clearly represent the policies and explain their reasons to the group. But if the policies are *contrary to professional standards* then the leader either may need to intervene with the agency on behalf of the group for a change or reinterpretation of policy or to ask the group if it wishes to engage itself in this process, assuming it has the interest and the capacity.

ASSESSMENT AND SELECTION OF INDIVIDUALS AND GROUPS

This model is applicable to both the conditions whereby (1) an organization offers a particular group service or (2) a group already exists and requests services. The process of negotiation around the type of service is reasonably similar, with minor variants. In the case of the group-initiated request, the organization must determine whether it can offer the particular service requested and under the terms proposed; if a mutually agreeable composite can be worked out, then the group service is launched. In the case of the organization-initiated offer of service, there may be only one or a few types of group services suitable for the particular auspice. The offer having been made, it is then largely a matter of whether the prospective members are responsive to its terms, although some areas of negotiation are possible.

Before any offering is made, the target population needs to be identified and the special needs for and values of a group work service determined. Following this, there is a determination of the type of group most appropriate to meet these needs, which must be based on the nature of the potential membership: the kinds of common interests or concerns, age range, sex, capacities and limitations, cultural variants, physical location, and availability.

Based on these factors, the practitioner can determine the form of the offering, including such features as the optimum range of group size; number, length, and frequency of sessions; and time and place of proposed sessions. Before making a specific offer, the practitioner needs to appraise the probable receptivity of the intended members in light of the nature of the setting, the voluntary-involuntary aspects of joining, and the specifics of the offering. All of these steps add up to a *process of group formation,* which is not the same in its meaning as group composition; the latter refers to the selection of particular individuals, while the former is simply addressed to the organizational steps of formation.

Since one cannot know how a prospective member will behave in a given group based on his behavior one-to-one, there is no point in trying to determine what combination of particular individual characteristics would make for the most effective group composition. All that needs to be known is that there is a significant core of commonality, and that no prospective member is going to be clearly *harmful* to or *harmed by* the group experience. Thus, there is no need for individual assessments (other than on these two criteria) in order to form a group.

The question may still remain as to the necessity for these preliminary individual assessments for use *after* the group is formed, so that planned gains and methods to achieve them can be individualized. There are several reasons why such an approach is both undesirable and unworkable. First, it is the vastly complex network of relationships within the common-goal group that requires the prime attention of the leader. In this context, it is not possible or necessary for the leader to carry along in his head and into the group a collection of complex individual study, diagnosis, and treatment plan data; his attention is being focused primarily on group goal-achieving, and all that information will weigh him down and confuse his orientation to the group tasks.

It is also undesirable to collect all this data because of the nonpredictability of its carry-over into the group and because it creates a contaminating process whereby the members become aware of the leader's prior knowledge and judgments about them. This tends to create a self-fulfilling prophecy. If on the other hand, the leader simply acts as though he expects all the members, in their own ways, to cope with group tasks and expects himself to learn who they are from how they behave in the group, there is a sense, transmitted to the members, of a chance for a fresh start. The worker will learn what he needs to know about individual members by how they deal with group tasks. If a particular individual is having difficulty *in* the group, the practitioner may want to explore this with him after a group meeting; he may seek to learn what else is operating on a need-to-know basis and by joint agreement.

The historical stress on advance informational preparations has led both literature and practice into a pattern of spending far too much time on the planning stage of work and has resulted in a serious paucity of attention to and development of practice methodology—that is, how to actually help people. There is also a fundamental value clash in the advance data collection pattern with the value stance of this model—namely, that within a humanistic orientation, it is not believed possible to ever know from the outside what is truly best for another person from that person's interior view. All that a human relations counselor can offer is to help people to look more clearly and with greater strength and hope at the variety of coping options and the respective consequences available to them and to grant each person the right to make the choice and bear the consequences.

In this perspective, the entire assessment process, which takes place jointly with the group, is a significant part of its work at each session. It is an assessment of what concern the members have *in common,* based on how they describe, evaluate, and respond to their own and others' experiences in coping. This process becomes translated into a clear set of practitioner functions, which now become formulated as *perceiving, evaluating,* and *acting* in relation to the group as a whole and to individual members. But the behaviors on which the leader's assessments are based are the common experiences of the group as it works to achieve its goals.

There is, however, an extremely important area for further assessment which becomes the leader's central preparatory work for each session—the area of the group-as-a-whole. If commonality is a key to this model, then the practitioner's preparatory efforts for any first meeting with a group needs to concentrate along the following lines: What are the gains in social functioning appropriate for and realizable by this group? What are likely to be the main interests or concerns of the members in relation to the group purpose and function? What are the common life situations they are likely to face in their private lives? How can the leader most effectively elicit and/or propose these or other possibilities as a basis for coming to a common agreement at the first meeting around the range of potential goals? With which goal should the group start?

It is therefore in the area of *likely common content focus*—either interest or concern—that the leader must make his major preparation so that, for each meeting, he is steeped in the probabilities and, at the same time, receptive to different member-initiated possibilities. Regardless of their origin, these proposals will need group approval before they are taken up.

GROUP DYNAMICS

PROCESSES AFFECTING SOCIAL GROWTH OF INDIVIDUALS

The essence of this strongly group-oriented model of practice is that the key dynamics through which each member's social growth takes place are: (1) the engagement of the group with its tasks and (2) the engagement of each member with the group in this undertaking.

These simultaneous engagement processes are the most powerful moving forces to challenge individuals as members to perform social roles that are most comparable to the realistic demands of the pervasive social tasks in society. The necessity to engage oneself as a member with the group can only stem from a beginning commitment to its purpose and process; to the extent that members do not fulfill their part of this commitment, it is legitimate for other members or the leader to identify this and ask them to deal with it. Thus, the social demands of common-goal-achievement call forth the utmost in performance, and the group becomes a testing ground and a learning laboratory for each member in preparation for comparable tasks in his own life outside the group. It is thus important that the group, the leader, and the tasks present combined experiences that are challenging rather than protective, and group-oriented rather than self-oriented. While the atmosphere needs to be empathetic and compassionate, the objective base for this tone is group-task-achievement. The creation of internal strivings to rise to meet this demand begins with the initial commitment to the group's endeavors.

PATTERNS OF RELATIONSHIPS

A group leader must take into account the following basic *lines of force* (analogous with vectors in physics) as existing continuously, even if not openly or verbally expressed: relations between each member and each other member; each member and each subgroup; each member and the group-as-a-whole; each subgroup and each other subgroup; each subgroup and the group-as-a-whole; each member and the leader; each subgroup and the leader; and the group-as-a-whole and the leader.

STAGES OF DEVELOPMENT

In relation to the above complex dimensions of behavior patterns in the group, some fundamental time sequence can be perceived in the life of a common-goal group. Based upon the variables of purpose, function, structure, age, and length of group life, it has not been possible to locate any more complex schematization of stages of group development than beginning, middle, and end.

Beginning stage. This stage is most commonly the process of the first session, but it may continue beyond to the extent that the length of group life allows. The group members (1) become oriented to the new situation, (2) identify the reasons for joining and the work they will be doing, (3) experience uncertainties, fears, and hopeful anticipation, and (4) test out each other and the leader for responses.

The leader faces the tasks of (1) clarifying purpose, function, and structure, (2) establishing an agreement to proceed, (3) supporting early efforts, (4) offering conviction, and (5) facilitating task-selection and unification.

Middle stage. This is the main stage, or core, of the group's life. In a ten-week group, for example, it consists of all sessions but the first and the last, with some allowance for minor spill-over from the first and preparation for the last. The group now shows more open expression, greater involvement, and greater acceptance of the value of the experiences. It seeks more authority, develops roles and statuses, shows an ever-increasing ability to plan and function, has greater cohesion and stability, and, in general, is performing the function for which it was established.

The leader is guiding the group toward goal focus, clarifying tasks completed and still to be accomplished, facilitating the group's ability to do more for itself, supporting the group in this growing ability, and helping the group to recognize time limits and the implications of the approaching termination for achievement.

Ending stage. This is basically a final session in a short-term group and a somewhat longer period in a long-term group. The group shows varying degrees of task completion; varying levels of satisfaction resulting from this achievement; some frustration at ending; some difficulty in leaving the members, the leader, and the agency; and some combination of relief and happiness.

The leader is helping the group to (1) complete its tasks, (2) evaluate the total experience, (3) see the gains and the realistic problems remaining, (4) part company, and (5) think ahead to the future outside the group.

PRINCIPLES, METHODS, AND TECHNIQUES OF INTERVENTION

It is paramount that the methodology in the *middle period* of group development be at "stage center" and remain there for the indefinite future for a claim to be made for professional practice. One may know a great deal about the nature of group and individual behavior without it automatically following that one knows how to play a professional enabling role in enhancing the functionalism of such behavior. Not only must methodology become the center of attention but it must be organized in a systematic manner so that it can be applied in both a consistent and selectively determined manner, based on an internally coherent rationale leading to guides for action.

The systematization of a methodology of group work practice was first called for by Hurwitz [21] and later addressed in relation to theory-building by Vinter.[22] Although the impact of systems theory was likely not the direct cause for their concern (as it has not been for this writer), yet it is informative to see what another leading social work theoretician has said about the relation of systems theory to social work.

Gordon described the second law of thermodynamics as the underlying process that enlightened the way in which entropy (defined as *un*available energy) can be reduced in a system. He said that this famous physical law noted the tendency for "unattended systems to proceed to an increase in entropy," hence a decrease in available energy. This decrease in energy, which is a feature of *unattended* systems, is characterized, he said, by such features as disorder, disorganization, and randomness; *attended* systems, "aiming for growth and development," tend to increase available energy

---

[21] Jacob Hurwitz, "Systematizing Social Group Work Practice," *Social Work,* 1(3)63–69 (1956).

[22] Robert D. Vinter, "Problems and Processes in Developing Group Work Practice Principles," pp. 2–16.

and are characterized by such features as order, organization, and nonran-domness.[23]

Thus, as in role theory, communications theory, and small-group theory, all of which have usually been supportive of the practice wisdom of group work, so too has systems theory enabled us to see more clearly what was already easily available; but it may take on greater stature than that generated by social work theory. The message is clear, at any rate: an attended system, which yields more available energy, involves an organized methodology.

System does not, in human relations, imply a machinelike set of levers, in which a specific one is pressed to produce a specific result; rather, system must be seen as an organized base, with a set of mid-range guiding principles and interventive methods which are so complex in their cross-referencing requirements that there is considerable skill and art involved in deciding what to do when and why.

PROFESSIONAL PRESENTATION OF A LEADER

The group work practitioner, in the value system established, cannot be a routine operative who simply knows the right interventions to make at the right times. He needs to know, well before this, how to present himself in such a way as to be consistent with the values and assumptions by which he works. It is common knowledge in social work that *how* a practitioner does something in his work is at least as important as *what* he does. This concept of presentation of self is the undergirding "how" for all the detailed later "whats." The components of a presentation of self within this model are illustrated as implicit messages to the group.

1. *Compassion*—I deeply care about you.
2. *Mutuality*—We are here on a common human level; let's agree on a plan and then let's walk the path together.
3. *Humility*—Please help me understand.
4. *Respect*—I consider you as having worth. I treat your ideas and feelings with consideration. I do not intrude upon your person.
5. *Openness*—I offer myself to you as you see me: real, genuine, and authentic.

[23] William E. Gordon, "Basic Constructs for an Integrated and Generalized Conception of Social Work," Gordon Hearn (ed.), *The General Systems Approach: Contributions Toward an Holistic Conception of Social Work* (New York: Council on Social Work Education, 1969), p. 11.

6. *Empathy*—I am trying to feel what you are feeling.
7. *Involvement*—I am trying to share and help in your efforts.
8. *Support*—I will lend my conviction and back up your progress.
9. *Expectation*—I have confidence that you can achieve your goals.
10. *Limitation*—I must remind you of your agreed-upon obligations.
11. *Confrontation*—I must ask you to look at yourself.
12. *Planning*—I will always bring proposals, but I would rather have yours.
13. *Enabling*—I am here to help you become more able, more powerful.
14. *Spontaneity and control*—I will be as open as possible, yet I must recognize that, in your behalf, I need to exercise some self-control.
15. *Role and person*—I am both a human being like you and a representative of an agency, with a special function to perform.
16. *Science and art*—I hope to bring you a professional skill which must be based on organized knowledge, but I am dealing with people, and my humanity must lend the art to grace the science.

Without some reasonable combination of these qualities, the methodology to follow has little validity and does not achieve the intended results. In fact, presentation of self is a vital preliminary component of methodology in a humanistic approach.

A LEADER'S EFFORTS WITH THE GROUP AS A WHOLE

If the purpose of group work is to enable individuals to achieve greater self-realization through group experience, then the building of an optimum group experience as the vehicle for this growth becomes the first demand on the leader, even as he prepares for the formation of the group and then— most definitively—as he begins to work with it. If the group experience is to provide the central dynamic for individual growth, then attention to the quality of that experience becomes an imperative of the highest order.

The leader starts from the fact of the group as a potential living community, gathered around a common life situation. It is this common base which brought it together that is his prime focus of attention because it is the prime mover for whatever gains may be forthcoming for its members. He sees the group as the medium in relation to which the members are involved in action and reaction; it is the medium for both these actions and the leader's perceptions of and responses to them. Therefore, as he enables the group to carry out its purposes, he is engaged in a continuing process of *per-*

ceiving, evaluating, and *acting;* and this process occurs on two levels—namely, group-as-a-whole behavior and individual behavior in relation to the group.

The leader first needs to perceive what is happening. On this basis he evaluates the significance of any group or individual behavior; this then leads him, by means of a set of guiding principles, to determine both whether and how to act in relation to that behavior. The raw material of behavior to which he must direct his attention includes the following: words used with direct meanings; words intended as codes for other meanings; emotional tone of verbal expression; facial expressions; hand gestures; and body movements.

In connecting with these specific inputs, he, as well as the members, will need to become a skilled recipient of human communication before he attempts a professional evaluation. However, his training should give him the ability for sharper attunement to these attempts. Essentially, he will need to know first what a given member is *trying* to say to others—that is, the intended communication. This includes hearing, seeing, and feeling what the member is trying to articulate concerning: what he thinks, what he feels, and what he wants to do, and what he wants *others* to think, feel, or do. He must recognize that there are common human difficulties in expressing these things (and he too will have these difficulties), such as finding the right words to say what one means, using words meaning different things to different people, experiencing uncertainty and conflicts about what to say, having too many things to say, disguising a statement out of fear of how others will react, and expressing thoughts and feelings that appear to contradict each other.

On the receiving end, he and all the group members will also have additional difficulties, such as distorting a message by anticipating something in advance, blocking receipt of a message by being occupied with one's own thoughts and feelings, and reading one's own attitudes into the other's intentions. Based on these communicative considerations, the leader will be engaged in a process of hearing-seeing-feeling. As a result, he may, if he fails to grasp the message, *ask* the sender for a clearer one; or if he is unsure about the message, *check* to confirm or verify one of his readings.

His *evaluation* of a particular message is then simply a process of *making a meaningful connection between the message and the situational context in which it is offered.* This kind of evaluation occurs within the context of the *commonly perceived behavior* of the group, which is open for the members as well as the leader to see and respond to. Since the members will be dealing with what is within their awareness or easily called to awareness, the leader may reflect on what a particular message means to him; others in the group may be reading the message similarly, but the sender may be ignorant of its effect.

If the leader's reading is not confirmed by at least a segment of the group, it may be inaccurate, and therefore have little utility. Conjectures or hunches should not be offered as interpretations; the leader should have clear behavioral evidence before making such contributions to the group for either confirmation or rejection.

The goal-achieving process. Whatever goal has been chosen by the group for a given session, it is assumed that the leader's concurrence is indicative of his belief that this short-range goal will be useful in achieving the long-range purposes of the group. The goal for each session, or some continued series of sessions, becomes converted into the program content of the group experience during those sessions and takes the forms of specific activities, foci for discussion, or proposals for action. Thus the program is the *what* of group experience—the specific things the group has chosen to do.

Program content—whether focused on counseling, activity, or action—should be planned in a common effort by the group and the leader effort in order to provide the basis for a mutually agreed path to follow. The leader brings program proposals to the group which are appropriate in terms of the group's age level, purpose and function, history of reactions to prior content, concerns at a given time, and its relatedness to the mutual agreement. He comes prepared with proposals for both how to carry out the agreed-upon plans for the current session and what alternatives to consider for the following session. These proposals, in both instances, are for the purposes of stimulation and motivation, and arise out of concern for comprehensiveness and variety.

Generally, it is preferable for the group to plan some kind of program for the following meeting at the end of the current one. The pattern will tend to vary with the function of the group. In a counseling group a general area of concern is to build some anticipation and motivation for the following meeting, which thereby starts with an immediate sense of where to go and leads naturally to the task of identifying more specific subconcerns as its first order of business. This gives the group a clear basis for knowing where to start because it knows what has to be examined.[24] In activity and action groups, planning becomes about as time-consuming as the carrying out of plans. Entire sessions may be spent in planning, and about the same amount or less time spent in executing plans.

Despite his planning, the leader first asks the group for its own ideas. If there is little forthcoming, his plans are then useful as proposals to consider and to stimulate group thinking. If the group's suggestions are unrealistic or inappropriate to group function, he will need to point this out to the members. If, however, the group rejects the leader's proposals and prefers some still within range of acceptability, he would do well to go with the group's determination, assuming it has been reasonably well considered. In effect, the group acts, either formally or informally, on what to do. It would be impractical for the leader to insist on his own ideas if the group did not accept them, and it would also be in violation of the principle of mutuality. Groups can easily defeat leader-forced plans by apathy, willful nonparticipation, or playing games of accommodation.

The general range of usable program content is directly related to group function: in a counseling group, the range would cover the many possible concerns of a particular group; in an action group, content may include action directed toward the interests of the group itself or on behalf of the common welfare of larger community; in an activity group, the possibilities include social, athletic, cultural, educational, and community service programs.

As the leader engages the group in the goal-achieving process, he needs to be aware of his own attitudes and behavior, the group's attitudes and behavior, the group's reactions to him, and his reactions to the group. In this context, he initiates the processes of group deliberation, decision, and action.

Deliberation and decision. This process involves obtaining proposals from the group by asking for and presenting alternative choices and stimulating the thinking of others. Once proposals are available, the leader maintains the focus of discussion for deliberation by clarifying, concretizing, partializing, suggesting manageable aspects, presenting data as needed, and holding to relevancy. To reach a decision, he encourages free expression and interaction, separates external realities from feelings about them, confronts the

---

[24] Emanuel Tropp, "A Methodology of Group Counseling in Group Work Practice," *Child Welfare,* 50(4):18–28 (1971); also *A Humanistic Foundation,* pp. 103–13.

group with the challenge of purpose, asks it to look at the consequences of any action or of inaction, facilitates conflict resolution, identifies obstacles, and asks the group to come to decisions.

Action. Having decided what to do, the group is now faced with how to do it and with going about doing it. The leader clarifies group decisions, asks the group to take hold of them, confirms group commitment to them, and asks the group to abide by them. To help the group organize for action, the leader identifies group talents, suggests resources, encourages separation of responsibilities as needed, and asks for and suggests means for carrying out the plan. As the group engages in doing what it planned, the leader supports group efforts by showing his conviction and encouragement, reinforcing cooperative efforts, recognizing group achievement, noting and supporting progress, and sharing with the group the joys and frustrations of the efforts to achieve.

In the case of a group with elected officers, the leader serves in the capacity of advisor—in that he works "through the chair"—respecting the role of elected chairman, helping the chairman perform his role with increasing effectiveness and self-reliance, and helping the members see the responsibilities entailed in the democratic process.

LEADER ROLE IN RELATION TO GROUP BEHAVIOR

There are three criteria for determining and evaluating the performance of the group as a whole: group effectiveness, group vitality, and group responsibility. For each area—and they each have a bearing on the others—the leader has significant roles to play.

Effectiveness. The major criteria for group effectiveness can be seen as: accomplishing group purposes, accomplishing specific goals selected for those purposes, getting optimum results in quantity and quality, using time and effort in the most productive and efficient manner, demonstrating ability to cope with obstacles to achievement, obtaining optimum group participation, and making most productive use of internal and external resources. Low group effectiveness tends to lead to group dissatisfaction, disillusionment, deterioration, and, eventually, dissolution. High group effectiveness is not only the central gain in itself but is also productive of increased group vitality which, in turn, produces greater effectiveness.

Vitality. Major criteria in this area are seen as: group *responsiveness*, including such elements as interest, motivation, spirit, drive, enthusiasm, optimism, satisfaction; group *openness,* including freedom of expression, relaxation, spontaneity, genuineness, involvement, interaction; and group *cohesiveness,* which includes bond, loyalty, stability, intimacy, mutual respect, and mutual aid. These elements, identified as components of group vitality, are the *sources of energy that fuel a group to achieve its goals.*

Responsibility. There are lines of responsibility from the group in several directions: to its purposes, which means to carry out its agreement; to its members, which entails group respect for individual ideas and feelings and for the rights of the minority, and group expectation of member participation in fulfilling the agreement; to the agency and community, which includes functioning within laws and agency regulations, caring about how group actions will affect agency and community, and contributing to both, where possible and appropriate.

A leader's role. The leader's role in facilitating group effectiveness has been discussed earlier, under goal-achieving. His role in enhancing group vitality calls on him to stimulate, inspire, use humor, offer a sense of adventure, show enthusiasm, support group achievement, and offer himself both as a leader and as a person who is strongly invested in the process. To enhance group responsibility, the leader may confront the group with its agreements, with obstacles that get in its way, or with its own attitudes and behavior, use legitimate limits and authority, recognize and support responsible behavior, and demonstrate the connection between group responsibility and group satisfaction.

THE LEADER AND INTERPERSONAL BEHAVIOR
WITHIN THE GROUP

The members are involved not only with the group-as-a-whole and with particular group goals but also with each other in relation to goal-achievement. Those forms of behavior that are *instrumental*—that is, consciously directed toward common-goal efforts—provide the reality base for evaluating both the contributions a member makes to the group and the ways in which he is behaving in relation to meeting his needs. Included here are such behaviors as supporting and accepting others; accepting support and assistance from others; opposing and restraining others; handling opposition and restraint from others; engaging with others in resolving differences through assertion, compromise, or yielding; submitting to or rejecting appointed or elected authority figures; accepting others' inputs; and performing such roles as leading, following, and carrying out specific individual tasks. By the ways in which a member handles such interpersonal relations of an instrumental nature, he not only contributes to or hinders the group's efforts but also demonstrates his strengths, potentials, limitations, and means of coping. These are direct, commonly observable behaviors that can be used as criteria for evaluating the performance of any member.

In the course of performing these instrumental behaviors, each member also responds with unintended behavior which is expressive or emotional in nature. This behavior is interwoven with instrumental behavior and includes such action as showing like and dislike for others, attracting and repelling others, showing fear or eagerness, expressing anger and resentment, giving and receiving affection, expressing guilt, expressing pleasure or frustration, being dominant and insistent or withdrawn and suspicious, and showing emotional ties with subgroups.

The role of the leader in relation to facilitating instrumental interaction has been discussed in the section on group goal-achieving. The various forms of expressive interaction may aid or hinder instrumental behavior. When expressive behaviors are obstructing the instrumental process, the leader may have to ask the group to look at what is happening and how it is affecting its goal-achieving efforts. This confrontation is intended to enable each member to become more aware of and accepting of his behavior and how it is affecting other individuals and the group process, so that this can lead to more effective member performance. When expressive behaviors strengthen the goal-achieving process, the leader may need to bring this to the attention of the group and thus reinforce all members' understanding of the relation between individual behavior and group accomplishment.

THE LEADER AND INDIVIDUAL BEHAVIOR

Having specified that the leader's primary efforts are directed toward the functioning of the group-as-a-whole and then toward interpersonal segments of this functioning that are related to the group's efforts, a setting has now been created within which it is simultaneously clear and necessary for the leader to play a role in regard to individual behavior in the group. This line of leader-to-member is functionally related to the earlier relations of member-to-group and member-to-member. This does not mean that leader-to-member lines are not operating during those periods when the other lines are seen as central; in fact, it is unavoidable that they *will* be operating, *but*

primarily as instrumentally connected to the success of the group enterprise.
Of concern here are those conditions under which the leader is concerned
primarily with a particular member who needs some *special* attention from
the leader or from the group.

The underlying assumption is that *all* members derive various gains
from the productive efforts of the group, depending upon the extent and the
ways in which they involve themselves in those efforts. The leader needs to
perceive and evaluate the behavior of all members, not for the purpose of
collecting ''interesting'' information but rather for getting usable information about how members are or are not contributing to and gaining from the
group experience. In this light, *all* group-related member actions and interactions are useful as specific behavioral guides which can indicate
whether the leader needs to intervene on an individual basis and in what
way.

The leader's interventive actions with individual members is based on
the experiences developed within the group, rather than on knowledge of
how any member behaved in another situation prior to this group experience. By dealing with the member on a current-reality basis, the leader does
not intimate—verbally or nonverbally—that he knows all about the member's prior behavior, but shows only that he knows what the member has in
common with the others and is relating to him on the basis of events within
the group. This gives each member a sense of an opportunity for a fresh start
and allows for greater latitude in becoming whatever the group brings out in
him, rather than encouraging him to live up to, or fear having to live up to,
expectations based on prior behavior.

There are obviously a great many individual behaviors going on in a
group at any given time, but only some that a leader can and needs to perceive and evaluate. He does not evaluate simply for the sake of evaluation.
Not all individual behaviors call for reactions from either the group or the
leader. The leader reacts to individual members in both similar and different
ways, just as each member presents himself both in a role and as a person.
The leader's *similar* reaction-patterns are offered when the commonalities of
member actions are more significant than their differences. The leader's *differential* reaction-patterns are, accordingly, related to actions idiosyncratic
to an individual member.

Since the leader *must* be selective in this regard, he must have some
criteria for deciding which individual behaviors do *not* call for his special in-

tervention. These criteria are essentially three-fold: when the behavior is not interfering with group goal-achieving, when it is being handled satisfactorily by the group, or when it is so handled by the member. When *problematic* behaviors present themselves, the leader needs to determine whether they need special attention. Again, there are generally three criteria or categories of problematic behavior: those that hinder group efforts and must be handled for the good of the group, those that harm individual others, and those that create problems for the individual who initiates them. Some of the basic raw materials for perceiving those behaviors are: attendance patterns, interest, frequency and quality of participation, spoken content, facial expressions, tone of voice, body movements, emotional outbursts, and silence.

Another dimension is the *degree* of the behavior, for which other criteria appear: *how* severely is the individual harming himself or others, *how* adequately can the group handle it on its own, and *how* adequately can the individual handle it? If some intervention becomes necessary, the next question is whether the most effective help would be delivered through the group (indirect help) or through the leader (direct help).

In the complex action of the group process, the leader often must act in accordance with his perceptions and quick evaluations, without waiting for any open exploration—for example, to protect persons from serious harm. Yet, even in such situations, the leader, if time and other demands permit, can involve the member whose behavior creates difficulties. He can ask that member why he did something, ask the other members what it looked like to them and how it affected them, state what it looked like to the leader, and ask the member to cope with it. If this cannot be resolved within the meeting, the leader can see the member immediately after the meeting to work together, as openly as possible and in a mutual manner: to identify what happened and how it happened, to learn why the member acted in this way, to consider the possible resolutions and consequences, and to reach a mutual understanding of what needs to be done in the future.

In general, therefore, the leader's evaluation of his perceptions of individual behavior are neither merely based on his external observations (because it is perceived by others from within the group) nor on interpretations of what "lies beneath" the perceptions. The *evaluation* process consists of the following components: how did the member see his behavior, how did the group see it, how did it affect the group and the member, what did the member appear to be intending to accomplish with it, and, finally, *what con-*

nections and relational meanings can be established between the member's actions and the context in which they occurred?

As in legal rules of evidence, a tremendously important protection for both the member and the leader is the use of "witnesses"—i.e., the common perceptions of behavior on the part of others in the group. The purposes of the leader's actions that follow such an evaluation would be twofold: to enable the group to accomplish its goals and to enable the individual to learn to cope more effectively and with greater satisfaction of self and others.

Having perceived and evaluated a given individual's behavior and having determined that some form of leader intervention is necessary, the leader can use either indirect or direct helping processes. In *indirect* help, he can use the group's instrumental processes by asking the group to recognize the worth of an individual contribution, asking the group to use agreed limits with a member, asking the group to reflect back on how a member is involved in the goal-achieving process, and asking the group to look at individual behavior that blocks or facilitates process.

The leader also *directly* intervenes to help a member during the group session. This intervention is based on certain prerequisites: that the leader is aware of his own reactions to that individual and of the individual to him, that he is sensitive to that individual's needs and feelings, that he is respectful and empathetic, and that he shows a desire to better understand what is happening and how to be of help. The avenues of direct help, as expressed in terms of direct contact with the member during the group session, include approval, encouragement, affection, concern, stimulation, empathetic reflection, clarification, confronting the member with his role responsibilities, with the realities of the situation, and with his own behavior, and using legitimate leader authority to limit behavior that is contrary to others' welfare or asking the member to consider the consequences that will ensue if he persists.

If indirect help and direct help during the group session have not been productive, then some form of outside contact is indicated. This contact is most desirable as soon as possible after the group session, since it concerns group-related matters. It may be initiated by the leader or the member. If the leader seeks the member out, then the process has already been described in its essentials. If the member seeks the leader out on non-group-related matters, then it would be best for the leader not to get involved in a prolonged relationship. Such a relationship creates problems both for the leader and the member within the group because others will quickly identify the "special status" of the member being seen individually. If prolonged contact is indicated, referral to another professional counselor is in order.

In a group-related area, a persistent problematic behavior may require one or more intensive interviews with the member. The leader and member mutually explore how the situation tends to keep arising; the member's feelings about it; what he has tried to do about it; why his efforts have not been successful; what other alternatives there are and what their consequences are likely to be; which aspects can be handled now and which postponed until later; which aspects are external and beyond the member's control, and what can be done about them; which aspects are within his control, what strengths he has to cope with these on his own, what is there within him that interferes with this coping process, and what can he do about it; and finally what coping options remain as a result of this exploration. Possible coping options for any member are: acceptance of the external situation as a given, identifying new ways of handling himself and/or others, trying to effect some change in the situation itself, or dropping out of the situation.

THE RELATION OF GROUP WORK
TO CASEWORK

While group work and casework are two of the methods in the social work profession and while casework preceded group work in time as a professional discipline on the graduate level, group work is neither a historical derivative nor a theoretical extension of casework. It is more accurate to say that each had different origins and different paths of development which, although officially merged in a combined professional association in 1955, have continued since then along parallel but different lines because of both what they brought to the merger and what they needed to be in order to carry out their respective functions.

The raison d'etre of group work in its earliest forms has been richly elaborated by Schwartz,[25] and clearly re-inforced in the writings of others. Phillips noted that the essence of this rationale took shape in the settlement movement, and described the purposes of the settlement and its groups as a "method of social elevation . . . not through patronage but through mutual confidence and respect [to] elicit for better things the collective and cor-

---

[25] William Schwartz, "Group Work and the Social Scene," in Alfred J. Kahn (ed.), *Issues in American Social Work* (New York: Columbia University Press, 1959), pp. 110–37.

porate initiative of the people." [26] Falck states that "the history of social group work is almost totally different" from casework, and adds, "I can find nothing in Jane Addams that characterized the people whom she led as sick or pathological, needing a clinical kind of help." [27]

This beginning path continued to develop collective self-help as its central motif when group work was introduced to graduate schools of social work. This is clearly stated in the writings of the most representative first professional formulator, Grace Coyle. Even during the period from 1926 to 1955 (i.e., from the first group work master's degree graduates in social work to the formation of the joint professional association), when group workers-in-training were learning the same human behavior theories as caseworkers and were taking some courses in casework, the lines remained parallel rather than derivative. What did happen during those years was the laying of the groundwork for a professional merger as a result of the common undergirding by three forces—namely, a value system, a purpose-orientation, and a knowledge base.

However, one of the ways in which professional thinking became blurred was the substitution of the phrase, "social work with groups" for social group work. An NASW publication has noted that "there has sprung up a good deal of practice with groups that does not utilize the social group work method or any other well-formulated methodology," and this has often been referred to as "casework in a group." [28] Scheidlinger stated that social work with groups was ". . . beset by professional role conflicts and confused terminology . . . resulting in all kinds of work with groups," and added: "The question 'Who does what to whom in what kind of group and how?' is well worth asking at every step. . . ." [29]

The model in this paper, while sharing some common history, traditions, values; purposes, knowledge, and skills with the other social work methods is *far more different than it is the same when it comes to the crucial areas of knowledge and skill*. A group that is engaged in the pursuit of a common goal for the purposes of enabling its members to more fully realize

[26] Helen U. Phillips, *Essentials of Social Group Work Skill*, pp. 16–17, quoted from F. G. Peabody, "Social Settlements," *Conference of Charities and Corrections*, 24:330 (1897).

[27] Hans Falck, "Crisis Theory and Social Group Work," paper presented at the NASW Mid-Continent Regional Institute, Topeka, Kansas, p. 2 (mimeographed).

[28] Louise A. Frey (ed.), *Use of Groups in the Health Field* (New York: NASW, 1966), p. 14.

[29] Saul Scheidlinger, "Therapeutic Group Approaches in Community Mental Health," *Social Work*, 13(2):88 (1968).

their potentials for social functioning represents a very special social system that requires a highly specialized knowledge base and methodology because its prime target-focus is the group as a whole.

Attempts to prepare practitioners who are equally competent in casework and group work are operating either on the undemonstrated assumption that the two methods are essentially the same or the unstated assumption that the preparation and practice will be predominantly in casework, plus some familiarity with but not equal competence in group work, or the further unstated assumption that there is really not too much to know about one or both methods.

The increasing trend toward a systems-focused approach to practice is quite compatible with a view of group work as a distinct method because the very same conviction that competence derives from specialization in a delivery system would lead to a similar conclusion that this holds true for methods as well. Recently, the N.A.S.W. Council on Social Work in Mental Health Services recommended "that there was indeed a need for specializations in general (and for) specialization by method or function. . . ." [30]

Yet, despite the substantial requirements for competence in the group work method, it is quite feasible for caseworkers to undertake, with some training, some efforts in using a developmental group work approach as an auxiliary aid to their practice, just as group workers need to supplement their basic function with groups through some work with individuals outside the group but without the intensity and complexity that competent casework practice requires. While the centrality of emphasis and competence makes these two methods essentially different, auxiliary practice approaches within recognized limits can be used with real value. Of all the well-defined theories of casework practice, it would appear that this developmental approach is closest in value-set and style of work to Perlman's problem-solving model, although differing in some ways due to differing functions and lines of past development.

UNRESOLVED PROBLEMS

There are three major unresolved questions:

1. *Method of Choice: Casework or Group Work?* This apparently simple question is one of the knottiest to resolve and has tended to be either taken for granted or handled intuitively or practically.

[30] *NASW News,* 14(2):2 (1974).

2. *Choice of Group Work Modality: Counseling, Activity, or Action?* This choice has similar difficulties to those above and they are not amenable to simple resolutions.

3. *Research: Proof of Effectiveness.* There is no reliable research evidence to either validate or invalidate this model of group work practice. Taken in a larger context, there is question as to whether any other individual or group modality in interpersonal relations has been proven to be effective or ineffective. However, despite the difficulties, the charge clearly remains to find more efficacious ways of identifying the appropriate research questions and the suitable vehicles for evaluation. The complexity of this undertaking, however, must be openly recognized. It means the identification of valid target problems and the creation of suitable instruments to measure the cognitive, attitudinal, and behavioral movements that occur in the direction of improved social functioning.

CONCLUSION

Despite these unresolved problems, this developmental group work theory for practice is presented, based on its consistent application, its evolving systematization and internal coherence, and its demonstrated usefulness in a great variety of settings, over many years, with different kinds of populations. The fact that the gains have only been subjectively perceived by group leaders and members but not confirmed by objective research requires attention. However, in view of the comparable situation in other behavioral professions, it is still necessary and worthwhile to live by the conviction that direct personal experience with this method brings, and to keep working at sharpening it for more effective service.

BIBLIOGRAPHY

Allport, Gordon W. *Becoming.* New Haven: Yale University Press, 1955.

Frankl, Victor. *The Doctor and the Soul.* New York: Knopf, 1962.

Hurwitz, Jacob. "Systematizing Social Group Work Practice," *Social Work,* 1(3):63–69 (1956).

Matson, Floyd W. *The Broken Image.* New York: Braziller, 1964.

Parsons, Talcott. *The Structure of Social Action.* Glencoe, Ill.: Free Press, 1949.

Phillips, Helen U. *The Essentials of Social Group Work Skill.* Folcroft, Pa.: Folcroft Press, 1974.

Schwartz, William. "The Social Worker in the Group," in NASW, *New Perspectives on Services to Groups.* New York: NASW, 1961, pp. 7–29.

Szasz, Thomas S. *The Myth of Mental Illness.* New York: Dell, 1961.

Tropp, Emanuel. *A Humanistic Foundation for Group Work Practice,* 2d ed. New York: Selected Academic Readings, 1971.

Vinter, Robert D. "Problems and Processes in Developing Group Work Practice Principles," in *Theory Building in Social Group Work.* New York: Council on Social Work Education, 1960, pp. 2–16.

8

A TASK-CENTERED APPROACH [1]

CHARLES D. GARVIN, WILLIAM REID, AND LAURA EPSTEIN

Task-centered social treatment is a model of social work intervention aimed at helping individuals and families resolve problems in living. Whether used in individual or group treatment contexts, it has several distinguishing characteristics: (1) it is brief and time-limited; (2) its interventions are concentrated on alleviating specific problems which the clients and practitioners expressly contract to work on; (3) work on the clients' problems is organized around tasks or problem-solving actions the client agrees to carry out; and (4) research monitoring is an integral part of the service design and serves as a basis for progressive modifications of the model.

The time-limited, problem-oriented, and research-based features of the model are shared with several other approaches. The distinguishing feature is the conceptualization of "task," defined as what the client is to do to alleviate the problem. As Reid and Epstein indicate:

> The task represents both an immediate goal the client is to pursue and the means of achieving the larger goal of problem alleviation. In its initial formulation, a task provides a general statement of the action the client is to undertake rather than a detailed blueprint. [2]

---

[1] This is a considerably modified and expanded version of Charles Garvin, "Task-Centered Group Work." The authors also acknowledge the helpful comments of Harvey Bertcher and Maeda Galinsky on earlier drafts of this paper.

[2] William J. Reid and Laura Epstein, *Task-Centered Casework,* p. 21.

Examples of tasks would be that Mrs. Adams is to explore sources of child care for her child and that Mr. Brown is to develop a plan for retraining for his strenuous job after his heart attack.

In the casework application, the worker facilitates the client's selection of problem, determination of task, and task activity. In group work, the worker also helps the members to help each other. The group can also provide the context in which some tasks are performed. For example, a member of a group of former mental hospital patients may select as a task conversing with other members about social topics of mutual interest.

HISTORICAL DEVELOPMENT

The task-centered approach is an outgrowth of several developments affecting social work practice during the sixties: (1) increasing interest in brief time-limited treatment; (2) a trend toward use of more highly focused and structured forms of intervention, in part as a reaction against the diffuseness of prevailing modes of practice; (3) the failure of conventional forms of casework to demonstrate effectiveness in controlled studies; and (4) a movement toward grounding treatment approaches in empirical data rather than in speculative theory—a movement reflected, for example, in applications of behavioral approaches to social work.

The task-centered model was derived from a time-limited, short-term casework approach, tested by Reid and Shyne at the Community Service Society of New York.[3] In that study, comparable groups of troubled families were given contrasting forms of service: one group of families received planned short-term treatment limited to eight casework interviews within a four-month period; the other group received long-term treatment which provided a substantially larger number of interviews and continued for twice as long. The families that had received the briefer service were found to have made *more progress* by case closing than the families that had received extended service.

Despite its relative success and obvious promise, the short-term approach tested in the experiment still left much to be desired. Its principal shortcoming was the lack of a well-developed treatment technology. Early model-building efforts were, therefore, directed at constructing a more systematic and more thoroughly articulated design for brief treatment. To this

[3] See William J. Reid and Ann Shyne, *Brief and Extended Casework* (New York: Columbia University Press, 1969).

end, the practitioner's treatment efforts were conceptualized as a set of methods to help clients carry out actions or tasks to alleviate problems of specified types. In part, the evolving model represented an attempt to synthesize Perlman's view of casework as a problem-solving activity, Studt's conception in individual and group contexts of client tasks as a focus of intervention, and Hollis' efforts at classification of treatment methods used by caseworkers.[4]

The contention that a task-centered base for practice with families and groups, as well as individuals, was sound had been made by several authors.[5] These authors have viewed this base as a unifying one leading to a more generic practice mode. Harriet Bartlett, for example, in her efforts to provide a common base, stated that the worker's ways of perceiving social situations "takes into account *the coping efforts of people to deal with life tasks and problems as related to the demands of their environment and the consequences to both if there is a serious imbalance."* [6]

Studt has stated that "the emergence of a task-focussed approach to practice could have major implications for the way we conceive all the dimensions of practice." She defends the task concept by pointing out its validity as a "behavioral" concept with specific referents, as a "process" word with its time-extended framework, and as a "situation" concept because of its articulation with particular contexts.[7] She introduced the idea that client tasks may be more enhanced when seen as extending beyond the confines of a single method because "the task concept . . . permits us to differentiate among the uses of methods in a variety of cases and to account for repeated patterns of method adaptation as they appear in practice." [8]

In addition to drawing on the concept of task as defined by Reid and Epstein, Bartlett, and Studt, the applications of the task-centered model to groups also incorporate its time-limited aspects. As Reid and Epstein point to the literature on short-term treatment of individuals as leading to their conceptions, similarly a literature and body of experience has emerged

---

[4] Helen Harris Perlman, *Social Casework: A Problem Solving Process* (Chicago: University of Chicago Press, 1957); Eliot Studt, "Social Work Theory and Implications for the Practice of Methods," pp. 22–24, 42–46; Florence Hollis, *A Typology of Casework Treatment* (New York: Family Service Association of America, 1968).

[5] See Charles Garvin, "Education for Generalist Practice in Social Work; *Education for Social Work;* Studt, "Social Work Theory."

[6] Harriet M. Bartlett, *The Common Base of Social Work Practice*, p. 162.

[7] Studt, "Social Work Theory," p. 23.   [8] *Ibid.*

regarding short-term groups.[9] It is interesting to note that many short-term group experiences have focused on specific client tasks to resolve particular problems—even though the practitioners may have used other terms to describe their foci. Such groups have dealt with a wide range of tasks including those of planning following abortion,[10] dealing with children's developmental problems,[11] responding to the needs of children with cerebral palsy,[12] accepting medicine and psychiatric treatment,[13] helping hospitalized schizophrenics to leave the hospital,[14] and helping AFDC mothers respond to the school problems of their children.[15] One of the authors of this paper was also consultant on a project to use short-term groups to help unwed mothers to decide whether to place their child and to make plans for the life they wished to pursue after the birth of the child.[16]

In the last five years, work on the task-centered approach in casework has become centered at the School of Social Service Administration, the University of Chicago, where a series of projects has been conducted. In addition, there have been several companion projects in social agencies in the United States and abroad. Also, task-centered groups have been conducted in Chicago, utilizing conceptualizations developed by Garvin at the University of Michigan School of Social Work. Garvin had seen the possibility of utilizing selected elements of the group work approach developed at that school to generate a model of task-centered group work. These elements include the individual members as the focus of change, a concrete goal orientation, a member-worker contract, and the incorporation of research monitoring in the service design.[17]

[9] For an early summary of such literature, see Alexander Wolf, "Short-Term Group Psychotherapy," pp. 219–55.

[10] Alice Ullmann, "Social Work Services to Abortion Patients," *Social Casework,* 53:481–87 (1972).

[11] Olive Crocker, "Family Life Education: Some New Findings," *Social Casework,* 26:106–13 (1955).

[12] G. Boles, "Simultaneous Group Therapy with Cerebral Palsied Children and Their Parents," *International Journal of Group Psychotherapy,* 9:488–95 (1959).

[13] E. Hoch and M. Dennis, "The Role of Group Psychotherapy in a General Medical and Surgical Hospital," *Journal of Maine Medical Association,* 5:192. (1955).

[14] W. Partridge, "Deadline for Family Care," *Mental Hospital,* 5:21–24 (1960).

[15] Elizabeth Navarre, Paul H. Glasser, and Jane Costabile, "An Evaluation of Group Work Practice with AFDC Mothers," in Glasser, Sarri, and Vinter (eds.), pp. 387–403.

[16] Elizabeth Kaplow and Nancy F. Terzieff, "An Experiment in Group Services to Unmarried Parents," mimeographed (Toronto: Children's Aid Society of Metropolitan Toronto, June 1971).

[17] See Charles Garvin and Paul Glasser, "Social Group Work," 2:1263–72.

VALUES

More than other helping professions, clinical social work is concerned with the treatment of individuals and families who have not sought, and may be reluctant to accept, the services of a professional helper. Delinquents, abusive parents, and public-assistance recipients offer the more obvious examples of persons who are likely to have help thrust upon them. More subtle examples can be seen in family agencies and mental health clinics to which recalcitrant children and spouses may be brought in tow by another family member.

The paradox of giving help to those who do not want it has created a number of unsolved value dilemmas for social work. Most of these can be summed up in the central question, "How far do we go in trying to bring about change in people who may not wish to change?" Social work theorists have attempted to answer this question by asserting the client's right to self-determination or autonomy and then by qualifying this right in ways that are not always clear. Moreover, discussion of value considerations has tended to be on a highly abstract plane. Practitioners have been left with the task of implementing vague—and often contrasting—principles that have not been articulated into specific guidelines.

The most distinctive features of the value premises of task-centered treatment concern the issue of client self-determination. The model places a high premium on the client's autonomy, particularly his right to freedom from imposed or deceptive treatment. Guidelines have been developed in which value principles are spelled out in specific operational terms.[18]

A central construct in this scheme of values is the client's expressed request for service after he has had an opportunity to consider his initial perception of need in relation to the worker's offerings. The practitioner does not presume to know what is best for the client or what his problem "really" is. The problems the worker treats are restricted to those the client acknowledges and verbalizes a willingness to work on.

This principle is put into operational terms through the treatment contract, an explicit verbal understanding reached by the client and practitioner prior to the inception of any systematic effort to help the client. By spelling out agreements between the practitioner and client on problems to be treated and later tasks to be undertaken, the contract protects the client from help

---

[18] Reid and Epstein, *Task-Centered Casework,* pp. 15–19.

for a condition he may not wish to change or from treatment for an unacknowledged problem, such as an underlying personality disorder. Contracts can be modified to incorporate new problems that may emerge as treatment gets underway, but such modifications must also be in the form of verbal agreements between the practitioner and the client.

The client's autonomy is given additional protection through principles concerning the right to privacy and the right to know how help is to be offered. A contract to help a client with a specific set of problems does not give the practitioner license to roam through his psyche. Areas of the client's life that do not pertain to the problem at hand are none of the worker's business, or none of the business of fellow clients in a treatment group. Since even simple problems may have complex ties to various areas of a client's life, it is difficult to distinguish between relevant inquiries and needless prying. Yet some distinctions can be made and practitioners can, at least, be advised to approach areas not obviously related to the problem under consideration with caution and respect.

A person who turns to a professional for help has a right to know the broad outlines of what the professional proposes to do and why he plans to do it. This does not mean that a practitioner has to reveal all of his ruminations about diagnostic and treatment possibilities or to keep the client posted every step of the way. But clients should be given sufficient information to be able to make knowledgeable decisions about whether they want to participate and how. The worker hopes that the client will be more collaborative than cooperative. Thus the task-centered practitioner is asked to explain to clients, in some detail, what this form of treatment consists of, how it may be applied in a particular instance, the worker's assessment of the problem, and how the worker might be able to help.

These principles can be applied with relative ease to the self-dependent, nondeviant adult. Dilemmas arise when clients are socially deviant, mentally ill, retarded, or children. Here the social worker is often under pressures from the community to do what he thinks is needed rather than what the client may wish. While the task-centered practitioner is reluctant to impose goals upon such a client, still some amount of actual imposition often ensues, particularly if the practitioner is a representative of some authority whom the client wishes to please.

Still, the practitioner of this model does not proceed with treatment unless some problem can be found that clients expressly agree to try to work on. If such a problem cannot be found, the clients should be permitted to go on their way. This approach concludes, therefore, that, while there are many facets and factors to any problem, the client is the best judge of what to work on first, which pain should be alleviated initially, which pressure from others in the social network should first be heeded, and in what sequence multiple strains in careers and roles should be dealt with.

In some cases, the practitioner must remain active in order to carry out protective or other functions. When this happens, the worker should make clear that he may have to take certain actions the client may perceive as not helpful. "Help" is always something the clients *themselves* think may do them some good. When the social worker ceases to be a helper and becomes the equivalent of a policeman, as is sometimes necessary, clients should be forthrightly advised of the change in roles.

In addition, the task-centered model is undergirded by a philosophy of knowledge that gives a superordinate role to the methods and products of science. An earlier statement of this position is apropos here:

> We hold that knowledge acquired through application of systematic methods of in-quiry, that is, through formal research, is of greater value than knowledge ac-quired through other means, including expert opinion, practice wisdom, uncon-trolled observations or deductions from theory. We recognize the limitations in quantity of available research-based knowledge and we are also aware that other forms of knowledge serve essential functions. But only through research-based knowledge, we think, can we develop progressively effective treatment models.[19]

This position has had major consequences for the development and application of task-centered casework. First, the initial conceptualization of the model was based on a substantial body of research on brief, time-limited treatment approaches, as reviewed in Reid and Shyne.[20] Second, further de-velopments of the model have been guided by the results of a continuing program of research. Third, systematic methods of data collection, including continuous review and recording of task progress, are integrated into the practice of the model. Finally, in making use of contributions from the be-havioral sciences and from other treatment approaches, primary interest is in work that has been empirically grounded through formal research.

BEHAVIORAL SCIENCE BACKGROUND

The task-centered model is primarily a technology for helping people iden-tify and alleviate psychosocial problems. Thus of central importance is (1)

---

[19] *Ibid.*, p. 36.   [20] Reid and Shyne, *Brief and Extended Casework.*

knowledge that might help explain how such problems come into being and how they change and (2) knowledge of methods by which individuals can be helped to define and carry out problem-reducing tasks. The most fruitful source of relevant knowledge about problem change has resulted from research on interpersonal treatment, including studies comparing brief and extended forms of treatment,[21] investigations of brief treatment alone,[22] research on terminations from open-ended treatment,[23] and findings on the rate of progress in long-term treatment.[24] This body of research has provided support for the central propositions in our theory of problem change:

1. The problems most clients bring to social agencies represent temporary disequilibria in steady states.
2. These problems are likely to become alleviated in response to reequilibriating forces, particularly the client's motivation to change and the actions he may take.
3. Most of the change in these problems is likely to occur within a relatively brief span of time, generally not more than two or three months.
4. After reequilibriation has occurred, the client's motivations, actions, and other change forces will diminish, making additional increments of change more difficult to achieve.

The above propositions represent a different use of systemic concepts than that found in crisis theory. The latter theory deals with an upset in the individual's equilibrium related to a hazardous event. This upset is pronounced and usually time-limited.[25]

While the task-centered model can be applied in crisis situations, it is also intended for chronic conditions where the specific source of motivation for the client to seek help is difficult to determine. It is hard to fit such cases into crisis theory as it is usually conceived. The task-model assumes, how-

[21] Reid and Shyne, *Brief and Extended Casework;* J. M. Schlein, "Comparison of Results with Different Forms of Psychotherapy," in C. E. Stollak, B. C. Guerney, Jr., and M. Rothberg (eds.), *Psychotherapy Research* (Chicago, Rand McNally, 1966), pp. 156–62.

[22] Howard J. Parad and Libby G. Parad, "A Study of Crisis Oriented Planned Short Term Treatment," part I, *Social Casework,* 49:342–55 (1968); L. Bellak and L. Small, *Emergency Psychotherapy and Brief Psychotherapy* (New York: Grune & Stratton, 1965).

[23] Irving A. Fowler, "Family Agency Characteristics and Client Continuance," *Social Casework,* 48:271–77 (1967).

[24] Hans. H. Strupp, Ronald E. Fox, and Ken Lessler, *Patients View Their Psychotherapy* (Baltimore: Johns Hopkins University Press, 1969).

[25] Reid and Epstein, *Task-Centered Casework,* pp. 80–82.

ever, that these persons have experienced some subtle breakdown in their capacity to manage their problems. They appear to desire to reduce the intensity of their problem to where it can be "lived with," rather than to secure more extensive changes. The amount of change secured appears to restore the client's equilibrium so that motivation is not present for further work.

Given this formulation of problem change, the role of the practitioner is to enable the client to take action to alleviate his problems as constructively as possible within a limited period of time. The question then becomes: what forces can be mobilized in individual or group treatment contexts to help clients take the most effective action? The task-centered model does not draw upon methods related to any one change theory, but attempts to incorporate methods from different theories. Thus, it draws on psychoanalytic and cognitive theories for methods of helping clients gain insight into psychological obstacles preventing task accomplishment; on social learning theories as a basis for reinforcement and modeling techniques to facilitate task accomplishment; on communication theory for methods of task-centered work with couples and families; and on small-group theories regarding how individuals interact in small social systems to facilitate each other's problem-solving, decision-making, and task performances. In general, the principle is to adapt from whatever theories may help clients carry out tasks.

With most theoretical approaches to social work practice, it is assumed that a worker should be in possession of some *particular* body of knowledge of human behavior or the social environment in order to practice a given model at some minimal level of competence. Thus, the psychoanalytically oriented practitioner is expected to have knowledge of psychodynamic theory. In the task-centered model, a different position is taken. The theory and methods *essential* for the practitioner to know are contained in the exposition of the model itself. It is assumed that practitioners who use the model will know more than the model explicates, but the question of precisely what kinds of additional knowledge may be needed is left open. Certain guidelines for the acquisition and utilization of additional knowledge may be offered, however. First, the elements that comprise this practice framework direct the practitioner to certain kinds of literature. Thus, when constructs such as interpersonal conflict and group structure are wed, it is assumed that the practitioner has or will acquire some familiarity with theory and research relevant to them. Second, practitioners should make an eclectic use of behavioral theory and research as needed to help clients identify problems, and to help them formulate and carry out problem-solving tasks. For example, a practitioner may utilize one of many theories of depression to help a depressed client figure out the kinds of actions that may be taken to alleviate this emotional distress. This will be done in relationship to the client's identification of the sources of such distress. While practitioners are free to use theories of their choice, it is necessary that they test their theoretical notions quite carefully against case data. In other words, the worker must respect the value placed on the supremacy of empirical data. For this reason, an inductive approach is preferred—that is, one that moves from the facts of the case to whatever formal theory, if any, might be best able to explain the facts of the purposes of treatment.

FEATURES OF THE MODEL

Before describing task-centered work with groups, the major features of the casework model from which it was derived will be reviewed. During the first sessions of casework, the problems perceived by the client are elicited, explored, and clarified. The practitioner and client then seek agreement on the problems to which their work will be directed. Once the decision regarding problems has been reached, the worker and client then choose client tasks—that is, what the client is to do to reduce the severity of the problem or eliminate it altogether.

Following this task definition, a decision is made on the length and frequency of service. The subsequent work of the practitioner is then devoted toward helping the client complete the chosen task. Finally, in the last, or next-to-last interview, the client is helped to specify his task-attainment, apply what he has done to other problems, and define future tasks that might be undertaken indefinitely.

It is not the intention of this paper to give any greater detail than the above on the rationale, methods, supporting theories, or evaluation of outcomes of task-centered casework. Rather, the intent here is to specify how small-group processes may be used to help clients accomplish tasks related to their problems. In this respect, the basic practice assumptions of Reid and Epstein are accepted.

In task-centered work with groups, the steps to be taken by the worker will vary from the task-centered casework model because of the worker's use of the group process in helping the members formulate and attain tasks.

These steps will be noted here and described subsequently in greater detail.

1. Preliminary interview. Task-centered group work starts with an individual interview in which problems are elicited, explored, and clarified. The worker and client thereby reach agreement on the problem(s) which will be addressed. In addition, if the worker thinks that the client can be helped to attain tasks through group processes, this possibility is presented, and acceptance or rejection of group treatment secured. An orientation to group participation is provided and the member's reactions to discussing problems and formulating tasks in a group are elicited. Responses that indicate severe anxiety or other adverse reactions must be reduced prior to group participation. Under some other approaches to group work, this preparatory work is done in the group, but the task-centered group work model with its short-term emphasis requires that the group help with members' tasks almost immediately. In this interview, the worker also describes the general outlines of task-centered group work.

2. Group composition. The worker decides upon group composition, a process which does not usually involve the clients, and which requires a decision on the range of client attributes to be considered as well as the size of the group.

3. Group formation. In the first group meeting, and sometimes in later ones, the members are helped to tell each other about the problems they will seek to reduce or eliminate through formulating and accomplishing tasks.

4. Group processes for task accomplishment. Once tasks are agreed upon, the practitioner works with the members so they can help each other to accomplish tasks within the agreed-upon period of time. It should be remembered that client tasks may include the client's modification of his or her own behavior, the behavior of significant others, or the functioning of social institutions.

5. Termination. At the end of the determined time period, the group members are helped by the worker to assess each member's task completion and his or her subsequent responsibilities in view of the degree to which this completion has been attained.

THE PRELIMINARY INTERVIEW

In task-centered group work, the process of exploring the client's problems and reaching agreement on the target problem occurs in the same way as if the client were to receive casework service.[26] During this phase in casework, the problem may be narrowed in scope and its characteristics delineated. In group work, however, these processes are delayed until the client is in a group, as the group members can help each other with these processes as well as help to choose tasks based on the nature of their respective problems.

In the initial interview a decision is also made as to the value of task-centered work for the client. Reid and Epstein suggest that certain types of clients are not appropriate for their casework model, and their exclusion from task-centered group work appears valid for the same reasons.[27] These include clients with problems which do not appear to relate to specific tasks, such as emotional reactions with unknown origins, psychogenic conditions, and habit disorders. In addition, in this interview a decision must be reached by client and worker as to whether the client will receive service through casework, group work, or some other alternative. While writers have discussed criteria for this choice, new investigations must be undertaken to determine the conditions under which either task-centered casework or group work is appropriate because of unique aspects of these approaches.[28]

In all situations the client's informed choice of individual or group treatment should be a central factor. In helping a client to make a choice, the worker considers problems in confidentiality, the client's ability to interact in group situations, and the demands the client is likely to make on the worker and other group members. Yalom found that persons are likely to be satisfied with their therapy groups if the following conditions exist:

1. They view the group as meeting their personal needs.
2. They derive satisfaction from their relationships with other members.
3. They derive satisfaction from their participation in the group task.
4. They derive satisfaction from group members vis-à-vis the outside world.[29]

---

[26] *Ibid.*, p. 147.   [27] *Ibid.*, p. 55.

[28] For discussions on choice between individual and group treatment, see Charles Garvin and Paul Glasser, "The Bases of Social Treatment," in Glasser, Sarri, and Vinter (eds.), *Individual Change*, pp. 496–98; Irving D. Yalom, *The Theory and Practice of Group Psychotherapy*, pp. 156–79.

[29] *Ibid.*

In the preliminary interview the client is oriented to participation in a task-centered group. There is a consideration of the ways in which each group member can describe his situation to others so help can be secured to clarify the problem and identify tasks to be undertaken. This discussion helps the client to understand how the group members, with the assistance of the worker, seek to help each other define tasks. It also gives the worker information regarding the amount of help each client may need in making use of the group.

Early experiences with task-centered group work indicate that the problems dealt with through the casework model can also be approached through group work. Reid and Epstein have developed a tentative typology of these problems which consists of the following categories.[30]

1. Interpersonal conflict. This is defined as any conflict occurring in the interaction between two individuals. Examples include parent-child and marital relationships, as well as teacher-pupil and employer-employee. The group is a useful place to identify and work on such problems because of the opportunities offered to practice performing interpersonal tasks.

2. Dissatisfaction in social relations. This category includes concerns about interpersonal relations. These concerns are focused around the behavior of the individual client rather than on the interaction between the client and others. Examples include the inability to make friends, as well as deficits in handling situations requiring aggressiveness or tact. Again, the group is an excellent place to identify relevant tasks and to carry out some tasks.

3. Problems with formal organizations. This category may include some of the elements of interpersonal conflicts or dissatisfactions, but in relation to an organization. The distinguishing feature here is that the difficulty is with a type of position in an organization rather than the idiosyncratic characteristics of the individuals involved. In task-centered group work it is possible that other group members may have similar problems so that joint tasks might evolve that involve social action to change policies of welfare organizations, school systems, hospitals, and so forth.

4. Difficulties in role performance. These problems include the client's concerns about meeting expectations related to roles the client has achieved—such as student, employee, or group member. Such roles can often be simulated in a group as a means of further task specification.

[30] Reid and Epstein, *Task-Centered Casework,* pp. 42–48.

5. Problems of social transition. Persons in our society are often involved in moving from one social position to another. Examples are leaving an institution such as a hospital, graduating from college, and securing a divorce. Tasks for dealing with associated problems are often plural and include decisions about attempting the transition and learning the skills associated with the transition. Frequently, groups will be composed of members experiencing a similar transition and thus will facilitate identifying tasks and securing support in task performance.

6. Reactive emotional distress. On occasion, clients will identify a problem in terms of their emotional reactions to a situation. This often occurs when the client does not believe he can do much to alter the situation although it is a concrete one such as a death or an illness. The client may then choose tasks which effectively discharge emotions or desensitize them. On occasion, groups may also be formed of persons experiencing common emotional distresses, although the possibility of mutual reinforcement of the undesired emotion must be considered.

7. Inadequate resources. When clients require concrete resources that can be secured by clients through task achievement, the problem falls into this category. Here also, clients in a group may often share similar needs and can help one another in identifying tasks relevant to obtaining resources such as money or housing.

GROUP COMPOSITION

There is considerable discussion in the literature regarding principles that should guide the composition of treatment groups. Many of these principles may appropriately be considered for task-centered groups.[31] In field tests of task-centered group work, the size of the groups was the same as that recommended for other therapeutic groups—from five to eight members—and this appeared to work well. This size allowed for discussion to develop in the group to help members identify and achieve tasks. The group was not so large as to prohibit any member from receiving needed help. In the experience of the writers, groups whose members have considerable homogeneity of problem can be slightly larger than those heterogenous in this respect.

The issue of homogeneity versus heterogeneity is a basic one whenever group composition is considered. It is proposed that task-oriented groups

[31] See Harvey J. Bertcher and Frank Maple, "Elements and Issues in Group Composition," in Glasser, Sarri, and Vinter (eds.), *Individual Change*, pp. 186–208.

will be more effective agents when the tasks of members are similar rather than different. Thus, for example, a group of adults on probation might have more ideas about the kinds of tasks relevant to remaining out of prison than persons not in this role. A task approach, however, can occur with groups with heterogeneous tasks when the members can see other similarities among themselves. A group of divorced adults may be motivated and able to help each other with tasks related to such varied problems as parent-child relationships, settling remaining conflicts with ex-spouses, obtaining new friendships, and—if they can appreciate commonalities derived from the divorce experience itself—coping with social stigma attached to their divorced status.

Task-centered groups will usually be formed groups. Family work is also possible, but the latter will not be considered here. Such groups will *always* depend on voluntary membership and can occur in both residential and nonresidential settings. Membership will almost always be closed, as members should optimally be learning together to specify problems, select tasks, and work on tasks. There may be some occasions, however, when members will be willing to help a new client to go through these phases which the older member has already accomplished. Because of this possibility, workers should not be rigid on the question of an open versus a closed group.

GROUP FORMATION

In the initial group meeting the members are asked by the worker to help each other to select the target problem to be worked on in the group. The worker acknowledges that initial work has been done on this in the pregroup interviews, and states that, as members form relationships among themselves, they may reevaluate their choice of problems. In some cases the statement of problems may remain the same. In other situations members may be hesitant to choose certain problems when they actually become acquainted with each other or, on the other hand, the comfort with which some members express problems may free other members to do the same. Members will begin to develop interpersonal ties as they seek out "commonalities and compatabilities with respect to personal values and attitudes, to group purposes, and to activities and tasks." [32] Garland et al., have

[32] Rosemary Sarri and Maeda Galinsky, "A Conceptual Framework for Group Development," in Robert D. Vinter (ed.), *Readings in Group Work Practice* (Ann Arbor: Campus Publishers, 1967), pp. 78–79.

termed this phase "pre-affiliation," as members may also still be resolving ambivalences regarding a commitment to the group.[33]

The process for determining the target problem will occur during the formation phase of the group. This process is as follows: [34]

1. The array of problems with which *each* client appears to be concerned is elicited.
2. The different problems or various aspects of problems are defined in behaviorally explicit terms. Here, the group members can be particularly helpful to one another. The group can be given examples of explicit and nonexplicit statements, and members can help each other to give more information. For example, a nonexplicit statement was given by a group member who stated, "I don't get along with my son." That member was helped, through questions and examples, to state, "I don't know what to do when he laughs when I tell him he's going to get into trouble with the friends he's usually with."
3. The target problem is then selected through the combined efforts of the client, the worker, and the other group members. As in task-centered casework, the problem the client is most interested in resolving is normally the one selected. In the group, however, additional variables are introduced as the client may decide to work on certain problems because of their similarity or dissimilarity to those of other clients. The worker may also suggest an order of precedence when several members have similar problems and when this ordering will facilitate the members' helping each other in the identification of tasks. The worker, however, should avoid suggesting an ordering of problems because of the special needs of a particular client, particularly when this is a disservice to others. All members may benefit, however, when one member chooses to work on a particular issue early in the group's life, if this same issue is likely to concern others later.
4. The target problem is classified by the worker, using the problem categories described earlier. The same rationale as that used in the casework model is applicable—boundaries are set for assessment and treatment planning is facilitated. As research further identifies

[33] James A. Garland, Herbert E. Jones, and Ralph L. Kolodny, "A Model for Stages of Development in Social Work Groups," in Saul Bernstein (ed.), *Explorations in Group Work: Essays in Theory and Practice* (Boston: Boston University School of Social Work, 1965), pp. 21–30.

[34] For the casework process, see Reid and Epstein, *Task-Centered Casework,* pp. 58–60.

connections between classification, group composition, and group processes for selecting and working on tasks, the findings can be shared with the group. At the current stage of knowledge it is unlikely that group members will be able to use the classification, except as it may illuminate the range of possible problems to be considered. The worker, nevertheless, applies the classification as he continues to plan how to help individuals to help each other. The classification can then serve as the basis for hypotheses regarding the choice of interventions in the group.

5. The target problem is specified through further exploration. This is a phase in which characteristics of the problem are delineated and the scope of the problem narrowed. Here again, group members may, on occasion, respond better to each other than to the worker in providing further information or scaling down too broad a problem.

6. Another possibility that the group often offers is that it provides the place where the first attempts to accomplish some tasks may occur even though the plan should always include the eventual accomplishment of the tasks outside the group. Many of the problem categories described above suggest tasks that can be performed first in the group. Such categories include, for example, problems in interpersonal conflicts, dissatisfaction in social relations, and difficulties in role performance.

GROUP PROCESSES FOR TASK ACCOMPLISHMENT

Utilizing conceptualizations of Vinter [35] and Garvin and Glasser,[36] the worker can choose among three types of interventions to help members accomplish their tasks: direct, indirect, and extragroup. Within the task-centered framework the client system is always viewed as the individual. It is the *problem alleviation and related task accomplishment of the individual group member that is the ultimate criterion of success*. Direct means of influence are defined as interventions with the worker's intent to secure change in an individual member. Indirect means are defined as interventions through which the worker expects to effect modifications in group conditions which subsequently affect one or more members.[37] Extragroup means of influence include activities conducted on behalf of clients outside the group.

[35] Robert D. Vinter, "The Essential Components of Group Work Practice," in Vinter (ed.), *Readings in Group Work Practice,* pp. 8–38.

[36] Garvin and Glasser, "Social Group Work," pp. 1263–72.

[37] Vinter, "Essential Components," p. 18.

For purposes of consistency in the use of the task-centered approach, Reid and Epstein's classification of casework activity is utilized as a means of describing the worker's direct means of influence in groups. Thus, workers can use the techniques of exploration, structuring, enhancing awareness, encouragement, and direction in interacting with individuals in groups as well as in dyadic situations.[38] Although the communications from the worker who uses these techniques can also have effects on group processes, these interventions still resemble worker communications in a casework situation and can have similar consequences.

The most significant contributions of task-centered group work are the indirect means of influence—that is, worker actions ranging from those that change group conditions to those that help members accomplish tasks. Indirect means of influence include manipulating group composition, helping to define group purpose, and modifying group structures and group processes. Compositional issues have been described above, but the other worker actions in this category will now be described:

1. Helping members achieve consensus regarding group purpose. By "purpose" is meant short-term objectives related to the group's goal of helping members attain tasks. As such, group purpose may be considered analogous at a group level to client task at an individual level. A group purpose in the traditional sense is most likely to emerge when members have highly homogeneous problems and tasks. For example, a group was formed to help members achieve tasks related to leaving a mental hospital. One purpose for a group meeting was to disseminate information about hotels for ex-patients. At another meeting the purpose was to help members learn about employment opportunities. When members have dissimilar problems or tasks the purpose is often a more abstract one, such as "helping each other to work on tasks." On occasion, members with dissimilar tasks may be helped through a common group purpose. For example, a group was composed of members with the following tasks:

Mrs. A: Decide whether to remain with a hostile employer.
Mrs. B: Break off a relationship with an undesired suitor.
Mrs. C: Work out with her husband a greater authority role for herself in the family.

[38] For an explanation of these techniques, see Reid and Epstein, *Task-Centered Casework,* pp. 139–75. These are partly chosen from Florence Hollis, "Explorations in the Development of a Typology of Casework Treatment," *Social Casework,* 48:335–41 (1967).

Mrs. D: Help her daughter with interpersonal problems the daughter is experiencing in school.

Mrs. E: Help her parents to accept the fact she will no longer live at home.

These members negotiated a purpose for several group sessions of learning how to be more assertive and learning how to deal with feelings of anxiety surrounding assertiveness.

Achieving consensus concerning group purpose is classified as an indirect means of influence because group norms, expected behavior of group members, and structures and processes in the group are strongly determined and selected by reference to group purpose. As decisions are to be made on these issues, information on group purpose can be used to choose among potential alternatives. For example, the purpose of discussing and evaluating alternative approaches to child-rearing has many implications for these other dimensions. Members will begin to speak with candor about their ability to respond to their children's behavior. An appropriate group structure which might emerge would be for some members to record their experiences with the suggested child-rearing alternatives.

2. Helping members with group structures. Group structures influence the ways in which groups can help members to determine and fulfill tasks. Among the structures which should be considered are the communications structure, the sociometric structure, the normative structure, the division of labor, and the leadership structure.[39]

The communications structure refers to who in the group speaks to whom about what. Communication structures can enhance task accomplishment if maximum participation is attained in group problem-solving, if no member withdraws from the communications network, and if information regarding definitions of tasks and attainment of tasks is clearly transmitted among the members. A task-oriented communication structure will include ways of sharing information on tasks selected and the state of accomplishment of tasks. This might be in the form of written charts shared within the group or in opportunities provided for members to report on progress to one another.

The sociometric structure is the affectional pattern within the group: member's feelings regarding other members and the subgroups that form as

[39] Garvin and Glasser, "Social Group Work," p. 1269.

a result of these emotions. Subgroups can be constructive if the members can help one another in relation to their tasks. Such subgroups can create barriers to task attainment if they hinder the emergence or accomplishment of group purposes. Members should learn to support one another in relation to their tasks: individuals who are members of antagonistic subgroups or who are isolated from relationships with other group members may not secure needed support and are often lost from the group. Subgroups often emerge around common tasks and similar progress in task accomplishment. The worker must identify the effect of these subgroups on task accomplishment and call to the attention of the relevant members structural problems that arise.

The normative structure refers to the pattern of belief among group members about appropriate behaviors in the group. Underlying this structure are values held by members about what is desirable and undesirable, acceptable and unacceptable. Norms which further the work of task-centered groups are those which support the value of defining and working on tasks, as well as the value that members should help one another in this endeavor.

Groups also develop a division of labor. In some groups, selected members take responsibility to record tasks; other members help clarify tasks. Others reinforce their fellows for fulfilling tasks; and still others may, in some groups, take on such roles as arranging for the time and place of meetings, checking on the needs of absent members, and serving refreshments.

The leadership structure describes the location of leadership activities. One of these activities is to define and further group purposes; the other is to enhance group maintenance and reduce intragroup tensions.[40] In task-centered groups some members may share with the worker responsibilities for focusing the group on its purposes and others will help in the reduction of tensions which may arise as members struggle to achieve their tasks.

The worker has several means he can utilize to help members change group structures in order to enhance the attainment of group goals. The practitioner will at times call the attention of members to such problems in order to help them seek solutions; at other times the worker may use a program to

[40] For a comprehensive treatment of this approach to leadership, see Robert F. Bales, "Task Roles and Social Roles in Problem-Solving Groups," in Eleanor E. Maccoby, Theodore M. Newcomb, and Eugene L. Hartley (eds.), *Readings in Social Psychology,* (New York: Holt, Rinehart, and Winston, 1958), pp. 437–46.

enhance group purposes. Programs which have been used successfully include role plays, films which model approaches to task attainment, and
games which contain—in simulated form—some of the task problems on
which members are working. The worker may also use reinforcements of
behaviors as a means of changing structures; examples include rewarding
members for leadership acts, new ways of communicating, or behaviors
consistent with new norms. The worker may also use some structures as a
means of modifying other structures—for example, calling attention to
group norms which are contrary to the existence of hostile patterns among
subgroups.

3. Helping members with group processes. Another dimension of indirect means of influence is the worker's effect on group processes. Among
the major processes of interest are problem-solving processes, group-control
processes, and program processes.[41]

Problem-solving process in groups has been a major interest to group
workers as well as social scientists, and a number of models are in existence. Among those which will be of use to a task-oriented worker will be
Bales' and Strodtbeck's concept of phases of group problem-solving and
Maple's concept of shared decision-making.[42] Problem-solving approaches
will usually be used to help members decide which tasks to undertake to alleviate problems. The members will begin this process by securing information as to the skills and resources necessary for task accomplishment. They
will then evaluate alternative tasks in terms of the effects on themselves as
well as others. The necessary sequence of steps to perform the task will then
be analyzed. Throughout, the worker must be aware of when the members
are ready for a new phase of problem-solving and what help in focusing they
require. As shall be seen later in the report of a clinical trial of the model,
these are essential ingredients to success.

Control processes—those in which members seek to influence each
other's behavior—can facilitate task achievement. For example, the worker
will try to help the group establish norms that are supportive of members'

---

[41] A comprehensive review of the worker's effects on group processes is contained in
Charles D. Garvin, "Group Process; Usage and Uses in Social Work Practice," in Glasser,
Sarri, and Vinter (eds.), *Individual Change,* pp. 209–32.

[42] Robert F. Bales and Fred L. Strodtbeck, "Phases in Group Problem Solving," in Dorwin
Cartwright and Alvin Zander (eds.), *Group Dynamics: Research and Theory* (3d ed.; New
York: Harper & Row, 1968), pp. 380–98; Frank Maple, "Shared Decision Making: A Systematic Approach to Setting Goals," mimeographed, undated (Ann Arbor: University of Michigan).

work on tasks. These norms will include limits on the introduction of extraneous material, expectations that members will work on attaining tasks, and encouragement to members to frankly present information relevant to their tasks. When group norms exist, members discover ways to secure conformity with these norms. The worker's role is to see that group norms articulate with treatment objectives as well as professional ethics and values. There are times, however—such as when a member is scapegoated for his problem—when these control processes limit task attainment; these negative situations must be watched for by the worker.

Program processes are those that are established through an activity: taking a tour, followed by a discussion; role-playing a work situation in order to learn to handle competition; engaging in a problem-solving process on child management—all have beginnings, middles, and endings, and the nature of these sequences can often be predicted. Task-centered group work must eventually include propositions regarding the effects of various program tools on problem specification, task selection, and task accomplishment. Role-playing, for example, may be useful in all these ways. Problems can be identified through dramatizing interactions, tasks can be selected through observing examples of tasks that are role-played, and task performance can be rehearsed through the same medium. Engaging in such activities as meeting another group or having social events may constitute task accomplishments for persons whose problems lie in dissatisfaction in social relations. A social-action program is an appropriate example for persons experiencing problems with formal organizations.

The agenda for a task-centered group meeting has similarities to the task-centered casework interview.[43] If members have similar tasks they can rotate reporting on work accomplished since the previous session. Members can be helped to reinforce one another, to discuss any required alternative approaches, or define new subtasks.

When members' tasks differ from one another the focus of group discussion will often be on one member; meanwhile, that member proceeds through steps which are similar to those taken in task-centered casework.[44] Members can help each other by supplying reinforcement and coaching. They can also suggest alternative approaches, and further define tasks. For this type of group the membership is best kept to five (or fewer) members, so that no member waits too long without receiving help. Depending on the

---

[43] See Reid and Epstein, *Task-Centered Casework,* pp. 176–80.   [44] *Ibid.*

member's potential for postponement of gratification, some may have to wait until the subsequent meeting to secure full group attention if such help is based on a rotational procedure.

Progress in task-centered group work—especially for problems involving interpersonal conflict, problems with formal organizations, and problems of social transition—often requires the worker with or on behalf of the client to interact with individuals and systems outside of the group. The following are some types of interventions which are appropriate in this context:

1. The worker may collaborate with other persons and organizations to create opportunities for tasks to be performed. Thus, the child whose task is to perform certain classroom activities will require a teacher to make relevant assignments.
2. The worker may assist relevant others to supply reinforcement to the client for task performance. The teacher in the example above can be helped to give the child praise for completed tasks.
3. The worker may have to utilize whatever legitimate authority is possessed to change situations which prevent clients from fulfilling tasks. He may press for the modification, for example, of school rules or even for the removal of a teacher who fails to permit or record appropriate tasks.

In all of these instances, the worker will consult with the client before utilizing extragroup means of influence. The client's values in these matters are crucial, as are his perceptions of possible effects of such actions. The reason for including these actions within the model, however, is that task-centered work must recognize that client's work on tasks cannot be abstracted from other components of the life space of the client.

TERMINATION

In task-centered group work the issue of termination is raised in the first group session when the number of meetings, length of meetings, and their frequency are presented. The next to the last group session is also devoted to an evaluation of progress in fulfilling tasks. Group members can then reinforce each other's achievements, particularly for performance of tasks which are repeated.[45] Members are also encouraged to help each other to state the kinds of things each can do to stabilize their problem situations at the level of improvement secured through task accomplishment. This is particularly

---

[45] This relates to the concept of open and closed tasks. *Ibid.* pp. 115–16.

important when members have learned through the group some new ways of acting that are relevant to performing tasks.

It is important that there be discussion of feelings about the group experience so that members can be helped to deal with those feelings which make termination difficult. Such feelings may relate to leaving other members as well as the worker, and include guilt reactions, feelings of rejection, and fear of the emotional consequences of relinquishing the gratifications of treatment. Unusually strong feelings on the part of members may require longer time intervals between the last few meetings. Such a change in the spacing of meetings can allow some emotions to diminish while members are simultaneously learning to become independent from the group.

When the members' tasks involve developing interpersonal relationships, the group or a subgroup within it may wish to continue as a social club. The worker can help such a group to affiliate with a community facility (such as a community center, community mental health program, or an educational institution). If some members wish to work on additional tasks after the group is terminated, arrangements can be made for another group experience for them.

REPORT OF A CLINICAL TRIAL

In keeping with the intention to develop treatment principles from clinical research, an early formulation of the task-centered group model was put into clinical trials between January and June, 1974. The practitioners were first-year students in a social treatment course which combined class, field, and research.[46]

Data on the problems, processes, and outcomes were obtained in the form of structured recordings and audio tapes. At this point, a preliminary analysis was made from the written records. Twelve students attempted systematically to apply the adaptation of task-centered casework to groups.[47] Twelve groups were formed; usable information was obtained from ten.

[46] Laura Epstein and William J. Reid, "The Coordinated Social Treatment Project," paper presented at the Annual Program Meeting of the Council on Social Work Education, San Francisco, California, February 25–28, 1973.

[47] The development of these structured programs and conclusions drawn from their use are reported in the cases of Ron Rooney, Susan Annis, Rita Klees, and Carol Jabs. The following term papers have organized some of the concepts related to these structures: Ron Rooney, "An Exploratory Study of Cohesiveness in a Task-Centered Group," SSA 304, April 1974; and Rita C. Klees, "The Use of Role Playing As a Treatment Technique in Task-Centered Casework with Children," SSA 304, April 1974.

The clients were active in the agencies cooperating with the project and providing the practicum: one adult out-patient community psychiatry setting and three inner-city public elementary schools. Nine groups were composed of boys and girls, mainly black children of poor families. There were a few white children and a few of middle-class status. Ages of the children ranged from nine to fourteen years. All the children's groups had not more than a three-year age spread. School classrooms and grade levels were grouped together, since referrals were initiated by teachers—often for their own pupils—or by friendship groups in the same class. Four of the nine children's groups were self-referred. Composition was both co-ed and exclusively boys or girls. The one adult group from the psychiatric clinic was composed of seven young black women, aged twenty-two to thirty-one years, who were self-referred applicants for treatment.

Sixty-six clients were seen in the groups for a total of sixty-eight sessions. Average group size was seven members. The average number of sessions was also seven.

In the children's groups, teachers' reasons for referral were congruent with the children's own perceptions of their problems. The main reasons for referral and self-referral were fighting among peers and academic underachievement. Pre-teen girls, however, were troubled with problems relating to sexuality and conflict with mothers and sisters. Tasks in the children's groups clustered into three main categories: (1) those dealing with improving academic performance, (2) those dealing with improving relationships with peers, and (3) with the teen girls, those dealing with reducing dissatisfactions with their own behaviors or those of significant others. Tasks in the adult group were desired actions such as: to talk up to husband, to budget, to go back to college, and so forth. As in the case in the task-centered casework model, these tasks were derived from the sense of the target problem; and target problems were specified sectors of the client's perceived "problem in living."

Ratings of task achievement were obtained from judgments of the student practitioners. In many intances this judgment reflects checks made with teachers. Although there was substantial variation in task achievement among individual group members, the present recordings do not always clearly designate the situation of each member at closing. Hence the ratings reported are generalized for the group as a whole. Despite its shortcomings, the available rating information is instructive. In three groups the members, on the average, achieved their tasks at a rating of substantial or better. In four groups the average was at a level of partial task attainment; in three, the average was minimal achievement of tasks.

Analysis of the reports suggests three conditions which were characteristic of the high-achieving groups: (1) specific behavioral target problems, such as "too few friends," and "grades too low for graduating," (2) tasks containing verifiable, public acts, such as "to learn friend-making skills," and (3) structured programs, based on group purposes, intended to shape successive increments of the desired behaviors. These increments were labeled subtasks. The successful structured programs were single-minded, narrow, and highly meaningful to the members. In one of these groups, role-playing was the program for the purpose of teaching and learning friend-making skills. In two of the successful groups, collecting and selectively disseminating semipublic records of problems and achievements was the central content of the group program. In the successful groups, indirect influences—in the form of group processes—drove the group forward to task achievement.

All the practitioners attempted to carry out the mandate of the model to be specific about the target problems and to devise observable tasks. The less successful and unsuccessful children's groups floundered upon high diversity among members' target problems and tasks. No unifying themes emerged. These groups revealed high intragroup conflict, strong leadership rivalries, and lack of commitment. Neither practitioners nor members could bind or organize the divisive group processes. The adult group presented a mixed picture at termination. Some members had clearly progressed, others had not. The information available on the adult group does not lend itself to any convincing explanation at this point, although a loose quality in directing the group emerges in the recording.

What is clear in the successful groups is that their members behaved as if they knew what they wanted, wanted what they said they did, and worked hard to get it. The poor-achieving groups spent their time in process-oriented discussions and behaviors, and in "having fun." It is not known what factors in group composition and in the climate set by the various agencies, and what features of practitioner style contributed decisively to low achievement. It is clear, however, that groups which focused on specific actions designed to overcome obstacles to task achievement did better than those which focused on process.

In addition to these usual task-centered procedures, however, the fact that the group mode was being suggested to the client necessitated acquainting the client with what he or she could expect in the group itself. Both clients and practitioners made a judgment about the appropriateness of the group. Clinical observations of the present sample strongly suggested that where this pregroup phase was casual and vague, the groups met in a climate of anxiety and members had crossed purposes which were never well resolved. Where target problems were identified and expectations clear, the individual members' tasks, nevertheless, had to become known to—and the property of—the group, and subject to change created by group processes. Thus, while the pregroup interviews were analogous to task-centered casework's familiarizing and problem-search phases, the initial group session was most closely analogous to the initial casework interview.

The middle phase of the group, roughly sessions two through five in the present sample, is the direct counterpart of task-centered caseworks' middle phase: an "obstacle course." Here, interferences with achievement were identified and means to overcome them were devised and rehearsed, consequences were anticipated, reinforcement and advice were provided, and effects examined. To enable the group to achieve, the practitioner needed to attend meticulously to repetitive reworking of rules and norms as the highest priority process. Other intragroup interactions in the successful groups were viewed with reference to how they did or did not advance the tasks—rather than a "good experiences"—with the goals of self-perception, perception of one's effects on others, self-actualization, and so forth.

The best performance was in groups which possessed high degrees of cohesiveness. At present, this cohesiveness is attributed to the relative homogeneity of target problems of the members.

The expectation in the task-centered groups was that the problem-reduction work would take place outside, not inside, the sessions. The sessions themselves were a stimulus and a place to acquire skills of whatever sort were needed to accomplish the tasks. Two high-performing groups evolved the practice of providing additional individual sessions for members having a particularly hard time; also, conferences were held with families and teachers. The practitioners in these groups evolved a profitable use of consulting pairs, composed of two group members who met inside or outside the sessions for mutual aid and who reported to the group on their discussions and actions.

Two examples may suggest the flavor of these groups. Group number 10 consisted of three boys and three girls, all thirteen years old, students in the eighth grade, with one month to go before graduation. All were in danger of failing but were thought by their teachers to be capable of doing the work. The goal of the group was for its members to pass and graduate. Pregroup interviews with each child and each mother established the expectations. In the pregroup interviews, the initial group session, and "consulting pair" discussions, each child's deficiencies, capabilities, and needed work were pinned down. An assessment sheet was devised, which each child kept and displayed, to identify what he had to do and what he had been able to do. To enhance the task focus, part of each session was given over to "consulting pairs" conferences.

Following the second session, the student-practitioner noted: "Clara did all her assigned work, she says, but did not keep her records properly. She is not enthusiastic and is in a mood to leave. Gloria not only did all her assignments but got good grades. She didn't keep her records either but devised a system of her own. Ronald did part of his work but the teacher will not accept his bibliography. . . ." Four of the six graduated. The same format used with another group achieved five out of six graduates.

Group number 5 did not fare this well. This was the clinic group of seven women who all had reactive depression. They viewed their problems dissimilarly. One was adjusting to getting a divorce, another to getting over having been deserted by a boy friend; another suffered from what the practitioners labeled "housewife syndrome—children getting to her." In some instances, members' tasks were explicit: to tell a husband his good points and also what she wanted; to make a budget in order to straighten out the family finances; to get back into college. Other tasks were "soft"—for instance, to "find ways to handle a depressing situation." By the initial session, several members had not been able to identify tasks. Attendance was erratic for some members. One dropped out. The practitioners strove to elicit efforts of the group to assist members, but these efforts resulted in uneven group performance and an absence of cohesiveness. Several of the members achieved substantial progress on tasks but others did not.

Future work must be directed to refining the techniques that were found most successful in these trials and to collecting information of a more definite nature about the characteristics of task-centered group practice.

NEXT STEPS

In this paper, task-centered work with individuals and with groups has been described. Topics discussed included selecting members for task-centered group work, composing task-centered groups, and sequencing the way in which group members help each other to define and work on tasks. Also presented was an analysis of worker interventions appropriate to working with groups with the purpose of helping members attain tasks. The paper concluded with the report of a clinical trial.

A number of issues have yet to be resolved regarding the extension of the task-centered model to groups. These will have to be settled by experience and research. Among the major questions are:

1. What are the limits as well as possibilities of task-centered work with groups?
2. Do criteria for inclusion of members in other types of social work groups hold for task-centered groups?
3. Under what conditions will homogeneity or heterogeneity of members with regard to problem or task be most helpful toward completing tasks?
4. What types of worker interventions into group and extragroup processes will most facilitate the ways in which task-centered groups help members?
5. If many persons can respond positively to either task-centered group work or casework, what other considerations—such as, timing, benefits of individual versus group experience, and costs—should be used in choosing between individual and group methods?
6. Finally, how can individual and group methods utilizing task concepts best be conceptualized and taught as one integrated approach within a comprehensive social treatment paradigm? It is recognized that the student and practitioner might well be equipped with a range of service models, and how this can be accomplished is a major task for educators—in agencies and schools—in the future.

BIBLIOGRAPHY

Bartlett, Harriet M. *The Common Base of Social Work Practice*. New York: NASW, 1970.

Garvin, Charles. "Education for Generalist Practice in Social Work: A Comparative Analysis of Current Modalities," *Journal of Education for Social Work*. In press.

——. "Task-Centered Group Work," *Social Service Review*, vol. 48 (December 1974).

Garvin, Charles and Paul H. Glasser. "Social Group Work: The Preventive and Rehabilitative Approach," in *Encyclopedia of Social Work,* 2 vols. New York:
NASW, 1971.

Glasser, Paul H., Rosemary Sarri, and Robert Vinter (eds.). *Individual Change
Through Small Groups.* New York: Free Press, 1974.

Reid, William J. and Laura Epstein. *Task-Centered Casework.* New York: Columbia
University Press, 1972.

Studt, Eliot. "Social Work Theory and Implications for the Practice of Methods,"
Social Work Education Reporter, vol. 16 (June 1968).

Wolf, Alexander. "Short-Term Group Psychotherapy," in Lewis R. Wolberg (ed.),
Short-Term Psychotherapy. New York: Grune & Stratton, 1965.

Yalom, Irving D. *The Theory and Practice of Group Psychotherapy.* New York:
Basic Books, 1970.

9

SOCIALIZATION THROUGH SMALL GROUPS [1]

ELIZABETH MCBROOM

The process of socialization is as pervasive as interpersonal relationships: whenever two or more people interact to influence each other, inputs and outcomes of change are assumed.

For this reason, socialization is an inevitable component of all theories of social work with small groups and of practice based on those theories. The model developed in this paper is an effort to identify, order, and operationalize those elements of socialization theory which have most specific relevance for social work practice with groups.

Definitions of socialization have ranged from those that are simplistic or succinct to those that are complex and include many variables. Alex Inkeles offered two brief definitions: "the process by which animal child becomes social man," and "socially relevant learning." [2] More extended statements define socialization as the process whereby an individual acquires attitudes, values, ways of thinking, needs, dispositions, the personal-social attributes of successive developmental stages, and, ultimately, the culture of groups in which he seeks membership.

The term socialization has come into wide use in the general vocabulary as well as in professional communications, and is subject to varying

---

[1] With appreciation for assistance and support to the library of the Western Australia Institute of Technology; the Reid Library, University of Western Australia; Royal Perth Hospital; University of Southern California; and Peter Jordan.

[2] Alex Inkeles, "Society, Social Structure and Childhood Socialization," in John Clausen (ed.), *Socialization and Society* (Boston: Little, Brown, 1968), p. 76.

definitions. The following alternate meanings are specifically excluded from the theoretical model developed in this paper:

1. In group work literature, socialization has often been described as the province of groups under lay auspices for informal education and character building, with Boy Scouts, Four-H clubs, and settlement houses as common examples. In that usage, socialization groups are differentiated from treatment groups. This paper will suggest applications of socialization theory to treatment groups.

2. Earlier writers have feared or actually encountered threats that the term will be taken in a political rather than a social and developmental context. Socialization has been equated with socialism as "alien" political philosophy. In the repressive climate of the early 1950s, when Charlotte Towle's *Common Human Needs* was burned by an official agency of the U.S. government, one of the charges was that it contained a reference to "socialization of children." In 1959 Robert Merton found it necessary to establish that a serious study of the socialization of medical students to meet expectations in their social roles as physicians did not constitute advocacy of socialized medicine.

3. The term has become a synonym for recreation or fraternization. This use is also common in clinical practice, as when a psychiatric prescription for socialization is discovered to mean "dances, music, and card games." Though learning social and sports skills may be an important part of socialization, the term is not used here in that narrow sense.

4. The term may be used pejoratively to denote "brainwashing" or forceful persuasion. A social work student, for example, may protest that he is being "socialized" to accept repressive agency policies that damage clients. This meaning, too, occurs in professional literature. For example, one attempt to quantify socialization outcomes utilized a continuum on which extremes of *highly criminal disposition* represented low socialization, while high socialization was operationalized as *highly rule-respecting, self-denying, and conforming behavior* (emphasis added).[3]

At developmental turning points through the life cycle, people confront new demands associated with changes in self and altered relationships in

---

[3] H. G. Gough, "An Interpretive Syllabus for the California Psychological Inventory," in P. McReynolds (ed.), *Advances in Psychological Assessment* (Palo Alto, Calif.: Science and Behavior Books, 1968).

their social networks. Social survival depends on some consensus regarding present and emergent goals and means of goal attainment. This consensus depends, in turn, on the individual's voluntary acceptance of group ways and meeting the requirements necessary for social functioning. Central to this process, to which the term socialization is applied, is the selective acquisition of knowledge of self and significant others in social interaction. This learning embraces the current values, attitudes, interests, and skills of groups to which a person belongs or aspires. It depends on feedback from an agent who models and teaches and whose approval is important. Drawing from the analysis of child-rearing, in which parents are agents and children are recruits who learn important social roles, the socialization model for social work conceptualizes social workers as agents and social agencies as settings for a process that may be developmental—normative for the individual's life stage; compensatory—for those deprived of social learning opportunities and experiences in the appropriate stage; or a corrective process—termed resocialization.

Early in the twentieth century, two American social philosophers, William James and George Herbert Mead, and a pioneering social theorist, Charles Horton Cooley, drew attention to the ways in which individual personality develops in primary groups. This subject became the focus of serious scientific study and a burgeoning scholarly and professional literature beginning in the 1930s. Similar themes underlie the development of theories of socialization and of small-group processes. These include the distinguishing characteristics whereby interaction in a group leads individuals to perceive themselves as interdependent entities in pursuit of goals guided by group norms and interpersonal bonds strong enough to contain disintegrating influences within the group.[4]

Socialization theory, in addition to its early roots in philosophy and the ideas of the symbolic interactionists, has drawn on the fields of social psychology, developmental psychology, psychoanalysis, cultural and comparative anthropology, and social structural theories of sociology.

One landmark publication of high relevance to the current subject is the 1955 work by Parsons and Bales, *Family, Socialization, and Interaction Process*. The authors' professed purpose was to conceptualize the nuclear family as a small, highly differentiated subsystem of society in which

---

[4] Morton Deutsch, "Group Behavior," in *International Encyclopedia of Social Sciences* (New York: Macmillan, 1969), 6:265.

parents' family roles as socializing agents interpenetrate with their roles in other systems, and in which children are socialized for and into extrafamilial roles. Of special interest is the extent to which Parson's theory of socialization as a family process drew on the empirical work of Bales and his associates, which was designed to analyze the structure and interaction process of small, task-oriented groups.[5]

Two recent anthologies have made available to social work students and practitioners the evolving social science formulations on this vast subject.[6] Specific references to social work are rare in these two collections, even by contributors in the Goslin volume who deal with treatment programs for specific groups. The rising interest of the profession in socialization theory related to social work practice, on the other hand, is indicated by the three articles on socialization in the 1971 edition of the *Encyclopedia of Social Work*.[7] The previous edition, published in 1965, included no comparable subject heading.

In sum, socialization in the group and by the group is a natural process, constantly evolving. The process has become, implicitly, a source of practice principles in social group work. The problem for development of theory and theory-based practice is to understand the process in its natural settings, to identify elements specifically appropriate to professional methodology, to rationalize them, and to construct predictive models.

The socialization model for social work practice may be conceptualized as follows: The major problem focus is inadequate opportunity for role-learning in the social network. The social worker's challenge, therefore, is to provide opportunities for changed role performance and interaction in novel situations. The targets of change are the self-concepts, internalized values, and expectations of self and others. The social worker, functioning as an agent of socialization and change, actively teaches, models, invites participation, works for definition of mutual responsibilities, and helps to accelerate learning and competence in social roles.

Considering the group as a means and context for socialization tasks,

[5] Talcott Parsons and Robert F. Bales, *Family, Socialization, and Interaction Process.*

[6] John Clausen (ed.), *Socialization and Society;* David Goslin (ed.), *Handbook of Socialization Theory and Research.*

[7] Catherine Chilman, "Socialization and Interpersonal Change," Margaret E. Hartford, "Socialization Methods in Social Work Practice," and Martin B. Loeb and William E. Berg, "Socialization, Social Structure and Personality," in *Encyclopedia of Social Work,* 2:1295–1310, 1311–15, and 1315–24.

enlarged understanding of the process involves identifying present and emerging social roles in which members are expected to engage during cycles of increasing autonomy and responsibility, followed eventually by disengagement.

As indicated above, the family is pivotal in theoretical approaches to social work with small groups, since it is the "target client group" as well as a major source of socialization and small-group theory. Much earlier work has assumed stability or slow change in family form and function. This assumption is now challenged by large-scale social experiments in other countries and more sporadic and unsanctioned ones in Western countries. In the United States, fatherless families constitute a significant portion of all child-rearing efforts, and other new forms, as well as childless families of varying sexual relationships and compositions, exist everywhere. These developments suggest that practice is far ahead of theory—most family treatment theory presumes the orthodox family of Parsonian properties and regards deviations as pathological. The pervasive influence of ecological concerns prescribe a secular change in which few—rather than more—children are the condition of species survival. This inevitably exerts powerful pressure on sanctions expressed in laws governing family mores. It also makes the developmental opportunities for children a matter of public concern.

Professional resources and practices that assure and extend these opportunities will be evaluated in terms of outcome, but they will also be supported by increased social value and economic rewards. Families will be the object of professional practice involving socialization theory, as will groups of persons in parental roles.

CORE VALUES

The central philosophy of socialization makes it congenial to professed democratic and social work values. The primary consideration is the emergence of selfhood and self-realization through social connectedness. This is the pervasive theme of Erik Erikson's writings on identity—that climax of development which comes with the sense of the continuity and significance of self and is affirmed by those whose recognition is of supreme importance: family and other primary groups. Though the value of self (the individual) is central, man does not flourish or even survive in isolation from his fellows. Therefore, society and social groups are viewed not as aversive to individuality but as the essential means of enhancing individual potential to its utmost. Thus, in addition to whatever competence strivings are innate, all humans are continually involved in a process of meeting—according to the variables of endowment and opportunity and the still incompletely explored interaction between them—the expectations of others. This is a complex process, and the fact that so many achieve so much is regarded by scholars as awesome.

Though some writers have bracketed socialization with behavioral modification, the essential difference between them lies in the important symbolic processes which account for the emergence of the social self as a consequence of interaction between the individual and significant others in his network. As a theory of development of self, therefore, socialization is an alternative to—rather than an element or subsystem of—classic stimulus-response reinforcement theory.[8]

Meyer has discussed the provision of human services as an indicator of social responsibility or social control, depending on provider and aim.[9] Some discussions have specifically equated socialization with social control. That is not the philosophical framework of this paper, which addresses the development of the person rather than conformity to institutions. Indeed, the value recognized in major theoretical writings is a view of the needs of society which is consonant with the person as the site of human values. A vital aspect of individual potential which has recently received increased attention in adult education and social work programs is the evidence that socialization is a lifelong process. Major social learning and role changes do, in fact, occur after childhood. A related value, which postulates openness of social systems and of the future, is the recognition that many are socialized for roles as change agents. This is essential to the viability of any system and is contradictory to ideas of monolithic conformity and to maintenance of the *status quo ante* as an important human or professional activity.

BEHAVIORAL SCIENCE BASE

Since the early years of the twentieth century, socialization theory has drawn on formulations of creative thinkers, observers, practitioners, and experimenters in many social science disciplines. It has contributed to and drawn on small-group theory and the empirical work that has expanded under-

---

[8] Goslin, *Handbook of Socialization Theory*, p. 17.
[9] Carol H. Meyer, *Social Work Practice* (New York: Free Press, 1970), p. 95.

standing of group process. Cooley, an early theorist who published his *Social Organization* in 1909, noted the influence of primary groups, especially the family and children's play circles, on attitude formation. Kurt Lewin, in the 1930s, introduced the group as a setting for research in social science, with particular attention to the psychology of social influence.[10] Contributions from psychology have characteristically reported on manipulation of influences in the laboratory, while sociologists carried out field studies in natural settings. Social psychologists were the first to combine field and laboratory methods.

These pluralistic sources of theory have led to parallel emphases on the interpersonal processes involved in socialization and on its social-structural aspects. The symbolic interactionist tradition stemming from G. H. Mead, for example, emphasizes interactional process in role relationships and is therefore classified as an interpersonal rather than a social-structural theory. Smith has contrasted these two approaches by differentiating the construct of socialization as a process whereby personality and selfhood emerge in the course of role-taking in progressively focused interactions from the notion of socialization as a means of "getting equipped to occupy a series of niches in the social structure." [11] These perspectives might also be contrasted in the extent to which each is dynamic or the degree to which each emphasizes the role of recruit and agent. Self-changes in the recruit—or emergence of self—is central to the interpersonal perspective. The social-structural view tends to emphasize the agent as equipper.

The converging streams of theory-building from social science are illustrated by the works of Inkeles, the sociologist, and Gladwin, the anthropologist: both proposed social competence as the outcome or aim of the socialization process.[12] Psychologist Robert White contributed three classical and somewhat controversial essays on the wellsprings of competence and its relevance to human development.[13] Foote and Cottrell have investigated and

[10] George C. Homans, "Study of Groups," *International Encyclopedia of the Social Sciences,* 6:259–64.

[11] M. Brewster Smith, "Competence and Socialization" in Clausen (ed.), *Socialization and Society,* p. 276.

[12] Alex Inkeles, "Social Structure and the Socialization of Competence," *Harvard Educational Review,* 36:265–83 (1966); Thomas Gladwin, *Poverty USA* (Boston: Little, Brown, 1967).

[13] Robert W. White, "Competence and the Psychosocial Stages of Development," Nebraska Symposium on Motivation (Lincoln: University of Nebraska Press, 1960); "Motivation Reconsidered: The Concept of Competence," *Psychological Review,* vol. 66 (1959); "Ego and Reality in Psychoanalytic Theory," *Psychological Issues,* vol. 3 (1963).

reported on "interpersonal competence," and have identified health, intelligence, empathy, autonomy, judgment, and creativity as its components.[14] Interpersonal competence so constituted could be taken as an ideal model for possible translation into criteria for measuring outcomes of treatment or practice.

The prototype of the socialization process has been child-rearing in the family. Rich contributions to theory have come from scholars of human development. Child-rearing has long been a major activity investigated by anthropologists; they have produced a wealth of cross-cultural data showing how children develop personalities consonant with the survival needs or value tenets of their group at a particular time and place. From the socialization perspective, certain traits—such as sex, aggression, and physical mastery—have been overstudied. At the same time, there has been relative neglect of important questions on the development of individual qualities pertinent to social relationships and learning, as well as the characteristics of family and other groups in which these processes occur.

Goslin characterized the main thrust of socialization as the investigation of the processes whereby individuals learn effective participation in social interaction—that is, interpersonal competence—and of the differential functions of individuals and groups.[15] Acknowledging individual differences, group survival requires a minimum—though not rigidly fixed—conformity to social norms and value standards. This definition suggests that social work practice and research can both profit from and contribute to the development of predictive models for behavior in groups and of groups per se.

Finally, Inkeles has proposed a matrix in which he relates socialization elements to life stages and to relevant aspects of social systems.[16] His purpose was to illustrate a mode of analysis of the relationship of the social structure to the socialization process. At the risk of distortion, which occurs when a conceptual scheme is lifted out of context, this matrix will be used as a framework for considering clients whose needs might be served by social group work following a socialization model. The elements have been widely used as major variables in socialization theory and research; they are: issue, agent, content, and task. The life stages he addresses are infancy, childhood and adolescence, adulthood, and old age.

[14] Nelson N. Foote and Leonard S. Cottrell, *Identity and Interpersonal Competence* (Chicago: University of Chicago Press, 1955).

[15] Goslin, *Handbook of Socialization Theory*, p. 2.

[16] Alex Inkeles, "Social Structure and Socialization," in Goslin (ed.), *Handbook of Socialization Theory*, pp. 618–20.

CLIENTS AND AGENCIES

Since socialization is a lifelong process to which all social organizations inevitably contribute, the strategy for planning professional services is guided by ecological and economic considerations. Socialization theory suggests a framework for relating services to life stages and concentrating them at those turning points that introduce changed social responsibility or altered opportunities and expectations. This life-cycle orientation also suggests strategies for organizing and offering social work services to populations in need or at risk because primary agents are, or have been, inadequate or absent. Additional populations stand in need of new services because of technological changes which result in rapidly shifting opportunities and successive loss of significant social roles during a life span that has increased remarkably.

Inkeles has identified as the socialization *issue* of infancy the state of helplessness and dependency on adults with the *objective* of survival and progression to the next stage. The infant's *task* is to gain body control and physical mastery and to learn language, a process which invokes the critical symbol system as well as the physical skills involved.

Infants are not organized into social groups, but the recital of issue, objective, and task immediately suggests the relevance of social group work based on socialization theory with parents of infants and young children. There is currently a surge of interest, worldwide, in parent education for child health and efforts to advise on "parentcraft." The messages which bombard young parents are often confusing, and lead to insecurity. The results of health education have been disappointing, with research showing minimal change in behavior resulting from classes and informational brochures. The socialization model for social work with groups would suggest structure and process to make available peer support and reinforcement from direct primary interaction, with the aim of increasing parents' competence and confidence to foster the developmental tasks of their infants.

Even agencies charged with special responsibilities for social services to parents, however, have not maximized the potential for help through groups, even where need appeared obvious.

Two populations have been the focus of social work interventions. The dynamics in these families are different; the extent to which intervention strategies should vary from families in which the intent is to support normal development has not been explicated. Parents of mentally retarded infants and young children have a different role with high and stressful demands in carrying out their socialization task. A recent study of how social workers in public health carried out the agency's mandate to help such parents found no groups organized, though parents were requesting help in groups.[17] Another special category, poignantly related to the objective of survival, is parents who have battered or abused their infants. Group intervention has been invoked with these parents, with preliminary evidence of effectiveness.[18]

The *issue* in late childhood and adolescence is the individual's capacity to adapt to change and society's uneven sanction for his assumption of adult roles. The adolescent's *task* is to manage changes in self and social expectations without disruption, and the *objective* of agents, who are outsiders now augmenting family, is to move the adolescent toward adult roles. The *content* is the values of the culture, specific earning skills, mature relationships, and adult responsibilities.

The social worker may well be one of the new extrafamilial agents who helps the adolescent with these complex tasks or who provides second chances for those already in serious difficulty because they have failed to manage the changes or encountered intolerable strain and dissonance in their efforts to achieve autonomy and emancipation. The content of socialization at this stage is also fraught with social and emotional complications. Many a youth needs, preferably in peer groups, a chance to compensate for earlier lacks in socialization in order to establish mutuality in sexual relations and carry out the social responsibilities entailed. Historically and currently, this has been the age span where most positive results have been reported and where much social group work effort has been concentrated.

The *issue* in adulthood is the individual's capacity to assume mature roles and serve as a responsible model for the next generation. The adult's *task* is to fit in and function with a range of expectations; there is less tolerance for failure than is accorded to youth. He must learn highly specific skills, often through depersonalized and "warehoused" procedures, and without the opportunity for peer support. The *objective* is competence in family and occupational roles, and the *content* is integration of the values, skills, and relationships for which the adolescent was striving.

Socially, adults are a burdened and neglected cohort; opportunities for

---

[17] Zonia Tappeiner, "Public Health Practice in the Socialization of Mentally Retarded Children," (D.S.W. dissertation, University of Southern California, 1972).

[18] C. Henry Kempe and Ray E. Helfer (eds.), *Helping the Battered Child and His Family* (Philadelphia: Lippincott, 1972).

personalized help with the tasks in selected peer groups have been almost nonexistent. This is true, as well, of adults in special statuses, including public-assistance recipients, where a few group opportunities for enhancing competence have been available. In fact, certain proposed research studies of the process have not been carried out because no group programs were established.[19]

Though they do not apply the terms used in this paper, two reports of efforts to help recipients of public assistance in groups describe the application of socialization principles. Wiltse and Fixel explored problems and need for social services and effectiveness of such service in the California State Department of Social Welfare.[20] Their design called for clear definitions of leader role and group purpose to be explicitly stated. It was expected that mothers would achieve more competence in coping with present and future problems, and that the agency would learn more effective ways to help clients. Group attendance was facilitated by supplying carfare and money for child care. The group was forthrightly discussed with clients as a basis for the decision to participate. Realistic control of survival needs emphasized the parental aspects of the worker's role. The worker knew the reality problems of the actual living situation and was able to provide needed tangible services. Differences reported in group members included increased interest and self-esteem, and ability to take responsibility and use community health facilities. They were more realistic and confident, and at the time of termination they acknowledged gains to be due in part at least to their group experience.

Navarre and her associates in Michigan reported research sponsored by the Children's Bureau to evaluate group practice with AFDC mothers.[21] The purpose was to influence parental behaviors in a group which had in common entrapment in poverty and frustration. Parents whose children had school difficulties related to parent-child interaction were invited to give and take help in time-limited groups which had as their goal individual change in attitudes, feelings, and behavior in relation to the purpose of the group—

[19] Wynn Tabbert, "The Development of Social Competence: A Comparative Analysis of Social Work Practice" (D.S.W. dissertation, University of Southern California, 1972).

[20] Kermit T. Wiltse and Justine Fixel, *The Use of Groups in Public Welfare* (Sacramento, Calif.: State Department of Social Welfare, 1963).

[21] Elizabeth Navarre, Paul H. Glasser, and Jane Constabile, "An Evaluation of Group Work Practice with AFDC Mothers," in Paul Glasser, Rosemary Sarri, and Robert Vinter (eds.), *Individual Change through Small Groups* (New York: Free Press, 1967), p. 7.

specifically, to help mothers support their children in achieving better school adjustment. Spin-offs were found in other gains in child-rearing effectiveness. Group participation had increased mothers' task performance, including child care and decision-making ability at home.

Success of the intervention was measured by behavior of children whose mothers attended the rehabilitation groups. While findings were inconsistent, the interpretation was that workers had succeeded in individualizing the group process sufficiently for each member to change differentially. A finding wholly consistent with the socialization model is that group work practice requires specificity and clarity of group goals and the means to achieve them, specificity of method, timeliness, and adequate coverage. The question of how to set priorities in the face of multiple, interrelated problems was unresolved.

Perceptions of the aged have been highly susceptible to cultural shifts. Old age in America has been regarded as an affliction, rather than an achievement. A beginning, however, has been made in social group work, taking into account useful aspects of socialization theory. Seguin, in a creative contribution to gerontology, has pointed out that as older people themselves become more self-actualizing, the *content* may be significant political, economic, and aesthetic roles.[22] Since role availability is a social-structural problem, the *task* may not need to be relinquishment of roles and associated rewards, but rather a succession of roles and competence in them. As in earlier life changes, the *issue* is adaptation to bodily change and related social expectations. Important *agents* are peers and those the aged person has earlier socialized. There are special difficulties for the aged, since peers tend to be devalued and the reference group often consists of younger people.

So much for hazards along the life span. Social group work is well equipped to help, but has left a vacuum that has been filled by agents and agencies of questionable qualifications and motives, or by massive recourse to drugs to meet otherwise unfulfilled relational needs. For all the groups mentioned, the agency of choice would be a community-based health and family agency where neighbors could fill multiple roles as planners, directors, helpers, and client-group members.

[22] Mary M. Seguin, "The Small Group as Agent of Socialization: A Model for Social Work Practice with Older Adults," paper presented at the 97th Annual Forum, National Conference on Social Welfare, Chicago, 1970.

Specialized groups often perceived in need of socialization include those who enter or leave the "other world" of total institutions: army, prison, hospital. Like people at developmental turning points, they meet major changes in self-perception and social expectations. These social factors are compounded for patients who suffer an actual change in self or self-image that occurs with the loss of a body part or a body function. Social group work under institutional auspices offers promise for many of these people. The socialization model has been explicitly applied in psychiatric hospitals and halfway houses to anticipate and support patients' return to more autonomous community roles.[23]

Goslin emphasized the importance of socialization settings as a source of external sanctions. Without them, the socialization process is impeded; socialization becomes impossible for the individual in isolation. There is a direct connection between interaction and motivation. Therefore, primary groups are the optimal setting for socialization; they promote maximal feedback and the chance for alternatives and experiment without disaster.[24]

This section, while not identifying existing agency auspices appropriate for practice of social group work purposefully based on socialization theory, has emphasized problems of systems and settings which are of high concern throughout the profession. If socialization theory is taken seriously as a guide to professional service which will enhance and extend opportunities for development of self and progressive engagement in vital social roles, the practice must be carried out in rationally designed service systems.

ISSUES OF TYPOLOGY AND STRUCTURE

One of the major issues involved in constructing a typology of groups for which socialization theory may provide appropriate guides to practice, concerns its basic sources in the family as the prototype of socialization setting and process. Emergent theory views the family as a small primary group, rather than a social institution. Group processes apply to the family as a continuous and autonomous group served in social work practice.[25] The family

[23] John A. Williams, "Ego Psychology: Its Application to Work with Socialization Groups—Chronic Patient," in *Ego Psychology: Its Application to Social Work with Groups in the Mental Hospital* (Washington, D.C.: U.S. Department of Health Education and Welfare, National Institute of Mental Health, 1963).

[24] Goslin, *Handbook of Socialization Theory*, p. 20.

[25] Margaret E. Hartford, *Groups in Social Work* (New York: Columbia University Press, 1972), pp. 24–26.

has been studied also as the prototype of the socialization pro(
uitous and has "first crack" at the infant and child in his
sionable stage. Talcott Parsons created a landmark with h
structural analysis of the family, for which he drew on empir
process in small task groups.[26] As a conceptual tool for opening the family
to social analysis, his scheme proved a useful supplement to the psychoanalytic theories of development and stress in the family triangle, which had
formerly claimed almost exclusive attention of social workers who essayed
to diagnose family problems. Like other theoretical formulations, however,
the Parsonian model in its turn was misused with the seductive assumption
that the structure of the nuclear American family, with its ascribed age and
sex roles, was timeless and universal.

Because of the influence of the work done by Parsons on both small-
group and socialization theory, it is briefly reviewed here with examples of
contemporary research which have led to reexamination and modifications.
These research findings have also contributed to socialization theory and
have direct application to social work with small groups.

Parsons identified the primary function of the family as providing a
social group in which the child can be totally committed and fully dependent
for the early stages of life while he internalizes the culture of his society.
The family can carry out this function because adult members have extrafamilial roles of strategic importance to their personalities. He proposed
that the primary connection of the family to the occupational system through
the husband/father's earnings from his occupation is the strongest differentiating feature in determining the ascribed status of all family members. The
father is the instrumental leader because of his occupational role as a component of his familial role; the woman's role as housewife, on the other hand,
is modal for the married woman with small children. She does not seriously
compete for status and earnings. Women's occupational roles, therefore, are
expressive and supportive to those of men.

Parsons made these differentiated sex roles the major axis of family
structure. The other criterion of role type is generation, or biologically given
power, especially when children are young. The sexual differentiation, he
stated, is qualitative, and appears in social interaction systems and small
groups, regardless of composition, according to the empirical findings of

[26] Parsons and Bales, *Family Socialization.*

Bales. Parsons explained that biological function forces males to specialize in the instrumental direction. He thereby arrived at his famous fourfold differentiation of role types: the father is the instrumental superior, technical expert, and executive leader; the mother is the expressive superior, cultural expert, and charismatic leader; the son is the instrumental inferior, inadequate technical performer, and cooperator; the daughter is the willing, accommodating, and loyal member. Parsons further stated that learning these ascribed roles must precede learning achieved roles. His dictum was influential in evaluations of development and concern that growing children achieve comfort in conventional sex roles.[27]

Later criticism of the structural theory of Parsons comes from many sources. One example is Chilman, who saw rigid definitions of sex-appropriate and age-appropriate behaviors as decreasing in validity, although remnants of this rigidity remain under pressures of poverty, racism, and militarism. Chilman cited G. H. Mead's interpersonal focus in role relationships as flexible and sensitive, in contrast to the idea of social structure as the major role determinant. She assessed the interpersonal aspects as more fulfilling and suitable than structural determinants for a transitional society.[28]

Many contemporary writers are advancing alternative ideas about family structure. Billingsley and Giovannoni, for instance, pointed out that the one-parent family is a particular type of social group for which services specific to needs should be provided, with no assumption of underlying pathology. They suggested studies of one-parent families that turn out well, with identification of how this result was achieved, as a pattern for social work services with other families. Agreeing that a major social function of the family is socialization of children, they pointed out that millions of children are now being reared in one-parent families in which there are wide variations of economic status, behavior, marriage patterns, and the extent to which children are developing wholesome identities.[29]

There is, of course, dissent from the Billingsley formulation. Sussman, in particular, pointed out the extent to which single-parent families lack flexibility and reserve. According to him, such families suffer increased strain;

[27] *Ibid.*, especially pp. 13–15
[28] Chilman, "Socialization and Interpersonal Change," p. 1301.
[29] Andrew Billingsley and J. M. Giovannoni, "Family, One-parent," in *Encyclopedia of Social Work*, 1:367.

are deprived of communication power and modeling, except for verbal modeling; and lose out on contacts in the neighborhood and formal socialization systems because they contain only one parent. All this affects the child's ability to handle normative demands, and there is less interaction experience and affectional need-meeting.[30]

Hill and Aldous have postulated a shift from parental to marital roles as the central focus of family life. Marital roles, neglected and postponed during the child-rearing period, must be confronted, as women have opportunities to become change agents as well as agents of socialization, and as fathers take more active family roles. They point to joint participation with more mutuality—rather than a pattern of role segregation—in family life. Furthermore, the family of orientation has never served as agent of socialization to marital roles, since the child can only observe the spouse system and cannot participate in marital roles. Alternative role-performance models occur in family life education, marital counseling, and formal socialization and resocialization agencies which transmit a range of alternatives, rather than behavioral prescriptions.[31]

Turning from general considerations about family structure to the particular topic of sex role, many current writers recognize that sex roles are themselves products of earlier socialization and represent society's requirements which dictated the ways in which members were restricted or encouraged to become self-reliant in childhood. It has been customary in many periods and many cultures to train daughters of the family to be obedient, responsible, and nurturing. Girls in the American middle class have characteristically been trained to be less aggressive, more emotional, less bossy, and more compliant in preparation for their chief role as mate. This is in contrast to boys, who are expected to compete in occupational roles. These factors in sexual identity operate from the first days of life. Sex-related behaviors conform to sex role expectations, which have had the strongest social reinforcement. Parents unconsciously encourage differential behaviors in sons and daughters from birth.

Margaret Mead has noted the constraints on identity which have operated in most child-rearing systems, so that behaviors of the opposite sex are incorporated as a negative ideal and rejected for self. The crossing of sex

[30] Marvin B. Sussman, "Family," in *Encyclopedia of Social Work*, p. 1:336.

[31] Rueben Hill and Joan Aldous, "Socialization for Marriage and Parenthood," in Goslin (ed.), *Handbook of Socialization Theory*, p. 943.

lines, even in occupational choice, has produced turmoil.[32] Treatment accorded to boys and girls at the oedipal phase already differentiates and dichotomizes male-female personality. Mead's primary thrust, however, is the generational hierarchy—rather than the sexual dichotomy—in family structure. She traces a development from slow-changing cultures in which authority derives from the past and adults learn from their peers, to predicting that the young will take on new authority in apprehension of an unknown future. This is in sharp contrast to the time when grandparents represented physical and cultural survival and provided complete models of life.[33]

Other questions about traditional parental power, authority, and roles in socialization appear in the reports of those who have observed alternate family forms. Bettleheim suggests major revision of accepted ideas about the age of peer influence in his comments on "crib mates" in an Israeli kibbutz.[34] The importance of the peer group begins to make a deep impact in the first days of life. Babies watch each other and mourn if one is removed. Their relationship is described as a twinlike interdependence; infants of both sexes share all vital steps in development. Older crawling infants play together successfully without supervision, and from the age of two may comfort each other. The structure of the kibbutz forces children to grow as part of their group, so that peers early supercede the importance of parents, and toddlers lead an active group life.

One of Parsons's purposes was to show the family as a unique group having elements in common with other groups. Analogies between the family and small task-oriented groups were based on the fact that the family is always a small group in which leadership and other specialized roles are related to effective functioning. Bales summarized the comparison of family and experimental groups by noting that the role differentiation that arises in social interaction is dependent upon the problems confronted and the resources available for solution. The result is the construction of a common symbol system and culture. The need for guiding behavior in a changing situation is always perceived and expressed by some before others. There is a sequence, with intervening time lags, of problem recognition, proposed solution, and consensus.

[32] Margaret Mead, *Culture and Commitment: A Study of the Generation Gap* (London: Bodley Head, 1970), p. 41.
[33] *Ibid.*
[34] Bruno Bettleheim, *The Children of the Dream* (London: Thomas & Hudson, 1969), p. 86.

The foregoing examples, selected from recent studies, emphasize the fact that the structural formulation of Parsons is obviously irrelevant to millions of contemporary families, both as to components and specified roles. The pioneering observations of Bales have been supplemented by much experimentation and experience in social group work, as well as in laboratory settings. The work of Parsons and Bales has, however, been the stimulus for much of what is known and done in efforts to apply theory in social work practice with major types of groups: families, youth groups, and groups in a variety of treatment agencies and institutions. Analysis of dynamics and treatment principles developed in family groups awaits application and testing for relevance in other types of groups.

GOAL ACHIEVEMENT

Much human action today, from work with nursery school children to mushrooming management-by-objectives courses for rank-and-file bureaucrats, is guided by conscious effort to work toward goals which have been made explicit as the first stage of the endeavor. As elaborated below, the validity of stated objectives has not yet received comparable attention. However, goals are intrinsic to the culture of a group, its "design for living."

A central goal, variously recognized and expressed, is achieving a state of well-being for the group and its members. Well-being, as White has expounded, goes beyond the state of satisfied need and freedom from tension; it takes in the human aims of achievement, competence, and effectance. In other words, the development of social responsibility appropriate to age stage is a necessary component of self-satisfaction and self-activation. These perspectives give direction to individual purposes sought and realized in group experience, as well as to professional purpose with groups, from young children to older adults. Intrinsic to but more complex than the aim of survival are the understanding and skills of social relationships and social responsibilities. This knowledge and skill is essential to ensure survival of the oncoming generation, as well as for continuing actualization of the self.

To define, order, and progress toward these goals, each group establishes patterns of normative regulation, expectations, and sanctions. It is a principle of democratic activity in groups that the goals of benevolent or paternalistic others are not imposed (as they must be at certain stages of family development), but that goals should develop out of group interaction and early decisions of members. This principle is governed by the more general principle that socialization is a process that serves society and individuals—that human beings are most human when social skills are maximized. Whenever a system is aversive to such development, change in the system itself—rather than change in individual members—becomes the primary goal.

Hartford, a student of socialization and group process, has furnished useful criteria on member and group change. With regard to personal change, the purpose is always self-development of members, enhancement of social role performance, or provision of compensatory opportunities. Developmental socialization is achieved only through engagement, significant attachment, interaction, and commitment to important roles over time. Groups, involving as they do a commitment to the collective, therefore have more pervasive effects in reinforcing and supporting individual change than can a single counselor.[35]

Noting few research answers and missing conceptual links in theory on how small organized groups can take social action to change the system, Hartford nevertheless states that for this purpose, too, the group draws strength from members. It brings changes from within through organized collective action that raises more than individual voices for a group goal of external change. Since members are attempting to bring their activity together for common achievement, the process is directed toward identified and developing goals. These goals develop within the group as individuals sustain their involvement and increase cooperation and loyalty.

A special case of developing purpose is Spergel's description of street gangs, based on group work method. Here the goal is returning the group to behavior defined as acceptable to the neighborhood, to discovering satisfaction in more conventional patterns, and adapting to the world of work. *Simultaneously*, more realistic school programs are encouraged and work plans altered.[36]

ASSESSMENT AND SELECTION

The formal and systematic use of socialization principles in assessment and inclusion of members has been tested and reported too sparsely to make a contribution to theory. Given that many people could be aided in engagement with central life tasks in small groups, there are few specific leads as to

[35] Hartford, *Groups in Social Work*, p. 40.
[36] Irving Spergel, "Street Gang Work," in *Encyclopedia of Social Work*, 2:1489.

how such groups should be constituted. The family, street gang, and other preformed groups allow for selective exclusion of individual members only as a matter of social judgment, with far-reaching consequences. The more crucial decision as to which families or other groups could be most appropriately helped by professional services based on this model should be decided on the basis of the indicated need or desire for change and the resources available.

Deutsch has pointed out, as a highly generalized principle, that peoples' preferences for interaction with others of similar attitudes, interests, backgrounds, and status are subject to alteration by factors of competition, complementarity, and differentiated task requirements.[37] This statement needs refinement to yield practice principles which will indicate the limits of heterogeneity. Two examples from hospital settings illustrate contrasted outcomes:

1. A young man suffering from a progressive and deforming illness was included in a social work treatment group. All other members were older women in far advanced stages of the illness. For obvious reasons, it was not possible for these patients to become a positive reference group for him, and he assessed the experience, concurrently and in retrospect, as a negative episode in his illness and treatment career.

2. A group organized for patients with a progressive and fatal illness included members of both sexes, divergent ages and disease stages, and a spouse, parent, or adult child of each. This group, unlike the other, was diverse but not unbalanced. It offered sufficient complementarity to permit the interaction to become supportive for all members.

There is no evidence for including or excluding members from socialization groups on the basis of assessment or diagnosis of individual personality. Given the opportunity and sanction for group help with socialization, formed groups would probably succeed best if they are open and ongoing, with members selected and continuing on the basis of recognized bonds of interest.

A classification for groups in the socialization model would deal with members who were:

37 Deutsch, "Group Behavior," p. 265.

1. Unsocialized. This category consists of members whose lifetime social opportunities have been minimal. Some unsocialized persons will have low potential or ability for group interaction; some will be able to respond with adequate support from the milieu, as well as from the group leader and members.

2. Inadequately socialized. This includes those with more stability, with promise or potential for competence. Developmental damage is not so severe as to prevent relationship, response, and learning. These members will be helped by social work in peer groups organized specifically for socialization, but will go through a long period of distrusting and testing the worker and fellow members.

3. Socialized to specific subcultures. These are persons whose role performance was adequate to earlier expectations, but because of changed opportunities have become inadequate. Such persons tend to show little initiative to find or use help in adapting to change. The major focus of treatment is on opening connections to rewarding new opportunities and teaching appropriate and effective behaviors.

Groups of patients with changes resulting in altered self-image and expectations of self and others, especially in rehabilitation settings, may need help in groups led by collaborating professional teams.

Some applications of the model for social work with groups of mentally handicapped, both the mentally ill and the retarded, have been reported. For example, Emerson and his associates at Harbor View House, a community rehabilitation center for the mentally ill in San Pedro, California, have used the terms constructive and instructive socialization to describe their active efforts to teach and develop relationships adaptive to the needs of the group.[38] They see socialization as essentially a nurturing process, in which the feedback in group relationships creates consistent awareness of the consequences of acts. Staff consciously serve as models, especially in their work roles. This occurs within a structured milieu where expectations are made explicit, and all members are pursuing realistic programs of self-support.

Such programs are important at a time when there is widespread dissatisfaction with outcomes of the medical model for treatment of mental ill-

[38] Archie Emerson, "The Long Way Back: Methods in the Community Rehabilitation of the Chronically Mental Ill," paper presented at the International Association of Rehabilitation Facilities, Miami Beach, Florida, 1973.

ness, even for some patients who have had intensive long-term care, and when pressure is mounting for community treatment. Many mentally ill and mentally retarded clients have gained confidence and competence for encounters in their communities after they have experienced professional and group support in learning to meet the ongoing expectations of daily life.

The fact that socialization is a developmental process suggests that groups with socialization goals are more extended in time than those addressed to crises. Development is a process of unfolding that is accelerated only with peril, and socialization groups should also be "obstetrical" in the sense of standing by to see that there is minimal interference with health and natural processes.

The family as a prototype suggests a range and extremes of group size for social work based on socialization theory. The primary group by definition is one that allows for face-to-face interaction and the operation of all possible dyadic subsystems. The well known formula of $\frac{1}{2}(N^2 - N)$ for calculating the number of these subsystems shows that the number reaches 21 for a group of seven and increases to 28 for a group of eight. This number may well represent the limit of complexity a worker can tolerate. For adequate interaction and socializing effects, the group of four with its six possible subsystems is a desirable minimum.

GROUP DYNAMICS

A great deal is known about the essential processes by which a collection of individuals becomes a human group through the interaction of its members— that is, a unit of a number of individuals with stabilized status and role relationships at a given time whose values and norms regulate behavior that has consequences for the group.

Phases of families as small groups have often been invoked, and much recent literature on the family is developmental; stages are traced from family inception in courtship through old age and widowhood. Most of these formulations refer to the traditional nuclear family. Hartford has described aspects of family process-reformation—new members, disintegration in conflict and crisis, and reintegration and termination—which show phase similarities to small groups composed of nonrelated members.[39]

The point of interest here is purposeful professional activity in relation

[39] Hartford, *Groups in Social Work*, p. 66.

to the group life cycle. Parsons believed that the phases in therapy and socialization are basically the same as in task performance, but that the order is reversed—the therapist's attitudes progress through permissiveness, support and denial of reciprocity, to manipulation of rewards. The fundamental discontinuity in the socialization process draws its crucial significance from the internalization of important objects through interaction in the social system. Each phase requires extensive reorganization of personality.[40] With a formed group, member roles are in a latent phase in intervals between meetings. The conspicuous feature of phase-specific aspects of socialization, as identified by Parsons, is this discontinuity. It is not a linear process, and integrating processes always need a chance to catch up with consequences of a given step in differentiation. The only alternative is destruction of the system.[41]

The task-solution process presumes a stable state of the system, including the assumption that the goal is given. Problems include coping with environmental exigencies to bring about achievement of the goal and coping with integrative consequences of these activities. The person's learning process does not differ in its basic phase pattern, but a stable state is disturbed so that the given goal is not fully attained.

Parsons regarded socialization as "task oriented with phase achievement as its goal." [42] The important difference between task-oriented and other formed groups and the family is that the leader with power and instrumental responsibility in the group does not purposefully frustrate the goals of a member, as is necessary at times in any family in the course of a child's development. If a member's performance is inadequate, on the other hand, the leader does not act permissively and supportively—he does not suspend sanctions or accept the member regardless of his shortcomings. The leader also responds to appropriate overtures to goal attainment and does not make positive rewards on the basis of performances extraneous to the system. This describes the leader's role, or intervention in the formed group. By contrast, the parent frustrates, suspends negative sanctions for inadequate performance, is oversupportive, and rewards performances appropriate for other systems because he is socializing the child for roles in other systems.[43] Bales's analysis attempted to identify the inception of role differention for

---

[40] Parsons, *Family Socialization*, p. 40.   [41] *Ibid.*, p. 29.   [42] *Ibid.*, p. 200.
[43] *Ibid.*, p. 201.

clues to its forms and rationales in short time spans as a model for understanding the process in more complex structure.[44]

These studies, which set forth the theoretical basis for the process of socialization within the family, also attempted to identify similarities and differences in that process in other types of groups. A major variable, which promises ongoing contributions to theory, is further specification of similarities and differences between the roles of social worker and parent. These should include both acknowledged and unadmitted parallels. It is a general principle that termination occurs when group goals have been achieved. The family's socialization task customarily ends with the expulsion of its fully socialized members. The end phase of a socialization group comes when socialization has been advanced. Part of the ending process is an assessment by the group of the degree to which its goals have been achieved. The phases will be better understood when there are more available data from social work practice on goal setting in terms of socialization theory and reports on members' assessments, with rationales for success and failure.

PROFESSIONAL ROLES

An important issue germane to development of this practice model is the identification of appropriate professional roles, their differentiation from valid activities of aides and lay helpers, and the public visibility of these distinctions. It is in the light of this issue that professional social work methods and intervention techniques with small groups is viewed in the development of the socialization model.

Generalized principles regarding the agent which Inkeles set forth are well fitted to social work practice. Knowledge of a socially required goal is prerequisite to the professional task of selecting or devising practices that lead to goal attainment. This involves the balancing of pressure sets: social imperatives, traditional techniques, and the worker's own ideals and personal needs. Group members also influence the worker's style and success by imposing their own distinctive and unique needs.[45] These pressures impinge on all worker activities: planning, execution, assessment of ongoing processes, correction of course, and evaluation of outcomes. Tropp, who has considered pressures on the worker, described his differentiated role as a "guest of the group" who must respect its organizing purpose and integrity

---

[44] *Ibid.*, p. 259.   [45] Inkeles, "Society, Social Structure," p. 91.

as well as each member's role. Because the central group dynamic is member-to-member helping, the worker's role is that of enhancing group effectiveness and the expectations of each member. A worker must present himself as a real person with a real function—authentic and free of mystique. For this he needs self-awareness, with a delicate balance of plan and spontaneity.[46]

The worker's role also varies by client group and the readiness of members to exchange information and support each other. The role differs with a group of adolescents, parents, or patients faced with altered life styles because of physical deficits. Developmental stage and coping capacities of members are major variables in shaping worker role.

Northen has specifically delineated a worker role in relation to the goal of increasing members' social competence. She has included recognition of members' capacities, reducing obstacles, and providing opportunities for their exercise and a milieu that supports them. The worker's personal influence is likewise important as members develop their ability to interact effectively by means of increasingly realistic perception of self, other persons, and social institutions, and as they derive satisfaction from growing social competence. The worker makes a direct contribution to this goal through his role in purposeful discussion leading to decision-making. Further, a worker may *prescribe* new perspectives and behavior, and *demonstrate* ways to implement decision.[47]

Hill and Aldous, drawing on research findings relating to interpersonal competence, have attempted to translate family activities that influence children's social learning to leadership roles in small *ad hoc* groups. They consider as necessary some of the instrumental roles which they label idea man, planner, problem-solver, policy-maker, decision-maker, scheduler, allocator, and evaluator. This listing leaves a gap for practice, in that some of the roles are appropriate for professional and some for member leaders. The expressive marital or family roles which importantly affect children's social learning include those of lover, sex partner, confidante, companion, listener, ventilator, tension-dispeller, face-saver, and ego-builder. They are considered less applicable to leadership roles in small *ad hoc* groups.[48] These ob-

    [46] Emanuel Tropp, "Social Group Work: The Developmental Approach," in *Encyclopedia of Social Work*, 2:1248.
    [47] Helen Northen, *Social Work with Groups,* pp. 77–78.
    [48] Hill and Aldous, "Socialization for Marriage and Parenthood," p. 893.

servations do, however, suggest interesting possibilities for social work research to extend socialization theory and identify family roles of varying relevance to formed groups, as well as shifts between worker and member roles under varying conditions.

Bales may have anticipated and provided guides for such work with his recognition that the development of a common culture and socialization of new members in groups demands the integration of allocations of power and assets with role specialization. There are marked differences in affect between family and other social groups. In the latter, positive affect is in such short supply that the problem becomes that of allocating enough to the task leader to protect him from loss of power. Negative feelings are inevitable, resolution of ambivalence is a problem, the member regarded as deviant is in danger of becoming the target of hostility, and the leader is always to some extent a deviant.[49]

Bales's formulation, too, suggests direction for social work research that will contribute data directly applicable to practice with family and formed groups and specify indicators in each for integration of role, power, and effect. These have not been developed for the professional role in practice with small groups. It should be noted that there are differences in professional roles with treatment groups from those often studied and reported in social science. The latter presume that members with certain basic abilities, knowledge, attitudes, interests, and personality dispositions are ready to combine as an effective group for coping with the confronting tasks. The reports also tend to present the assumption that group members will be compatible and attractive to each other.

ACCOUNTING FOR PERSONAL CHANGE

Social psychologists have devoted extensive study to group influence on individuals and to accounting for and measuring the extent and endurance of change.

Sherif and Sherif theorized that group properties, including norms and common goals, define group identity, which in time becomes binding on members and in important groups becomes part of individual conscience.[50] Cottrell suggested a point in time: the self system changes when the defining

---

[49] Parsons and Bales, *Famply Socialization,* p. 305.

[50] M. Sherif and C. W. Sherif, "Group Formation," in *International Encyclopedia of Social Sciences,* 6:282.

responses of its referent others change. These may be internalized and may contradict real people in the current situation. Further investigation is needed of the way in which changing situational fields produce changes in self-other systems, as well as more sophisticated concepts for analysis of situational fields. These observations parallel the increasing professional recognition of the need for more understanding and prescriptive ability in dealing with environments and settings. They interact with worker role and style to permit novelty in stabilized relationships, and change as well as stability in interaction processes.[51]

In the socialization model, the worker would expect change to result from clients' developing and reacting to explicit expectations, identifying with and imitating role models that occur under conditions of substantial and intimate contract, and getting positive and negative sanctions from the worker and group members. Within a group and in broader planning of services, it is vital that there be second chances to compensate for social conditions that confront members with discontinuity and rapid change.[52] Wolins has made the same point about the socialization process in groups in children's institutions: safety is an important condition of growth. A safe environment is one in which failure at newly attempted tasks is not devastating.[53] Even Margaret Mead, who sees little role for adults as socialization agents in the future, still insists that they will be necessary to construct safe and flexible environments.[54]

This suggests that an important part of the worker's role is specifying and developing settings and situations for the group that are favorable for the socialization process. The settings, in turn, enhance or detract from worker's effectiveness.

WORKER TECHNIQUES AND SKILLS THAT INFLUENCE CHANGE

Minuchin has described in detail efforts with families to promote socialization. The program was inaugurated when studies revealed regression in

[51] Leonard S. Cottrell, "Interpersonal Action and the Development of the Self," in Goslin (ed.), *Handbook of Socialization Theory,* p. 567.

[52] Inkeles, "Society, Social Structure," p. 94.

[53] Martin Wolins, "The Benevolent Asylum: Some Theoretical Observations on Institutional Care," in Donnell M. Pappenfort, Dee Morgan Kilpatrick, and Robert W. Roberts (eds.), *Child Caring: Social Policy and the Institution* (Chicago: Aldine, 1973), p. 93.

[54] Margaret Mead, *Culture and Commitment,* p. 86.

delinquent boys on their return to former settings after intensive individual and group treatment in an institution. Families were divided into subgroupings to clarify and simplify observations. The workers, while encouraging release of affect, interrupted mounting aggression, and shifted from being an observer to playing a family role while another family member observed. The worker's *modeling* role included giving clear expression of feeling. There were also many activities intended to help deprived families meet survival needs.[55]

Much earlier, Overton and Tinker pioneered in the use of group work consultation to enhance skills in working with the family as a group—that is, to see the family as a special group consisting of subgroups and factions which shift over time and which occasionally push a worker into the role of referee, or compete for his support. They identified a process of *learning family functions*—such as how to talk, act, and plan as a family—through group interviews.[56]

The modeling role is an important part of all socialization transactions. Cottrell has essayed an unusually profound conceptualization of how the model produces changes in another. Drawing on the phenomenon of "taking the role of the other," which G. H. Mead first described as internalizing an empathetic response, he traces the incorporation of roles perceived and experienced in social interaction. Research techniques are not sufficiently refined for the study of internalization of the interaction process to the point of determining when the learning becomes assimilated as part of the self or describing the selection process involved.[57]

CLIENT'S ROLE

The client's role as group member in producing change is enormous, with the limits not yet fully explored. The kibbutz experience dramatically suggests the power of the peer group in basic personality and character formation and its importance as a socializing influence, beginning with the cribmate relationship. Granted that this development proceeds in a nurturing environment which protects against the threat of interruption, self-control early develops out of the infant's compelling desire to maintain the willing

[55] Salvadore Minuchin et al., *Families of the Slums.*

[56] Alice Overton and Katherine H. Tinker, *Casework Notebook* (2d ed.; St. Paul, Minn.: Family Centered Project, 1959), pp. 105 ff.

[57] Cottrell, "Interpersonal Action," pp. 545–46.

companionship of his peer group. This companionship is, from the early months of life, more important than the infant's own family in meeting his emotional needs.[58]

Socialization is a two-way process; and the group, as an agent, may also be greatly changed as each member creates stimuli for those who undertake to change him. Cottrell applied G. H. Mead's concept of the "generalized other" to the influence of group members: participants construct expectations of the group as a whole and perceive and react to their own behavior from the perspective of this collective image. Thus, each member guides and evaluates his behavior from the perspective of collective standards, expectations, and goals.[59]

This powerful group influence suggests modifications in the worker's role. Margaret Mead, referring to the family group, asserts that peers present more potent models than their elders and are better guides to the system. Youth also strongly seek peer models, and the parental expectation that children will go away from them and achieve beyond them has become a cultural norm.[60] As well as the age span over which member roles are important, further work needs to be done in investigating gangs and other natural groups, both for their identity-serving functions and elements of initiation rights in relation to family forms and for differentials posed by social class variables.[61]

OUTCOME CRITERIA

As socialization is a developmental process over time, outcome studies share the disadvantage of much longitudinal research on human development, chiefly the comprehensive and accurate assessment of effects of intervening variables.

Generally, compared with individual changes, there are few reliable and valid criteria of group effectiveness which are external and concurrent. The internal indicators include the viability of the group under varying conditions, member satisfaction, and member change in knowledge, skills, attitudes, and behavior. Deutsch emphasized that Kurt Lewin's field theory

---

[58] Bettleheim, *Children of the Dream*, p. 66.
[59] Cottrell, "Interpersonal Action," p. 556.
[60] Margaret Mead, *Culture and Commitment*, p. 40.
[61] Henry S. Maas, "The Role of Member in Clubs of Lower-Class and Middle-Class Adolescents," *Child Development*, 25:241–51 (1954).

conceptualized a reeducation process as involving a change in culture. The chain seems obvious: an individual who comes to accept a new value system must come to value his membership *in a group* to whose culture it is central.[62]

In social group work following the socialization model, values central to the group's culture would be related to competence—that is, the extent to which behaviors for effective interaction, or meeting expectations of self and others for social role performance, have been learned. The specific skills of competence are subject to rapid obsolescence, but the issue of ability to meet social expectations remains constant.

INTERVENTION PROCEDURES AND SOCIALIZATION

Insights from theory suggest strategies for locating and composing groups. Several developmental theories, including those of Sullivan and Erikson, suggest that peer groups rise to the peak of their influence during puberty. In alternative cultural organizations, they may already be important for toddlers engaged in the struggle to attain autonomy. Thus, little children have been observed to help and model for each other with toilet-training and other early social learnings and efforts at self-mastery. Even infants seem to draw security from intense observation of their cribmates, and this experience may set the stage for their being open to influence from wider groups. The basic issue, Bettleheim recognizes, is whether protection from the destructive forces of isolation and a social behavior which this early and deep validation from peers affords will go beyond attachment, and become bondage.[63]

Chilman has provided a partial answer by tracing basic themes of the life cycle as they emerge from the dual needs of individual self and membership in human groups. Though she sees the issue as not completely resolved, she suggests that the maturing person is increasingly competent to deal with the bipolar drives between self and social relationships, but continues to encounter pressure peaks during developmental crises.[64]

These writings, along with many others cited, while not related to the specifics of individual techniques, suggest that professional leadership lies in allocation of resources to groups most in need of socializing interventions, and that the need is to develop environments, settings, and resources both

[62] Deutsch, "Group Behavior."   [63] Bettleheim, *Children of the Dream*, p. 307.
[64] Chilman, "Socialization and Interpersonal Change."

more widely accessible and more specifically guided by theory. Wolins is in accord with this strategy when he suggests that professionals treat too much, model less successfully than those who represent a narrower developmental gap, and function most effectively as back-up consultants.[65] The social worker's role, in the light of these conditions, may emerge as one in which he maintains direct contact with groups, especially near peers, but devotes most of his time and expertness to facilitating and directing others who are selected on the basis of personal qualities suited to influencing and forwarding the socialization aims of specific groups. This represents a variant opinion about the direct role of the worker, which will be further discussed as one of the unsolved problems in this model.

WORK WITH GROUPS AND INDIVIDUALS

Perlman has asserted recently that clinical social work may utilize the method called casework with individuals or group work with formed or natural groups or a combination of these in any given unit called a case; and that, because transactions between individuals and the group are continuous, the methods may alternate or overlap.[66] This statement suggests that the boundaries which defined and separated the two methods may be disappearing, and that future practice will invoke them more flexibly, serially, or concurrently, as the needs of the case may indicate.

Certainly the theoretical base identified for social casework does not differ from that discussed in the foregoing sections for work with small groups.[67] The generalized aim was identified as enhancing social competence. The techniques of the worker (agent) included teaching, modeling, inviting participation, providing feedback, and enlisting cooperation.

The client was expected to internalize new expectations, acquire new self-conceptions, observe, participate, take roles, and develop motivation for being active in the process. The worker was expected to provide a model, explanations, feedback, and opportunities and alternatives for expanding and improving role performance.

Because group work is at a level of complexity beyond that of the one-

---

[65] Wolins, "Benevolent Asylum."

[66] Helen H. Perlman, "Confessions of an Ex-Clinical Social Worker" (University of Chicago, School of Social Service Administration, Occasional Paper No. 5, 1974).

[67] Elizabeth McBroom, "Socialization and Social Casework," Robert W. Roberts and Robert H. Nee (eds.), *Theories of Social Casework* (Chicago: University of Chicago Press, 1970).

to-one relationship, different selection procedures or preparation may be required for those who seek mastery of the method. Workers deal with subgroups, and have less direct control of the process because the group itself is both context and means of change. The group, therefore, supercedes the worker in influence and relationship, the lines of communication are less direct and more complex, and the issues of confidentiality differ.[68]

The very terms of socialization theory suggest that group work is usually the method of choice: the social interaction aspects of personal change are enriched and accelerated in the group as a socializing environment. The goal of social competence assumes functioning in a group rather than in isolated activities. Indeed, socialization as the organizing principle of the individual's social development embraces all those processes which enable him to participate in his groups. It is only through social interaction that the self rises and takes on meaning. Erikson has conceptualized the developmental climax of identity as the realistic self-esteem which comes with the attainment of culturally significant mastery and socially recognized gratification.[69] This is manifestly impossible to achieve in the absence of significant group attachments since all important human objectives and gratifications are interpersonal. Applied to professional practice, the group encourages explicit selection of other members as well as workers as role models, offers opportunity for role choice, and increases a member's understanding of expectations. Individual members, in turn, can affect the motivation of others and influence future expectations.

Granted that group work is a method of choice in the socialization model, there has been relatively less use of group work as a service to the populations at risk described as major targets for this model: new parents, and those whose role will be deviant because of atypical developmental needs or limitations of a child; deprived and displaced adults; persons facing major changes or loss in family and work roles, body image, or body functions; and those experiencing radically altered social expectations and opportunities.

The linkages between social casework and social work with groups are in the similarity of their theoretical bases, with the group method indicating promise of more effective outcomes. Despite this promise, and perhaps because of added complexities, there is less practice and less reported expe-

[68] Bernard Davies, "Groups in Social Work," *New Society,* vol. 14 (November 1968).
[69] Erik H. Erikson, *Identity, Youth and Crisis* (New York: Norton, 1968), p. 49.

rience of group treatment than of individual treatment with those identified as in need of social work guided by socialization theory.

UNSOLVED PROBLEMS

Just as the linkages between social casework and social group work based on socialization theory are strong, the unsolved problems are similar. One is the ethical dilemma of expanding competence and coping ability while avoiding conformity and preserving culturally rooted group differences. This dilemma embraces questions of appropriate socialization models, behavioral expectations, recognition of value differences, and professional acceptance of responsibility for activities intended to produce change. In recent years, these troubling questions have tended to become more complex, rather than having moved toward solution. They bear on help to deprived groups as well as to deprived individuals. As social change is accelerating and pervasive, the status quo is vanishing. Learning to meet expectations of established roles becomes irrelevant; it may place a limitation on available alternatives for an unpredicted future.[70]

Hartford has expressed concern that our efforts may lead toward adapting individuals to a malfunctioning society or motivating them to strive for unattainable goals.[71] Instead, socialization in the family and in professionally led groups should produce a resiliency to change and courage to view the options of an open future. This has long been an expressed aim— often failed in practice—in progressive correctional institutions. It has always been more difficult to strengthen youth for the challenge beyond the walls than to reward conformity to rules within the facility. While recognizing the rapidity of change, it is well to note the warning, advanced by Inkeles, that we may be approaching a fluid state in which no society can endure.[72] The limits on change from an individual perspective were given by Parsons, who stated that the human personality is a system of the behavior of organisms of a particular species, hence bound by the exigencies inherent in the organism as a biological system.[73]

Even limitations set by the organism, however, may be less fixed than

[70] Annette Hamilton, "Blacks and Whites: Cultural Change in Australia," *Arena,* vol. 30 (1972).
[71] Hartford, "Socialization Methods," p. 1313.
[72] Inkeles, "Social Structure and Socialization," p. 616.
[73] Parsons and Bales, *Family Socialization,* p. 393.

they appeared to Parsons. Though human biochemistry has apparently remained unaltered since the Stone Age, current breakthroughs in knowledge about the potentials of human consciousness suggest future major changes in behavioral theory to guide practice in social work and other human service professions.

The question of who shall model is related to persistent problems of task allocation which affect practice and professional education. The question may be formulated for answers by research on patterns of collaboration between professional and technician. These will probably be found less in division of task on the basis of assumed complexity and more in patterns of communication, information sharing, and individual temperments and work styles.

It is obvious that the organization of social agencies in most communities today fails to make services accessible to populations in need. This gap suggests the use of groups in social work in the second role specified by Hartford in which the institution, community, or society is the target of change.[74] The accessibility of services, like the accessibility of social roles to potential candidates, is a pervasive unsolved problem of professional practice. It explains, in part, the low achievement to date of parent education classes and suggests that rising standards of practice must be reflected in the design of care-giving systems, as well as the practice of social work within them. The two are interdependent: resources are futile if they are unattractive or inaccessible to those who need them. It follows that social group work services should underpin health education efforts intended to be preventive—to increase, for example, the probabilities of infant survival and optimal development to the next stage. Group learning of new roles (as parents, or as persons accommodating to major physical impairment) can help individuals find appropriate modes of expression and social function.

Meier made a similar point in discussing unsolved problems of family planning—namely, that knowledge, motivation, and environment are all necessary to effective performance, but that the services intended to help families toward goal achievement remain a disorganized patchwork, often assuming individual pathology. They have not become a rationally designed system. Thus, there are many failures to reach those who are indifferent, discouraged, or antagonistic, or to organize group work with young people

---

[74] Hartford, "Socialization Methods."

who may be ready to make differential use of family and population concerns.[75]

Modifying the behavior and attitudes of those in clients' environments,
including the agency where the work is done, has been identified as an integral part of rehabilitation and prevention. We are not yet at the stage of having solid, tested knowledge on this question. Research has begun to produce
guides to practice. One report on "creating an environment" suggests a pattern for combining setting design and operation with direct work with small
groups.[76] This project was not carried out by social workers, but the plan
could be replicated and alternative patterns developed. Endeavors by worker
groups to change agency policy through recognized group process have also
been reported.[77] It is sobering to realize that such efforts, like the popular
social simulation games, confront us with convincing evidence that our
knowledge of change is inadequate, and that models of ideal environments
can backlash with destructive force, like the delayed mutilating effects of
some wonder drugs. Because environments may stigmatize certain groups,
Loeb and Berg have conceptualized one aspect of socialization as affecting
personality by changing class relationships, redefining appropriate role-
enactment, and making resources available for socialization into those
roles.[78]

For the more immediate question of dealing with and relating to the
complexity of ongoing groups, it has been suggested that computer monitoring may reveal relationships and effects still undetected by grosser methods.
This, too, is a field for social work research, guided by the considerable
knowledge gained in the past.

More theory-based research is also needed to measure change as the
outcome of purposive activity intended to support the individual's search for
a tolerable, satisfying self system. More reliable guides for group work
focused on this process could be created if the determinants and timing for
incorporating others' response as ego's own could be more precisely identified. This process is of a complexity beyond stimulus-response learning.[79]

[75] Gitta Meier, "Family and Population Planning," in *Encyclopedia of Social Work*, 1:385.
[76] I. I. Goldenberg, *Build Me a Mountain: Youth, Poverty, and the Creation of New Settings*
(Cambridge, Mass.: MIT Press, 1971).
[77] Rino Patti and Herman Resnick, "Changing the Agency from Within," *Social Work*,
17:48–57 (1972).
[78] Loeb and Berg, "Socialization, Social Structure," p. 1342.
[79] Cottrell, "Interpersonal Action," pp. 566–67.

However, further work should add to our understanding of behavioral change under social influence. It should give more dependable cues for assessing the congruence of socialization models, affective elements, coalitions, and origins of status. There is already evidence that the small group is the milieu of choice for professional activity based on socialization theory. That activity would aim essentially to help individuals develop the self-concept and interpersonal skills which can prevent disruption at life's major turning points. It would also aim to help them replace behaviors that become inadequate or destructive under changed conditions, and to find ways to reconcile the multiple role conflicts and cope with major role shifts of adult careers.

BIBLIOGRAPHY

Chilman, Catherine. "Socialization and Interpersonal Change," in *Encyclopedia of Social Work*.

Clausen, John (ed). *Socialization and Society*. Boston: Little, Brown, 1968.

Encyclopedia of Social Work, 2 vols. New York, NASW, 1971, 1972.

Goslin, David A. (ed). *Handbook of Socialization Theory and Research*. Chicago: Rand McNally, 1969.

Hartford, Margaret E. "Socialization Methods in Social Work Practice," in *Encyclopedia of Social Work*.

Loeb, Martin B. and William E. Berg. "Socialization, Social Structure and Personality," in *Encyclopedia of Social Work*.

McBroom, Elizabeth. "Socialization and Social Casework," in Robert W. Roberts and Robert H. Nee (eds.). *Theories of Social Casework*. Chicago: University of Chicago Press, 1970.

Mead, George H. *George Herbert Mead on Social Psychology*, Anselm Strauss (ed.). Chicago: University of Chicago Press, 1965.

Minuchin, Salvadore et al. *Families of the Slums*. New York: Basic Books, 1967.

Northen, Helen. *Social Work with Groups*. New York: Columbia University Press, 1969.

Parsons, Talcott and Robert F. Bales (eds.). *Family, Socialization, and Interaction Process*. Glencoe, Ill.: Free Press, 1955.

10

CRISIS INTERVENTION WITH FAMILIES AND GROUPS

Howard J. Parad, Lola Selby, and James Quinlan

Perhaps more than at any other time in the history of social work, today's professional climate fosters new departures from traditional treatment techniques in clinical practice. This paper is addressed to one such area of practice innovation—namely, time-limited crisis-oriented work with families and groups.

In recent years, formulations of time-limited crisis-intervention, preventive-intervention, and emergency and brief therapies have received growing attention in the literature of social work and social and community psychiatry. In fact, social work has even been defined in terms of its efforts at crisis management: "Generally speaking, social work can be visualized as centering on the management of cases with the objective of alleviating a crisis in the life of an individual, family or group." [1]

The theoretical approach under discussion in this paper concerns time-limited crisis-oriented social work practice with families and other natural and formed small groups, as well as the linkages between family, group, and individual crisis modalities.

---

[1] Joint Committee on Mental Illness and Health, *Action for Mental Health* (New York: Basic Books, 1961), p. 151.

COMPONENTS OF A CRISIS-ORIENTED APPROACH

Crisis intervention focuses on a wide range of disequilibria phenomena affecting the biopsychosocial functioning of individuals, families, and groups. Included are problems relating to disordered communication patterns, disrupted role networks, and dissonant value orientations, which can sometimes create situations in the lives of people that precipitate a crisis reaction. The causes of these dysfunctional phenomena are of course as varied as the families and the individuals who experience them, and as complicated as the neighborhoods and larger social systems in which these families, individuals, and groups live.

A detailed review and critique of crisis intervention is beyond the scope of this paper. Since a number of authors have provided overviews concerning the basic theory, practice aspects, and historical development of crisis intervention, this paper will not cover the same material.[2] To set the stage for the presentation that follows, however, the main features of crisis intervention will be outlined. There will be some discussion, also, of recent literature and contemporary crisis-intervention practice, particularly with families and groups.

Within a broad range of preventive and remedial social work practice efforts, crisis intervention may be defined as a process for actively influencing the psychosocial functioning of individuals, families, and small groups during a period of acute disequilibrium.

The historical origins of the crisis approach, including the important contributions of Lindemann, Caplan, and Jacobson, have been traced by Parad and Golan in recent reviews.[3] Crisis intervention basically has two goals: (1) to cushion the immediate impact of disruptive stressful events and (2) to help those directly affected, as well as significant others in the social environment, mobilize and use their psychological capabilities, interpersonal skills, and social resources for coping adaptively—rather than maladaptively—with the effects of stress. This paper will focus attention on time-

---

[2] Naomi Golan, "Crisis Theory," in Francis J. Turner (ed.), *Social Work Treatment: Interlocking Theoretical Approaches* (New York: Free Press, 1974) pp. 420–57; Howard J. Parad, "Crisis Intervention," in *Encyclopedia of Social Work* (2 vols.; New York: NASW, 1971) 1:196–202; Lydia Rapoport, "Crisis Intervention as a Mode of Brief Treatment," in Robert W. Roberts and Robert H. Nee (eds.), *Theories of Social Casework* (Chicago: University of Chicago Press, 1970), pp. 313–52.

[3] Golan, "Crisis Theory"; Parad, "Crisis Intervention."

limited crisis-intervention activities with families and small groups rather than with individuals.

In the crisis literature, crisis has been defined as "an upset in a steady state," and as an emotional reaction on the part of an individual, family, or group to a threatening life event. An emotionally hazardous situation, so interpreted by the person (s) involved, creates stress which becomes unbearable at the point when some precipitating event places demands on the person(s) for coping resources not readily available. A severe anxiety state sets in, and is not easily dispelled because of lack of effective problem-solving means. The crisis state results when new solutions to problems in living are called for, and habitual coping means do not suffice.

As pointed out by a number of writers, crisis intervention has important macroscopic implications as well as implications for individuals—for instance, during a period of crisis (1) a person may become a carrier of ill health, a pathogenic agent, a sort of mental illness "typhoid Mary" influencing others in his social orbit, (2) crisis victims are especially vulnerable to other carriers, and (3) crisis victims are particularly susceptible to influence because of their feelings of helplessness. Such influence may be helpful or detrimental.

Crisis intervention is primarily an "approach" rather than a theory that has been validated by rigorous research. The state of crisis is a temporary upset in equilibrium characterized by immobilization of problem-solving abilities and other aspects of daily functioning. Crisis is not a disease; hence, a crisis-state is not considered to be pathological. It can and does happen to most people some time in the course of their life.

The main elements of the crisis configuration may be outlined as follows. First, there is a stressful event or precipitating stress. This may be a hazardous circumstance or experience involving accidental, environmental experiences such as the sudden death of a loved one or an accident; developmental maturational stresses, such as reaching puberty, entering school, getting married, becoming a parent, or retiring; or transitional situational stresses, such as getting or losing a job, moving, or some other important life change.

The perception of the stress is the second element in the configuration. The stressful event may be perceived as a threat to important life goals, security, or affectional needs. Obviously, not all stress leads to a crisis, even though the two terms are often equated. A stressful event becomes a crisis only when it is perceived as menacing important security or affectional needs and overtaxing the person's available problem-solving resources.

The third element is the response phase, which is characterized by an acute period of disequilibrium. The person, family, or group evidences rising tension and marked discomfort and disturbance in thinking, feeling, and day-to-day behavior. Familiar routines are disrupted. Coping capacities are overburdened, and feelings of helplessness and inability to manage within the predictable future are paramount. There are feelings of considerable pressure and anxiety.

By far the most important, and probably the most neglected, aspect of the crisis configuration is the resolution phase. The problems posed by the stressful event, which have been perceived as threatening and which are responded to with the signs of disorganization known as the crisis-state, are resolved adaptively or maladaptively. Each resolution influences subsequent stress periods. The aim of crisis intervention is to help individuals, families, and groups, through appropriate differential assessment and intervention techniques, to move toward adaptive and away from maladaptive resolutions.

During the response phase of the crisis sequence, the individual, family, or group is both vulnerable to further breakdown and amenable to positive and corrective influence, hence the familiar observation that crisis involves both danger and opportunity. The duration of the crisis state is considered to be time-limited because no one can stay in a state of severe disequilibrium indefinitely. Important variables affecting outcome include the nature and perception of the stressful event, the coping and response patterns of those affected, and the availability of individual, familial, and group supports and problem-solving resources.

The stages of the crisis sequence include the reaching of a significant turning point requiring the use of new coping mechanisms; the experiencing of increasing anxiety and tension as this turning point is reached, often requiring the mobilization of new or previously hidden resources; and, finally, the establishment of a new equilibrium. The new equilibrium may represent a level of psychosocial functioning as adequate as, better than, or less adequate than the precrisis level of functioning.

Encounter with crisis burdens the individual, family, or other small group with a range of emotional, cognitive, and behavioral tasks which must be mastered. These tasks, varying enormously from stress to stress, have been only partially documented through systematic empirical research. Particularly studied, for example, has been the phenomenon of coping with the birth of a premature baby.[4]

Studies of bereavement have emphasized the importance of coping with the normal tasks of "grief work." These include disengagement from emotional bondage to the deceased by working through the feelings associated with the normal misery of mourning. Family members who exhibit maladaptive grief reactions (for example, inability to face the reality of loss, overidentification with the memory of the deceased, and morbid preoccupations) can frequently be helped by social work practitioners toward adaptive coping and mastery of the grief tasks.[5]

A word should be said about the dimensions of time and crisis in crisis-oriented intervention. Not all brief service work is crisis-oriented; nor is all brief service time-limited by plan. On the other hand, crisis-intervention services are, because of the temporary nature of the crisis phemonenon, usually time-limited, and so planned formally or informally. There are four logical service categories with respect to the dimensions of crisis and time as operationalized in practice: (1) planned short-term treatment (PSTT), crisis-oriented services, (2) non-PSTT, crisis-oriented services, (3) non-crisis PSTT services, and (4) services that are neither PSTT nor crisis-oriented. The paradigm shows the similarities and differences among these four forms of service.

As illustrated in the paradigm, crisis-oriented PSTT involves conscious use of the following service components:

1. Early accessibility at the time of the request for help, preferably within 24 to 72 hours following the application or referral for assistance.
2. Use of time limits, either in the form of a specific or approximate number or range of interviews or weeks of treatment. This is determined at intake, preferably by joint decision of client(s) and worker, and is utilized during the crisis response and resolution phases.
3. Use of task-centered and problem-solving techniques.
4. Focused attention to the crisis configuration, including the

[4] David M. Kaplan and Edward A. Mason, "Maternal Reactions to Premature Birth Viewed as an Acute Emotional Disorder," *American Journal of Orthopsychiatry*, 30:539–52 (1960).

[5] Erich Lindemann, "Symptomatology and Management of Acute Grief," *American Journal of Psychiatry*, 101:141–48 (September 1944). Reprinted in Howard J. Parad (ed.), *Crisis Intervention*.

A Paradigm for Classifying the Use of the Crisis
Approach and the Time Dimension

	PSTT [a]	Non-PSTT
CRISIS-ORIENTED	(1) Early accessibility at time of request for help (within 24 to 72 hours of the "cry for help") (2) Use of time limits (specific number or approximate range of interviews or weeks—determined at intake to be utilized during crisis response and resolution phases) (3) Use of task-centered techniques (4) Focused attention to crisis configuration (precipitating event, perception of threat, response, and resolution) (++)	(1) Early accessibility at time of request for help (within 24 to 72 hours of the "cry for help") (2) Open-ended orientation toward time dimension; duration of contact may be informally brief (no time contract made during intake phase—that is, first or second interview); or contact may be "long-term": crisis intervention may be regarded primarily as point of entry into an extended treatment service (3) Some attention to elements of crisis configuration (+ −)
NONCRISIS-ORIENTED	(1) May be short or long waiting period (2) Use of time limits: contract for specific, predetermined number of interviews, determined at intake (3) Use of task-centered techniques (4) No special attention to crisis configuration (− +)	(1) May be short or long waiting period (2) Open-ended orientation toward time dimension; no use of PSTT limits (3) No special attention to crisis configuration (4) May be oriented to specific or diffuse goals (− −)

[a] PSTT = Planned Short-Term Treatment activities.

Most crisis intervention work would fall in cell 1 (++), although some service activity in some agency settings would fall in cell 2 (+ −).

precipitating or stressful event, the perception of the threat as hazardous to life goals, the disequilibrium response, and, finally, the resolution, hopefully leading toward an adaptive solution to the problems imposed by the crisis situation.

Documentation of the use of PSTT with families and other small groups is to be found in recent publications. Lang, for instance, discussed the use of

Quick Response Units as part of a planned, short-term, crisis-oriented service in each of the district offices of the Jewish Family Service in New York City.[6] Operating on the assumption that all applicants can profit from an immediate-access short-term service, the Quick Response Units avoid waiting lists (often families are seen the same day they apply), make frequent use of home visits and collateral field visits, limit the family-crisis intervention to approximately six weeks, place heavy reliance on the positive contagion of hope in brief interventions, give considerable attention to the termination process, and often plan follow-up interviews within a three- to six-month period.

Also relevant in this context is the 1970 FSAA survey of family agency cases which documented that (1) planned short-term services appear to be more cost-effective in certain groups of cases, (2) more family members were involved in treatment (as compared with the 1960 FSAA survey), (3) there has been increased use of group treatment, and (4) a considerable decrease in the time elapsing between the client's request for help and the assignment to a family counselor.[7]

In their recent literature review, Pool and Frazier outline a variety of family-oriented crisis modalities used in situations where the identified patient is either a child or an adolescent.[8] Brief family-crisis-intervention approaches are frequently employed in dealing with mental health emergencies. For example, a tightly structured family-crisis service is offered by a psychiatric emergency program for children, focused on an explicit time plan for managing the immediate problem. Prompt intervention is offered, involving a good deal of direct advice to aid family members in crisis. Children's self-destructive behavior is interpreted to family members as a sign of "blocked communication," erupting in a crisis episode.

Others have reported similar attempts at short-term family-crisis intervention in diverse programs concerned with a range of problems. Virtually all of the articles reviewed by Pool and Frazier offer descriptions of programs and techniques—rather than rigorously designed research—aimed at scien-

---

[6] Judith Lang, "Planned Short-Term Treatment in a Family Agency," *Social Casework,* 55:369–74 (1974).

[7] Dorothy F. Beck and Mary A. Jones, *Progress on Family Problems* (New York: Family service Association of America, 1973).

[8] Michael L. Pool and James R. Frazier, "Family Therapy: A Review of the Literature Pertinent to Children and Adolescents," *Psychotherapy: Theory, Research, and Practice,* 10:256–60 (1973).

tific study of such persistent problems as criteria for seeing the family as a group, differences between those families who accept and those who decline family therapy, and objective differential measurement of the efficacy of crisis approaches and other therapeutic modalities.

To summarize, crisis means a loss of equilibrium. When beset by internal pressures or external stresses which disrupt a prior homeostasis, individuals, families, and social networks can move into a state of crisis. The essence of crisis is a struggle—a struggle to cope with and master an upsetting situation and regain a state of balance. Homeostasis, viewed as a steady state, is a dynamic and not a static concept. Balance means that dynamic forces, often in opposition, are in a state of equilibrium.

With the emergence of such notions as Hartmann's concept of "optimum frustration," [9] and Erikson's focus on modal problems which must be coped with before further growth can take place, crises are now viewed as part of the normal growth process, the management of which determines either further growth or regression. [10]

Crisis intervention is usually time-limited, has limited goals, and is focused on the identification of the precipitating stress, the clarification of relevant circumstances, conflicts, and dilemmas, consideration of problem-solving means and alternative solutions in the here and now, and evaluation of actions taken toward crisis resolution. To be effective, crisis intervention needs to be readily available and properly timed. Support systems within the individual's family or within a relevant group context need to be utilized or, if unavailable, need to be developed.

Social work, along with other helping disciplines, has become increasingly aware of the family and group contexts of individual disorders in psychosocial functioning, particularly at times of crisis. Family therapy is becoming an established practice in the repertoires of social workers and other mental health professionals. Likewise, there is a growing interest in group phenomena, group support systems, and nonkinship group social systems. Knowledge in these areas has begun to influence crisis intervenors, thus enlarging their thinking about group-crisis experiences and the use of groups as therapeutic contexts.

[9] Heinz Hartmann, *Ego Psychology and the Problem of Adaptation* (New York: International Universities Press, 1958).

[10] Sallie R. Churchill, "Preventive Short-Term Groups for Siblings of Child Mental Hospital Patients," in Paul Glasser, Rosemary Sarri, and Robert Vinter (eds.), *Individual Change Through Small Groups* (New York: Free Press, 1974), pp. 362–74.

SOME NEW PERSPECTIVES

Recent literature and experiences of the authors reveal some new perspectives emerging with respect to crisis and crisis intervention. There can be collective crisis as well as individual crisis: groups, both family and nonkinship, can experience crisis.[11] Other persons who are significant to an individual in crisis are both affected by and affect crisis-resolution efforts; the individual is not viewed in isolation, but rather as part of a family and/or group milieu.

Social systems theory, an important knowledge base for virtually all of the theoretical approaches discussed in this book, emphasizes the interaction-transaction-feedback mechanisms important to crisis resolution. People are seen to be involved in social networks which have some influence on crisis precipitation, perception, and resolution. Groups can provide support and reinforcement and can contribute to system changes which will enhance the social functioning of individuals and their groups.

Time-limited and structured help via familial and nonfamilial groups can be utilized for therapeutic purposes and problem-solving. Active participation of individuals and groups in crisis resolution helps to mobilize strengths, offer hope, allow for emotional discharge and ventilation, and enlarge the arena of alternative courses of action available to those affected by the crisis impasse.

PHILOSOPHICAL CONSIDERATIONS

The crisis approach involves a humanistic framework that values the dignity of each person and recognizes people's need for an appropriate balance of inner autonomy and external structure, expressiveness and control, privacy and social interaction, and responsibility for self as well as for society.

Within the crisis approach there is great attention to each person's capability for problem-solving, and beyond that for further awareness and growth. There is much wisdom in Carl Roger's dictum: "You don't have to be sick to get better." Even though capacity for growth is a vital ingredient of the crisis-intervention process, experience indicates that people with chronic difficulties in coping with the complexities of life can also be supported in their problem-solving efforts.

[11] Allen Barton, *Communities in Disaster* (New York: Doubleday, 1969).

Help should be available to people who need it—ideally, when and as they need it; that is, in a way that makes the help readily accessible and meaningful. Thus, the social work practitioner and the agency he represents should respond to the person's need as it relates to his or his group's crisis predicament rather than expecting that the client's definition of crisis will be fitted to the agency's function and administrative arrangements.

From a philosophic standpoint, programs of primary prevention are of importance—for example, the use of crisis consultation in schools during the pre-onset stage of problem development.[12] Also valued is secondary prevention and related case-finding techniques during the early stages of problem development. It is recognized, moreover, that many people can profit from crisis approaches at the teritary preventive level, particularly those who require protective services. In such instances, the persons involved need help in coping with immediate crisis-producing pressures so that they can mobilize themselves for further efforts at rehabilitation, growth, and change.

Warm, emphatic, outreaching approaches from caretaking agents and important others can be of much assistance in crisis work. "Reach out and help" rather than "wait and treat" is the crisis intervention motto.

BEHAVIORAL SCIENCE BASES

Just as the term theory is used more in an honorific than in a scientific sense when applied to the crisis approach, so the behavioral science bases supporting crisis intervention are not characterized by a unifying, consistent, systematically validated body of theory. The crisis approach relies on a mix of behavioral science perspectives. The reason why the crisis approach encompasses, accommodates, and even encourages a diversity of theoretical orientations is that its fundamental concept of equilibrium is as open to diverse influences as the theory of change itself.

The behavioral science foundations of the crisis intervention approach include psychoanalytic ego psychology, developmental theories, Lindemann's ideas concerning adaptive and maladaptive grief work, Caplan's formulation of the crisis state, system and social network theories, communication theory, stress theory, theories of induced change, problem-solving and learning theory, studies of cognition, social learning theories,

[12] Lola B. Buckley, "The Use of the Small Group at a Time of Crisis: Transition of Girls from Elementary to High School" (D.S.W. dissertation, University of Southern California, 1970).

theories of interpersonal influence,[13] and other strands of theory regarding human motivation, behavior, and change. Some of these are explanatory theories of human behavior; others are conceptual orientations to ways of changing behavior that themselves accommodate different notions concerning the dynamics of human behavior.

The authors of this chapter have been most influenced by ideas drawn from ego psychology and systems theory; they also make use of theories related to stress, growth and development, and learning.

In practice, most crisis-intervention workers are eclectic. Individual social work practitioners often package diverse psychosocial, behavioral, and humanistic orientations for use in working with individuals, families, and groups in crisis situations. The psychosocial approach in social work practice has typically relied on the formulation that appropriate awareness and expression of feeling, combined with appropriate cognitive insights, leads to improved psychosocial functioning. The social worker oriented toward the psychosocial model draws heavily upon psychoanalytic ego psychology.

Behavior-modification approaches, based on social learning theory, are now being utilized by some social work practitioners. The basic principles of behavior modification, as applied to social work, have been presented in a number of recent publications.[14]

On the other hand, those preferring a humanistic approach often tend to minimize the importance of cognition and learning theories in favor of greater emphasis on getting in touch with feelings, thus enhancing emotional expressiveness and body awareness. These workers might lean toward use of Gestalt techniques.

The unraveling of the puzzle of what makes people change and what makes some people responsive to some approaches and not others is far beyond the scope of the present paper. There have as yet been no empirical studies concerning which theories and techniques are most applicable and helpful in crisis intervention.

---

[13] Ross V. Speck and C. L. Attneave, "Social Network Intervention," in Jay Haley (ed.), *Changing Families.*

[14] See, for instance, Peter Alevizos and Robert P. Liberman, "Behavioral Approaches to Family Crisis Intervention"; Sheldon Rose, "A Behavioral Approach to the Group Treatment of Parents," *Social Work,* 14:21–29 (July 1969); Richard B. Stuart, "Behavior Modification: A Technology of Social Change," in Turner (ed.), *Social Work Treatment,* pp. 400–19.

TARGET POPULATIONS AND ORGANIZATIONAL AUSPICES

Crisis intervention with families and groups includes the following target populations: (1) individuals in crisis, (2) those associated with persons in crisis, and (3) those in collective crisis.

On a macroscopic scale, crisis intervention, using the techniques of generic crisis intervention as presented by Jacobson, and mental health consultation as detailed by Caplan and by Beisser and Green [15] may be directed to populations at risk. Crisis intervention is thought to be appropriate for people of all ages, ethnic groups, and social classes. In short, crisis intervention is applicable to people with widely different psychodynamic and sociocultural characteristics. The only requirements are that the clients must be in a state of crisis or affected by persons in crisis, be willing to seek or be referred for help, and be able to sustain a relationship with a helping agent for a relatively brief period.

The settings within which crisis-intervention activities are carried out are as varied as the population groups served. These include a wide range of social work, mental health, and medical services; walk-in emergency services; outpatient, psychotherapy, and medical clinics; hospitals; and self-help programs.

Much of the social service activity routinely carried out in hospital outpatient clinics involves the use of brief crisis-intervention techniques. Family service agencies, pursuing their mission to help families in distress and to assist in the promotion of sound family life, are apparently increasing their use of brief and planned short-term crisis-oriented approaches.[16] Public schools, where school social work and guidance personnel daily see children in crisis, are an important setting for the delivery of direct crisis-intervention services as well as mental health consultation services. Suicide-prevention services and hot lines provide a variety of crisis-intervention activities through an immediate access policy to persons and families in trouble. These include telephone services—using techniques of creative listening and referral—to help persons who ordinarily would not come for in-person crisis

[15] Gerald Jacobson et al., "Generic and Individual Approaches to Crisis Intervention," *American Journal of Public Health*, 58:338–43 (1968); Gerald Caplan, *The Theory and Practice of Mental Health Consultation* (New York: Basic Books, 1970); Arnold Beisser and Rose Green, *Mental Health Consultation and Education* (Palo Alto, Calif.: National Press Books, 1972).

[16] Beck and Jones, *Progress on Family Problems*.

counseling. Travelers-aid services have long utilized crisis-oriented techniques with their clientele. Free clinics, with their emphasis on informality and antiestablishment practices, provide a natural setting for crisis-intervention programs. These programs are often staffed by volunteers, paraprofessionals, and those who themselves have experienced recent life-crises and are often able to help others undergoing similar predicaments. Marital counseling and court conciliation services; multipurpose agencies offering a package of legal aid, health care, budget counseling, and other personal services; foster homes and half-way houses; public welfare agencies; adoption and child-placement agencies; crisis hostels providing community care programs as alternatives to mental hospitalization; mobile psychiatric and home-treatment crisis service units; and correctional settings—all these, and more, offer crisis services to a wide spectrum of individuals, families, and groups under stress.

Many of these agencies emphasize a reaching-out approach, and crisis intervention takes place in the client's own home or within his natural social habitat. Many of the people served in these programs would ordinarily be stereotyped as unmotivated for entry into more traditional service-delivery systems that may have lengthy waiting lists, complex application forms, elaborate psychosocial study procedures, cumbersome conferences, and other institutionalized rituals which would not articulate with their general life style or urgently felt needs at a time of crisis.

SMALL GROUPS ADDRESSED BY THE CRISIS APPROACH

TYPES

The crisis approach is used with nuclear and extended families, and with natural friendship or common-interest groups, including a wide variety of gangs and clubs that are not family-related.

Crisis intervention is utilized within a broad spectrum of formed groups, including groups of children and teachers in school settings, work groups, interest groups, and therapy groups. These groups meet on an intra- or extramural basis; again, the common denominator is the experience with crisis. It has often been observed that people who are simultaneously experiencing crisis are able to be comfortable with each other within a group setting, despite the social distance factors that would usually separate them during noncrisis periods. The encounter with crisis is also a social leveler when communities are struck by natural disasters.[17]

[17] Barton, *Communities in Disaster*.

Crisis intervention is often practiced within institutions, including crisis hostels and halfway houses that provide transitional care for mentally disordered individuals in the process of being reintegrated into family and community lifes. In detention facilities, crisis intervention is often combined with techniques of crisis induction and used as part of delinquency-control programs.

Newer developments include crisis intervention within protective-service settings, where the precipitating stress is the knock on the door by the protective-service worker announcing that a complaint requiring investigation has been made. Self-help groups, such as Parents Anonymous, are becoming increasingly important. The group method seems preferred for helping many of these parents, especially those who have a tendency to abuse their children. Crisis intervention is also the treatment of choice for rape victims, often through self-help programs.[18]

While crisis intervention involves a warm, empathic reaching out, and a "search-and-find" approach, participation by clients in crisis programs is primarily voluntary. This is so because mutual aid, within a family or group setting, requires the exercise of free choice and a reasonable commitment to the change process. On the other hand, social workers in protective or correctional settings, operating as agents of social control, often present clients with a Hobson's choice as to whether they wish to avail themselves of crisis intervention or face possible detention or court action.

Membership in crisis groups may be open or closed, depending on the situation and need. Although there are no fixed criteria, groups of people sharing a crisis experience in common tend to have open memberships.[19] This also seems to be the pattern in many crisis clinics such as the Benjamin Rush Center of the Los Angeles Psychiatric Service.[20]

Groups are typically time-limited, although time factors are not universally agreed upon. An offer of up to six sessions per person seems to be the usual procedure in most agencies. There is no empirical validation for the choice of this arbitrary number; it seems to derive from the earlier writings of Lindemann and Caplan, who frequently stated that most crisis states are limited to a period of four to six weeks.

[18] Sandra S. Fox and Donald J. Scherl, "Crisis Intervention with Victims of Rape," Social Work, 17:37–42 (January 1972).

[19] Herbert Blaufarb and Jules Levine, "Crisis Intervention in an Earthquake," Social Work, 17:16–19 (July 1972).

[20] Martin Strickler and Jean Allgeyer, "The Crisis Group: A New Application of Crisis Theory," Social Work, 12:28–32 (July 1967).

The size of groups varies, but small groups, with memberships ranging from four or five to no more than ten or twelve members, are considered more manageable.

With regard to the elusive problem of group composition, there appear to be no specific criteria, although occasionally agencies set up criteria of exclusion; for instance, persons who are seriously homicidal or suicidal may be excluded because they are too hazardous to themselves or others. Such criteria need further study by crisis workers. The only agreed-upon criterion is the requirement that group members are expected to be in a crisis or connected with an individual in crisis or part of a social network affected by a crisis situation. Groups may be started for the significant others of individual-therapy patients when it is thought that these others are important in providing support and resources for the patient—as, for example, mentally disordered individuals who are seen in groups with their families in order to develop an after-care plan.

Speck and Attneave, and Flomenhaft and Kaplan, among others, have investigated the importance of extended-kinship groups and social-network groups.[21] Social-network intervention has been suggested as a variant of crisis intervention with families. All members of the kinship system or relevant network, perhaps including friends and neighbors of the family, may be assembled at one time at one place. According to one author, a typical middle-class urban family can assemble about forty such persons.[22] The network meets with a team of network intervenors, and the goals are to stimulate, reflect, and focus the problem-solving potential within the network and to help it become more of a life-sustaining community.[23] Among the anticipated network effects are shared new experiences, which create new bonds, and new forms and uses of social relationships. These latter are often a badly needed antidote to depersonalized loneliness, which can produce crisis proneness.

Flomenhaft and his colleagues have pointed out that social networks beyond the immediate family offer relationships in which meaningful social contacts and reciprocal aid for family development, especially at time of

[21] Speck and Attneave, "Social Network Intervention;" Kalman Flomenhaft and David Kaplan, "Clinical Significance of Current Kinship Relationships," *Social Work,* 13:68–75 (January 1968).

[22] Speck and Attneave, "Social Network Intervention."

[23] Flomenhaft and Kaplan, "Clinical Significance of Kinship."

crisis, can be available to constituent units.[24] Crisis intervention in social work practice should include, these authors have argued, an assessment of nuclear- and extended-family relationships which may be constructive or detrimental to the functioning of the client or family on whom attention is focused. Often there is a need to work directly with extended family members who comprise the relevant network.

PURPOSES

The varied and often interrelated purposes of crisis-oriented groups include the following:

1. Avoiding hospitalization or institutionalization through the development and properly timed provision of support systems and ego-mobilizing help.
2. Helping people make constructive use of institutional care by dealing with certain problems in daily living which might develop into emotionally hazardous situations.
3. Dealing with crises of hospitalization, surgery, catastrophic events, death, terminal care, and dislocating experiences.
4. Dealing with crisis events superimposed upon chronic situations—that is, acute eruptions within members of chronically disordered families or groups.
5. Dealing with crisis reactions to life-cycle developmental stresses such as the "empty nest syndrome" or retirement.
6. Dealing with crisis reactions growing out of relationship and role difficulties, such as the addition of a step parent to a one-parent family.
7. Resolving family conflicts (marital, parent-child, family communication and interaction) where crisis reactions are involved.
8. Mobilizing personal, group, and social-network resources in order to meet needs during the period of disequilibrium.
9. Problem-solving for resolving a crisis and restoring ego functioning.
10. Orienting to a program or a life situation which is new, during a transitional crisis.
11. Helping with crisis responses to termination, transfer, discharge, or placement.
12. Expanding people's coping means and alternatives.

[24] *Ibid.*

ASSESSMENT AND SELECTION OF INDIVIDUALS
AND GROUPS

The use of groups and the selection of members is at present typically based on considerations of expediency, agency function and setting, personal preferences of workers, practice wisdom, available staff, and a few theoretical rationalizations. Northen has discussed the need for a balance of homogeneity and heterogeneity—that is, the group must be homogeneous to the extent that it has enough common bonds to enable its members to relate to each other, and heterogeneous enough so that there are sufficient stimuli to enhance the growth of its members and of the group as a whole.[25] Obviously, too, the purpose of the group plays an important part in the selection of members.

The individuals in the group differ in terms of vulnerability to crisis and crisis-coping ability; hence, individual assessment is necessary. It is desirable that both worker and group members participate in this assessment process. The worker, with the help of the individual or the group that feels the collective crisis, may have to determine who in the social network needs to be included. Again, there are no clear-cut diagnostic classification schemes available other than the indication of an existing crisis state, and the fact that the discomfort flowing from the crisis usually binds members together in a group problem-solving effort.

PRINCIPLES, METHODS, AND TECHNIQUES

Before discussing the principles, methods, and techniques of group crisis intervention, it is necessary to review the focus and structure typically used in individual-oriented crisis intervention. The following four steps, found helpful by many practitioners in individual counseling, provide guidelines for and linkages with small-group crisis counseling. This patterned approach is based primarily on ego-psychology and problem-solving theories.

Step I: The Search for the Precipitating Event and Its Meaning to the Client
1. When did the discomfort begin, or when did the client start feeling worse?
2. What recent change has occurred that represented a threat to instinctual needs or a threatened or actual loss of a significant role or relationship? How does the client interpret this event?

---

[25] See Helen Northen's paper in the present volume.

3. What reminders have there been of a previous situation that was upsetting?
4. Why is the client coming for help now?
5. What nonverbal cues as to affect and the impact of current distress does the client exhibit in discussion of recent and past events?

This line of inquiry provides clues for identifying the client's personal/social dilemma: the conflict situation with which he is currently struggling and which has thrown him into a crisis. Findings from this inquiry enable the crisis counselor to formulate the dilemma for the client—that is, to make conscious the problem which is stimulating the client's distress and confusion.

Step II: The Search for Coping Means Utilized by the Client
1. What did the client try to *do* to cope with the stress produced by the precipitating event?
2. What means of coping has the client used in the past in similar situations?
3. Where is there a lack of "fit" between the particular dilemma (problem-to-be-solved) and the coping means the client has employed?

This line of inquiry helps the client and worker to identify what has been tried by way of resolving the problem and what has not worked.

Step III: The Search for Alternative Ways of Coping that Might Better Fit the Current Situation
1. What different approaches to modifying the problem might be feasible to try out?
2. What outside resources might be needed and tapped for helping to resolve the problem/dilemma?
3. What new plan for action can be tested out *now?*

This line of inquiry helps the client to mobilize new problem-solving efforts and to take action on the basis of consideration of new alternatives.

Step IV: Review and Support of Client's Efforts to Cope in New Ways; Evaluation of Results
1. What worked, what did not work, in client's experimentation with new approaches to solving the problem?
2. What additional efforts might pay off?
3. When does the client begin to show signs of relief, improved ego functioning, and readiness to carry on alone?

This line of inquiry brings closure to the problem-solving experience, hopefully underscoring the gains made by the client.

SMALL-GROUP DYNAMICS

Within a family or group context the same four steps are utilized, with appropriate efforts at involving other family or group members in each stage: (1) the search for the precipitating event and its perceptual meaning to the client(s); (2) the search for coping means which have been utilized by the client(s) and appraisal of the extent to which these have or have not worked; (3) the search, with particular emphasis on suggestions from group members, for alternative ways of coping, and the resources that might benefit the current situation; and (4) a review and support of the family or the group members' efforts to cope in new ways, with evaluation of results in terms of day-to-day living experiences; then helping toward an early termination which has been planned in the initial time structuring. It is often desirable to add a post-termination follow-up for feedback purposes.

Throughout this process the social worker is active in defining the purpose of the family crisis session or group meeting and the means that can be used for achieving these purposes. The worker must actively focus on the relevant issues and stay within the stages outlined above: negotiating the contract; modeling; giving advice when appropriate; helping with reality-testing; supporting, stimulating, encouraging; confronting when necessary; formulating the dilemma (outlining the precipitating event, discovering how it has been perceived, and identifying analogous conflicts it has stirred up from the near or remote past and the key tasks that must be worked on); clarifying alternatives and their consequences; staying within the time limit and using time dynamically to heighten the family's or group member's motivation and ability to focus on goals; helping to consider the resistances and obstacles, from within and from without, that interfere with goal achievement; considering ways of manipulating the environment; helping to determine who shall be included; and sometimes engaging in risk-oriented crisis induction to provoke a crisis either in the client(s) or in significant others within the relevant social network.

The role of each family or group member is of central importance. The crisis victim must have goals or be able to become aware of them as well as obstacles to their achievement. Each individual is assumed to be suffering enough discomfort from a crisis reaction or reaction to others in crisis that he will want to, and be amenable to, change and influence, in terms of being responsive to the interactions within the group as well as the interventions from the therapist within the family or group context. Particularly relevant is the willingness to try new coping means with encouragement, stimulation, and perhaps some confrontation from other group members and the therapist. Crisis resolution is often speeded when the client is able to involve his significant others in coping efforts.

In response to the worker's and members' help, the client must be able to develop, within a reasonably brief time, cognitive recognition of his dilemma and some awareness of his feelings. He must be able to utilize not only the help of the other family or group members but also the assistance of other natural and professional networks.

To recapitulate briefly: Because of the sense of urgency inherent in crisis and the constraints of time limits, the group process is usually accelerated in crisis group counseling; the worker generally takes on a very active directive role in cutting through resistances and unproductive discussions in order to hold to a goal-oriented focus to maximize change opportunities within a tight time structure. Little has been written as yet concerning the motivational problems of engaging either individuals or groups in crisis intervention.

Factors relevant to the group dynamics within the crisis counseling group include common awareness of stress and pressure; consciousness of need for crisis resolution to reduce pressure and anxiety; an awareness that others have similar responses to crisis, which tends to provide a feeling of support; sharing of ideas regarding possible alternatives; use of other resources which engender hope—always a critical variable in any helping effort, but particularly important to the success of time-limited crisis activities; balance of confrontation and support; satisfaction in problem-solving and in regaining mastery and control, with heightened self-esteem resulting from feeling in command of the troublesome situation.

The group dynamics may occasionally work against the individual whose needs and pace are not harmonious with those of the group, where there is lack of comprehension of group objectives, or where individual animosities and scapegoating mechanisms are not or cannot be controlled by the group and the worker.

The crisis group has advantages not found in individual crisis intervention, such as group support, companionship, and shared information about community resources. Group members can also be very helpful in suggesting alternative coping techniques to others in the group. Individuals can be encouraged to express feelings and to identify with the problems of others.

LINKAGES

In general, the theoretical notions about individual crises have been carried over to group- and collective-crisis phenomena. Unfortunately, no clear criteria have been developed about when a given client is best served by an individual or group method, any more than there are validated criteria for assigning individuals not in crisis to a group modality. The trend, however, seems to be toward the importance of viewing individuals as part of family and other social systems and networks.

Developments in family, group, and systems theories have emphasized the importance of utilizing the small group for social learning and therapeutic purposes. Most of the crisis literature, however, is directed to work with individuals, and there is a scarcity of articles on group-crisis phenomena. Informal checking of agency programs indicates that crisis counseling is more practiced than written about.

The newer developments involving an extension of the individual approach to group-crisis intervention include: family-crisis intervention in a wide variety of social work and mental health settings; [26] multifamily crisis group therapy; psychiatric emergency home-visiting teams, operating on a mobile basis to reach out to homicidal, suicidal, gravely disabled, and other individuals and family groups experiencing domestic crisis; [27] crisis hostels providing transitional living facilities for mentally disordered persons, either following a period of hospitalization or as an alternative to hospitalization; network therapy; and multiple-impact therapy, which involves highly concentrated, intensive crisis intervention on the part of multidisciplinary teams.

Many of these developments reflect greater sensitivity to stressful events in the life cycle, and opportunities for preventive intervention with individuals and families. Moreover, there is greater awareness of the importance of involving families in situations where an individual is the identified patient; increasing recognition of the importance of working with institutions utilized by people in crisis, such as hospitals, clinics, foster homes, and

---

[26] See, for example, Churchill, "Preventive Short-Term Groups."

[27] Joel Foxman, "The Mobile Psychiatric Emergency Team," in Parad, Resnik, and Parad (eds.), *Emergency . . . Aid.*

halfway homes; more receptivity to the need for developing new facilities to provide additional sources of support to individuals and families in crisis, such as respite homes for relieving pressures on families of the mentally disordered and the retarded; and, generally speaking, broader understanding of the applicability of crisis concepts to work with a wide range of settings and target populations.

In short, crisis intervention has many of the attributes of a social movement. Crisis intervention is ubiquitous; it can be used in any social work or social welfare setting and with any target population under stress. Increasingly, crisis intervention is becoming an interdisciplinary effort in many programs; crisis teams consisting of social workers, psychologists, psychiatrists, mental health nurses, and psychiatric technicians are now routinely assigned to inpatient emergency facilities, crisis hostels, and mobile home treatment psychiatric service.

UNRESOLVED PROBLEMS AND ISSUES

As indicated in the foregoing discussion, after some fifteen years of theoretical development and application, crisis intervention's usefulness has been well demonstrated in practice by the helping professions. Its applicability in a wide range of settings with a diverse clientele seems to be established. Clients of any agency or institution can experience crisis; crisis can be a kind of common denominator among people. Despite crisis theory's demonstrated usefulness, however, crisis intervention is still unevenly practiced, and given little or no attention in some settings. Its theoretical constructs are still far from being sufficiently refined through a cumulative body of knowledge and research. Such tasks are not simple, as Golan points out, because "the crisis approach is rooted in several disparate bodies of theory and practice, some of which developed quite independently and others which have converged, fused, and in some cases, separated again to go off in new directions." [28]

While there are a number of exploratory-descriptive studies of family crisis phenomena, there are relatively few experimentally designed investigations of family crisis intervention. One of the most important is the research conducted by Langsley, Kaplan, and their colleagues at the University of Colorado, Department of Psychiatry, who combined the elements of

[28] Golan, "Crisis Theory," p. 420.

task-oriented time-limited service (an average of five office and one home visit during a three-week period); conjoint family therapy (with emphasis on negotiating role conflicts, including the roles of significant others within the extended family); immediate-access crisis intervention (family members were seen immediately after the request for hospitalization for the identified patient); and, if necessary, referral to ongoing support systems.[29] This multidisciplinary team of action-oriented researchers found that brief family-crisis intervention was in certain respects more effective than, and in other respects as effective as, traditional hospital treatment services to a control group of inpatients.

Another experimentally designed project of major importance is the study conducted by Reid and Shyne at the Community Service Society of New York.[30] While not specifically addressed to crisis intervention, the task-centered, time-structured approach utilized by social workers with the experimentally treated families contained features basic to a family-crisis approach—for instance, active focusing on specific achievable goals within a brief, predefined period. The families treated in this way generally fared as well as, if not significantly better than, those treated by a traditional open-ended approach.

There is much need for further experimentally designed investigations of family crisis work, as well as of crisis approaches used with nonkinship groups.

In the social work literature, until very recently, most of the writing about crisis theory and crisis intervention had been done by caseworkers with individual clients in mind. Very little has been written by social workers about the use of crisis groups, although in the last decade there has been an expansion of such group intervention.[31] Recent developments in the use of crisis-intervention techniques with families and nonfamily groups have been written about more often by members of allied helping professions than by social workers, possibly because such practice has frequently developed in interdisciplinary settings. In any event, general theory about crisis as

[29] Donald G. Langsley and David M. Kaplan, *Treatment of Families in Crisis*.

[30] William J. Reid and Ann Shyne, *Brief and Extended Casework* (New York: Columbia University Press, 1969).

[31] The first article in a social work journal on the use of groups in crisis intervention was Strickler and Allgeyer, "Crisis Group." See also Jean Allgeyer, "The Crisis Group: Its Unique Influence to Divergent Racial, Cultural, and Socio-Economic Groups," *International Journal of Group Psychotherapy* 20:235–40 (April 1970).

applied to individuals is now being carried over to situations of collective crisis—that is, to families in crisis and/or community groups in crisis. These linkages need much more thorough examination and consideration than has yet been accorded them.

There still are no clearly articulated and empirically verified criteria as to when individuals in crisis are best served by individual or group approaches, although the trend seems to be toward viewing individuals as parts of social systems and social networks which can be utilized as support systems. Developments in family therapy, small-group theory, system theory, and social-network theory underscore the importance and usefulness of the small group as a therapeutic and support system resource. Some of these considerations have been taken into account in the last decade as practitioners have experimented with crisis work with families, multifamily groups,[32] multiple-impact therapy,[33] psychiatric emergency teams, network therapy, and programs such as crisis hostels, halfway houses, and other transitional living facilities for vulnerable and disaffiliated clients. Moreover, there seems to be increasing awareness on the part of helpers of the potential impact of stressful events inherent in the life cycle and in certain situational events on both individuals *and* families.

The earlier literature on crisis theory proposed that crisis intervention seemed to be inappropriate for individuals and families who were "crisis-prone" and whose life style was one of constant chaos. This assumption needs further testing. There seems to be practical experience confirming the usefulness of crisis intervention at times when crisis situations are superimposed on chaotic life styles; individuals and families in such predicaments can get at least temporary relief from unbearable pressures, as can people with better organized egos. Caplan's idea of "emotional first aid" would seem to have universal applications. For chronically disordered persons the idea of "help as needed," intermittently if necessary—rather than the goal of "cure"—is congenial with the crisis approach.

The nature and duration of crisis deserves further study and attention. One group of researchers is considering the concept of crisis matrix—as op-

---

[32] Jane Donner and Anita Gamson, "Experience with Multifamily, Time-Limited Outpatient Groups at a Community Psychiatric Clinic," in Harvey H. Barten (ed.), *Brief Therapies* (New York: Behavioral Publications, 1971), pp. 260–76.

[33] Agnes Ritchie, "Multiple Impact Therapy: An Experiment," in Howard J. Parad (ed.), *Crisis Intervention.*

posed to a single hazardous event—as better describing what happens in many situations which create a crisis state for people.[34] The usual crisis diagram indicates a precrisis state, a slump in social functioning when some hazardous event precipitates the emotional state known as crisis, and then some point of resolution. For many people, however, there may be more than one pressure point in a series of related events and pressures, any one of which could become "the last straw." For instance, a person facing and undergoing surgery endures a series of stress points—the point at which the diagnosis and recommendation is made, the point at which surgery is scheduled, the surgery itself, the introduction to a prosthesis, and a return to a work or social role or a necessary role reorganization. This matrix of interrelated events could precipitate an individual or family crisis. The implications of this enlarged perspective of the process of crisis development deserves further study. What stages in a series of related events might be most likely to precipitate a crisis state in an individual or group? What does this suggest regarding timing of help, and possible anticipatory preventive strategies? And who should be involved?

The matter of time and timing is still a moot question in crisis work. Based on practice wisdom, there seems to be general agreement that there should be early access to help, and that help is best timed at the onset of a crisis experience. But how many contacts, how frequently spaced, and for what duration per family or other small group session is not clear. Practice tends to be flexible, based on expediency and worker style. There seems to be no magic in the six-week's pattern first suggested by Caplan. There are many variations in practice, from marathon or multiple-impact weekend groups to once-a-week sessions over six to twelve weeks. Any additional light on the subject of number of contacts, frequency, and spacing should be useful to crisis intervenors.

Much more needs to be done to clarify the application of crisis theory in community situations and in formed groups. Most projects thus far reported have been descriptive of a particular practice experience rather than a formal research effort. The question of open or closed groups (which is most useful, and in what circumstances?) needs further study. What criteria should guide selection of group members? A basic assumption in crisis

[34] For further explication of the crisis matrix concept, see Gerald F. Jacobson and Stephen H. Portuges, "Marital Separation and Divorce: Assessment and Preventive Considerations for Crisis Intervention," in Parad, Resnik, and Parad (eds.), *Emergency . . . Aid.*

theory is that any human being can experience a crisis if he is faced with a problem that calls for a solution beyond his usual coping means. What shadings of difference are there, however, among individuals and groups, in what is interpreted as an unbearable pressure or threat? Do ethnicity, social class, cultural values, or life style have any bearing on such interpretations of life events, and on whether help can best be utilized in a one-to-one or group context?

Very little has been written about crisis intervention with children. What types of events or life experiences are likely to be most stressful for children? [35] Does the crisis approach work with children? Can problem typologies be developed that better illuminate childhood experiences? To what degree are the crises experienced by children related to family dysfunction, or the malfunctioning of social institutions, such as school?

Many other questions need to be asked with reference to further development of crisis theory. What variables affect client utilization of a crisis-intervention approach? How important are such factors as age, sex, race, socioeconomic status, education, former contact with helping resources, source of referral, individual or group intervention? What measures of the effectiveness of crisis intervention can be developed? What variations in crisis-intervention and time-structuring techniques are possible? And what theoretical frames of reference for explaining behavior seem most applicable? If some kinds of crisis-producing hazards can be anticipated, how can effective preventive measures be instituted? How can groups serve in this process? How can a clear differentiation be made between the acute (recent) and chronic (long-standing) problems as crisis precipitants, and what difference does this make in the process of crisis intervention? And a final basic question: What are the essential goals and objectives in crisis intervention which necessarily affect practice procedures and worker's role?

Answers to questions like these should enrich all of social work practice, not only that segment labeled crisis intervention. Moreover, an in-depth understanding of crisis and crisis-resolution processes should add new dimensions to thinking about social work purposes, goals, and techniques, especially in relation to crisis intervention with families and other small groups in problem-solving, task-centered efforts.

[35] See Irving Berlin, "Crisis Intervention and Short-Term Therapy: An Approach in a Child-Psychiatric Clinic," in Harvey Barten and Sybil Barten (eds.), *Children and Their Parents in Brief Therapy* (New York: Behavioral Publications, 1973), pp. 49–62.

BIBLIOGRAPHY

Alevizos, Peter and Robert P. Liberman. "Behavioral Approaches to Family Intervention," in Howard J. Parad, Harvey L. P. Resnik, Libbie G. Parad (eds.). *Emergency Mental Health and Disaster Aid*. Bowie, Md.: Charles Press, in press.

Allgeyer, Jean. "Resolving Individual Crises through Group Methods," in Parad, Resnik, and Parad (eds.). *Emergency Mental Health and Disaster Aid*.

Caplan, Gerald. *Support Systems and Community Mental Health*. New York: Behavioral Publications, 1974.

Golan, Naomi. "Crisis Theory," in Francis J. Turner (ed.). *Social Work Treatment*. New York: Free Press, 1974.

Haley, Jay (ed.). *Changing Families: A Family Therapy Reader*. New York: Grune & Stratton, 1971.

Langsley, Donald and David Kaplan. *The Treatment of Families in Crisis*. New York. Grune & Stratton, 1968.

Parad, Howard J. (ed.). *Crisis Intervention: Selected Readings*. New York: Family Service Association of America, 1965.

Parad, Howard J., Harvey L. P. Resnik, and Libbie G. Parad (eds.), *Emergency Mental Health and Disaster Aid*. Bowie, Md.: Charles Press, in press.

Rapoport, Lydia. "Crisis Intervention as a Mode of Brief Treatment," in Robert W. Roberts and Robert H. Nee (eds.). *Theories of Social Casework*. Chicago: University of Chicago Press, 1970.

Selby, Lola G. "Social Work and Crisis Theory," *Social Work Papers,* vol. 10 (1963).

Strickler, Martin and Jean Allgeyer. "The Crisis Group: A New Application of Crisis Theory," *Social Work,* 12:28–32 (July 1967).

11

PROBLEM-SOLVING IN SMALL GROUPS

MARY LOUISE SOMERS

Problem-solving characterizes the formulations of social group work practice across the spectrum of fifty years. Although no one approach has emerged as a comprehensive, fully explicated, unitary formulation labeled "a" or "the" problem-solving approach to social work with small groups, major components of problem-solving are germane to the formulations from the earliest to the most recent. In some formulations, the entire sequence of steps in problem-solving becomes apparent; in others, one or more steps may be lifted for special consideration and examined in detail. Inevitably, the purpose for which the group was formed influences the content and process of the problem-solving component. But whether the purpose is one with clear social goals or is weighted more heavily toward individual change and growth through the group process, problem-solving intent and efforts by the group, individuals, the social worker, and all of these participants in concert are pertinent to the problem-solving work of the group and the hoped-for outcome.

It is instructive to review two definitions germane to the inquiry carried forward in this paper—the dictionary definitions of the concept of "problem" and the explication of the concept of "group problem-solving" found in the current literature of social psychology. These definitions and explications form the context and specification of meanings that are used throughout this paper. It becomes readily apparent that the series of definitions of group problem-solving have their counterparts and parallels in the several approaches to group problem-solving found in the social group work literature.

The definitions of problem presented in Webster's Third New International Dictionary span the range of usages that have characterized social work practice with small groups over the last fifty years:

> Problem—a question raised or to be raised for inquiry, consideration, discussion, decision, or solution; an unsettled matter demanding solution or decision and requiring considerable thought or skill for its proper solution or decision; an issue marked by considerable difficulty, uncertainty, or doubt with regard to its proper settlement; a perplexing or puzzling question; something that is a source of considerable difficulty, perplexity, or worry; a cause of trouble or distress.

Since the underlying behavioral and social sciences exert considerable influence on the development of social work formulations, it is interesting to note the findings of a major analysis of experimental studies of group problem-solving. The authors emphasize that several years of empirical studies have yielded important substantive groundwork, and some strong possibilities that a theory of group problem-solving may eventually be formulated. Such a prospective theory must illuminate a range of problems and situations, including those of individual problem-solving in a social context as well as those of common action emerging from common interests and concerns. It must also take into consideration the initiation and persistence of group problem-solving, a range of models, and comparisons of individual and group problem-solving processes and outcomes. An eventual theory of group problem-solving must take into account the research findings and methods that address individual motivations and interpersonal reactions and responses as well as the group processes and phases pertinent to small group problem-solving efforts and outcomes. [1]

The range and diversity of usages of problem and of group problem-solving in social work with small groups reflect the complexities that appear in the dictionary definitions and in the literature of social psychology. In social work practice, however, the complexities are even greater, since the literature of social psychology deals for the most part with laboratory groups

[1] See Harold H. Kelley and John W. Thibaut, "Group Problem Solving," in Gardner Lindzey and Elliott Aronson (eds.), *The Handbook of Social Psychology* (2d ed., vol. 4; Reading, Mass.: Addison-Wesley, 1969), p. 1–88. In the first edition, published in 1954, these authors attempted to sort out major variables that influence group problem-solving; fifteen years later, on the basis of additional research, they placed issues and phenomena in a theoretical context moving toward the formulation of a theory of group problem-solving.

under experimentally controlled conditions, and without the presence of a social worker with particular professional ethics, values, and goals that affect the group problem-solving process.

It should be no surprise that problem-solving components appear with such ubiquity and persist with such strength throughout the formulations of the social group work method. The social and intellectual history of the United States is replete with examples of the pragmatic philosophy and experimental approach that form the matrix in which problem-solving is embedded, and that provide the source of its essence and continuing energy.[2] Indeed the very same pragmatic philosophy and experimental approach forms the matrix for the development of some major aspects of all of social work philosophy and practice.[3] It seems that problem-solving is so germane to social group work that the two are almost inseparable—the one assumes the other.

If this assertion of the vitality of problem-solving as a major component of the formulations of the social group work method is borne out in the examination of these formulations over the span of fifty years, it is important to uncover the sources from which that emphasis sprang, to trace the patterns and persistence of the earlier emphases, and to discover the modifications that have evolved as the formulations have been influenced by developments in society, in social welfare and social work practice, in the underlying behavioral and social sciences, in social work and allied professional education for social work, and by research in the underlying sciences and in practice. Such explication may offer clues as to why no unified, comprehensive, fully developed problem-solving formulation has yet emerged in social work with groups comparable to that in other methods, developed so admirably by Helen Harris Perlman in her *Social Casework: A Problem-Solving Process* and ably reflected in Irving Spergel's *Community Problem Solving: The Delinquency Example*.[4] If problem-solving is indeed ubiquitous to the prac-

[2] The following volumes of social and intellectual history of the United States present detailed discussions of the pervasive influence of the philosophy of Pragmatism and of the experimental approach: Eric F. Goldman, *Rendezvous With Destiny* (New York: Knopf, 1953), pp. 155–60; Richard Hofstadter, *Social Darwinism in American Thought* (rev. ed.; Boston: Beacon Press, 1955), pp. 123–42; Gail Kennedy (ed.), *Pragmatism and American Culture* (Boston: Heath, 1950), pp. 1–111.

[3] See Carel Germain, "Casework and Science: A Historical Encounter," in Robert W. Roberts and Robert H. Nee (eds.), *Theories of Social Casework* (Chicago: University of Chicago Press, 1970), pp. 11–12.

[4] Helen H. Perlman, *Social Casework; Irving A. Spergel, Community Problem Solving*.

tice of social work with groups, perhaps it is time to consider and work toward a consciously articulated, comprehensive, unified formulation of a problem-solving approach.

The clarification and articulation of the components essential to a comprehensive formulation and the discovery of linkages and of gaps among problem-solving formulations of social casework, social group work, and community work may provide additional understanding of similarities and differences in assumptions, theories, and propositions characterizing the three methods long identified as major in social work practice.

To proceed with the inquiry and to accomplish these ends, several tasks must be addressed in an orderly fashion. A selection of major or landmark writings dealing with social group work will be examined for each of five decades beginning with 1920, and for the first half of the seventies, to determine the nature and extent of the emphasis on problem-solving that characterizes writings of each decade. Consideration will be given to the influences of societal concerns, philosophical considerations, the behavioral sciences, intra- and interprofessional developments and professional education for social work that permeated the particular decade. Efforts will be made to describe the target populations and organizational auspices, the classification of small groups, the purposes of the groups, the attention to assessment and selection of individuals and groups, the attention to group dynamics, the explication of principles, methods, and techniques of intervention, and to linkages with social casework, community work, and other professional disciplines. The paper will conclude with the summarization of trends in theoretical formulations of problem-solving in social work with small groups and will suggest further inquiry to be pursued.

FORMULATIONS—SIX DECADES

THE TWENTIES

The decade of the 1920s laid the groundwork for the development of the formulations that emerged in the 1930s and 1940s as initial statements of the social group work method. The richness and depth of thought of such scholars as Herbert Croly, John Dewey, Mary Parker Follett, and Eduard Lindeman emphasized the process of inquiry or problem-solving as basic to the work of small groups of citizens who participate responsibly and creatively to clarify and implement the social goals of a democratic social order. Their views of the developing sciences of society held that these sciences could become truly significant only if they inquired about, examined, and interpreted "human activities undertaken to accomplish definable but adaptable human purposes." [5]

The work of these social philosophers and scholars is embedded in Pragmatism, the dominant philosophy in the United States during the first two decades of the Twentieth Century. Four of its major emphases influenced the development of a problem-solving emphasis in group work: (1) the idea that the individual can influence, manipulate, change, or even control his environment; (2) emphasis upon philosophy as the experimental study of the uses of ideas and knowledge, and a belief in the effectiveness of ideas and in the potential and power of novel ideas; (3) the emergence and dominance of William James' humanistic views within Pragmatism, and his emphasis upon the individual as central and upon the individual knower as actor; and (4) John Dewey's more socialized philosophical theory that took the form of Instrumentalism, which became "both a social theory and a social influence," to the effect that ideas are plans of action, that genuine understanding comes only from direct participation in events, and that intelligence is a major, effective instrument in modifying the world. [6]

The humanistic, individual orientation of William James and the social orientation that characterized John Dewey's thoughts were united in the emphases upon social consciousness and upon man's ability to change his social environment. Individual and social goals were to be accomplished through an experimental approach to the search for knowledge, and through the use of *human action* to test ideas, their consequences, and their effectiveness. In essence, these social philosophers believed that social science would contribute to social betterment through helping the participants of small problem-solving groups to become conscious of what they were trying to accomplish, of their ways of work, of obstacles in their path toward their goals, and of how well their methods were adapted to what they wished to accomplish. With such consciousness, individuals and groups might become better able to control their own behavior, "insofar as control was equivalent to self control." [7]

[5] See especially Herbert Croly's introduction to Eduard C. Lindeman, *Social Discovery: An Approach to the Study of Functional Groups* (New York: Republic, 1925), p. xii.

[6] Richard Hofstadter, *Social Darwinism in American Thought*, p. 123–42.

[7] See especially Croly's introduction to Lindeman, *Social Discovery*, p. xv. Croly elaborated this point, as follows: "Social science would consist, that is, in a body of recorded, interpreted social practice which would be taught in the form of a method rather than in the form of a social

The explication of individual problem-solving as stated by John Dewey has become classic and is often equated with the scientific method. It is the major framework for formulations of the problem-solving process in social work, and therefore merits special attention. Dewey cast his presentation within the conceptualization of five phases or aspects of reflective thinking, emphasizing that such thinking originates in a "state of doubt, hesitation, perplexity, mental difficulty," and procedes as "an act of searching, hunting, inquiring to find material that will resolve the doubt, settle and dispose of the perplexity." [8] His continuing emphasis upon the importance of both the uncertainty and the inquiry is legendary. His analysis of the process of reflective thinking which goes between the initial uncertainty and the end resolution—that is, the process of inquiry—is as follows:

> (1) *Suggestions,* in which the mind leaps forward to a possible solution; (2) an intellectualization of the difficulty or perplexity that has been *felt* (directly experienced) into a *problem* to be solved, a question for which the answer must be sought; (3) the use of one suggestion after another as a leading idea or *hypothesis,* to initiate and guide observation and other operations in collection of factual material; (4) the mental elaboration of the idea or supposition as an idea or supposition (*reasoning,* in the sense in which reasoning is a part, not the whole, of influence); and (5) *testing* the hypothesis by overt or imaginative action. [9]

It is important to note that Dewey recognized the initial emotional reactions to a difficulty that is *felt* or experienced, and emphasized that it was essential to inhibit the natural tendency to *act* immediately before the problem is identified and clarified intellectually, and the process of inquiry set in motion and completed. These emphases on the feelings involved, the tendency toward immediate and possibly irrational action in response to a felt difficulty, and the importance of problem identification, clarification, and exploration have permeated the problem-solving formulations of social work, both individual and group, in very specific and explicit ways, as has the importance attached to collection and examination of facts (including the recognition of feelings as facts), the imaginative consideration of alternative solutions and their consequences, the decision to try one or some combina-

---

encyclopedia. It would become the articulate and methodical conscience of the individuals participating in a society—the reflection of the steady and discriminating attention which human beings had achieved with respect to their own social activities" (p. xvi). For further elaboration, see p. xix.

[8] John Dewey, *How We Think,* p. 12.   [9] *Ibid.,* p. 107.

tion of alternatives, the evaluation of the results, and further work toward integration of that solution or further search for and testing of alternatives, with further evaluation.

In the early 1920s another major thinker and writer was coming into prominence in the world of those who were endeavoring to formulate and influence social thought and to connect that thought with action in the everyday lives of people. Mary Parker Follett, deeply grounded in the study of economics, political science, and philosophy, was concerned with the psychological (dynamic) view of organizations in the practical implementation of the ideals of a democratic social order and in the inner workings of business and industry. In her volume *The New State* she expressed her belief that social progress in a democracy depends on the group, not the crowd, and that "the group process contains the secret of collective life, it is the key to democracy, it is the master lesson for every individual to learn, it is our chief hope for the political, the social, the international life of the future." [10] She viewed the essence of group process as *creating,* and emphasized the necessity for differing points of view in groups (constructive nature of group conflict), and the importance of eliciting, considering, and working with all points of view. She offered her cogent analysis of the four possible consequences of the confrontation of differing interests or views in groups: "(1) voluntary submission of one side; (2) struggle and the victory of one side over another; (3) compromise; or (4) integration." [11] Her interpretation of integration—the ideal in group process—was that it always involves invention. The group members, working together, invent a solution that no one individual came with, a solution that is *qualitatively* different. The process involves *growing* a solution that includes at least some component of the major desire of each diverse interest, but develops some new elements or qualities, not previously present, usually having to do with the relationships among the initial interests or with a larger interest to which all can become committed.

Follett was deeply involved in one of the major thrusts among the social scientists of her time—that social scientists should not engage in abstract speculation, but should study the behavior of people, especially in groups, and should attempt to bring about and deal with problems in the practical, everyday, social relationships among human beings. Until the time

[10] Mary Parker Follett, *The New State* (New York: Longmans, Green, 1926), p. 23.
[11] Mary Parker Follett, *Creative Experience,* p. 156.

of her death in 1933, she was engaged in writing and in work with some of the leaders in industrial relations in both the United States and England. Thus, in her lifetime she had encompassed work in the problems of democracy and government, social problems, social administration, and industrial organization and administration. All of her writings reflect an emphasis upon the psychological as well as the collective nature and demands of the social process in groups, and upon the creative essence, potentials, and vitality of group problem-solving in the building of a better social order within the United States and internationally. She believed such efforts to be the true responsibility of every citizen of a democracy.

The group problem-solving implications of Follett's work and thought are so lucid as to need no comment or elaboration. In the next two decades they became a major source of reference and inspiration for those writers who formulated the initial statements about social group work.

Eduard C. Lindeman further developed the process of social investigation within and through small groups. Like Follett, he stressed how essential it is to recognize diverse interests, to elicit their expression and consideration, and to work through to group solutions that involve elements of social discovery, new qualities, new learning, and ways not heretofore conceived or developed.[12]

At about this same time, Harrison Elliott brought out his *Process of Group Thinking,* which aimed to present a methodology by means of which democracy could be made to function in everyday life. In Elliott's view, "The aim of democracy is to secure the active participation of every individual up to the limit of his capacity in the conduct of all his social, vocational, and political affairs." [13] His analysis of the procedures and conduct of group thinking brought together thought and action, within the Dewey tradition, and found specific ways to implement the ideas of Follett and Lindeman, underlining the importance of the contribution of the ideas of each individual in reference to the question, problem, or task at hand, and the potential of ordinary people to work together in the development of creative ideas that could grow only through the give and take of the social process of the group.

It is interesting to note that the first study of what actual leaders of groups do in the course of their daily work came at the end of the 1920s.

---

[12] Lindeman, *Social Discovery.*
[13] Harrison Elliott, *Process of Group Thinking* (New York: Association Press, 1928), p. 1.

Margaretta Williamson offered the first careful job analysis of group workers. There was examination of both implicit and explicit problem-solving functions and efforts of the social worker by himself, with group members, with other staff and colleagues, with board and committee members, and with citizens of the community. Again, a more elastic, changing democratic social order was emphasized as both context and goal of such a problem-solving process in and through small groups, within organizations, and within the community.[14]

Thus it is clear that in the 1920s the philosophical base of group problem-solving was articulated. The basic belief in the small group as an entity and instrument to serve the individual and society at one and the same time became a dominant theme. Individual interests could be met by acting in concert with others, and the rights and responsibilities of individuals could be preserved and actualized. A democratic social order was thought to depend upon the proper functioning of small groups that reflect and implement the rights and responsibilities of individual members of society, and social progress was believed to depend upon an educated and responsible citizenry. Individuals and small groups were envisioned as creative problem-solvers in their own behalf. The notion that such problem-solving work was their democratic right and responsibility became crystal clear. Respect for individual differences and the creative use of such differences in group problem-solving emerged with striking clarity.

The *behavioral science* base was further delineated through the insistence upon the use of knowledge derived from both individual and group psychology. The emphasis upon the interaction among thinking, feeling, and doing was quite clear. Individual human beings were envisaged as personalities capable of realization and growth; small groups were viewed as functioning social entities, capable of development and growth, and capable of influencing their individual members and the larger social environment.

Specific articulation of a problem-solving process, almost synonymous with the scientific method, was advanced as germane to the responsible thinking and acting of individuals and groups and as essential for the survival and implementation of a democratic social order. The emphasis upon the *testing* of this formulation in the crucible of use in everyday life of everyday citizens—and not as some esoteric, abstract, design—was para-

---

[14] Margaretta Williamson, *The Social Worker in Group Work* (New York: Harper, 1929).

mount. The continuing, reciprocal interaction between the individual and his social environment was remarkably clear in its essence and import.

It became evident as well that these social philosophers and scholars of the 1920s believed in the importance of voluntary participation of individuals in small problem-solving groups, and that such groups might be formed within a range of organizations or might arise within the social fabric as autonomous social entities whose goals were related to the interests and needs of individual members and to the production of changes within selected aspects of the social environment.

THE 1930s

Dominated by the Great Depression and its consequences, the decade of the 1930s marked the beginnings of the major efforts to define and formulate the social group work method as such, and these efforts revealed attention to certain aspects of the group problem-solving process as essential to the practice of group work. The major themes of the work of the 1920s reappeared, especially the emphasis upon the small group as an essential instrument for individual and social problem-solving in a democracy and the importance of the scientific study of small groups in everyday life. This latter theme became particularly prominent in the 1930s and was developed especially by Grace L. Coyle and Wilber I. Newstetter, who pioneered in social work the use of scientific approaches toward understanding the nature and dynamics of the social process in small groups.

The landmark volume by Grace L. Coyle *Social Process in Organized Groups* appeared in 1930. While her effort was clearly an analysis of the universal processes of small face-to-face groups and not an attempt to formulate the social group work method, it is noteworthy that she devoted a major chapter to "The Process of Collective Thinking," [15] that she drew upon the work of Dewey and Follett, and used a range of groups as examples to illustrate her points. Individual participation and growth, combined with the accomplishment of social goals, were described as inevitably intertwined in such groups if the discussion method were properly used—that is, the process of collective thinking that insured creative problem-solving by the people most affected and involved. Her analysis dealt in detail

[15] Grace L. Coyle, *Social Process in Organized Groups*, pp. 173–213.

with the interaction of human and situational factors in the group-deliberation process and with the actual process of group decision-making.

It should be noted as well that in her volume *Studies In Group Behavior* Coyle devoted attention to methods of problem-solving that a group leader should use in handling social interactions of the members and in assisting the group to deal with problems of group control, to develop and implement its program based on the members' interests and needs, and to deal with the ebb and flow of positive and negative feelings that characterize the fabric of group life.[16] Illustrations were drawn from records of groups with an educational or recreational purpose that met in settlements, community centers, national program agencies, public schools, churches, and trade unions. Several of her emphases reappeared in other writings of this decade: active, responsible participation of the individual throughout all problem-solving efforts, the development of social attitudes and abilities to work with others who held diverse ideas and interests in the achievement of agreed-upon social goals, opportunities for the individual to develop new interests and new skills through the problem-solving process, and the training and experience in active participation in group and community affairs.[17]

The major thread of the problem-solving process appeared as well in the very creatively developed set of papers dealing with group work in the 1935 *Proceedings* of the National Conference of Social Work. In a paper that is not always given the credit it deserves, Wilber I. Newstetter distinguished among three uses of the term social group work—to designate a field of social work practice, to describe a process, and to describe certain techniques or conscious efforts used by a social worker.[18] In his further delineation of the group work process and of techniques, he emphasized the

---

[16] Grace L. Coyle (ed.), *Studies in Group Behavior* (New York: Harper, 1937), pp. 6–13.

[17] Near the end of this decade there appeared a volume of papers published under the auspices of the National Association for the Study of Group Work, edited by Joshua Lieberman, *New Trends In Group Work* (New York: Association Press, 1938). This volume reflected strong concern with methods of implementing democratic philosophy in everyday living. There is evidence of the interrelatedness of individual growth and social goals, including the problem-solving components of the process, and of the group worker's responsibility for assisting small groups to deal with social problems, including those inherent within their own group life and those problems of the wider community that "threaten further social progress and even civilization itself."

[18] Wilber I. Newstetter, "What is Social Group Work?" *Proceedings of the National Conference of Social Work, 1935* (Chicago: University of Chicago Press, 1935), p. 291.

discovery and use of individual interests through the use of the discussion method, the adjustments of the relationships of people and ideas that must characterize the process, the working together toward the solution of some common problem, and the interrelatedness of individual growth and social goals through the *group process,* implemented through the group *work* process as he defined and described it. His analysis of the conscious efforts of the social worker emphasized problem-solving activity by the worker in his own thinking, and in his ways of *doing with* the group participants.[19] In addition, he placed very strong emphasis on the use of an *inquiry process*—of observation and fact-gathering, and on the necessity for openness with regard to the solutions or decisions that the group would develop together. The worker should not have predetermined outcomes that he tries to suggest or impose upon the group; instead, he should work with the group each step of the way, responding to their reactions and responses to each other, to the exchange of ideas, and to himself.[20]

In that same volume, Grace L. Coyle's paper on group work and social change was given an award by the editorial committee for being the most important contribution to the subject matter of the Conference. She developed the theme of the group process as "a significant mode of social action" and emphasized the responsibility of the individual as a participant in social problem-solving in implementing, sustaining, and improving a democratic social order. Group work was identified as a force for social change. Again, the emphasis on free discussion of all points of view in reference to social issues and social problems appeared with clarity, as did the point that the worker assists the group in the identification and clarification of issues and problems, in the elicitation and consideration of all points of view, and in the implementation of the *group's* responsibility to make individual and/or group decisions about any actions they wished to undertake.

In *Group Adjustment—A Study in Experimental Sociology,* Newstetter, Feldstein, and Newcomb reported on their research on the social process of small groups of children in a summer camp. From the findings, the authors drew a number of implications for group work. Several of these reflect and deal with detailed suggestions, guides or tentative principles that the group leader should use in such group problem-solving aspects as discovery of in-

---

[19] *Ibid.,* pp. 292–99.
[20] Grace L. Coyle, "Group Work and Social Change," *Proceedings of the National Conference of Social Work, 1935* (Chicago: University of Chicago Press, 1935).

dividual interests and needs, development of program, the individual and his adjustment to the group, and social purposes; and dealing with group conflicts and controls germane to the group problem-solving process and outcomes in reference to agreed-upon social goals.[21]

During the 1930s those writings that revealed a strong emphasis upon the validity and use of the group problem-solving process retained and elaborated the *philosophical base* laid down in the 1920s. There was essential agreement with the following philosophical themes: (1) the growth of the individual and the achievement of social goals are intertwined and inseparable in philosophy and in practice; (2) the group problem-solving process, ideally developed and implemented, affords the opportunity for the members to invent a social solution, integrative in quality, that no one member would have been able to develop on his own; and (3) the process of inquiry that is pertinent to the process necessitates openness, and the consideration of alternative means and alternative outcomes.

The *behavioral science foundations* continued to emphasize knowledge derived from individual and group psychology, with the conviction that these sources must be used in combination if the participants and professional worker are to understand the dynamics of social process in the small group, including those processes related to collective thinking, problem-solving, and decision-making. As in the 1920s, both cognitive and emotional components were deemed essential for problem-solving actions in small groups, and there was concern with rational and irrational aspects of thought.

A newly articulated emphasis began to emerge with clarity during the 1930s. Coyle, Newstetter, and others presented the social worker as an active problem-solver in his own *thinking* process and in the actual *doing* that is involved in assisting small groups to clarify, deal with, and solve a range of problems undertaken by their members. There was agreement that the best way for a social worker (who was to be a researcher as well) to learn about the nature and dynamics of the social process in small groups was to become engaged as an active participant-inquirer, to work with the group, and to observe, assess, and interpret the group problem-solving process. This meant that the participant-inquirer must assist the members and himself

[21] Wilber I. Newstetter, Marc Feldstein, and Theodore Newcomb, *Group Adjustment: A Study in Experimental Sociology* (Cleveland: School of Applied Social Sciences, Western Reserve University, 1938), pp. 105–31.

to become conscious of the process and of their own relationships and behavior, to the end that the process and outcome might be improved, as well
as the future problem-solving capabilities of the individuals, of the group as
a whole, and of the worker himself.

The writings of this decade confirmed the decided bent toward the use
of small groups in which the members are voluntary participants—whether
those groups are informal or are structured in formal work situations or in a
wide range of organizations and associations within educational, recreational, or political auspices.

The interrelated purposes of individual and social problem-solving
through the structure and dynamics of the small group persisted strongly
throughout the decade. Emphasis continued to be placed upon the importance of the needs and interests of individuals of society, in their reciprocal
interactions, in reference to the problem-solving process. Continuing recognition of individual growth through responsible participation in group problem-solving remained clear. However, there were efforts to articulate, with
greater specificity, the ways and means by which the social environment influenced individual and group problem-solving, and the ways and means by
which the social environment might be affected or changed by individuals
acting in concert to achieve agreed-upon goals. The planful, conscious
awareness and activities of the social worker in parallel and collaborative
problem-solving with the group appeared as a strong motif in the writings
toward the end of this decade. The beginning articulation of the social group
work method highlighted both the separate and joint opportunities and responsibilities of the worker and the group in the problem-solving process
and outcome.

THE 1940s

The decade of the 1940s was dominated by World War II and its after-
math. Social group work practice and the developing formulations of the
method were strongly influenced by the events and thought that permeated
the society and social work of the time. A review of the group work literature of the period reveals continuing and intense concern with ways to
implement democratic philosophy and principles. This was particularly
prominent during the first half of the decade when the battle against totalitar-
ianism and dictatorship permeated all aspects of life. The thread of group

problem-solving, and the essential nature of its contributions to the full implementation of a democratic social order, were very clear.

Within the writings dealing with social group work, several other major themes appeared as well: (1) the contributions of the method to improving relationships among individuals of differing racial and ethnic backgrounds; (2) contributions of the method to the discussion of intergroup and world problems; (3) a growing emphasis on therapeutic uses of the method and concern with similarities and differences among social work, therapeutic group work, and group therapy; (4) increasing interest in similarities and differences between social casework and social group work; (5) increasing recognition of the possible use of the method with groups in which membership is not voluntary; and (6) increasing, specific concern with professional issues and interests, such as professional identification, searching for the essential or core knowledge, principles and skills of social group work, and consideration of a variety of ways to improve the quality of practice.[22]

With the growing concern about similarities and differences between social casework and social group work, with some experiments in collaborative services,[23] and with the burgeoning of group work specializations in schools of social work, came increased interest in the use of social group work for the treatment of individuals who were suffering from emotional conflicts and who were experiencing severe problems in coping with various responsibilities and demands of everyday life. Although the behavioral

[22] Between 1940 and 1945 the American Association for the Study of Group Work (AASGW) published through Association Press five yearly volumes of papers. The titles suggest the major concerns of the time, and a review of the contents revealed the major themes delineated in the text: *Main Currents in Group Work Thought* (1940); *Group Work in a Year of Crisis* (1941): *Group Work in War Time* (1942); *Group Work and the Social Scene Today* (1943); *Group Work Horizons* (1944). From 1945 to 1946, by which time the AASGW had become the American Association of Group Workers (AAGW), a professional association, the volume published by AAGW was entitled *Toward Professional Standards*. The papers reflect the search for the knowledge, principles, and skills germane to group work in all settings, and with a variety of groups formed for a range of purposes; the search for specific professional identity; and special concern with cultural and intercultural factors and relationships, with youth in a post-war world, and with ways to improve the quality of practice, including the use of supervision, process recording, and research.

[23] See especially Gertrude Wilson, *Group Work and Case Work: Their Relationship and Practice* (New York: Family Welfare Association of America, 1941) and the report of a symposium sponsored by the AAGW, *Group Work—Case Work Cooperation* (New York: Association Press, 1946).

science base of social group work retained the emphasis upon the combination of cognitive and emotional aspects of individual behavior, and the necessity to use knowledge derived from both psychology and sociology in order to gain understanding of both individual and group functioning, there emerged a strong push to search for the meaning or significance of individual behavior within the context of the group.

In the majority of schools of social work at the time, the most widely used personality theory was Freudian in its derivation, although a small number of schools drew upon the thought and work of Otto Rank. With the move toward possible uses of group work in the treatment of individuals, the concern with more detailed knowledge and understanding of personality became clear, and this concern was manifest in the writings. At the same time that Freudian theory of personality development was widely used by social group workers who were graduates of schools of social work, there was growing interest in field theory as a basis for understanding the dynamics of group process. The efforts to articulate theories dealing with individual development and change, and with group development and change, were beginning to appear among group work writers, especially in the late 1940s. There continued to be a strong conviction that workers needed to understand and deal with both individuals and groups, and that individual and social goals were intertwined in social group work, although one or the other might be more prominent in work with a particular group for a particular purpose.

Amidst all these developments and their elaborations, the strong emphasis on the group problem-solving process continued to flourish. The last three years of the decade brought an especially significant period in social group work writing; and within several major contributions produced at that time, the emphasis on the group problem-solving process was very clear. In some of the writings, the problem-solving efforts were turned to work on the problems of individuals who were using the assistance of other group members and of the worker to deal with some aspects of difficulties and to work toward solutions that were individual, and not group, in the sense that the individual would decide and would follow through; but no group solution was involved for the group as a group.

In a collection of papers published in 1947, Grace L. Coyle continued to emphasize the social goals inherent in group problem-solving and the importance of such small-group efforts in the implementation of a democratic social order.[24] The following year brought her volume, *Group Work With American Youth—A Guide to the Practice of Leadership,* in which she identified six basic assumptions of group work and dealt with major aspects of group leadership in recreation or education within leisure time agencies.[25] She continued to portray the leader as a problem-solver in his own thinking as well as in his actions. His process of inquiry as he seeks to understand the members includes his search for the meaning of their behavior, individual and group, and underlines the need for the group leader's use of careful observations and knowledge from psychology, social psychology, and sociology. Her particular emphasis and detailed application of some of the findings of research on small groups becomes prominent in this volume. Her chapters dealing with "Achieving Democratic Control" and "The Art of Program Making" are especially rich in the analysis of the way the leader engages the group in problem-solving, from the point of identification and clarification of the problem through the phase of considering various alternatives, choosing one to try, and evaluating the results; there is further problem-solving as the group moves forward to new alternatives or to new problems and tasks.

The year 1948 also brought Harleigh Trecker's volume on social group work.[26] He formulated several basic principles of social group work practice, and delineated a threefold problem-solving approach for the worker: (1) the process of evaluating his own work carried on through the writing and study of process records of his work; (2) the use of evaluation criteria that indicate a problem-solving approach by the worker—his statement of objectives, evidence of his ability to engage the group in solving its own problems, and an evaluation of how the results do or do not reflect the objectives; and (3) the importance of the worker's engagement in continuing study and research on the many unsolved problems identified in practice.

The last year of the decade brought writings that further emphasized understanding and dealing with the individual within the group, including the problem-solving aspects. The publication of *Social Group Work Practice*

[24] Grace L. Coyle, *Group Experience and Democratic Values* (New York: Woman's Press, 1947).

[25] Grace L. Coyle, *Group Work with American Youth: A Guide to the Practice of Leadership* (New York: Harper, 1948).

[26] Harleigh Trecker, *Social Group Work: Principles and Practices* (New York: Whiteside, 1948).

by Gertrude Wilson and Gladys Ryland marked a bringing together of knowledge of work with individuals and work with groups, and an integration of dynamic personality theory within the knowledge and expected competence of the worker. It also offered an unsurpassed analysis of program media and their purposeful use by group workers in the service of goals related to individual and group development and to individual and group problem-solving. Problems of individuals and of the group were considered appropriate for attention. This approach to practice emphasized the worker's responsibility to understand the dynamics of group life and factors of individual and group difference, and to engage the members in solving problems, in developing programs and in evaluating their own accomplishments and failures in reference to their goals. These authors believed that "the decision-making process is the central core of the social group work method," [27] and this component became central in their analysis and synthesis of what constitutes the social group work method. While the emphasis upon understanding and working with the individual was very strong, the emphasis was retained on the individual and social goals that could be accomplished through the use of group work and especially by means of its problem-solving aspects.

During this decade, emphasis upon voluntary participation in groups continued. But within the gradual movement toward recognition of the importance and validity of therapeutic uses of groups, there appeared some major threads of interest in groups in which membership might not be voluntary. The point was made that while the initial decision to join might not be voluntarily made by the individual, the actual participation could become voluntary through the meaning of the experience and outcome to the group members. Such problem-solving groups were thought to be helpful to individuals suffering from severe emotional conflicts and problems in coping with the demands of living. The problem-solving efforts might be directed toward problems of individuals or toward a group problem. Both children and adults were thought to be appropriate members of such groups in which the problems to be worked on might well include selected emotional problems of individual members, or problems of dealing with day-by-day demands in the particular life situation of the individual.

In 1949 Gisela Konopka focused attention on the use of social group

---

[27] Gertrude Wilson and Gladys Ryland, *Social Group Work Practice,* p. 66.

work in the study and treatment of children in a child guidance clinic and in an institutional setting.[28] She emphasized the importance of the worker's competence in discussion-leading as a means toward assisting group members to work on problem-solving—individual and group. Her continuing emphasis on the use of program as a tool within the careful framework and philosophy of the Wilson-Ryland book was clear, as was the use of concepts from psychoanalytically based ego psychology in understanding and dealing with the individual and with groups in their problem-solving efforts.

In 1947 Newstetter distinguished between the social group work process and what he termed the social intergroup work process that he viewed as one major component of community organization. Through the social group work process it is intended that individuals should satisfy selected personal needs, that this process should be a "dividend" to society as well, that individuals should, in that way, learn to relate effectively to other groups in the community, and that "groups should learn to participate responsibly in the community process of furthering social action which seems to them important." [29] He defined the social intergroup work process as focused on the "adjustmental relations between groups and not the personal needs of the members of our inter-group who are there primarily as representatives of some other group or groups," and as focused on "specific social goals selected and accepted by the groups involved." [30] The problem-solving framework continued in both instances of Newstetter's delineation, with attention to the social worker's own problem-solving thinking in his study and assessment of the individual, group, and community and to the engagement of individuals and groups in problem identification and clarification, selection for work, and in the process of searching for and selecting alternative solutions, trying them out, evaluating the results, and moving to the next problem or task.

The organizational auspices that continued to appear prominently within the literature dealing with group problem-solving efforts were settlements, community centers, youth-serving national program agencies, and, to some extent, churches and public schools. Institutions for dependent, ne-

[28] Gisela Konopka, *Therapeutic Group Work with Children (Minneapolis; University of Minnesota Press, 1949)*.

[29] Wilbur I. Newstetter, "The Social Inter-Group Work Process: How Does it Differ from Social Group Work Process?" in *Community Organization* (New York: Russell Sage Foundation, 1947), p. 20.

[30] *Ibid.*, p. 22

glected, and delinquent children also were mentioned more frequently as settings in which social group work might make important contributions, including the use of small groups for working on problems of individuals,
problems shared in common by several individuals, problems in the functioning of the group as an entity, and problems germane to the social context
of the living situation, such as a cottage or section within the larger institution.

Toward the end of the decade, in part as a result of services to soldiers
in psychiatric hospitals during and after World War II, the literature began
to reflect a marked interest in the use of social group work in hospitals, both
medical and psychiatric. The following decade produced major attention to
these settings as appropriate ones for the use of the method in its problem-
solving thrusts and accomplishments.

By this time, earlier emphasis on the group worker as a participant-
inquirer had evolved to one in which the practitioner was urged to evaluate
the progress of the group and of its individual members in reference to the
particular goals of service. Close observations of individual and group behavior, attempts to assess the meaning of behavior through the use of knowledge derived from the behavioral sciences, and analyses of the nature and
influence of the community and of cultural factors on individual members
and on the group as a group were articulated as salient features of methodology in the problem-solving aspects of practice.[31]

In late 1949 a report on the function of the professional group worker
was accepted by the Executive Board of the American Association of Group
Workers.[32] This report, culminating in a one-page statement that became a
major reference point for practitioners and scholars, emphasized individual
and social goals as the proper focus of attention in social group work. It also
emphasized several aspects of the problem-solving process in small groups:

[31] In a small pamphlet, Saul Bernstein developed an instrument for evaluating progress of the
group and of the individual, and for evaluating the individual member's contributions to the
group: *Charting Group Progress* (New York: Association Press, 1949). Bernstein's criteria included such group problem-solving dimensions as "handling conflicts, leadership and participation, cooperative planning, group thinking, acceptance of differences" (p. 8). This method of
evaluation was offered as an experiment within the spirit of inquiry and search for improved
means of evaluating the use of social group work and of assessing some of its results.

[32] See "Final Report of the Committee on the Function of the Professional Group Worker"
(Grace L. Coyle, Chairman, AAGW, 1949). Also, Grace L. Coyle, "Social Group Work,"
in *Social Work Year Book* (New York: AASW, 1954), p. 480–81.

(1) the sharing of knowledge, and integration of ideas and differences in group decision-making; (2) the value of recognizing and dealing with differences in backgrounds and values of individual members; and (3) the responsibility of small groups to assist in solving community problems and in improving the democratic social order. Within this problem-solving framework the necessary knowledge included concepts from the modern behavioral and social sciences dealing with individual and group behavior, social conditions, and community relations. The group worker was charged to use his understanding of personalities and of program as he engaged the members in using their own capacities in individual and group problem-solving, whether efforts were focused on personal or social growth of the members, on participation as responsible citizens of a democracy, or on the group as a whole acting responsibly to change its social environment.

THE 1950s

The decade of the 1950s was characterized in the larger society by fears of Communism and by McCarthyism, resulting in tendencies to pull sharply away from social goals. Examination of the writings of the period reveals a tendency to continue and to elaborate upon some of the major concerns of the late 1940s. During this decade, the National Conference of Social Work selected for publication each year a small number of papers presented at the annual meeting. Analysis of the content of these volumes and of other collections of papers published during this decade shows that the major professional concerns of social group work fell into the following categories: (1) the expansion of the use of social group work into medical and psychiatric hospitals serving children and adults, with analysis of the similarities and differences in the method resulting from the different purposes and settings; (2) concern with reaching and serving hostile, confused, acting-out teenagers through the social group work method, with analysis of modifications essential for accomplishing these aims; (3) concern with individual and group autonomy, and problems of conformity in a period of shrinking social experimentation; (4) emphasis upon improving practice through better use of a range of technical knowledge and skills; (5) concern with the question of whether social group work had moved too far too quickly into a treatment focus and had virtually abandoned its long-time commitment to social goals; (6) some efforts to define researchable problems in social group work; and

(7) collaboration between casework and group work in service to individuals.[33]

The social group work literature of the 1950s maintained a continuing emphasis upon the group problem-solving process as a very important aspect of the method, and lifted various components of that process for special attention. In one of the major publications of this decade, Helen U. Phillips emphasized the use of the social group work method in working toward social goals. As she developed her explication of the skills that the worker must use if he is to fulfill social values and social purposes, she emphasized the use of the group problem-solving process in communicating and dealing with feelings of the individual member, the group, and the worker, and in helping the group members to make responsible decisions, to deal with interpersonal relationships, and to develop and use programs that would implement their agreed-upon goals. Throughout her presentations she recognized "two major purposes of group work, namely the individual growth of group members and the development of the group as a whole for social usefulness." [34]

In 1953 Alan F. Klein restated the principles of democracy and underlined the importance of the social group work method in the realization of the aims of a democratic social worker. In his introduction to the volume, Trecker noted that "this book, more than any other, puts the 'social' in social group work, because a major portion of it deals with group work's social goals and aspirations." [35] The group problem-solving process was fully developed through the emphases upon social goals, upon practical problem-solving within the group itself and in reference to problems encountered in the social environment of the members, upon the analysis of cultural influences that affect the group and individual members, and upon ways in which workers might assist members to deal constructively with problems of cultural and value conflicts in groups. A major thrust of Klein's presentation

[33] Three collections of social group work papers were published during the 1950s: Dorothea F. Sullivan, *Reading in Group Work* (New York: Association Press, 1952); Harleigh B. Trecker, *Group Work Foundations and Frontiers* (New York: Whiteside; William Morrow, 1955); and Harleigh B. Trecker, *Group Work in the Psychiatric Setting* (New York: Whiteside, and Morrow, 1956). The same identified concerns appear with regularity in the volumes of collected papers.

[34] Helen U. Phillips, *Essentials of Social Group Work Skill* (New York: Association Press, 1957), p. 167.

[35] Alan F. Klein, *Society, Democracy, and the Group* (New York: Woman's Press; Whiteside, and Morrow, 1953), p. vii.

was the importance of social group work in assisting small groups of adults to become inquirers and social problem-solvers in fulfilling the responsible roles of citizens in a democracy.[36]

During this decade as well, the rising emphasis upon the use of group work to treat troubled individuals became clearly evident, and the problem-solving emphasis turned more toward dealing with individual members' personal conflicts or interpersonal relationship difficulties; thus the personal growth side of the dual emphasis became more prominent.[37] Concern about what seemed to some scholars as the tendency of social group work to formulate and attempt to deal with "global goals" began to appear with some frequency; and, especially toward the end of the decade, the move toward greater specificity and precision of goal, particularly of treatment goals for each individual member of the group, became apparent. Such concern with specificity and precision of goal was, of course, linked to an effort to gain greater specificity and precision of outcome. There was evidence of attention to such considerations as making the group purpose and goals conscious in the minds of the individual members as well as in the worker's mind, and keeping the individual and group problem-solving goals, processes, and accomplishments clear in the minds of all concerned. Factors in group composition were given attention, especially in reference to the specific goals for the group treatment of individuals with identified problems, and emphasis was placed upon the use of individual interviews to bring members into the group through an intake process.

During the 1950s the behavioral and social science knowledge used to undergird the problem-solving components of social group work practice retained essentially the same base brought forward from the 1940s. However, it was increasingly emphasized that group workers must understand the dynamics of both health and illness of the individual in his development throughout the life span, must learn specialized knowledge needed for par-

[36] *Ibid.*, pp. 44–147, 309–34

[37] The problem-solving thread was evident in Gisela Konopka, *Group Work in the Institution* (New York: Association Press, 1954), p. 45. She emphasized that dependent, neglected, and delinquent children in residential care, as well as physically, mentally, or emotionally handicapped children, have special need to develop the capacity to participate, to learn to take responsibility for decision-making and the consequences of their decisions, to increase their abilities "to contribute to decisions on grounds of rational thinking and through group deliberation," and to develop increased respect for and constructive ways of dealing with differences in racial and ethnic backgrounds and in values (p. 46).

ticular settings (such as medical and psychiatric), and must learn specialized knowledge of the nature and effects of particular handicaps from which individuals suffer and with which they must cope in social adaptation. Thus the behavioral and social sciences, as well as medicine and psychiatry, played an even more important part in the content considered essential for social group workers. At the same time, the retention of the emphasis on social goals required continuing development and use of knowledge from the social sciences dealing with social problems and the social environment.

In all instances, the fifties brought attention to the burgeoning knowledge of small-group structure and dynamics that the social sciences were producing—most especially, that which was developed through the experimental research and laboratory approach of social psychology. The emphasis upon ego psychology—psychoanalytically oriented—that permeated much of social casework in this decade, was also permeating social group work. The worker was urged to develop his own self-awareness to a high degree, to become fully conscious of his part in the problem-solving process, and to assist the group members as individuals and the group as a whole to become conscious of their parts in the process. He was also expected to develop professional control of his own part in the process and to assist the group members to develop and implement their own responsible controls of their behavior. His own evaluation and his engagement of the group in evaluating its own progress were expectations of the worker, and he was urged to move into research efforts that would begin to provide improved knowledge of practice, improved practice skills, and improved evaluative measures.

It should be noted here that the 1950s brought major research on group problem-solving by Robert F. Bales and other social scientists whose work was studied, tested, and applied in several of the professions. Such seminal scientific work influenced social workers to apply these methods and findings in order to refine their knowledge and understanding of the problem-solving process in small groups and to improve their ability to assist small groups to improve their problem-solving abilities, process, and results.[38]

---

[38] For the social science research methodology and findings, see: Robert Freed Bales, *Interaction Process Analysis* (Cambridge, Mass.: Addison-Wesley, 1950); Harold H. Kelley and John W. Thibaut, "Group Problem Solving," in Gardner Lindzey (ed.), *Handbook of Social Psychology,* 2 (Cambridge, Mass.: Addison-Wesley, 1954), and the up-dating of their article in Gardner Lindzey and Elliott Aronson (eds.), The *Handbook of Social Psychology,* vol. 4, 2d ed.; (Reading, Mass.: Addison-Wesley, 1969). For applications of the problem-solving process

The 1950s saw major efforts of social group work scholars and educators to study, select, and use the findings of the burgeoning research on the structure and dynamics of small groups, and on phases of group development. Along with the greater specificity deemed important for understanding and working with individuals through the use of groups formed for treatment purposes, there was a major thrust toward gaining and using greater specificity and depth of knowledge dealing with the nature, functioning, and life cycles of small groups as entities. Such knowledge was embedded in the matrix of field theory; and by the end of the decade, the beginning recognition and use of concepts derived from systems theory became apparent.[39]

THE 1960s

The decade of the 1960s was marked by social revolution that attempted to realize social justice for minority groups in the United States and reflected the rising expectations and demands of oppressed people throughout the world. It brought as well the assassinations of political leaders who had carried the hopes and aspirations of many people for a more just and socially enlightened society that would support and strengthen individual talent and social development. It brought involvement in the Vietnam War that further undermined the beliefs of many people in the integrity of their government and in other of their society's institutions, and the aspirations of many youth were sapped as they contemplated their future.

By this time, the philosophy of Existentialism was clearly evident in American thought, particularly among young people. For many, the focus on the moment and the attempt to express something of their creative selves, thus controlling at least some aspects of their own destinies, seemed the major priority. Attempts of many young people to overthrow the pressures and demands for academic and work achievement—placed upon them with such unrelenting and pervasive force in the late 1950s—expressed their determination to live their lives in ways that would not be bound by work

(or inquiry) to education, see Herbert A. Thelen, *Dynamics of Groups at Work* (Chicago: University of Chicago Press, 1954) and his *Education and the Human Quest* (New York: Harper & Row, 1960).

[39] See especially Grace L. Coyle and Margaret E. Hartford, *Social Process in the Community and the Group* (New York: Council on Social Work Education, 1958); and Mary Louise Somers "Four Small Group Theories: An Analysis and Frame of Reference for Use as Teaching Content in Social Group Work" (D.S.W. dissertation, School of Applied Social Sciences, Western Reserve University, 1957).

alone, and their refusal to support what they viewed as a machinelike existence.

Examination of the social group work literature of the 1960s reveals clear recognition of these forces and events and shows, as well, continuity and elaboration of themes that characterized the earlier demands. The 1960s brought a proliferation of formulations of the social group method, intensive work on the refinement and testing of some, and the development of others that differed from earlier formulations in their basic assumptions and in the philosophical framework within which they were cast. At the same time, there were approaches that were quite eclectic in their origins and in their development. It was during this decade that a sociobehavioral emphasis began to appear more frequently in group work formulations, issuing some major challenges to the framework of psychoanalytically oriented ego psychology that had dominated the teaching of the method since the late 1940s and early 1950s. The use of social systems theory continued and expanded as a basis for the group-dynamic components.

As background upon which to view the persistence of the problem-solving process in the formulations of the 1960s, it is instructive to examine the major themes that characterized the papers selected for publication by the National Conference on Social Welfare in yearly volumes dealing with social work practice.[40] The following themes evolved: (1) continuing concern with the use of the social group method in an expanding range of services and settings, with various age groups, and with children, adolescents, and adults who suffered from a variety of physical, mental, emotional, and social handicaps; (2) the application of group work knowledge and skills to work with short-term groups and family group treatment; (3) the use of group work method to facilitate constructive intergroup relations, and to assist individuals and groups to deal with differences and conflicts in values and to deal with problems in social and religious discrimination; (4) intense concern with figuring out the basic principles, the essential core of the social group work method, and intensive analysis of selected technical aspects of the method; (5) consideration of the structure of group services and pro-

---

[40] See *Social Work with Groups, 1960* (New York: NASW, 1960); *New Perspectives on Services to Groups: Theory, Organization, Practice* (New York: NASW, 1961); see also the eight volumes of selected papers, including those dealing with social casework, social group work, and community organization: *Social Work Practice* (New York: Columbia University Press, 1962–1969), published for the National Conference on Social Welfare.

posals for restructuring services to more effectively meet priority needs of selected populations that lacked essential services; (6) a major question as to whether practice and formulations reflected and expressed in essence a maintenance, equilibrium model—rather than a disequilibrium model—essential to support and implement social change; and (7) growing concern with the question of whether social group work should be retained as a separate method of social work practice or combined in some way in a common method that would include the basic concepts and principles of the three traditional methods of social casework, social group, and community organization.

The emphases germane to a pragmatic philosophy and scientific method persisted in the problem-solving formulations of this decade, accompanied in some instances by a strong move toward an empirical base for evaluating outcome and to theory-building. However, an Existentialist philosophy and a strong humanistic tradition were also reflected in the writings.[41]

The behavioral science foundation of psychoanalytically oriented ego psychology remained very strong and pervasive in its influence. Several of the problem-solving formulations emphasized the use of the social group work method to assist individuals to develop selected ego functions essential to effective problem-solving.[42] There was evidence of some movement toward the use of sociobehavioral theory as well, with strong attachment to a research approach to practice, including problem-solving aspects to the total process.[43]

This decade was especially rich and productive in the development of social group work formulations. In the paper, "The Social Worker in the

[41] The work of William Schwartz is cast within an existential and systems-theory framework, while that of Emanuel Tropp is within a framework of a humanistic tradition and a psychology of self-actualization. See William Schwartz, "The Social Worker in the Group," *The Social Welfare Forum, 1961,* Proceedings of the National Conference on Social Welfare (New York: Columbia University Press, 1961), pp. 146–77; see also Emanuel Tropp, *A Humanistic Foundation for Group Work Practice* (New York: Selected Academic Readings, 1969).

[42] See especially Gisela Konopka, *Social Group Work: A Helping Process* (Englewood Cliffs, N.J.: Prentice-Hall, 1963); Saul Bernstein (ed.), *Explorations in Group Work* (Boston: Boston University Bookstores, 1965); Grace Ganter, Margaret Yeakel, and Norman A. Polansky, *Retrieval from Limbo: The Intermediary Group Treatment of Inaccessible Children* (New York: Child Welfare League of America, 1967); Helen Northen, *Social Work with Groups.*

[43] While ego psychology is a prominent feature in Robert D. Vinter (ed.), *Readings in Group Work Practice* (Ann Arbor, Mich.: Campus Publishers, 1967), there also are indications of a sociobehavioral approach based on learning theory.

Group,'' Schwartz emphasized the reciprocal need and relationships between the individual and society and proposed a formulation for work with groups covering a wide spectrum of services. The problem-solving process is especially apparent in his analysis of five tasks of the social worker. Included are a search for the problem upon which the group and worker agree to work together, the detection and working through of obstacles to problem work and solution, and the contribution and use of data that assist in working on the problem. Evaluation as an aspect of problem-solving is implied in reference to specific requirements and limits of the contract or working agreement, and in reference to social values brought and shared by the social worker in his problem-solving work with the group.[44]

In 1963 Gisela Konopka, in her book *Social Group Work,* analyzed certain problem-solving components of the worker's role, dealing in particular with "Assessing and Establishing Objectives in Social Group Work (Diagnosis)" and "The Helping Process of Social Group Work (Treatment)." [45] She emphasized a problem-solving approach to conflict-resolution in groups, she emphasized that the worker "uses the scientific method: fact finding (observation), analyzing, diagnosis in relation to the individual, the group and the social environment," [46] and performs his function through "enabling members to involve themselves in the process of problem solving." [47] Her emphasis upon the social group worker's conscious participation in the problem-solving process, and upon his conscious thinking through of that process, reflects that thread which has persisted through the preceding decades.

In 1965 a collection of papers developed by faculty of the Boston University School of Social Work included Saul Bernstein's analysis of conflict in groups and of the social worker's dealing with conflict, and Louis Lowy's analysis of decision-making in social group work.[48] These authors made important connections with the formulation of phases of group development in social work groups, as explicated in another paper in the same collection. In another paper, there is a clear preference for a problem-solving approach to the process of exploration and to the development of a working agreement in social work practice with individuals and groups.[49]

[44] William Schwartz, "The Social Worker in the Group."
[45] Gisela Konopka, *Social Group Work,* pp. 79–153.   [46] *Ibid,* p. 166.
[47] *Ibid,* p. 168.   [48] Saul Bernstein (ed), *Explorations in Group Work,* pp. 54–90.
[49] *Ibid,* pp. 10–18.

In 1967 a collection of readings by faculty of the University of Michigan showed a major commitment to the scientific method in the delineation of an approach to practice, in the specific use of knowledge from social psychology in defining and understanding the nature and dynamics of small groups, in its detailed approach to diagnosis of the individual and of the group, in its analysis of the nature and use of program activities, and in its emphasis upon research in the practice itself to improve the quality of both practice and service. This set of papers is permeated by a commitment to and a thorough explication of an orderly, systematic approach to practice that in essence reflects the scientific method of problem-solving.[50]

The end of the decade brought publication of Helen Northen's *Social Work with Groups,* which develops in detail both parallel and collaborative components of problem-solving that characterize her explication of the social group work method. This work expresses, analyzes, and explicates a comprehensive problem-solving approach to practice. Within the framework of psychoanalytically based ego psychology and a psychosocial view of the individual person in his dynamic relation with others in small groups and in the community, she emphasized and analyzed the small group as a problem-solving medium; she also described the social worker's activities that assist the group to function to its fullest capacity in its problem-solving abilities and accomplishments, including an evaluation process that is central to a valid and useful termination.[51]

In his volume, *A Humanistic Foundation for Group Work Practice,* Tropp emphasized a "common-goal group" as the special, traditional, and unique contribution of the social group worker, and the importance of the small group in the normal development and socialization of individuals and in implementing a democratic social order. Within a framework of a humanistic tradition and of the psychology of self-actualization, Tropp's writings offer a concept of problem-solving that includes: (1) a *common goal,* defined as one which members share for the group as a whole; (2) *common decision* as the process of deliberation and decision-making by the group as a whole toward the accomplishment of the general goal or any specific objectives related to that goal; (3) *common action* as coordinated efforts by the members toward carrying out these decisions.[52]

[50] Robert D. Vinter (ed), *Readings in Group Work Practice.*
[51] Helen Northen, *Social Work with Groups.*
[52] Emanuel Tropp, *A Humanistic Foundation for Group Work Practice.*

Careful analysis of the formulations of writers during the decade makes it clear that each dealt with some problem-solving components. In some instances, comprehensive explications of a complete problem-solving framework and process permeated their work. Their formulations addressed a wide range of major social problems, types of clients, fields of practice, and organizational auspices. They also included a wide spectrum of types of groups, including formed and pre-existing (both family and nonrelated members).[53] Consideration was given to groups with open and closed membership and to voluntary and nonvoluntary participants. Short-term and long-term groups were considered to be appropriate in reference to specific purposes. Size was thought to be an important factor in planning for and composing groups for problem-solving purposes. Both residential and nonresidential settings were considered appropriate for problem-solving groups.

The group purposes explicated in these formulations ranged from groups formed for treatment of individuals to those formed to change selected aspects of their environment. Some formulations gave full attention to specific diagnostic assessment of individual motivation and capacity—particularly within a framework of ego assessment—and also included a detailed analysis of the group dynamics and of phases of group development within a framework of social-systems theory. All of the formulations gave close attention to phases of the problem-solving process, however defined by each, and to its individual and group components.

Probably one of the most outstanding characteristics of the work on problem-solving in this decade was the intensive effort to make the components and the process specific, to clearly define the domain, the conscious intent, the techniques, the results, and the evaluation of each outcome in reference to specific goals, and to state clearly the working agreement between the group members—individually and as a group—and the social worker. There was evident a growing, concerted effort to refine problem-solving knowledge and skills, and to provide groundwork essential to theory-building and theory-testing through research.

A second outstanding characteristic was the major emphasis placed

---

[53] See especially, Mary Louise Somers, "Group Process Within the Family Unit," *The Family Is the Patient: The Group Approach to Treatment of Family Health Problems* (New York: NASW, 1965), pp. 22–39. Aspects of the group problem-solving process were highlighted and explicated in reference to the family as a small group.

upon the social worker's conscious awareness of himself as a problem-solver—in his own thinking, planning, and doing—and in his collaborative work with the group as he engaged with them in problem-solving. The formulations differed from each other in the emphasis given to whether the social worker and group members were seen as a worker-client system in their mode of relating and working, or whether they were viewed as colleagues who were collaboratively seeking to identify and explore jointly selected problems, working together to engage in problem-solving, and evaluating the outcomes in reference to agreed-upon goals. In all of the formulations the parallel processes of problem-solving carried by the worker, by individual members, and by the group-as-a-whole were made clear, along with the collaborative problem-solving jointly and consciously planned, achieved, and evaluated by the worker and the group. All formulations emphasized the importance of making the members conscious of the specific ways in which the problem-solving experience and outcome in the social work group could be used to improve their problem-solving efforts outside the group.

The proliferation of formulations in the 1960s served to advance the refinement of various components of the problem-solving framework for social group work practice. Major problem-solving aspects were more fully explicated, analyzed, tested, modified, and elaborated, but synthesis also went on. The more eclectic formulations were cast quite comprehensively within a problem-solving framework, while others presented strong ties to problem-solving within more limited but quite specific parts of the whole. The usual processes of separation, individuation, elaboration, modification, synthesis, and reintegration seemed to be working their way.

THE 1970s

The early years of the decade of the 1970s were characterized by a crisis of confidence in the leaders of government and in social institutions, accompanied by a crisis of rising unemployment and spiraling inflation. The major formulations of the social group work method that appeared between 1970 and 1975 continued to show the trend toward increasing specificity of treatment goals, worker activity, and evaluation of goal accomplishment. Continuing and increasing use of the findings of social and behavioral science research characterized some formulations, along with further movement toward empirical methods of testing and evaluating practice procedures and their outcomes. Growing interest in behavior analysis based on learning theory was clear. At the same time it was possible to identify long-time commitments to personal and social goals, and to further elaborate formulations that fell within the existential and humanistic philosophies and within the self and self-actualization psychologies. Problem-solving components were clearly discernible, threading their way among the formulations and retaining an important emphasis and place.

In the early part of this decade, Margaret Hartford's volume dealing with groups in social work brought together, and integrated for use in practice, selected social science findings about the nature and dynamics of small groups. Connected directly with Coyle's *Social Process in Organized Groups* published forty years before, Hartford's work updated, developed, and refined components of social science knowledge that had persisted as useful for social group work practice during all the years of its development. In particular, one chapter dealt in detail with a major aspect of group problem-solving—the process of deliberation and decision-making in small groups.[54] Application of selected findings of social science research to these aspects of the problem-solving process were shown to enable the group members and the social worker to improve the nature and accomplishments of their problem-solving efforts.

Three publications carried forward and elaborated previous work of their authors and continued to emphasize the problem-solving process. Saul Bernstein and his associates at the Boston University School of Social Work underlined the long-time theme of bringing together individual and social goals through a problem-solving approach and process.[55] William Schwartz and several associates further defined and analyzed the problem-solving activities of the social worker, of the group members, and of the worker and group in concert.[56] Several faculty of the University of Michigan School of Social Work continued to demonstrate a problem-solving framework and method of approach, focused upon specific behavior change.[57] Their efforts

[54] Margaret E. Hartford, *Groups in Social Work*, pp. 229–43.

[55] See Saul Bernstein (ed.), *Further Explorations in Group Work* (Boston: Boston University Bookstores, 1971), pp. 119–46.

[56] William Schwartz and Serapio Salba (eds.), *The Practice of Group Work* (New York: Columbia University Press, 1971), especially: Schwartz, "On the Use of Groups in Social Work Practice," pp. 13–18; Lawrence Shulman " 'Program' in Group Work: Another Look," pp. 221–40; and Goodwin P. Garfield and Carol R. Irizarry "The 'Record of Service': Describing Social Work Practice," pp. 241–65.

[57] Paul Glasser, Rosemary Sarri, and Robert Vinter (eds.), *Individual Change Through Small Groups*.

contributed in major ways to the development of precision in all aspects of the problem-solving approach and process, including the evaluation of specific behavioral change in reference to specific goals of change. They continued their major emphasis upon the individual members' and workers' conscious awareness and conscious use of several aspects of the treatment process: problem identification and description, their own engagement in procedures designed to produce behavior change, the evaluation of accomplishments, and connections of behavior within treatment groups with behavior in other social situations.

By the mid 1970s, two emerging formulations using a problem-solving framework and approach pushed forward the growing emphasis upon specificity of identified and selected problem, specificity of assessment, plan, and procedures, and precise evaluation of the actual behavioral changes that occurred through the implementation of the treatment design and procedures. Within a problem-oriented, problem-solving approach, Sheldon Rose set forth a comprehensive presentation of the ways in which group dynamics may be used to facilitate individual behavior change, within a framework of behavior-modification based on learning theory.[58] In collaboration with the authors of a task-centered approach to social casework, Charles Garvin developed the formulation of how a task-centered approach to practice might be worked out in small groups.[59] The conscious collaboration of the group members and social worker in all aspects of the problem-solving process and in all tasks that support and implement the process, and the presentation of the worker as a practitioner-researcher, appeared to be within the long-time stance, tradition, and heritage of the problem-solving framework and process in social group work.

SUMMARY AND IMPLICATIONS FOR FURTHER INQUIRY

Examination of social group work formulations over a span of six decades reveals that a problem-solving framework and process are indeed pervasive in their influence and persistence. The earliest formulations were embedded in the process of inquiry, often articulated as the scientific method or an orderly, systematic way of thinking and doing, of moving from the known to

[58] Sheldon D. Rose, *Treating Children in Groups* (San Francisco: Jossey-Bass, 1973).

[59] William J. Reid and Laura Epstein, *Task-Centered Casework* (New York: Columbia University Press, 1972). See also the paper by Charles Garvin, William Reed, and Laura Epstein in this volume.

the unknown. Interwoven in this process of inquiry or problem-solving, broadly defined, are a strand from scientific thought and method and a strand from the democratic ethos. Both of these are joined with another prominent strand that might well be termed a creative one that reaches for and uses the social opportunities and experiences that characterize small groups and that facilitates the development of integrative solutions. These strands are interwoven in the problem-solving framework and process by the worker's recognition of the need for methodology, as well as philosophy, if inquiry, democratic beliefs, and creative developments are to be realized in the problem-solving process.

Essentially, over a span of fifty years the problem-solving framework and components of social group work formulations have been strongly influenced by the philosophical tenets of Pragmatism, the Instrumentalism of John Dewey, Existentialism, and Humanism. The formulations of the early decades were influenced by the figure-ground and whole-part concepts of Gestalt psychology, followed by the prominence of psychoanalytic theories of personality development—both Freudian and Rankian—and later by the cognitive, affective, and competence concepts of ego psychology. From the social sciences, especially social psychology, came concepts dealing with interpersonal relations and other dynamics of small-group life, based in field theory and in social-systems theory. Some recent formulations are strongly influenced by sociobehavioral and behavior-modification theories, while others are based in psychologies of the self and of self-actualization.

Throughout the span of more than fifty years, ten major themes appear with regularity in the formulations of the group problem-solving process in social group work. Whatever modifications appear—and there are several that are quite obvious—these persist. Five of the themes deal with the nature and dynamics of the group problem-solving process and five with the role of the social worker with a problem-solving group.

The persistent themes that mark the nature and dynamics of group problem-solving throughout the formulations of the social group work method are the following: (1) personal and social goals in combination are germane to group problem-solving; if one of these dual goals is emphasized, the other is recognized and often used as context; (2) ideally, a problem-solving group searches for knowledge, including knowledge of facts and of feelings as facts; learns from experience; works on ways to achieve its goals; and continuously questions and tests its process and its achievements: consciousness of time and of its own process of learning and development permeate its work; (3) problem-solving work, in dealing with relationship conflicts, generates improved understanding and feeling among the members of a group, and thus facilitates more effective and productive problem-solving: the reciprocal nature of cognitive and emotional strands of the process is clear; (4) a wide spectrum of groups, organized for various purposes in a variety of settings, serving individuals who represent all age groupings and a broad range of strengths and difficulties (including physical, mental, emotional, and social) can and do effectively and productively use a group problem-solving process in their work; and (5) group problem-solving efforts may result in individual opinion or action, in collective opinion or action, or both.

Five of the persistent themes deal with the role of the social worker: (1) problem-solving work goes on in the social worker's mind before, during, and after each encounter with a problem-solving group and/or with any one of its members; collaborative problem-solving work goes on between the social worker, the group, and individual members in their engagement with each other; parallel problem-solving work goes on among group members—on their own—between and during meetings; (2) the self-observation capacities and abilities of the social worker and of the group members must be stretched and fully employed in the problem-solving work of the group and of individuals; (3) the active participation of all members and of the social worker is essential to effective and productive group problem-solving; (4) the social worker's responsibility is to assist the group and individual members to do the problem-solving work to the greatest degree possible; he should stimulate and guide the problem-solving process, but should not intrude upon problem-solving that the group and individuals are able to do on their own; and (5) the social worker assists the group members to maintain a reality focus in their problem-solving work, and to evaluate their achievements in reference to agreed-upon goals.

It is clear that during the last twenty years, social group work scholars have devoted their major attention to making more precise the analysis, synthesis, and testing of the dimensions of group problem-solving that deal with personal growth and change. The social-goals aspect has not been worked on to the same extent, nor has it been as precisely developed and operationalized, descriptively and prescriptively, as has the personal-goals dimension of problem-solving. It is also clear that the groups emphasized in the early years were mainly those which might be termed consumer, self-help, educational, and citizen-participation in character, and voluntary associations growing out of the democratic ethos and the place of responsible citizenship in implementing a democratic social order. The early problem-solving formulations also emphasized personal growth and change through social participation and responsibility. It has been within the latter half of the fifty-year span that the emphasis in problem-solving groups has turned sharply to that of dealing with the personal conflicts and problems of individual members, many of whom suffer from illnesses or other types of handicaps. However, the social-goals component tends to persist. While aspects of such problem-solving work are considered by some scholars to be in the realm of community organization and not social group work, the social-goals component does persist as a concern of social group work, although not so thoroughly studied and formulated in recent efforts.

This examination of the problem-solving components of social group work formulations over a fifty-year span reveals that the concept and process known as problem-solving, broadly defined, serves as a unifying force, and brings into some closer articulation several of the formulations that are disparate in their assumptions, theoretical underpinnings, or goals. The problem-solving framework and components tend to lead to some eclecticism among the various formulations. As a sequence of steps—orderly, knowable, and testable—the problem-solving process is woven through all aspects of pregroup planning, assessment, treatment (however named and defined), and evaluation that continue to characterize the social group work method. While each formulation indicates that these orderly steps are not always taken in progression in the actual situation, there is recognition of the usefulness of the problem-solving framework and process for the thinking and doing of group members and of the social worker in their separate, parallel, and collaborative work. In its essence, problem-solving carries the conviction that man can know and do something about obstacles, difficulties, and personal and social problems, and that the small group that looks at once two ways—toward the individual and toward society—can become an effective and productive instrument for man's personal and social use. The potential for creative development of integrative solutions to personal and social problems lies especially within the essence and functioning of small-group process.

The question of the development of a unitary, comprehensive formulation that can be named "a problem-solving approach" remains unresolved. In good inquiry and problem-solving style, the alternatives should be identified, explored, tried out, and evaluated. In view of the existence and demonstrated usefulness of a problem-solving framework and the components of the process as a unifying feature among social group work formulations, and in view of the substantive groundwork that has already been accomplished, a next step might well be some attempts to formulate a full, comprehensive, unitary problem-solving approach to group work practice. Next steps must be taken, however, with some consideration of questions. Will the development of such a proposed unitary formulation, so labeled, build upon or detract from, in substance and in process, the unifying and eclectic features and functions that a problem-solving framework and its components have continued to serve in the development of social group work formulations of varied stance and character? What are the most productive and effective ways for formulations to continue to be articulated, modified, refined, and tested, with both the differential and integrative features and processes fully and freely at work?

BIBLIOGRAPHY

Coyle, Grace L. *Social Process in Organized Groups.* New York: Smith, 1930.
Dewey, John. *How We Think.* Boston: Heath, 1933.
Follett, Mary Parker. *Creative Experience.* New York: Longmans, Green, 1924.
——. *The New State.* New York: Longmans, Green, 1926.
Glasser, Paul, Rosemary Sarri, and Robert Vinter (eds.). *Individual Change Through Small Groups.* New York: Free Press, 1974.
Hartford, Margaret E. *Groups in Social Work.* New York: Columbia University Press, 1972.
Northen, Helen. *Social Work with Groups.* New York: Columbia University Press, 1969.
Perlman, Helen H. *Social Casework: A Problem-Solving Process.* Chicago: University Press, 1957.
Spergel, Irving A. *Community Problem Solving: The Delinquency Example.* Chicago: University of Chicago Press, 1969.
Wilson, Gertrude, and Gladys Ryland. *Social Group Work Practice.* Boston: Houghton Mifflin, 1949.

12

THE STATUS OF THEORY

HELEN NORTHEN AND ROBERT W. ROBERTS

Social work with groups has a short but rich history, and many of the themes contained in this volume had antecedents in the works of the profession's pioneers. For instance, there was an early and continuing commitment to research on *process and outcome*. Earlier writers also shared with today's theoreticians concern about purposes and goals; and the goals of yesterday, like those of today, ranged from informal education to socialization and normal development to rehabilitation or therapy. Pioneer group workers also had a commitment to influencing both groups as entities and individuals in groups—a dual emphasis that is most contemporary. Because so many of the topics and issues discussed by the authors of this set of papers were recognized and debated by earlier group work scholars, it is only appropriate that a review of the status of theory for social work with groups begin with a brief presentation of landmarks in the development of such theory.

A profession is dependent not only upon knowledge developed from the experiences of its practitioners but also from relevant knowledge borrowed from other disciplines. And one part of a profession, such as work with groups, is dependent also upon developments within other component parts of the profession. Thus, an examination of the antecedents of today's theory necessitates an examination of these sources, as well as those internal to group work itself.

Philosophically, group work has had its roots deeply imbedded in the democratic ethos, as expounded by such leaders as Eduard Lindeman, John

Dewey, and Mary Parker Follett. Certainly, it has always been humanistic in outlook.

Theory for social work with groups was propelled ahead by several major contributions from other disciplines. John Dewey's explication of the problem-solving process, both in its individual and collective manifestations, captured the attention of early social workers who were interested in groups. Knowledge about the functions, structure, interaction, and development of small groups was developed by sociologists and social psychologists. Interwoven with the strands of problem-solving and small-group theory have been the contributions of knowledge concerning the motivations, development, and behavior of individuals in their social situations. Freudian psychoanalytic theory and later ego psychology were perhaps the most influential. The "group-as-a-whole" became a basic concept; emphasizing the interdependence among the elements that comprise the whole, it was a forerunner to modern systems theory.

During the 1920s social casework was being defined in relation to other forms of social work, and the generic and specific aspects of casework were delineated. There was recognition that there was generic knowledge and skills applicable to all forms of social work, one of which was group work.

The use of research methodology was one important means for developing theory. Wilber I. Newstetter and his research associates undertook one of the earliest experiments in social work. Studying disturbed children in a therapeutic camp, they identified the processes in group relations that lead to satisfactory group adjustment. Concurrently, Clara Kaiser was developing a system for recording the worker's part in the social group work process: from these records, principles of practice were developed. Grace Coyle's doctoral dissertation, published in 1930, was a masterful description and analysis of the extant theory of organized groups. It is interesting to note that Coyle selectively incorporated concepts from Freudian psychoanalytic theory into her elaboration of social process. Subsequent study and research by numerous social scientists has confirmed the soundness of this early work, and has also provided a greater body of tested knowledge.

In group work, the 1930s was a decade characterized by the publication of numerous definitions of social group work. Elucidated were ideas concerning a variety of purposes for the use of group work methods, including normal growth and development, informal education, recreation, and psychotherapy. Through efforts to define the phenomenon, there began the difficult process of separating out a social work approach to the use of groups that differed from their use in education and recreation and of clarifying the relationships between casework and group work. Gertrude Wilson's research on the relationship between casework and group work led to generalizations about the generic values, purposes, knowledge base, and methodology, as well as the major differences between the two methods of practice.

By the late 1940s there had been sufficient development of theory for group work that numerous books were published, including those by Coyle, Konopka, Redl and Wineman, Slavson, Trecker, and Wilson and Ryland. The major efforts of individuals and professional associations were directed toward the development of a unified theory of social group work, with emphasis on demonstrating its applicability to varied functions, client populations, and fields of practice. Even when the functional theory of casework was adapted to group work by Helen Phillips, there was a focus on the common—rather than the distinctive—knowledge and skills required for this approach. In 1949 the American Association of Group Workers (AAGW) adopted a definition of group work that had general acceptability and was widely quoted as an official position of the professional organization.[1]

With the emergence of the National Association of Social Workers (NASW) in 1955, the refinement of theory for group work within the general working definition of social work practice accelerated rapidly. Work with groups became fully established within the profession. Between 1959 and 1963 the Committee on Practice of the Group Work Section of NASW developed an updated working definition of social group work practice.[2] In the process of developing this statement, it became apparent that there were theoretical differences that needed to be recognized and understood. From an analysis of ten short definitions and two papers submitted to the committee, William Schwartz concluded that there were three different models of practice, each with its own implications for how practice is defined. These models were labeled as a medical model, a scientific or problem-solving model, and a reciprocal model.[3] A few years later, Catherine Papell and

---

[1] American Association of Group Workers, "Definition of the Function of the Group Worker" (New York: AAGW, 1949).

[2] Margaret E. Hartford (ed.), *Working Papers Toward a Frame of Reference for Social Group Work* (New York: NASW, 1964).

[3] William Schwartz, "Analysis of Papers Presented on Working Definitions of Group Work Practice," in Margaret E. Hartford (ed.), *Working Papers Toward a Frame of Reference for Social Group Work,* p. 60.

Beulah Rothman concluded that there were several different theoretical models of group work method. They identified these as: remedial, similar to Schwartz' medical model; reciprocal, similar to Schwartz' of the same title; and a social goals model, unrelated to any of the three identified by Schwartz.[4] These two efforts to analyse theoretical differences stimulated varied efforts to put together systematic descriptions of practice theory.

In recent years an increasing number of books have been published on social work practice with groups; these reflect many common ideas, but also many different ones. Since 1960, social group workers have also made major contributions to the development of theory for practice with family units. In addition, several books have been published recently that have as their major purpose the development of theory that is applicable to work with individuals, groups, and communities.

These earlier contributions to theory for social work practice with groups serve as a foundation for today's theory-building. Partly because of this shared history, it is clear that the ten position papers contained in this volume do not represent ten distinct and mutually exclusive theories. Thus, the authors share much in the way of foundation knowledge from behavioral sciences, they accept many of the same propositions, and agree on certain purposes and techniques. They combine these common ingredients in different ways, however, and vary in the emphasis they give to the knowledge they share and what they add to it. Portions of certain approaches are very similar, yet attempts to reduce the ten approaches to a smaller number of clusters of approaches were not successful because there are large enough areas of disagreement or difference between any two of the papers to make a merger of them impossible.

A comparative analysis of the approaches was difficult for many reasons. Each author describes the essence of his theory quite differently, in spite of the many ideas that seem to be generic to several approaches. The authors also vary in the level of abstraction and specificity on which their approaches are described. The extreme complexity of groups and of practice with them, and the many dimensions from which such complexities are analyzed, led to the conclusion that a comparison of the position papers as totalities would do injustice to their component parts. Attempts to use content-analysis procedures were also unsatisfactory because specific statements

[4] Catherine Papell and Beulah Rothman, "Social Group Work Models: Possession and Heritage," *Journal of Education for Social Work,* vol. 2 (1966).

often assumed meanings that were different from those communicated when the statements were read in the context of the total papers. The problem was solved by a compromise procedure, one wherein a content analysis was performed using the topics suggested as categories of organization. Once this analysis was done, the papers were reread as total entities as insurance against attributing positions to the authors that might seem unwarranted.

The analysis that follows is thus not a comparison of theoretical approaches as totalities but an examination of similarities and differences between authors on specific topics and issues contained within the outline provided to authors as a suggested guide for their task of theory construction.

HISTORICAL ANTECEDENTS

The authors trace the historical antecedents of their approaches to widely varied sources, although a number of common themes emerge. Usually, credit is given to earlier social workers and to scholars from other disciplines—particularly, philosophy, psychology, sociology, and social psychology. They vary, however, in what they consider to be the major antecedents.

Four authors report that their approach grew mainly out of the earlier work of other social workers, supplemented by selected contributions from the behavioral sciences. Thus, the *organizational context* approach traces its development primarily to the earlier formulations of group work practice by Robert Vinter. *Task-centered* practice with groups has been built upon research on short-term treatment, more particularly task-centered casework. The *psychosocial* formulation has evolved from both the diagnostic or psychosocial theory of casework and from those group workers who incorporated both psychological and social insights into practice with small groups, including families. The *developmental* approach recognizes the contributions of earlier writers about social group work who emphasized developmental purposes and the achievement of group goals.

Three of the authors trace their approaches almost equally to earlier writers from social work and from the behavioral sciences. *Problem-solving,* as a component of practice, could not be developed without the crucial formulations of educational philosophers such as John Dewey and Mary Parker Follett, or the social work pioneers who utilized these concepts in practice. Hartford has traced her work to the contributions of social philosophers, educators, ego psychologists, and social scientists, but she gives attention as well to those social workers who used this knowledge in the development of practice in which the group is the primary instrument of help. In its historical roots, *functional* social work is most divergent from the other approaches in that it is derived from the psychoanalytic theory of Otto Rank.

Three of the approaches in this volume trace their historical roots predominantly to theories formulated by other disciplines, with the interest of building social work practice theory directly from this knowledge base. The *socialization* approach is traced back to diverse contributions made by social psychologists, sociologists, and anthropologists to knowledge of the process whereby people become socialized. *Stress theory* and *crisis intervention* came into social work primarily from social psychiatry. Finally, the paper on the *mediating* approach has its roots in a wide range of ideas: existentialism, philosophy, and small group and systems theory.

PHILOSOPHICAL AND VALUE CONSIDERATIONS

Despite a universal commitment to the scientific method and an at least partial dependence on the findings of empirical research for a knowledge base, the strongest disagreements among the authors center on their definitions of an appropriate philosophy of science and the criteria for labeling knowledge as factual. At one end of the argument are writers such as Schwartz and Tropp, who, identifying themselves as humanists and existentialists, reject logical positivism, the classical search for cause-and-effect relationships in human behavior, and mechanistic models for understanding mankind. At the other end of the argument are authors such as Garvin, Reid, and Epstein, and Glasser and Garvin, who emphasize the importance of restricting the profession's study to behavior that can be operationally defined, and give priority to research procedures that satisfy requirements of proof developed in laboratory and experimental sciences. Most likely, these disagreements would have been even stronger had this volume included papers more narrowly focused on behavior modification and encounter groups.[5]

[5] The reasons for not inviting partisans of these theoretical approaches were quite dissimilar. The original plans called for a paper on behavior modification. Input from a review of the prospectus by a scholar commissioned by Columbia University Press, however, convinced us that behavior modification does not represent a unitary theory of social work practice with groups. Instead, its contributions seem well on the way to being integrated into more general models, such as the sociobehavioral approach under development at the University of

The major differences between the two schools of thought appear to center around three basic questions: How is human behavior to be understood? What types of research are most likely to produce valid knowledge of human behavior? What are the legitimate objectives of empirical research?

Pushed to its extreme, the first question grows out of the ancient philosophical argument of free will versus determinism. Exaggerated positions that describe human behavior as entirely voluntary or completely determined are not held by any of the authors in this volume. Instead, those of the humanistic-existential persuasion admit some constraints on an individual's freedom to behave as he wishes. Those toward the other end of the continuum, through statements such as ". . . specificity in group work also enhances its ability to draw upon related research in the social sciences for the purpose of assessing *causal factors* in group work situations in order to select appropriate change targets" (Glasser and Garvin, italics added), imply that they believe that a great deal of human behavior is determined by contemporary and historical factors and that the amount of voluntarism enjoyed by humans is limited. That they do not believe in a completely deterministic view of human behavior is evidenced by their explicit commitment to client autonomy and self-determination.

Yet, if the effort that both Schwartz and Tropp have put into developing their position on this issue is to be accepted as important, the differences between the two schools of thought add up to more than a difference of degree. As Schwartz has stated and Tropp has implied, these differences may lead to rather extreme variations in how human behavior is perceived. Those at the deterministic end of the continuum, they argue, are wedded to an outdated concept of human behavior that is based upon a mechanical model of physics, one that emphasizes symmetrical cause-and-effect relationships and leads to a subject-object frame of mind. They would replace this model with one that views human beings as organisms that are constantly interacting and transacting with a multitude of systems, and one that views relationships between systems as symmetrical or reciprocal and involving mutual feedback.

Whether any of the theoreticians represented here would subscribe to

---

Michigan. The encounter-group approach, on the other hand, appeared to the editors to belong more to psychology than to social work, to deemphasize the development of a theoretical rationale for its operations, and to have little interest in the solution of problems in psychosocial functioning—the generally agreed-upon focus of social work practice.

the mechanistic model described by Schwartz is unknown. Unfortunately, none of them chose to develop in detail their philosophy of science. Attempts to make inferences about their beliefs based upon their use of certain concepts were not successful, largely because the small-group process, by definition, involves interactions between systems and because the use of systems concepts has become ubiquitous among social workers.

These differences in philosophy affect what various authors define as research, what they perceive as the objectives of research, and what they value in the way of knowledge sources. Those at the positivistic end of the continuum, for instance, state they give a "superordinate role to the methods and products of science" and "hold that knowledge acquired through application of systematic methods of inquiry, that is, through formal research, is of greater value than knowledge acquired through other means, including expert opinion, practice wisdom, uncontrolled observations, or deduction from theory" (Garvin, Reid, and Epstein). Ultimately, these theoreticians look forward to the development of a new breed of social worker, one who is a "practitioner-researcher" (Glasser and Garvin). Those who have identified themselves as humanist-existentialists express either a lack of concern about "rigorous research methods" and comfort with a definition of empirical that refs ". . . to accumulated knowledge from first-hand descriptions of the application of the described methods and first-hand responses that are seen, heard, and felt by" practitioners (Tropp); or, as is the case with Schwartz, an outright rejection of research that stresses determinism, rationalism, and objectivity. And so it goes with what are considered the objectives of research. Those describing the *organizational context* approach, for instance, are explicit in their expectation that research serves the purpose of "assessing causal factors" (Glasser and Garvin) and, along with those presenting *task-centered* practice, evidence a preference for experimental research that can evaluate the effectiveness of social work practice. Schwartz, on the other hand, has little interest in either of these research objectives, and would have research focus on ". . . processes, the nature of experience, the influence of feeling on human behavior, and the conduct of people in interaction."

The authors of the other six papers seem to occupy the middle ground on these issues. While some of them seem to be closer to one position than the other, there is no evidence to suggest that these issues are of major importance to them. Their writings give the impression that they are comfortable with both approaches to research and that the only criterion by which they assess research is its practical validity. This comfort with the various approaches to research may be attributable to the continuing influence of pioneer social scientists such as John Dewey, who combined observation of process with the experimental testing of hypotheses, or it may reflect an emerging synthesis of humanistic and experimental points of view.[6]

Other value issues which were addressed by most of the authors, or which the editors considered important, were the following: What is the client system served by the worker? Who sets goals or objectives? Can or should services be extended to nonvoluntary clients? What is the nature of the relationship between client, worker, and agency?

Although all of the authors reported a strong commitment to the integrity and worth of the individual, and to his right to self-determination, there was variation in the client system chosen as the focus for the worker's activities. Two of the approaches, the *task-centered* and the *organizational context,* define the client system as the individual; two others, the *mediating* and the *developmental,* see the group itself as the primary client. Interestingly, all of the authors who define a single system as the client either exclude or do not discuss family groups as appropriate targets, and focus most, if not all, of their discussion on formed groups. In contrast, three of the authors, Hartford, Northen, and Somers, focus on dual client systems, the individual and the group. These authors see individual and group goals as entertwined in all types of groups, but point out that one or the other system may be the primary focus for the worker in a particular situation. The other three papers do not address the issue.

All of the theoretical approaches describe some sort of transactional process between workers and client systems, be they individuals or small groups, for establishing goals or objectives. There are differences, however, in the amount of responsibility the worker carries for defining and establishing goals. Six of the papers describe processes where the group as a whole plays the major role in defining goals. The *task-centered* approach is alone in placing primary responsibility for goal-setting with individual clients, and two of the approaches, the *organizational context* and the *psy-*

---

[6] Irving L. Child has suggested that differences between the points of view expressed by these two schools of thought are narrowing in psychology and that an integration of the two is rapidly emerging. *Humanistic Psychology and the Research Tradition* (New York: Wiley, 1973).

chosocial, give a great deal of responsibility to the worker in defining goals. The issue is not discussed by those describing the *crisis-intervention* approach. The function of the agency hosting the group is, of course, another factor entering into goal-setting; and for both Ryder and for Glasser and Garvin, agency function is seen as a strong, if not impermeable, boundary that limits and shapes the range of goals possible for a given group. Schwartz has a unique perspective on this, and defines the worker's role as mediator between an agency and a group, with the ultimate goal representing a contract based upon consensus between the two systems.

Because social work is often called upon to extend services to persons who either do not perceive a need for services or those who openly reject offered services, an important value issue is whether the profession should or can effectively serve groups composed of involuntary clients. Three of the approaches (the *organizational context,* the *mediating,* and the *developmental*) take relatively strong positions opposed to serving those who do not wish to be helped, while two of the authors (Northen and Somers) argue that nonvoluntary clients can be worked with. The *crisis-intervention* paper is not completely clear on the point, and the *socialization* and *task-centered* approaches argue that while imposition of group services is never desirable, it is sometimes done. Neither Hartford nor Ryder address the issue.

Although some social workers are in private practice, most work under the aegis of agencies carrying specific mandates from the community. Given this fact, it is surprising that half of the position papers make little or no mention of possible conflicts between the needs and desires of clients and the purposes and functions of agencies. Two of the approaches, the *developmental* and the *organizational context,* take the position that the functions and values of the profession take precedence over those of the agency. Tropp, for instance, while recognizing the constraints of agency function on both workers and clients, defines some agency functions, such as a police function, as inappropriate for social workers. Glasser and Garvin, despite the central importance they place on agency functions as a way of classifying group services, are the most outspoken against agencies dictating priorities to social workers, arguing that the profession ". . . must not be coopted by organizational needs and interests" and that it is ". . . the right as well as the responsibility of professionals to set priorities for social work services." The *functional* approach continues to define agency function as legitimately restricting the goals and activities of workers and clients, but sees such functions as less fixed and social workers as more responsible for advocating organizational change than was true historically. Hartford states that the ". . . objectives of the service are set, at least at an abstract level, by the auspices," but that within these abstract objectives, workers and clients are free to develop more concrete goals. Schwartz admits to tensions between agency and client, but argues that to perceive the two only as adversaries is to ignore the forces in agencies that motivate them to move toward those persons they are designed to serve. The professional's strategy, he suggests, is to mediate the differences between the two systems and ". . . to help both parties readdress the work they were meant to do together."

BEHAVIORAL SCIENCE FOUNDATION

There is a pervasive theme accepted by all of the authors—namely, that knowledge of the structure, function, dynamics, and development of small groups is necessary for effective practice with small groups. In somewhat different ways and with different emphases, all of the authors use ideas concerning the structure of groups. Frequently included are concepts of types of group structures, group size, composition, roles and status, rules or governing procedures, division of labor, norms, subgroups, and sociometric structure.

The dynamics of groups—variously referred to as social interaction, symbolic interaction, interaction process, group process, social transaction—are discussed by every author. The process of determining group purpose and specific goals or tasks is also discussed by all of the authors. Four authors elaborate on interpersonal and group influence and contagion. The development of patterns of social relationships, including affective ties and identifications, is given specific attention by only three of the authors, as is the concept of cohesion. Other specific concepts described by one author each are social exchange and potency rewards. It is interesting that only two authors pay any explicit attention to unconscious motivating factors related to group structure and process. It is not clear whether some of these concepts are merely taken for granted, or whether the fact that they are not mentioned is a matter of theoretical differences among the authors.

It is notable that all of the authors emphasize the idea of group development. With some authors, however, group development is described as phases or stages; with others, these developmental changes are conceived to be phases in the helping or treatment sequence. The number of stages or phases varies from the triadic beginning, middle, and ending to nine phases, elaborated upon by Hartford. It is clear that development is an important concept and that there is some logical movement of individuals and the group from the time of first convening to termination. It is not clear whether differences in the number of phases are due simply to lack of evidence concerning the phases, to the different types of groups toward which the theory is directed, or to other factors. Hartford, who has developed this part of group theory most fully, applies basic knowledge of groups to a wide variety of groups in terms of purpose, structure, duration, and size. Other authors have limited their material to more specific types of groups. The idea of beginnings, middles, and endings, originally introduced into social work by the *functional* school, clearly has its roots in Rankian theory, but it is not clear whether Ryder and Tropp, who use these terms, attach these particular meanings to them.

Closely related to small-group theory is the conceptual framework for viewing social systems of different sizes and levels of complexity. A family or peer group is a system, and hence the attention given to small group theory can be considered within the sphere of systems theory. Use of systems theory is implied by authors who do not identify and elaborate on it. For Northen, for Parad, Selby and Quinlan, and for Schwartz, social system is a major construct used for understanding an individual as part of a group and the group as part of other connecting systems. Communication theory, which is closely related to systems theory, similarly is mentioned in several formulations, most frequently as a concept within small-group or systems theory, but it is not fully explicated by any author.

In *Theories of Social Casework* it was noted that psychoanalytic theory and ego psychology were accepted and used as a major behavioral science base by most of the theorists. This does not emerge as clearly for social work with groups. Although seven of the papers make some mention of concepts from psychoanalytic ego psychology, only two develop ego psychology as a major behavioral science base for practice. These are by Northen and by Parad, Selby, and Quinlan. The most frequently used concepts seem to be the coping and problem-solving capacities of the ego, developmental phases through the life cycle, and the interaction between people and their environment. Very little attention is given to the major construct of personality—its structure, functions, and levels of consciousness—except by

Northen and to a lesser extent by Parad, Selby, and Quinlan, by Hartford, and by Somers. Two authors, Ryder and Tropp, use the concept of the self rather than the ego, and Ryder uses several concepts from Rankian psychoanalytic theory. Freudian personality theory probably is inconsistent with the approaches developed by Ryder and Tropp, but it is not clear why other authors have given short shrift to this content.

Cultural values and cultural influences affecting individuals and groups are given attention by only two authors, a surprising omission since group work has its roots in work with people of different cultural and socioeconomic backgrounds. The significance of culture, as it applies to age, ethnicity, religion, and social class, in human development and social functioning is dealt with only by Northen. She is the only one to explicitly discuss the effects of prejudice and discrimination on development and behavior.

The dynamics of the process by which individuals, families, or groups presumably achieve their goals is a relatively neglected aspect of theory and research on practice. It is clear that all of the authors have the idea that attitudes and behavior are maintained or changed through interaction between people or between people and their environments. There is a paucity of elaboration of the specific dynamics that operate, but there is considerable food for thought in some of the papers. The most frequently mentioned dynamic, but by only four authors, was that of mutual or group support as a dynamic motivator. The idea that people attain their goals through sharing of feelings, ideas, experiences, or alternative ways of coping was identified by three of the authors. Beyond this, suggestions are made by one or two authors that positive changes are brought about by a particular type of group experience in which there are common goals and peer relationships; that interruption of dysfunctional patterns of thought, affect, and behavior may contribute to change; that cognitive clarification, reality testing, or self-appraisal are important influences; that release of or identification and sharing of feelings are components of change; and that learning a process of problem-solving in itself is a contributer to change. Description, analysis, and testing of these ideas concerning the dynamics of change is an important area for theory development and research.

Somers' paper makes a unique contribution by explicating the basic knowledge that underlies problem-solving as a purpose and process in social work. Half of the other writers consider problem-solving and decision-making as a knowledge base for practice. Another unique contribution is made by Glasser and Garvin in their application of organizational theory to work with groups. They see the type of organization as a major determinant of the type of services provided, the nature of clientele served, and the strategies of practice to be used. McBroom has done the most complete task of describing and explaining socialization theory and clarifying its application to practice with families and peer groups, and Glasser and Garvin have incorporated some of these concepts into their theory.

Within the common emphases, there are important theoretical differences in the selection and use of concepts from the behavioral sciences. Psychoanalytic ego psychology seems to be one controversial area. The use of behavioral analysis and modification perhaps is another, although it gets little attention in any of the papers. Somers mentions the use of behavioral analysis and modification as one recent movement away from the traditional concept of psychosocial functioning by a few social workers. Glasser and Garvin are the only authors who have incorporated this knowledge and the interrelated techniques into their eclectic approach to practice. Tropp seems to have eschewed most knowledge from the behavioral sciences in favor of an existential and humanistic philosophical perspective.

TARGET POPULATIONS AND ORGANIZATIONAL AUSPICES

Despite the number and diversity of theoretical approaches contained in this volume, there was surprisingly little variation in the target populations addressed or the organizational auspices considered appropriate. Although mention was often made of specific subpopulations, all of the approaches are intended to serve persons with a wide range of potential or actual problems in psychosocial functioning. Although most of the authors use the concept of psychosocial functioning, there appears to be large differences in how this term is defined. For most there appears to be considerably more focus on the social component than on the psychological. This is consistent with the paucity of attention to ego psychology in most papers.

Of the more general approaches, only two made statements that would exclude any of those served by the total profession. Northen states that task-oriented groups are best served by other approaches, and Tropp states that the *developmental* approach is not appropriate for work with families or for groups with goals other than the social growth of their members.

Three of the approaches are aimed at somewhat narrower—but still broad—target populations. Parad, Selby, and Quinlan describe an approach aimed at individuals, families, or groups in crisis or associated with others in crisis. Garvin, Reid, and Epstein report that the *task-centered* approach is designed to alleviate specific and well-defined problems which represent temporary disequilibria in steady states. Discussion of types of problems included in this definition shows that few problems are excluded, however, and the authors state as a proposition that most of the problems brought by clients to social agencies represent acute disorders. McBroom limits her target populations to those faced with socialization tasks or problems. When this is projected against all of the developmental stages of the life cycle and defined in a perfective as well as a preventive and rehabilitative way, it would appear to be appropriate for a very large proportion of those served by social work.

Although some of the approaches have been linked with particular auspices or settings in the past, no approach was described as appropriate for only a limited number of settings. Instead, either implicitly or explicitly, all of the authors suggest that their approaches can be used in a wide variety of primary and secondary settings.

TYPES OF GROUPS

One conclusion to be drawn from these ten theoretical approaches to social work with small groups is that the major sources of knowledge drawn upon are based on formal research and professional experience with formed rather than natural groups. All ten papers state that the theoretical approach under discussion is applicable for work with formed groups, and most of the discussion of conceptual material and most of the examples refer to formed groups. These approaches also place a great deal of emphasis on groups with closed memberships: nine of the papers explicitly talk of such types of groups, none states that such groups are excluded from service. Most of the approaches are seen also as appropriate for groups with open-ended memberships: seven specifically include such types of groups, two make no mention of them, and only one, *task-centered,* advises against work with open-ended groups under most circumstances.

Most approaches are seen also as relevant for work with natural or autonomous groups, although there is a variety of opinion about serving natural groups with related members—that is, families. Only one approach, again the *task-centered,* is considered inappropriate for work with natural groups of unrelated persons. Six of the approaches address family groups, although one of these, the *task-centered,* excludes such groups from the current discussion. Two of the authors, Ryder and Schwartz, make no mention of families. Both the *organizational* and *developmental* theories exclude families from their approach. Glasser and Garvin do not discuss their reasons, but consistently make a distinction between work with individuals, families, and small groups. Tropp, although he makes reference to family *groups,* rejects them from service under the *developmental* approach because of their hierarchical, rather than peer, power relationships. This structural difference leads him to the conclusion that ". . . family group counseling is built on the dynamics of a highly unique and specialized group system and requires a specialized knowledge base and methodology of its own."

Although most of the discussion focuses on work in open or nonresidential settings, none of the papers suggests that the approach under discussion is not appropriate for residential groups, and eight explicitly include residential groups.

A second major conclusion that can be made is that the papers give little attention to differences in practice related to different types of groups. Northen consistently, and Hartford to a lesser extent, discusses modifications required with family or unrelated natural groups, but the others only state that unspecified changes in worker activity are required with different types of groups, or they do not discuss the issue at all. Possible reasons for this lack of discussion may be the space constraints placed upon the authors, the belief that most if not all of the major constructs are applicable to all types of groups, or that not enough knowledge is available to spell out in detail the important differences in group process and worker activity for the different types of groups. The impact of differences in dimensions—such as closed and open membership, kinship or the lack of it among members, and residential and nonresidential settings—would seem to be exceptionally important for future research.

PURPOSES

A major stumbling block to making generalizations about similarities and differences in the goals and purposes of the various theoretical approaches lies in the fact that so many goals and purposes are described at high levels of abstraction. For instance, given considerable variation in wording, all but three of the papers make reference to a basic purpose of enhancement of social functioning. Five of the papers combine such abstract statements with descriptions of more concrete goals, but only the *task-centered* and *organizational context* approaches insist on definitions of goals at a level of specification that would make comparisons of goal achievement feasible.

Part of the difficulty faced by the authors was the number of systems with vested interests in defining group purposes and the tremendously complex interactions between these systems. As a minimum, five parties have a stake in such a process: the individual members of a group, the group-as-a-whole, the worker, the profession of social work, and, for those not in private practice, the agency hosting a group. At times, at least, the purposes of these systems are in conflict. The ways in which such conflicts are resolved, and whether they are resolved by a process of compromise or dominance of one system over another, are largely unknown. The *functionalists* have struggled long and hard with this issue, but do not appear to have a solution to the problem. Ryder's description of a process wherein individuals come to groups with idiosyncratic perceptions of need, followed by a stage where the group forms its own perception of need which is then tested against the agency's purpose or function, does not say much about final purposes. What happens when the different parties cannot reach consensus, even when aided by the most skilled social worker-mediator, is not clear, although some authors have mentioned the right of any client to reject services with goals not acceptable to him. Some have mentioned the responsibility of workers not to work for agencies with purposes that are incompatible with the values of the profession, or to participate in social action aimed at changing agency purpose or function.

It may well be that these issues and unsolved problems surrounding the establishment of purposes have led, in the profession and among these authors, to a growing commitment to the formal sharing of goals and purposes with clients, often in the form of a written or verbal contract.

A final way of comparing the purposes of the various approaches is in terms of systems in which change is attempted. The three systems most commonly mentioned were individual, interpersonal, and larger institutions surrounding the small group.

Despite the fact that some authors defined the small group as the client or system of primary focus, all ten of the approaches stated purposes related to individual members. These purposes vary from those described in *Theories of Social Casework* in that, although rehabilitation is considered important, more attention is given by more authors to the enhancement of normal growth and primary and secondary prevention. Variation exists, however, in the implied priorities that the various theories would give to these purposes.

There is even less variation in purposes related to interpersonal functioning. All of the approaches state purposes such as improving or correcting social relationships and role functioning. Enhancing such interpersonal skills or correcting existing difficulties in social relationships are often seen as leading to improvements in the internal state of individuals and contributing indirectly to changes in the broader society.

While no one voices the opinion that his approach to work with small groups will not in some way contribute to social change, only seven of the approaches mention purposes specifically related to social change. Within these seven, however, there is variation in the ambitiousness of their goals, the size and proximity of the institutions where change efforts are directed, and whether such purposes are primary or secondary. For the most part, however, social change objectives are directed at organizations and institutions in direct interaction with the client group, in some cases only the social agency hosting the group. Although Glasser and Garvin, Hartford, and Somers give considerable attention to purposes of social change, it is only the problem-solving approach that describes a process whereby small-group participation is seen as teaching skills and attitudes necessary for competent and active participation in a democratic government, and states the conviction that both personal and social goals are germane and omnipresent in small-group activities. Somers goes on to add, however, that for the last two decades scholars have emphasized aspects of small-group problem-solving relating to personal growth and change: "The social goals aspect has not been worked on to the same extent, nor has it been as precisely developed and operationalized . . . as has the personal goals dimension of problem-solving." The reasons for this, despite an increase in political and social action within the profession, are not clear. Wilson has described the conflict that occurred when AAGW was organized and many of the persons interested in task-oriented groups split off to develop the Association for the Study of Community Organization. The confusion and overlapping between what is considered to be group work and what is considered to be community work continues today, and it may well be that this volume's focus on small groups, rather than the larger groups usually addressed by community workers, may have led the authors to deemphasize purposes of social change.

ASSESSMENT AND CRITERIA FOR SELECTION

Discussions of assessment or diagnostic procedures are similar in that all of them focus primarily on selection of individuals for formed groups. Only one author, Northen, discusses in any depth diagnostic issues related to work with families and natural groups composed of nonrelated members.

Only one author takes the position that all persons are suitable for inclusion in groups. Ryder, describing the *functional* approach, states a value position that all people have the capacity to change, and thus an inherent capacity to work ". . . collectively on matters of common concern or like interest." Six of the other authors, including two (Schwartz and Tropp) who are opposed to diagnosis or assessment of potential group members, mention conditions which would make persons unsuitable for group membership. Only the *task-centered* approach excludes persons on the basis of clinical diagnoses or type of presenting problem; the others give criteria for exclusion related to the lack of capacity to participate in group processes without being harmful to others or in risk of being harmed by the group. Three of the approaches do not discuss whether some individuals should be excluded from group services.

Four of the papers do not discuss group composition, and another four argue for a balance between homogeneity and heterogeneity, often reflecting the principle cited by Northen that groups should be homogeneous enough to ensure stability and heterogeneous enough to ensure vitality. The position of the *task-centered* approach is not completely clear, but it is probably fair to conclude that this approach works best with members who are homogeneous with regard to problems and tasks.

Seven of the papers participate in the debate over whether or not there should be assessment or diagnosis of individuals as part of an intake and planning phase. McBroom and Tropp are opposed to such diagnoses; McBroom because she does not believe there is sufficient knowledge to select members on the basis of a diagnosis of individual personality, Tropp because he is philsophically opposed to the very concept of diagnosis. The five remaining approaches subscribe to assessment of individuals prior to admitting them to a group, but consensus does not exist about the dimensions on which individuals should be diagnosed. Some form of ego assessment is mentioned in three of the papers; two are explicit that assessment must look at social as well as psychological factors, and two state that past as well as present experiences are important. Although Northen notes that psychiatric diagnoses should be included as part of the assessment when they are available, none of the authors takes the position that social workers should formulate clinical diagnoses, even when groups are formed for psychotherapeutic purposes.

WORKER ACTIVITY

The attitudes of social workers are given little attention by the authors, an unexpected finding because usually attitudes are considered crucial influences of motivation and change. Perhaps, however, they are so interwoven with statements of values that further elaboration was not considered necessary. Self-awareness and self-discipline on the part of the worker are mentioned in six of the ten papers. Both are considered essential for the development of a helpful relationship between the worker and individuals and the worker and the group. The importance of relationships is developed to some extent in the same six papers dealing with self-awareness. But only four emphasize and elaborate on the qualities of relationship that are important as components of help or treatment. It is curious also that only a few papers focus on feelings and emotions of members in either the processes of assessment or treatment, with much greater attention being paid to overt behavior or cognitive understanding than to affect.

In the paper on problem-solving, Somers has traced the historical development of the construct and its use in group work. Problem-solving is defined as a sequence of orderly steps, knowable and testable, that are woven through the phases of pregroup planning, assessment, treatment, and evaluation. There is separate, parallel, and collaborative problem-solving work. In its application to groups, it requires collaboration between worker and group. The self-awareness and self-observation capacities of the members and the worker are used. Active participation of all of the members and the worker is essential to effective problem-solving. The worker's responsibility is to assist members to maintain a focus and to evaluate their achievements in reference to agreed-upon goals. Its potential is the achievement of integrative solutions to personal and social problems. In addition to Somers' paper, the *crisis-intervention, task-centered,* and *psychosocial* papers develop problem-solving both as sequential steps in identifying, coping with, and resolving personal and social problems and as a process that can be learned and applied to various situations. Although the worker's use of problem-solving is clearly evident in the paper on *organizational context,* it is not clear whether members' engagement in the problem-solving process is a major dynamic of change. Also, it is not clear whether problem-solving is perceived as essential to the formulations of either the *functional* or *mediating* models.

All of the authors develop some scheme that captures the interrelatedness of planning, diagnosis or assessment, help or treatment, and evaluation. Most of the authors view these sequences, not as separate sequential steps, but as overlapping and interrelated activities. There seems to be some difference between those writers who expect the social worker to take responsibility for some planning and diagnostic activity and the smaller number who limit the worker's responsibility for diagnosis to that which takes place in the group as a continuous process. In the instance of Tropp, the diagnosis is further limited to the commonly perceived behavior of members. Ryder's position is that the worker helps the group to diagnose and reassess itself. Schwartz seems to agree with this idea, since he views the worker as a moving part in a process, in which the movements of worker and members reverberate in a continuous process of change. The most fully developed explication is that of Glasser and Garvin, who describe a series of planful tasks in the interventive process, beginning with an initial assessment, decisions concerning the context for change, group composition, selection of interventive targets, strategies or plans for the achievement of desired results, and specific techniques associated with the strategies, the differential use of those strategies and techniques related to typology of organizational function, and five stages in the treatment sequence from intake to termination. In the *task-centered* and *crisis-intervention* practice, the steps in the process are very specific, for these formulations have been developed for particular clients, using very specific modes of intervention.

Description and explanation of the contribution of the social worker to the group is a complex task, requiring perhaps much greater elaboration than could be done within a chapter of a book. Authors responded to the items on the outline in different ways, so that comparison of formulations is difficult. The most frequently used term (by six authors) was that the social worker is a facilitator of change—a person who helps the members to engage in the group process and to do what they are able to do on their own. Several authors perceive the worker as an active participant in a continuous process in which there is mutuality of understanding and effort or collaboration between worker and members. That the social worker has some responsibility for directing and influencing the interaction is explicitly subscribed to by only half of the writers.

Most writers delineate a set of expectations that comprise the worker's role, but each one of these formulations is unique to the author. The most complete formulation is that of McBroom, who perceives the social worker as an agent of socialization who is a model, a provider of a safe environment, a specifier and developer of settings and situations of the group that are favorable to the socialization process, a leader of purposeful discussions, and an allocator of resources to groups in need of socialization. She is the only author to suggest that, although the social worker may provide direct services to people, priority is given to the facilitation and direction of the group leadership of others. The role of the worker as a mediator among members of the group and between the group and its environment is emphasized by Tropp and Schwartz. Hartford deals with this subject in terms of three stances from which a worker may select, often making flexible use of the directing, facilitating, and permissive stances.

Regardless of the framework used for describing intervention or treatment, there seems to be agreement among the authors that the client or member's role is an active one: he is not a passive recipient of help. This ties in with the perceptions of the worker's role as facilitating and supporting the members' efforts, and statements that the worker and client collaborate. The writers emphasize the importance of group structure and process as a major dynamic of change. They view the group as the means as well as the context for change. Group influence is a major dynamic for change. The reciprocal movements of worker and members reverberate in a continuous process of exchange or there is mutuality of understanding and effort between the worker and the members. McBroom points to the enormous power of the peer group in basic personality and character formation, and its importance as a socializing agent. Except for Tropp, who asserts that both individuals and groups are essentially self-directing, there is recognition that the individuals, the group, and the worker share in the effort to use the group to fulfill the purpose for which it was developed.

All of the authors list certain acts, procedures, or techniques used by the social worker, but these are diverse and not related to any classification system. Thirty different techniques are specified. The most frequently mentioned are support and encouragement, followed by the enhancement of awareness of self and reality. Other statements can be combined into such categories as clarification, negotiation of contract and content, exploration, structuring, direct guidance and advice, challenge or confrontation, provision of opportunities and use of resources, and reduction of obstacles. No pattern of techniques could be determined that would lead to conclusions concerning theoretical differences among the varied descriptions. Since it was rare for an author to relate techniques to theories concerning the process of change, this is an area that requires further development and research.

The purposefulness of time has been emphasized by five of the authors. *Task-centered* group work and *crisis intervention* are two forms of short-term treatment in which there is a planned use of time limits. This use of time differs from that of the functional approach in which there is strong emphasis on helping the group to assess and use the reality of each time phase as a dynamic of helping. In the *mediating* approach there is emphasis on the worker's responsibility for monitoring time. In a different sense, there is a strong commitment by most authors to focus on the current or here-and-now problems and functioning of group members. Only the *organizational* and *psychosocial* approaches consider the relevance of earlier experiences for diagnosis and treatment.

LINKAGES WITH OTHER METHODS

To the extent that the authors in this volume reflect the thinking of other social workers, there is evidence of a strong movement away from specializations based upon practice methods. Eight of the ten position papers take strong stands in favor of integrated or generic practice with individuals, families, and other small groups. Although Somers mentions casework and community work theories based upon problem-solving, she does not discuss whether she sees them, along with problem-solving group work, as forming an integrated practice theory. Only Tropp would like to see a continuation of group work as a distinct specialization. He argues that casework and group work had different origins and patterns of development, and have more differences than similarities in knowledge and skill.

Whether all of those who are for a generic practitioner with microclient systems would extend this to the incorporation of work with communities is unknown. Only three of the authors (Hartford, Schwartz, and Ryder) make unambiguous statements supporting an across-the-board integration of practice.

Whether one is committed to the integration or separation of methods, decisions must be and are made as to whether services should be delivered on a one-to-one or a group basis. Valid criteria for making such decisions are far from clear, however. Five of the papers do not address the issue, and four either state or imply that no criteria exist for such decisions. McBroom, on the other hand, states that because social competence can be developed only through group processes, the group method is usually the method of choice when clients have problems or needs related to socialization. Schwartz, in addition to stating that no criteria for differential use of methods now exist, goes further and argues that it is presumptuous for social workers to try to prescribe whether group or individual help is better for a client. The choice, he states, is rightfully left with the client.

SOME SUGGESTIONS FOR FUTURE WORK

The papers contained in this volume are evidence of the intensive development and expansion of theory for practice with groups within the last decade or so. As a whole, they reveal many areas of agreement about conceptual and empirical knowledge that is important for any who work with social work groups. They also illuminate differences between theoretical approaches and suggest next steps in theory-building and research. Finally, they raise important questions and issues for social work education.

Borrowing of foundation knowledge from a wide range of behavioral sciences is true for almost all of the authors. Some restrict such knowledge to those behavioral science theories that are compatible with a theory of human behavior or intervention that serves as an integrating core for their approach. Others borrow from a range of theories that are considered by many to be divergent, if not contradictory. A task for those who espouse such exaggerated eclecticism is to spell out in greater detail the relationships between conceptualizations that appear to be contradictory. Some suggested questions to be considered are: Have major constructs from opposing behavioral theories been integrated into a new theoretical scheme? If so, how has this been done? If contradictory propositions are contained within the same theoretical approach, how are such contradictions to be handled by practitioners? Are such propositions used differentially—that is, is one set of concepts considered preferable to another under a specifiable set of circumstances? Continued avoidance of such problems may lead to the expansion of theories lacking internal consistency and integration of component parts, or disillusionment with theory on the part of practitioners and a short-sighted reliance on technique that can only impoverish the research and knowledge base of the profession.

A lesser question stimulated by the papers concerns the use of psychoanalytic knowledge. The near absence of references to such time-honored constructs as the unconscious, transference and countertransference, and defense mechanisms is puzzling. Does their absence suggest a disavowal of dynamic personality theory by most of the theorists or is it that such constructs are so taken for granted that the authors did not think they needed to be explicated? If they are disavowed, it seems unlikely that there can be much integration with those casework theories that use constructs from psychoanalytic theory as central building blocks. If such a rejection of psychoanalytic theory holds for group work practitioners, this may explain some of the reasons for the lamented (but largely undocumented) tendency of caseworkers to seek theoretical guidance and training from group experts in psychiatry and psychology.

Looking beyond the internal components of these theoretical approaches, and remembering the strong commitment of most of the authors to integrated practice, it is obvious that the next major effort is to develop theories that will incorporate work with individuals, families, and small groups. A first step in this direction might well be an empirical investigation of what generalist practitioners are actually doing and how they are conceptualizing their work. Hopefully, such research will reveal techniques and concepts that cut across all levels of direct-service practice as well as provide leads for understanding when clients are best served by individual or group methods or the concurrent use of both.

The papers suggest directions for research on practice with small groups. For instance, study is needed of the frequency and nature of conflict in the purposes and objectives of individual clients, groups-as-a-whole, workers, the profession, and social agencies. When such conflicts occur, what are the ways in which they are resolved, and to whose advantage? Empirical investigation is also needed of how workers with varying theoretical orientations, practicing in various agency settings with different types of clients, compose groups, and whether differences in procedure or criteria result in important differences in group process and worker activities. A related question is whether and how group processes and worker actions differ with groups that vary on such dimensions as related or nonrelated members, natural versus formed memberships, open and closed admissions, short-term versus extended life spans, and goals of task achievement or growth of individual members. Finally, research is vitally needed on the question of how subcultures—based on such factors as ethnicity, life stage, social class, and gender—influence client motivation for and participation in group activities, group process and its effects, and worker actions.

The big need, however, is for research to determine if the theoretical orientations of practitioners make a difference in worker activity, group process, and outcome with different types of clients with different types of presenting problems in different types of agency programs. A basic question to be answered is whether all of these approaches are equally suitable for the full range of purposes, clients, and types of groups addressed by social work. If not, social work practice can become truly effective only when we are able to specify the conditions under which one approach is more likely to be successful than others.

Finally, a few words seem in order about the implications of this volume for social work education. The last ten years has seen a growing commitment among educators to train generic social workers, those who are competent to work with individuals, families, groups of non-related persons, and even communities. Simultaneously, there has been an expansion in the number and diversity of theoretical approaches within each of the traditional methods. A question that several of the authors raise is how workers can be educated and trained so that they can competently practice with all levels of client systems with an in-depth mastery of competing theoretical orientations. The answer to this problem is far from clear, but it seems obvious that social work education cannot add more content in the traditional two-year graduate program. It certainly cannot do more in less time, as is being suggested by those who argue that the basic professional should be trained at the undergraduate level. What seems more likely, if we are to upgrade the quality of social work practice and to insist upon depth as well as breadth of knowledge, is an increase in the length of professional social work education. While the master's degree will probably remain the modal degree for some time, it also is likely that more schools will offer and more social workers will take advantage of doctoral programs designed to educate advanced practitioners.

INDEX